A New History of Ware,
its people and its buildings

David Perman

*To Jean Hunt
with best wishes
David Perman*

A New History of Ware,
its people and
its buildings

Rockingham Press

First published 2010
by Rockingham Press
11 Musley Lane,
Ware, Herts SG 12 7EN
rockpress@ntlworld.com

**A catalogue record for this book is available
from the British Library**

ISBN 978-1-904851-36-3

Printed in Great Britain by
the MPG Group
Bodmin and King's Lynn

Dedicated to the memory of
Thera Alcock, Dick Brock, Joan Brogden,
Michael David, Maurice Edwards, John Fletcher,
Adrian Gibson, Michael Jennings, Nan Murphy,
Michael Ottley, Henry (Herbert) Page, Violet Rowe,
Hugh (Jumbo) Shayler, David Stockwell and others
who lived with me the history of Ware.

Two artefacts from Ware now in Hertford Museum.

Top: a typical piece of pottery of the Bronze Age 'beaker folk' (3000-2500 BC), the first farmers to arrive in this part of Hertfordshire. It was probably used for drinking ale or mead, and was found in the 1930s in a gravel pit off the Westmill Road (now the Gentleman's Field industrial estate).

Bottom: a 10cm bodkin or amulet with a fish head, made from a deer horn. It is from the Saxon or Viking period (890-900 AD) and was found at the Ermine Street crossing of the River Lea in 1974.

Contents

Maps, Plans and Family Trees

Introduction

When Edith Hunt wrote her book in the nineteen-thirties (publication was delayed by wartime paper shortages until 1946), she called it *The History of Ware*.[1] She was fully justified in that title. She did not mean it to be the definitive story of the town's past, in other words *the* history of Ware – in fact she did not attempt a narrative of the Ware story. What she did was to set down every scrap of the town's history that she had come across in extensive research, together with their sources, and thus made a sort of scrapbook revealing what she called "the chief links in the chain of our town's life story". Her intention was to show that the town did indeed have a history. Until publication of her *History*, there had not been a single book devoted to Ware and its past, although there had been pamphlets, magazine articles and the long section on Ware in the *Victoria County History of Hertfordshire*, which Mrs. Hunt used and readily acknowledged. But on library shelves Ware was neglected by comparison with Hertford, St. Albans or other towns in the county. It is to their credit that it was historians from these other towns – chiefly Herbert Caleb Andrews of Hertford (Mrs. Hunt's cousin) and Reginald Hine of Hitchin – who encouraged her to write *The History of Ware*.

This present book does attempt a continuous narrative of the town's history, from the Stone Age to the Present. That may seem presumptuous and foolishly ambitious, but the need for a narrative history of Ware has long been demonstrated. At numerous lectures, historical meetings and conducted tours of the town, people have shown their desire for a book that takes Mrs. Hunt's pioneering work further and places our local events in the context of wider history. Again it is not a definitive or exhaustive story, either in the historical facts and figures presented here or in the interpretation put on those facts. Others may interpret the facts quite differently. And so this is *a* history of Ware – but 'a new history' because many of the events have not been recorded before. That is the main title, but the subtitles are also important. The townspeople of the past contributed to the social, political, economic and religious history of the town but, as well as names, they also had occupations, families, identities and their own idiosyncrasies. They all have stories to tell. Now more than ever it is possible to tell those stories from the evidence available in libraries, museums and historical collections – all made far more accessible than in Mrs. Hunt's day – and from sources on the internet or world wide web (though the web always needs to be checked against other sources). The historical records of Ware are unusually rich and well preserved. That is but to be expected for such an ancient town.

But we have another rich resource, literally on our doorsteps. The town is especially well endowed with historic buildings, particularly timber-framed structures of the medieval period and malthouses from the more recent past. Because Ware was more fortunate (or perhaps successful) than its neighbours in escaping the comprehensive redevelopment of the nineteen-sixties and seventies, these ancient buildings still stand on streets which were well known to past generations and are there to be studied and appreciated, even though the uses to which they are now put are often different from those for which they were built. This is particularly the case with the malthouses or maltings which proliferated throughout the town in past centuries and have now been adapted for residential or business use. So the purpose of this book is to lay out a history of Ware with particular attention to the people of the town and its buildings.

It is a full and rich history and it could not have been told without the help and cooperation of a great many people – some of them no longer with us, as noted in the Dedication on page 5. Two bodies are the main guardians of Ware's heritage, and both the trustees and volunteers of the Ware Museum and the staff of Hertfordshire Archives and Local Studies have been exceedingly helpful and generous with their time in assisting my research.

Canon Hugh Wilcox kindly allowed me in Chapter 19 to draw on his extensive research into the trials and troubles of another former Vicar of Ware, Henry Coddington. Dr. Clive Partridge, who led most of the archaeological digs in Ware from 1966-80, informed much of what I have written about the town's early history and generously allowed me on page 15 to adapt one of his maps, first published in *Ware and Hertford, The story of two towns from birth to middle age* (Castlemead, Welwyn Garden City, 1994), co-authored with Robert Kiln. David Hillelson, archaeologist with the Heritage Network in Letchworth, read an earlier draft of the opening chapters and made some valid criticisms. And Diana Perkins was unstinting in the information she provided about the geology of Ware.

I wish to express my thanks also to the East Herts Archaeological Society for allowing me to use the drawings on pages 19 and 53, the Hertfordshire Building Preservation Trust for the drawing on page 80, Hetheringtons Countrywide Estate Agents and Richard Wells for the photograph of Place House on page 51, Adrian Grover for the photo on page 83 and Cecil Hewett for the drawing on page 52 from his book *English Historic Carpentry* (Phillimore, 1980). I am grateful to the Marquess of Salisbury for allowing me to reproduce a detail of Lord Burghley's map of the River Lea (now in the Hatfield House Collection) on page 97 and to the London Borough of Barking and Dagenham, Valence House Museum, for allowing me to reproduce the portrait of Thomas Fanshawe on page 93.

Finally, I wish to thank those friends who read the work in earlier drafts, who picked up many inaccuracies and infelicities and yet still encouraged me to go on and complete it – particularly Elisabeth Barratt, Edgar Lake, Romola Sturgess and Dr. Alan Thomson. Alan Murray proof-read and corrected the final draft with the greatest care. Despite all their efforts, any errors that remain are mine alone.

Ware, June 2010

1.
Facts on the Ground

It is usual to begin the history of a town with a little 'gee-gee' – Geology and Geography. I used to be suspicious of geology until I went on a Ware Society tour of the town, conducted by our local geologist Steve Perkins. He had us studying the pavements for York stone and basalt, the shop fronts for slabs of Greek marble and the walls of Christ Church for Kentish ragstone. It was an exciting evening.

But just as exciting is the geology of Ware and the immediate area. Quite near the surface we have a proliferation of chalk, flints, gravel, brick-earth and peat – and underlying these layers and deposits is the hundred-million-year-old heavy blue-grey clay called 'gault'. Gault clay occurs on the surface only in the far north-west of Hertfordshire – near Tring and Ashwell – but it is important for the whole county because it is impermeable to water and thus allows the chalk layers above it to be 'aquafers' which hold and store water. The gault clay was laid down in a warm sea which covered much of Europe; after that, the sea became clear of any mud or silt and the microscopic sea creatures (a form of algae) which lived in this sea sank to the bottom when they died. This is the makeup of chalk – composed of calcium carbonate from the skeletons of the algae. After the chalk had been laid down, movements in the crust of the earth raised it up and then lowered it into a brackish sea, so that a layer of clay, sand and pebbles – known as the Reading Beds – settled on top of it. After more earth movements, another layer of stiff clay – London Clay – was laid on top of this. About 30 million years ago, the surface was tilted and wrinkled into gentle folds and then in places the soft rocks were worn away. One wrinkle formed the London Basin, with the North Downs forming one rim of the basin to the south and the Chilterns forming the northern rim. In the Ice Age – or to be precise, one of the Ice Ages, about 200,000 years ago – a huge glacier covered Hertfordshire leaving behind pebbles, frost-shattered flints and other minerals. One of the most interesting of these is Hertfordshire Puddingstone, a conglomerate of pebbles and silica, which occurs in clumps – there is one in the grounds of Ware Priory and other examples were incorporated into the building of Scott's Grotto. Finally, on top of other geological layers there is the peat and top-soil washed down by the rivers and especially thick on the Meads of the Lea Valley between Hertford and Ware.

This geology has had a marked effect on the history of Ware. If you drive into Ware from Hertford on the A119, you are driving along the edge of an outcrop of chalk (a sort of first taste of the Chilterns) and you can see how large areas of chalk were mined for agriculture in the eighteenth century to 'sweeten' acid soils – these areas are now industrial estates. The Romans used chalk in building Ermine Street. And the eighteenth-century road builder, John Scott, used chalk as a road surface and excavated the chalk hillside to construct his remarkable grotto. Flints also occur in the chalk (one can see them in the ventilation shafts of Scott's Grotto) and our Stone Age ancestors skilfully fashioned these into tools. As for the coloured sands and clays of the Reading Beds, these accounted for the town's thriving brick industry in the nineteenth and early twentieth centuries. It is not generally known that an entire London surburb was built from Ware bricks taken by barge down the River Lea in the 1840s. More recently, the alluvial sand and gravel deposits around the town have been exploited by the construction industry and the resulting excavations put to different uses – for housing along Wülfrath Way (the former Brazier's Pit on the Watton Road), and as flooded nature reserves to the south-east of the town towards Great Amwell.

If the geology is fascinating, the geography is no less so. It mainly concerns the River Lea which has been at the centre of much of the town's history. The natural river is usually known as the 'Lea'; the name 'Lee' refers to the Lee Navigation begun in the eighteenth century. The Lea rises in Bedfordshire but it is not until Hertford that it becomes a major river, capable of carrying boats. After Hertford, the Lea is joined by the Beane (or Beneficican, as it was anciently called) and then on the Meads by the Rib. Between Hertford and Ware, the Lea Valley widens considerably and the river, flowing east-north-east falls by four metres (4.0894m or 13ft.5ins. to be precise). Before the Lee Navigation or Ware Lock were constructed, the river used to divide, one branch meandering across the Meads down a number of small weirs or cascades (now known as the Manifold Ditch) and the other branch falling over one larger weir at Ware itself. At Ware, the river turns south-east and passes through Stanstead Abbots and Stanstead St. Margarets, where it is now joined by the Ash (anciently called the Easnye). It then passes Rye House and Hoddesdon after which it is joined by the Stort just before it reaches Broxbourne. From there the Lea flows south through Cheshunt, Enfield, Edmonton and Hackney to its junction with the Thames, originally at Bow Creek but after the Limehouse Cut was made at the other side of the Isle of Dogs, nearer to the Port of London.

From the earliest times, the Lea was navigable as far as Ware and Hertford. It was a strategically placed river. To the south-west of both towns were large areas of clay thick with forests and few human settlements – areas now covered by Broxbourne and Hoddesdon woods and Enfield Chase. To the north-east were hundreds of small farms, stretching from Hertfordshire into Cambridgeshire, Suffolk and Norfolk and successfully producing cereal crops on fine light soils. This was (and still is) excellent wheat and barley country and Ware on the Lea formed a good inland port for shipping these cereals and malt to London and a distribution point for coal, wine, oil and other goods brought by river from London.

There were other links between the Ware area and East Anglia. Culturally, Hertfordshire is a hybrid county, the western half looking towards Bedfordshire and Buckinghamshire, while East Hertfordshire's links are with Essex or with towns farther down the Lea Valley. One can see this divide in the types of timber-framed buildings built in the Middle Ages. In Essex and East Hertfordshire, timber buildings have crown posts and vertical studs; to the west of Hatfield cruck-framed buildings are more prevalent. In earliest times – when the Saxons first settled in eastern England – people probably spoke an English dialect better understood by people living in Colchester or Bury St. Edmund than by those in Hitchin. In the earliest Saxon period, Ware came under the control of the Kingdom of Essex which included London and was closely linked to the Kentish kingdom to the south of the Thames. In the later Saxon period, Ware along with other towns and villages of Braughing Hundred were included in the Diocese of London (in the Archdeaconry of Middlesex), while the remainder of Hertfordshire came under the ecclesiastical jurisdiction of Lincoln Diocese.

2.
Early Wareites

Whether there was an ancient track crossing the Lea at Ware before the Romans constructed Ermine Street we do not know. But it is a natural crossing point for anyone travelling up the Lea Valley and wishing to continue their journey northwards. Once the ice ages were over and northern Europe became warmer – in roughly 10,000 BC – the upper parts of the Lea Valley would have been a thoroughly congenial place for hunter-gatherers to settle. The river provided fish and shellfish for food and reeds for plaiting as shelter or clothing; on the land there were flints to fashion into tools and weapons, trees to cut and use for shelter and for weapons, and clay and mud to daub on buildings and bodies. Men were now using spears and bows and arrows and there would have been plenty of game, coming down to the river from the woods on the high ground to the south-west and the north. It was during this period – known as the Mesolithic or Middle Stone Age – that wandering nomads who had crossed the land bridge from Europe, probably following herds of reindeer, began to establish communities. There is evidence of early Mesolithic communities in the valley around Broxbourne, where flint tools as well as organic remains such as wood, bone and plants, have been found in the peat layers excavated for gravel

At Ware too evidence has been found of a Mesolithic settlement, or perhaps something more substantial than a temporary settlement for hunter-gatherers. From 1976-80, Clive Partridge was excavating with the Hart Archaeological Unit (then linked to the East Herts Archaeological Society) prior to the development of the former Allen & Hanbury's sports field in Park Road for new pharmaceutical manufacturing buildings. Evidence of a small Roman town was found and beneath that an Iron Age settlement. These finds were expected and bore out the evidence of earlier excavations. But underlying both were clusters of flint flakes, prepared flint cores and scrapers – all artefacts typical of the Mesolithic period and dated by one expert to around 6,000 BC. They lay on top of the brick earth in a grey layer which was probably the original turf. After further excavations, pits, pot-holes and curved gullies were uncovered, with further worked flints and waste flakes in these various features. It was clear that this was a substantial Middle Stone Age settlement and excavations in the late 1980s confirmed the presence of scattered flint tools nearer the river. In their book, *Ware and Hertford: From Birth to Middle Age*, Robert Kiln and Clive Partridge say that it seems to have been more than the usual temporary hunting camp and "likely to have been a permanent base camp, perhaps approaching the size of a small village".[1] Elsewhere Robert Kiln had speculated that "Ware is one of the oldest continuously occupied sites in Western Europe".[2] It is an attractive idea but, despite the Mesolithic evidence, the facts do not bear out continuous occupation.

In about 3,000 BC the Mesolithic hunters began to be displaced by farmers, who herded cattle, pigs and sheep and planted crops. These Neolithic (or New Stone Age) people used smoother, better fashioned axes fitted to wooden shafts and a number of these have been found in the Ware area. But the Neolithic settlements tended to be away from the river valleys on higher ground, a typical site being that at Foxholes Farm near Hertford, excavated in the

1970s and 1980s. Characteristic Neolithic features in the landscape are 'long barrows' which are large communal burial mounds, and the large sites enclosed with banks and ditches known as 'henges' in which ritual and ceremonial activities were carried out. These are more common in West and North Hertfordshire than in the Ware area.

The next age of human development involved the use of metal to supplement the tools and weapons of stone, flint, bone and wood. The Bronze Age is thought to have started in around 2,000 BC when traders and immigrants introduced bronze (an alloy of copper and tin) from the Middle East. This was more or less contemporary with the Trojan wars chronicled by the Greek poet Homer in which bronze axes, swords and spears were the weapons on both sides. In Britain the introduction of metal was gradual. The first Bronze Age artefacts were pottery, belonging to a nomadic people known as 'beaker folk'. The name came from their peculiar drinking vessels, one of which was found in the 1930s in a gravel pit beside Westmill Road, Ware: it is inscribed with an intricate geometric pattern, similar to contemporary Greek pottery (*illustrated on page 6*). In 1972, the East Herts Archaeological Society found a small Bronze Age shelter at East Herts Golf Club, part of which was shortly to disappear under the Ware bypass. It consisted of a shelter and fire pit, with finds of flint arrow heads, a bronze pin and flint scrapers, probably for preparing skins. Compared with the Bronze Age finds in North Herts, at Foxholes Farm and at Broxbourne and Turnford, those in the immediate Ware area have been few. However, this may not be the complete picture. Recent excavations have been heavily dependent on developers, they are thus arbitrary from a research point of view and, in any case, are carried out against a deadline with little opportunity for exploring nearby sites. Aerial photography, on the other hand, has revealed ring ditches, many of which may have been Bronze Age burials, all over the area of Ware and Hertford.

The Iron Age

The Iron Age is an important but problematic period in our history. For one thing, it covered such a long period – from roughly 600 BC to 43 AD, from pre-history into history proper, from the time when our distant pastoral ancestors were beginning to use iron instead of flint and bronze to the invasion of the Roman Emperor Claudius, some 87 years after Julius Caesar had come and gone. It is a period in which we can put names to the chieftains or rulers of important parts of Hertfordshire, but what race these chieftains belonged to is still a matter of debate. Were they Celts as many people like to believe; or were they 'Belgae' which is what Caesar called them because they came from what is now Belgium; or should we simply call them 'Britons' because they lived in what everybody called Britannia? The debate continues.

An early Iron Age farmstead (or perhaps it was late Bronze Age) was found very close to Ware. It was discovered in September 1968 when members of the East Herts Archaeological Society were walking beside the trench opened for the pipes of North Sea natural gas: the site was on the high ground between Moles Farm and Thundridge, roughly a mile and a half north of Ware. A small pit was observed before the contractors filled it in and was seen to contain shards of pottery, flint flakes, stones used either for honing or heated and dropped into water as pot boilers, and many animal bones. The picture we have of the people who lived here is that they fed on young oxen and sheep and occasionally on wild deer, which they butchered

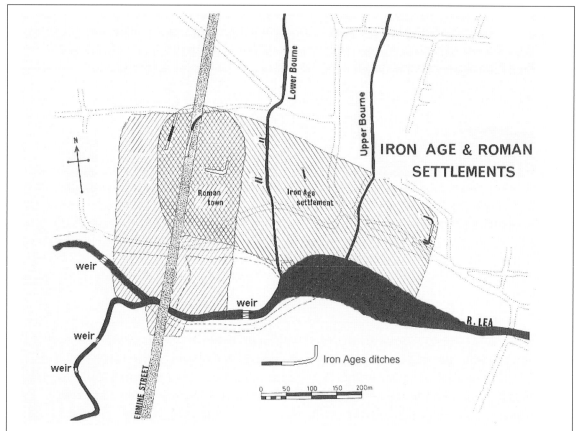

The Late Iron Age and Roman towns – adapted from Clive Partridge's map in Ware & Hertford: From Birth to Middle Age, page 26, but also showing the early weirs and the width of the river before the medieval land reclamation.

with sharp tools, and used large pots and bowls of coarse grey clay, which they had probably made by hand (i.e. not on a wheel) and fired in an open fire rather than in a kiln.

On the other side of Ware, on the Meads, workmen were laying a new water main in the nineteen-eighties and a local man ran his metal detector over a pile of spoil before the pit was filled in. What he uncovered was a Late Iron Age dagger guard, a beautiful object made of silver with the point of the broken dagger still in place. Whether it was broken by an enemy or by the modern pipelayers is not known. The dagger guard (or 'chape') has been cleaned and conserved and is now in the Ware Museum; the experts say it is similar to objects in the hoard of weapons of the fourth and fifth century BC found at La Tène in Switzerland, the heartland of the Celtic civilisation. The chape was found less than a mile from the Bronze Age and Middle Iron Age settlement at Foxholes Farm, excavated by Clive Partridge between 1976 and 1984 before gravel extraction. Occupation seems to have extended from Mesolithic right through to post-Roman, Saxon times but it is the Iron Age settlements which are in many ways the most interesting. 'Belgic' settlers arrived at Foxholes probably in the closing years of the second century BC and probably came by river. They lived farther up the hill than their Iron Age predecessors and the pattern of postholes, ditches, gullies and possible pits show that they farmed here and made their own 'grog tempered' pottery – i.e. with sand and crushed pottery sherds (grog) mixed in the unfired clay to make the vessels stronger. But Foxholes had a marked absence of coins or luxury goods, such as imported pottery, and none of the brooches found was dated later than 20BC. Other Late Iron Age sites in Hertfordshire had shown a drift of occupation from the hills and plateau down to the river valleys in the second half of the first century BC and Partridge concluded that the same may have happened at Foxholes.[3]

Indeed it is possible that it was to Ware that the Foxholes farmers migrated. Excavations of the Allen & Hanburys/Glaxo site showed that sealed beneath the Roman town was evidence of Late Iron Age occupation. 'Grog tempered' pottery was found stratified on the original land surface beneath Ermine Street and similar pottery was recovered from V-shaped ditches beneath evidence of Early Roman occupation. More of this pottery has been recovered in other parts of the modern town, in West Street and on the Buryfield Recreation Ground where Roman ditches and burials and Iron Age ditches have been found. Several British coins and fragments of Gallo-Belgic pottery have also been recovered from these Early Roman layers. So what sort of a settlement was Ware in the second half of the first century BC, at the time of the Roman invasions? What was its relationship with other, more prominent Late Iron Age settlements in Hertfordshire?

The reason why Julius Caesar invaded Britain in 54 BC and in the year before, when he was repulsed, was the anti-Roman stance being adopted by some British tribes. This had stirred up trouble for Caesar in Gaul and also interrupted the cross-Channel trade (according to the Roman writer Strabo) in corn, cattle, gold, silver, iron, hides, slaves and hunting dogs. Cassivellaunus, who was elected to lead the resistance to Caesar, is usually thought to be the chief of the Catuvellaunni, who were based north of the Thames, probably in Hertfordshire. Caesar's army landed at Deal and advanced inland, making a treaty with the Trinovantes at *Camulodunum* (modern Colchester) and accepting the surrender of some of the smaller tribes who informed him of the location of Cassivellaunus's fortress. Caesar advanced on this fortress or 'oppidum', which was probably at the hill fort beside the River Lea at Wheathampstead, where Cassivellaunus surrendered. Caesar concluded a treaty with him which limited his power to expand and then returned to Gaul. Cassivellaunus was thus a spent force and other chieftains arose in his place. From the coins they minted, we know that Tasciovanus and later Cunobelinus (Shakespeare's Cymbeline), who claimed to be Tasciovanus's son, were based in Hertfordshire – Tasciovanus at *Verulamium* (St. Albans) and Cunobelinus eventually farther north probably at Puckeridge/Braughing. Cunobelinus sprang to prominence with coins minted in the territory of the Trinovantes at Colchester and from there became the effective ruler of most of south-eastern Britain. The Romans left them alone and Cunobelinus enjoyed a long reign. But two of his three sons, particularly the third, Caractacus, provoked the Romans and in 43 AD the Emperor Claudius invaded and this time the Romans stayed.

During this period, Puckeridge/Braughing was an important Belgic settlement and, from the large distribution of bronze coins found there bearing his name, it seems to have become the eventual capital of Cunobelinus once he had become established. Later, Puckeridge/Braughing – we do not know its Latin name – was to become a major Roman settlement. It was not a fortified town or 'oppidum', but it was certainly the residence of a considerable number of wealthy and civilised people. This is borne out by the evidence of trade with Italy,

Southern Spain and Gaul. "That this trade was more than just a short-lived venture can be seen in the variety and quantity of imported goods," wrote the archaeologist Clive Partridge. "The amount of such items as flagons, jugs and especially mortaria must be an indication of the presence of people with Romanized tastes and habits, and in some numbers, if the amount of surviving material is anything to judge by".[4] In addition, Partridge pointed to the number of small bronze coins belonging to tribes in Northern, Central and Southern Gaul, which indicate the presence of 'middle men' or merchants whose visits were frequent enough for these coins to be accepted by their British customers. The trade routes from the Mediterranean were described by the Roman historian, Strabo – goods were brought by boat up the Rhone, via the rivers Doubs or Saône/Moselle to the Rhine and then across the North Sea. Partridge suggested that in Britain, this Gallic trade would have taken similar river routes – up the Thames and then the Lea, with Ware as the inland port, from which goods for Puckeridge/ Braughing would have been transported either overland or possibly pulled in shallow draught vessels up the River Rib.

What would Ware have looked like at this period in the Late Iron Age? The river crossing would have been where the Romans later located the crossing of Ermine Street; in other words just below what is now Ware Lock. Above this point the Lea ran in two channels and there were the weirs. We know where the weirs were because of the location of later flash and pound locks. The north bank of the river at this point was the main settlement – this is where the flint flakes of the Mesolithic community and the Late Iron Age ditches and pits were found. A little way downstream – where the Priory now stands – the river would have widened considerably, forming almost a basin or lake. We know from archaeological excavations that much of the land between the High Street and the river was reclaimed and built up in the early Middle Ages to form 'burgage plots' for rent or sale to merchants. Excavations behind 65-83 High Street revealed that the original land surface was at least a metre lower and there was evidence of Saxon riverside structures. Indeed the river's edge may well have come almost as far north as the present High Street and the Priory, both of which are constructed on natural platforms of gravel. We also know that the south bank of the river was notoriously porous with large tracts of the Amwell End area prone to flooding. Until the building of the railway in the 1830s, there was a 'barge basin' to the south-east of the Amwell End, an area later developed as a railway goods yard and now under modern blocks of flats. It is likely that this wide stretch of the river, south of the present High Street, was where boats and barges were unloaded, including those which had brought wine, jewellery and other luxury goods from Gaul and the Mediterranean. Thus Late Iron Age Ware covered a wide swathe of land, stretching from Harris's Lane in the west to the end of West Street and the Church Street/High Street junction in the east, and from the river almost as far northwards as Park Road.

3.
A Roman Town

Some years ago, I met an archaeologist from the Museum of London and asked if he would like to see the Roman artefacts in the Ware Museum. His reply was disconcerting. "I didn't know there were any Roman artefacts in Ware!" Excavation of the Roman town of Ware has been going on since the 1960s – or even since the 1830s if one uses a wider definition of 'excavation' – and yet little of this has found its way into national archaeological literature. There have been reports in Hertfordshire journals and a few longer articles – and there has been the book by Robert Kiln and Clive Partridge[1] – but there has not been the monograph or weighty academic volume one would have expected from such a well-excavated town. This is a matter of great regret locally for it seriously diminishes the town's history. It means that the enormous wealth of artefacts in the Ware Museum exists in a sort of academic limbo. It is also a significant loss to the study of Roman Britain. If the many excavations that have taken place since the 1970s had been brought together in one volume, then comparisons could have been made with other Roman towns and a critical analysis made of the Ware town layout, its pottery kilns, metal-working and other industries, the cemeteries, even the diet and diseases of the Romano-British Wareites.

Ermine Street

The Roman town at Ware is located on the crossing of Ermine Street with the River Lea. Unlike some other roads – Icknield Way, for example – Ermine Street does not seem to have existed before the Roman conquest. It was a classic engineered, military road, built to transport and supply the legions once they had penetrated northwards from London. It ran absolutely straight from London (exiting through what is now Bishopsgate) to just north of Ware. It then curved slightly to the north-north-east as it approached Puckeridge/Braughing, before resuming its straight course to Godmanchester and Chesterton (Roman *Durobrivæ*), then curved westwards to Stamford and Grantham before moving dead straight and due north through Lincoln (*Lindum*) and across the River Humber to York (*Eburacum*), capital of the northern province. Why it was called Ermine Street is a mystery – like the names of most Roman roads in Britain it is Saxon, not Latin.

Ermine Street was not the first road to be built by the legions north of the Thames – that would have been the 'Great Road' leading to Colchester (*Camulodunum*), the capital of the Trinovantes whose capture was a prime objective for the Emperor Claudius's legions. Ermine Street would have been built by the military as a 'territory-holding road' rather than one which penetrated into enemy territory but, as this was a peaceful part of the province, the road would soon have been adapted for civilian purposes, particularly for the imperial postal service (*cursus publicus*). For the imperial posts, a series of forts and stations were spread out along major roads with relay points (*stationes*) to provide horses for dispatch riders, who were usually soldiers, and vehicles for magistrates, as well as food, fodder, and accommodation. There was probably a small fort at Ware, or maybe more than one in the course of the 300 years the Romans were here. In 1977 Clive Partridge – heading an archaeological excavation on the Allen & Habury (Glaxo) manufacturing site in Priory Street – excavated a 'military style' ditch belonging to the first century AD and running north-south and parallel to Ermine Street. "This was in itself, an important discovery, because it may be taken as evidence for a Roman fort, or similar military installation, guarding the river crossing during the early years of the Roman Conquest"[2] The site of another (probably later) fort was excavated in 1998 by a group from Ware Museum, organised by the author of this book. It was to the north of the Roman town – at the Ridgeway and overlooking Wadesmill Road (Ermine Street) – and identified first in 1902 by the Hoddesdon historian, J. Allen Tregalles,[3] and then in 1939 by the Ware historian, Edith Hunt. It was arguably a 'turf camp' for legionaries to rest up in. Unfortunately any traces of Roman occupation were swept away in the 1960s development of the Kingsway area of Ware.

How much of Ermine Street survives locally and how was it constructed? To the south of Ware the line of the road can be traced on the ground as well as on Ordnance Survey maps. In the woods south of Hertford Heath, the Roman road exists as a wide green track known as Elbow Lane, on the same alignment as the main London Road which it joins to go through the village. Here on the gravelled surface of Elbow Lane, the agger (or embankment) of the Roman road seems to be 36 feet (11m) wide and roughly 1-2 feet high.[4] After Hertford Heath, traces of Ermine Street are lost as it crosses the fields to Rush Green and descends the slope of East Herts Golf Club into the Lea Valley. But in the valley at certain times of the year, when the grass is dry or dead, the agger of the road can be clearly identified, running from the Hertford Road beyond the New River and over the railway towards the River Lea.

It was just alongside the railway in 1952 that the first detailed observation of Ermine Street was made by John Holmes, a master at St. Edmund's College, Puckeridge.[5] The occasion was the digging of a trench to take a new sewer from Stevenage *en route* to Rye Meads. The section of the road which he observed had two side ditches, dug first with the material being thrown up into the centre producing the black soil shown in the diagram. The central section was then laid down with local materials – first, gravel with pieces of sandstone, then the final 'metalled surface' consisting of chalk and flints bound together with lime mortar. John Holmes measured the road width between the ditches to be 65 feet (roughly 20m). But he deduced that this was, in fact, a three-tracked road – the 7m wide central 'metalled' carriageway having a flat, hard surface for wheeled traffic and people on foot (such as legionaries), and two side

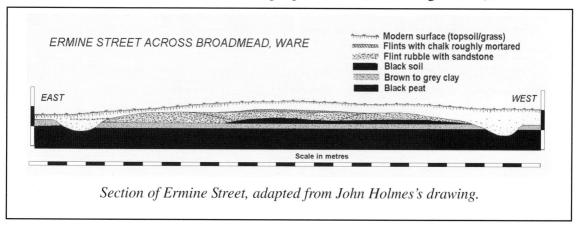

Section of Ermine Street, adapted from John Holmes's drawing.

tracks having a soft, sandy surface for horses and cattle. The next unveiling of Ermine Street occurred in 1974, in preparation for construction of a flood relief channel alongside Ware Lock. Martin Petchey observed that the road had been constructed and re-constructed in phases. The first phase was a fairly narrow early or military road, 11.3m (37ft) at its base with a usable road surface of 7.4m (24ft), but without side ditches; laid on top of this were later phases of construction. These widened the road to a carriageway 22.8m (75ft) wide with side ditches and a metalled surface of flint pebbles which had been repaired a number of times.[6] Interestingly, Petchey found buildings on this side of the Lea, particularly one small rectangular building near the water's edge – which we shall return to later.

The Romans ruled this part of Britain for 300 years and over that period the width and surface of the road changed radically. As archaeologists were able to excavate in the heart of the Roman town, even more radical reshaping of Ermine Street came to light. In 1989, Nicola Godwin carried out an excavation on the proposed site of Glaxo's P11 Building (in the north-east of the manufacturing site) and found a complex series of changes to the road. The earliest road was 12.5m wide, with flanking ditches but the road was subsequently re-laid. It contracted to 6.5m width, flanked by timber buildings, cobbled yards and hearths, the latter possibly evidence of industrial activity. These encroachments on the Roman road were possibly the result of locals wishing to entice travellers into buying their wares – like modern shopkeepers putting out A-boards. These features were overlain by a silt deposit, above which were further buildings of the Roman period and more signs of industrial activity. At this level the road had again been re-laid and was now only 5.0m wide.[7] These excavations at Ware are important because they provide clear evidence of how a major Roman road was modified as it approached the first river crossing north of London and then passed through a busy small town of traders and artisans.

There seems little doubt that both the military road and the later Ermine Street crossed the river by means of a ford. Before the construction of the first lock here in the seventeenth century, this part of the river opposite what is now Glaxo Manufacturing would have been wide and liable to flooding in the winter. That was because this was the confluence of the River Lea (later known as the 'Old Barge River', now as the Manifold Ditch) and the River Rib, which later formed the millstream of Ware Mill. There were a number of weirs here before the first lock was built. There was certainly a ford or ferry here in the medieval period, for in 1258 the men of Hertford came and blocked it (*ad impediendum transitum*) and most earlier historians assumed the ford was there in Roman times. In 1831, while constructing a new Ware Lock, the engineer William Chadwell Mylne discovered a bar of "firm hard gravel" running across the river, overlaid with a layer of peat in which a skeleton, steel yard, Roman coins and other objects were discovered.[8] In 1902, two local amateur historians – J. Allen Tregalles, the librarian at Hoddesdon, and Richard Benyon Croft of Fanhams Hall, Ware – debated whether the gravel bar Mylne had found was a natural ford formed by gravel brought down by the River Rib or a Roman construction, using gravel because no stone was available locally. There is thus archaeological evidence of a ford but no physical evidence has been found of a Roman bridge at the Ermine Street crossing. The main advocates of a bridge crossing were Kiln and Partridge, who in their book concluded that the small rectangular building, mentioned earlier, right at the water's edge was "a check point or toll house at the

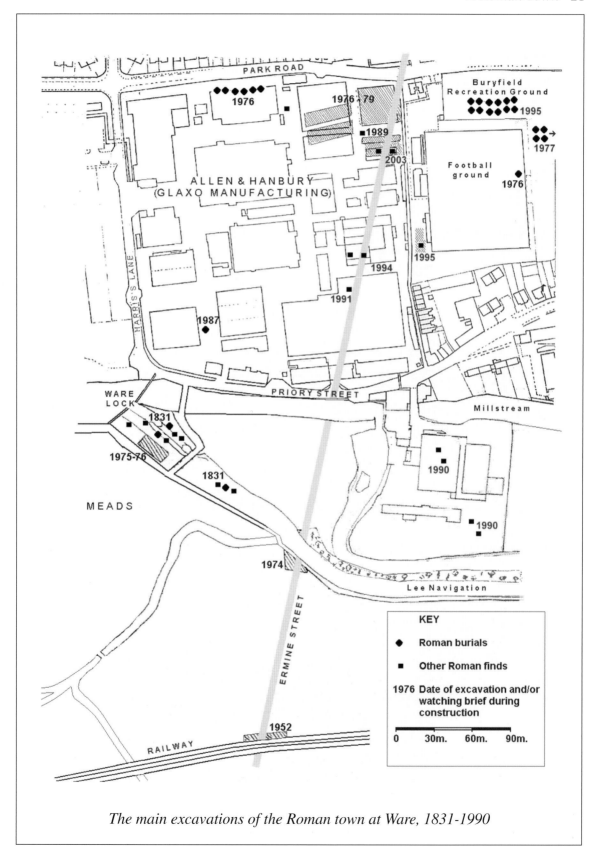

The main excavations of the Roman town at Ware, 1831-1990

south end of the Roman bridge" because a large number of small Roman coins had been found scattered on the chalk floor, as if they had fallen through the floor boards. But even they had their doubts for they admitted there are no known examples of toll houses in Roman Britain.[9] In fact, Martin Petchey, the archaeologist who in 1974 excavated this little building, proposed three possible uses –

i   a toll house for the bridge or ford over the Lea, which lay between the site and the rest of Roman Ware. Tolls, however, are not common in the Roman Empire.
ii a shop or tavern sited to attract customers before they entered the town.
iii a wayside shrine, dedicated to some water deity.[10]

One might pay tolls before crossing a bridge, but a shrine where one can placate the river god with a coin or two is needed before one plunges into the waters of a ford. In the case of the Ermine Street ford, the river god would have been 'Lugus' or 'Lygus' (the old, Celtic name for the Lea).

Living beside Ermine Street

We refer to the 'Roman town' at Ware but the people would not have been Roman. They were British, speaking a Celtic language akin to Welsh but with enough Latin to advertise and sell their goods – or at least in the early years. Once Christianity had arrived, there would have been more Latin speakers. These people were no doubt descended from the inhabitants of the extensive Iron Age settlement and river port where goods were landed for transport to the bigger settlement at Puckeridge/Braughing. There was a settlement beside the river long before the Roman engineers arrived and laid out Ermine Street. But once the road was established, the town would have grown as people realised the opportunities of providing rest and recreation for the legionaries, magistrates and other travellers and, like every other town which has offered R&R, this one would soon have developed market stalls, taverns, shops and industries.

But just living beside a Roman road brought its own rewards. The drainage ditches at the side and other layers of roadside debris have yielded interesting finds. These include an engraved copper bracelet, copper-alloy sewing needles, a pair of tweezers, part of a bone spoon, bone hair pins with engraved ends as well as numerous coins. The debris contained large quantities of pottery, from broken fragments of local greyware to sherds of shiny red Samian platters and bowls, which were imported from France. There were also quantities of volcanic rock, which were fragments of querns used for the hand grinding of corn into flour. This rock was imported from the Eifel region of southern Germany in the Roman period.[11]

In the absence of local stone, the buildings clustered around Ermine Street had timber frames, probably filled in with wattle or mud daubed walls. Post-holes discovered in various excavations since 1974 indicate a variety of building shapes and sizes – some mere sheds or lean-tos, others bigger, measuring up to four metres square. Near the river the buildings rested on foundations of rammed chalk, on the higher ground to the north the post-holes were often packed with flint. Many of the buildings would have been thatched but others show evidence of tiling – locally-made *tegulae* tiles have been found in large quantities. Indeed, the assemblage

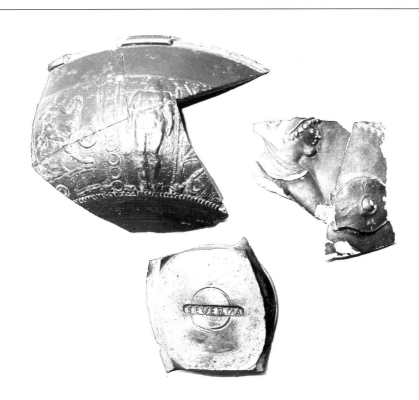

Examples of pottery found in the Roman town – anti-clockwise from top left, part of a Samian ware pot, the base of a Samian ware pot with the maker's name SEVERUS and part of a colour-coated pot showing a gladiator's head, arm and shield (Ware Museum).
Below: a selection of brooches, probably for sale to the passing legions (Ware Museum).

*Two of the triple vases, which may have been incense burners or altar vases,
found in the square building on the north bank of the River Lea (Ware Museum).*

of flanged *tegulae* and other tiles, bricks, sections of daubed plaster, ceramic, nails and other metalwork reads like the catalogue of a Roman builders' merchant. No evidence of a villa or other large dwelling or meeting house has been found at the Glaxo site, although there were reports that a tessellated floor was discovered just to the north in Watton Road in the 1950s when gravel was being extracted from the Brazier's pit. The pit now contains the housing estate of Wülfrath Way.

One fascinating building was revealed on the north bank of the ford, to rival the shrine on the south bank. Built probably in the late third century it partly covered the western drainage ditch of Ermine Street. It formed a perfect four-metre square with stone-filled post-pits at the corners and four smaller intermediate post-holes. Describing the building, Kiln and Partridge deduced from the finds that it was a temple. The finds included three triple vases (*above*), thought to be used as incense burners and altar lamps, fragments of thin bronze plates, often found as votive offerings in Roman temples, and a considerable scatter of small denomination bronze coins. All these were recovered from the layer of silt that had accumulated between the front of the building and Ermine Street. Also, from the fill of the north-western stone-packed post-hole, came the remains of a horse skull. Just to the rear of this square building a small arc of baby burials was found (these were the only burials allowed by law within a Roman settlement). "These finds recall many other finds of like material from Roman Britain, which are associated with Romano-Celtic temples. Horse and/or ox skulls were often buried as foundation offerings when these square cella-style temples were built".[12] This temple or roadside shrine was eventually demolished and superseded by three other phases of building, each creeping closer to the western edge of Ermine Street. Other evidence of religious practices included finds of miniature spears and knives and, in 2003, a complete brooch incorporating a crescent moon good-luck charm. We know from the burials that some of the people were Christian, but other religions coexisted with Christianity at that time.

Because the line of Ermine Street runs close to the eastern boundary of the Glaxo Manufacturing site, there has been little opportunity to explore what lay to the east of the road. To the west, however, there have been a number of discoveries, including some on the south bank of the river to complement the shrine beside the ford. There excavations carried out in 1975-76 (during work on the flood relief channel next to Ware Lock) revealed chalk rafts over the underlying peat on which buildings had stood, and from the slots and post-holes found in the chalk it is assumed timber buildings. Nearby were other signs of other timber posts and piles which may have indicated a wharf or similar Roman waterside structure. Finds from these excavations included pottery cooking pots, imported fine Samian ware, animal bones, an ox goad and – rarest of all, an iron leg shackle or slave chain. Whether this is evidence of the export or the import of slaves at Ware is not clear, but certainly there must have been slaves taken as well as employed in this part of the Roman Empire. One way the Romans had of controlling their subject people was to take some of their leaders' children as hostages and send them to Rome as slaves.

To the north of the river, we have a rough idea of the boundaries of the Roman town from the burials – by law adults could not be buried within town boundaries. In 1976, in the north-west of the Glaxo site next to Park Road, six burials came to light before the bucket of a JCB digger: they lay side by side in a line, all originally buried in wooden coffins (the nails were found even though the timber had rotted) and two still had the lead linings from inside the coffins. This was clearly an upper-class cemetery, since lead was a precious commodity in Roman Britain, and the archaeologists deduced that the deceased were Christians because the burials lay east-west. They dated from the period AD 320-400. On the same alignment but to the east of Ermine Street, twelve burials were found in 1994 on the Buryfield Recreation Ground just to the north of the former Ware Football Club – one of these burials was in a lead-lined coffin. Farther east, in 1977 while a new sewer was being laid across the Buryfield, the archaeologist Ivan Day (tragically killed in a motor cycle accident in 1983) observed four burials – two of them with grave goods consisting of an urn and a complete greyware beaker, other pottery sherds and a bronze finger ring. One of these burials was on the site of two earlier cremations. These burials to the north-west, north-east and east of the Roman town indicate its outer limits. There were probably many more burials in areas as yet unexplored, including the former Ware Football Club. A geophysical survey of the club's ground indicated that "it was genuinely free of large-scale archaeological features" but could well contain graves – and so these and any other smaller features were 'sealed' under the multi-storey carpark being built for Glaxo. That is regrettable since the football club could have covered Saxon as well as Roman graves, being on the boundary of the two settlements. One further burial was intriguing both because of its location within the town boundaries, and because of its identity. This was a stray inhumation, buried directly in the earth, found much closer to the heart of the town. It was of a girl of sixteen or so *(illustrated on p26)*, with perfect teeth, not ground down by grit in the coarse bread she would have eaten – and of course not rotted by sugar, which the Romans did not have. From her nearness to Ermine Street the diggers named her 'Ermintrude'.

Between the cemeteries and the Roman road there was plentiful evidence of industrial activity. But this appeared to date from late in the life of the Roman town. In company with other small towns in Britain, there seems to have been a period of neglect and possible abandonment of parts of the town during the later second and early third centuries (AD

175-250). However, at Ware there was one area of claypits, kilns and post-holes, suggesting at least one family of potters weathered this downturn and went on producing cooking pots and jugs from the local brick-earth. This pottery was a fairly distinctive type of greyware, similar to the widely distributed greyware from the late Roman kilns at Much and Little Hadham, but coarser. After the downturn of the early third century, industry seems to have picked up, with many small ovens and furnaces for smelting ore being discovered. In one place, there was a cache of bronze coin blanks, indicating that either there was a mint here or some of the townspeople were forging money. There was evidence of the manufacture of bronze rings and brooches, of toiletry items made of bronze and iron, knives, chisels and other tools of low-grade steel and pins (some very elaborately carved) made from animal bone. Other finds included a large number of 'hipposandals', the type of horseshoe with which oxen and horses were shod in Roman times. This was clearly a thriving industrial estate with a ready market nearby on Ermine Street. These finds were further confirmed

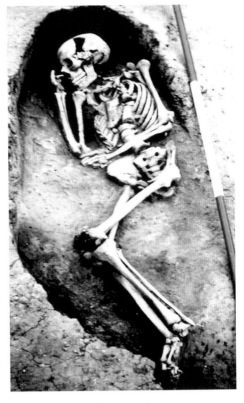

Ermintrude

by excavations in 1987, which also brought to light huge quantities of oyster shells.

The closing years of the Roman occupation are wrapped in mystery but the archaeological evidence at Ware has thrown up some intriguing questions. The usual date given by historians for the end of the Roman occupation is AD 410 when the legions departed, but there was instability throughout the country from the end of the fourth century. The 'barbarians' (as the records call the Saxons) had been attacking and overrunning the frontiers since AD 367. At Ware, above the workings associated with the late fourth-century industrial revival were signs of another, sudden economic downturn. Excavations on either side of Ermine Street revealed rough cobbled yards, surrounded by what must have been flimsy sheds, and nearby a square, timber-lined well, which contained the skeletons of pigs and dogs. Why were valuable animals thrown into a well, in itself a valued feature of the settlement? Was this evidence of sickness or maybe the pillaging of the period after the Romans had left? 'Dark earth' was found covering most of the Roman layers, as it has been at other Roman sites in Britain. There are two common explanations for the 'dark earth': one is that it showed the Roman towns were abandoned and became covered with centuries of agriculture. At Ware the evidence points to the alternative explanation, that more timber buildings were built on top of the Roman settlement and the 'dark earth' is the result of their rotting timbers. At least three phases of Roman structures were found post-dating the 'dark earth' and a wide range of continental imports of the fourth century seems to show that the Ware settlement was not completely abandoned. But life did not go on as it had under Roman rule. Late timber buildings were found which narrowed Ermine Street to less than four metres; there was also a series of large post-holes crossing the centre of the road in what appeared to be a barrier to stop or regulate traffic entering the town from the north. What does this tell us about life in what had been a thriving Roman, roadside town?

By AD 410 the legions had left and the British were running their own affairs and organising their own defences. Their enemies were Angles, Saxons and Jutes – all people from northern Europe – who

Evidence of a more grisly trade is this slave shackle found at Ware Lock in 1976 (Ware Museum).

may have been invited in by the British as mercenaries or may simply have arrived as invaders or settlers. By AD 441/442 Britain was under Saxon control, according to the *Gallic Chronicle*, but as this was written in France it may not be accurate. From the archaeological evidence, it seems that Ware was an exception to this blanket Saxon control. "In general, the evidence suggests that the Romano-Britons may have continued living in the Roman town at least throughout the fifth century," wrote Kiln and Partridge. "Then at some unknown time, perhaps in the sixth century, Saxon peoples arrived, choosing to settle in the area to the east of the Roman town, as Saxons were known to be reluctant to occupy previously built-up areas".[13]

A selection of Roman coins, from the 2nd to the 4th centuries AD (Ware Museum).

4.
The Saxon Settlement

The Saxon town of Ware is an enigma, a challenge and a marvel – all rolled into one. The enigma is the shortage of archaeological evidence, certainly as compared with the Roman town. But that should not surprise us. Saxon Ware lies under the streets and buildings of the modern town and to get at the archaeology one would have to demolish shops and office blocks still in use. This contrasts with the site of the Roman town which had either never been developed (as where Ermine Street crosses the Meads south of the river) or was occupied only by late Victorian industrial buildings scheduled for redevelopment by Glaxo Manufacturing. On the other hand, enough archaeological evidence is there for us to have a good picture of life in the so-called 'Dark Ages'. The challenge is to work out the shape and extent of the Saxon town and to relate it to the earlier Roman road layout and the later Medieval town. The marvel is that, during the six and a half centuries of Saxon rule, Ware leapt from being a small roadside settlement – a 'town' by contemporary standards but still small – to becoming the second richest and one of the most populous towns in Hertfordshire.

Despite the scarcity of Saxon remains and despite much of what was discovered remaining unpublished, we know the location and rough shape of the Saxon town. It lay mainly in the strip of land between the two Bourne streams – the Upper Bourne to the east and the Lower Bourne to the west. This is the area of what is now Baldock Street and the western end of the High Street. The lowest point is the gravel platform on which the High Street and Priory Street stand, comfortably above the River Lea's flood plain. It then rises by a good ten metres before it joins the original line of Roman Ermine Street, a little above the junction with modern Kingsway.

However, before we consider the excavations that have taken place in Baldock Street, we must look at a very important dig at the southern end of this strip. In 1977-78, just before Ware Library was modernised and extended, a small trench was excavated behind 87 High Street. Immediately, the diggers – Ivan Day of the Hart Archaeological Unit aided by local volunteers – came across two obstacles, a nineteenth-century brick wall and a brick-lined culvert, taking the Upper Bourne down to the River Lea. Nonetheless, what Ivan and team uncovered was fascinating. Below various floor levels and 1.2m. below the modern surface, were three large postholes which formed a right angle with a shallow depression in the middle. There were pits nearby – one of them containing sherds of late Roman pottery and Saxon grass-tempered ware. 'Grass-tempered' pottery is early Saxon, fifth to seventh century AD, and a regression from the smooth ware of the Roman period: grass or ferns were added to the pottery clay to give it strength, a technique also used by the Celts and found in parts of Africa. Roman coins of the 3rd and 4th centuries were also found. What was the building? Ivan Day described it as "a small rectangular timber building" but as it had been truncated by a ditch it could well have been large and imposing.[1]

On the same alignment – the gravel platform just to the south of the present High Street – other Saxon artefacts have been discovered. Behind 81 High Street, an excavation in 1987

Part of a grass-tempered pot of the sixth century AD, found in Baldock Street (left) and a medieval pot made on a wheel, from Black Swan Yard, Baldock Street (Ware Museum).

supervised by Nicola Godwin of the Hertfordshire Archaeological Trust found a fine triangular book-clasp: its intricate design was picked out with a silver inlay although the hook had been broken off *(illustrated on page 33)*. In the same area, though nearer the river, sherds of late Saxon pottery were found – 'late' because this was no longer grass-tempered and handmade but fine 'shelly' ware made on a potter's wheel. A few years earlier to the north of the High Street, at No.2 West Street, a Saxon silver penny or *sceat* of the mid-7th century was found in a medieval ash pit.[2] It seems to be important that all these Saxon finds were discovered alongside stray pieces of Roman pottery and, in the case of the Library excavation, late Roman coins. The Saxons did not usually take over Roman sites, but it may well be that this gravel platform, parallel with the river, was a favoured settlement for both peoples for landing fish and imports as well as watering animals and crops.

Who were these people? After the Roman legions had gone, Britain was invaded by tribes from across the North Sea speaking a variety of Germanic languages – Jutes (from Jutland) who settled in Kent, Saxons from Northern Germany settling in Wessex, Sussex and Essex and the Angles who took over the rest of the country: Norfolk, Suffolk, the Midlands and the north of England. They began to arrive in the early fifth century (the 400s AD) and then came in a rush. Once the Angles had begun to leave Schleswig-Holstein – partly to settle in Britain, partly to escape Attila's marauding Huns – it is reported that that area became depopulated. The Angles founded three important kingdoms, Mercia, East Anglia and Northumbria but, as with modern multinational companies, soon began to attack and swallow up their rivals. Ware was settled by the East Saxons who originally had their own kingdom of Essex, but this soon became a vassal state of Kent and then came under the rule of Mercia. The Mercian dynasty of Penda (626-655 AD) and his sons, Wulfhere and Aethelred I (675-704) were engaged in a long struggle with the kingdom of Northumbria, but they had little difficulty in conquering Essex, Kent and parts of Wessex. Situated on or near Ermine Street, Ware would have witnessed the frequent passing of the Mercian soldiers, crossing the Lea ford intent on conquest and plunder on their way south, or loaded with booty, prisoners and slaves on their way north to the Mercian capitals, Repton and later Tamworth. London became a Mercian capital later under King Offa (757-796).

When they first settled in this area, the Saxons had little interest in the Roman town or Ermine Street. They were farmers not townspeople. It has been said they avoided the Roman roads because they believed there were ghosts walking on them. But in time and particularly when the Mercian armies began their campaigns, the road regained its importance. A barrier of stakes may have been put across the road in the early fifth century, but in the centuries following Ermine Street was again in use, though diverted in an arc towards the east. This is the line of modern Baldock Street, which begins to curve towards the south-west before curving more sharply to the east as a result of medieval town planning. There have been a number of excavations in Baldock Street but not all of them have produced evidence of the Saxon settlement, or indeed of any settlement earlier than the 20th century. In Waggoners Yard, on the east side of the street, an excavation in 1983 revealed extensive disturbance from construction of a large Second World War air-raid shelter. All the same, beside the shelter were a number of small pits containing grass-tempered and plain sandy-ware pottery of early-mid Saxon date – "likely to be 6th to 7th century in date".[3]

On the opposite side of Baldock Street there have been three excavations, one of them of great importance. Nos. 17-21 Baldock Street (next to Black Swan Yard) became available to archaeologists in 1983 after the frontage of a Tudor building fell into the road. It happened on a Sunday morning! The Hart Archaeological Unit began excavations which revealed a series of post-hole and beam slot structures, predating the earliest Medieval houses on the site which in their turn had been replaced in the 16th-17th centuries. At least two phases of these simple wooden buildings were identified and they were on a different alignment to either the earliest Medieval buildings or the modern street frontage which shows a distinct swing towards the east. The earlier wooden buildings were aligned north-south, heading straight towards the river rather than towards what is now the High Street. Baldock Street then formed a detour from Ermine Street and at 17-21 there was evidence that it headed back and rejoined the Roman road at the ford.[4] A large number of pottery sherds and other finds dated this site to the mid Saxon period.[5] The two other sites on the west side of Baldock Street were disappointing. At No.11 Baldock Street, where an extension was being built on to the Salvation Army Hall, it was hoped there would be further evidence of the Saxon street frontage but the site proved restricted by standing buildings and services. No.49 Baldock Street – on the corner with Watton Road – was another restricted, small site and produced evidence only of 'back-yard' use from the 16th-19th centuries.

In the ninth century, the warring kingdoms of Saxon England faced a common enemy, the Vikings. The word is usually taken to mean 'pirates' but the Vikings included ship-borne raiders, traders or immigrants from all over Scandinavia. In the *Anglo-Saxon Chronicle* they are usually called Danes, but many of them came from Norway. They announced their arrival in Britain by an event which shocked the whole of Europe: on 8 June 793 AD they raided and sacked the monastery at Lindisfarne or Holy Island in Northumbria. For the next 200 years,

The Roman, Saxon and Medieval roads through Ware.

they dominated the history not only of England but much of Europe, including countries in the Mediterranean as far east as Constantinople (Istanbul). During the ninth century, the Vikings conquered the Anglo-Saxon kingdoms and took over most of the country. The *Anglo-Saxon Chronicle*, compiled from earlier, vanished sources at the end of the century, says that in 842 AD they caused great slaughter in London and Rochester and nine years later brought 350 ships into the Thames Estuary and expelled the Mercian king of London. The only kingdom to hold out was Wessex and its new king, Alfred (871-899), managed to turn the tide of war and conclude a truce with the Viking king, Guthrum. This was the Peace of Wedmore which established two areas of influence – Wessex and London for the Saxons and the Danelaw for the Vikings. The treaty began with these words: *First concerning our boundaries: up on the Thames, and then up on the Lea, and along the Lea unto its source, then straight to Bedford, then up on the Ouse to Watling Street*. So from 890, Ware on the north bank of the River Lea lay within the Danelaw – but only just. It was a frontier town.

But the Wedmore Peace did not guarantee peace. A large force of Vikings, who had deserted Guthrum and spent the last few years in continental Europe, arrived off the coast of Kent. In 894 AD they took their ships up the Thames and then up the Lea, and in the early months of 895 built a fort by the Lea twenty miles above London. In the summer of that year, a large army of Londoners and others marched north until they reached the Viking fort and a bloody battle took place. The *Anglo-Saxon Chronicle* says four of the king's thanes were killed – in other words, four of the English commanders – but it does not put a figure on the overall English or Danish death toll which must have been considerable. This was a real setback for Alfred who in the autumn rode up along the river (presumably with another army) and camped near the town, so that the Vikings could not prevent the townspeople from getting in the harvest. Then Alfred hit upon a way of driving out the enemy – he ordered the building of two forts, on either side of the river, and seeing them the Vikings realised they could not get their ships out. Whereupon, they made one of the rapid marches for which they were famous and took themselves and their followers across country to Bridgnorth-on-Severn. And so a major Saxon defeat was turned into victory.

It is an heroic story but it raises a number of questions. What was the town whose people needed protection to get the harvest in? It must have been Ware, which is indeed 20 miles up the Lea from the Thames – there was no other significant Saxon town in the area for Hertford, Stanstead Abbots and Hoddesdon did not exist then. Where was the Viking camp? The Edwardian historian, Richard Benyon Croft, believed it was at earthworks near Chadwell but most local opinion would locate the fort on Widbury Hill, where indeed an ornate Saxon strap-end was found by a metal-detector. Where were the two forts Alfred had built? Obviously downstream from the Vikings' stronghold, and probably at Great Amwell and Stanstead Abbots on either side of the river: it is reported that old ships' timbers were found at Stanstead Abbots when they were rebuilding the bridge. Finally, why did the Vikings sail up the Lea and why did the Londoners come out to dislodge them? The answer to both questions must be that the Vikings were threatening London with one of their famous rapid advances down Ermine Street. The Londoners must have come up the Roman road because there is no mention of them bringing up their ships. So Ware, in 895 was at the centre of a famous battle and a famous victory by Alfred the Great.

Seventeen years later, in 912 AD, his successor, Edward the Elder, set out to regain territory lost to the Vikings in the previous century. His strategy was to build forts or *burhs* from which he could take the fight into enemy territory and one of the first of these was at Hertford. The *Anglo-Saxon Chronicle* says: "after Martinmas, king Edward commanded the northern *burh* at Hertford to be built, between the Maran and the Beane and the Lea". The chronicle goes on to say that in the same year some of the king's supporters worked on the *burh* at Hertford on the south side of the Lea. Many of the *burhs* Edward built were new sites – Wareham and Wallingford are examples – but none was more clearly identified as a green-field site than Hertford. The *Anglo-Saxon Chronicle* for 912 gives it a unique topographical location – "between the Maran

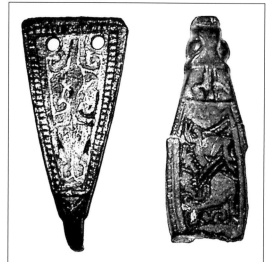

An intricately worked Saxon book clasp found on the river bank behind 84 High Street, and (right) a Saxon strap end found on Widbury Hill.

(Mimram) and the Beane and the Lea". The archaeological evidence also points to a green-field site. After reviewing three excavations in Hertford north of the River Lea and five to the south, Kiln and Partridge concluded: "it has to be said that none of these has produced evidence for occupation which could be said to be definitely earlier than the tenth century."[6] This is a puzzle for although the site of the two Saxon *burhs* was new, the name of Hertford was not. There had been an important synod of the church held at Hertford in 673, convened by Theodorus of Tarsus, Archbishop of Canterbury, under the auspices of King Aethelred of Mercia. It is mentioned in the *Anglo-Saxon Chronicle* and in the history of England by Bede, who wrote "we met at a place called Herutford", indicating that the name was significant. In 1973 Hertford Town Council and its citizenry celebrated the centenary of that synod which is commemorated in a sculpture on the wall of Castle Hall. All of this has been embarrassing to historians, some of whom have concluded that the synod of 673 was not held in Hertford, Hertfordshire, but at Hartford, Huntingdonshire.[7]

Was there another Hertford?

There is, however, another possible explanation which would put the site of the important synod back in Hertfordshire – in fact, at what is now called Ware! It was hinted at by the eighteenth-century historian, Nathaniel Salmon, who maintained that the name *Hertford* did not refer to 'the ford of the harts' but to the Roman military ford of Ermine Street over the Lea: his argument was that the prefix *Her-* was the Saxon word for an army.[8] Indeed, it can be argued that there never was a ford at present-day Hertford because the two *burhs*, built by King Edward and his supporters, would have been connected by a bridge which would make more military sense than linking fortifications by a wide-open ford. In fact all the other double *burhs* created by Edward – at Bedford (915), Buckingham (914), Nottingham (918) and

Stamford (918) – were linked by bridges. Bridge-building was one of the obligations or 'common burdens' laid upon any holder of hereditary land by the Saxon kings. Then the name 'Hertford' could well refer to the ancient ford two miles downstream at what is now Ware. It is well known that Saxon place names referred to a wide area and in the early tenth century the name 'Hertford' could have embraced the sites of the two modern towns, which are only 2.3 miles (3.7km) apart. If that is true, then the synod of 673 AD was in the town known now as Ware but then as Hertford. That would make historical sense since the town is situated on Ermine Street, linking southern England to the north, and the bishops present came from East Anglia, Kent, Wessex, Northumbria and Mercia. Once King Edward in 912 had built a fortified new town in this area, then the name of 'Hertford' would have become firmly attached to this royal *burh* or borough. When a century later, in the course of Saxon local government reorganisation, the old centre of 'Hertford' became included in a different local government area or Hundred, it was given a new name – 'Waras' referring to the weirs above and below the ford. 'Waras' has long been recognised as a late Saxon name and an odd one standing on its own without a prefix, such as 'Herutfordes-Waras'. Furthermore, one needs to look at the reason why Edward's supporters decided to build a second *burh* to the south of the river. Their motive may not have been the offensive one of the king, who intended to recapture territory from the Danes, but a defensive one – to defend the ford downstream. That would explain why in the Middle Ages the bailiff of Hertford Castle (on the site of the southern *burh*) regarded the ford at Ware as under his control and was even prepared to use force to assert his rights.

One other piece of evidence pointing to an earlier Hertford is in the name of Hertingfordbury. This hill-top village, a little over a mile to the west of the modern county town, was originally known as *Hertfordingbury*, or the 'stronghold of the people of Hertford'.[9] The transposition of the second and third syllables did not take place until 1507: it was known as *Herefordingberie* in Domesday Book (1086) and as *Heortfordingabyrig* in the will of the great landowner, Æthelgifu, in the late 980s.[10] But this is odd. Less than seventy-five years earlier, Edward the Elder and his followers had built two strongholds or *burhs* on the site of the present town of Hertford and it is unlikely these defences had fallen into disuse during that period. So why should there be another stronghold nearby for the people of Hertford, unless the name referred to an older Hertford. It is quite conceivable that, when they were under attack, the people of the 'other Hertford' or Hertford/Ware should retreat from their open town beside Ermine Street to a defensible hilltop a few miles to the west.

The Creation of the Shires

Edward's campaign to recover territory from the Danes, aided by his sister, Æthelflæd, 'the Lady of the Mercians', was successful. Most of the Midlands was soon subjected to Wessex-Mercian rule and the Northumbrian, Scots and Danish rulers of the remainder paid homage to Edward. By the time of his death he was in fact if not in name, king of England. But his successors could not hold on to his gains. They faced an even fiercer Viking onslaught by Sweyn Forkbeard and his son, Cnut or Canute. It was during Sweyn's bloody conquest of

The hundreds of Hertfordshire, formed in the tenth century. Hertford is the most well-contained of the hundreds. Ware was in Braughing Hundred which was kidney-shaped. Its boundaries included the River Stort to the south-east, the River Lea to the south-west and the River Rib to the west but the other boundaries made no geographical sense.

England south of the Wash in 1011 that Hertfordshire gets its first mention. The 'shire' system of government was a Wessex invention, extended to the rest of the country as a result of Edward the Elder's campaign. The procedure was straightforward: the king would march in with an army, build a fort or *burh*, garrison it and organise the surrounding countryside to provide the necessary manpower to maintain the fortifications. The *burh* would then become the county-town and give its name to the shire (except in the case of older kingdoms, like Norfolk, Suffolk and Essex). The system was formalised by the 980s, in the reign of Ethelred 'the Unready' (in Anglo-Saxon his name means lacking in good counsel which he did when he faced Sweyn's army). Later still the term *burh* was extended to any town which had once been fortified and was now a 'borough' with burgesses.

The shire, administered by a shire-reeve or sheriff, was divided into a number of 'hundreds', each containing a hundred 'hides' (a land unit roughly equivalent to 120 acres or 49 hectares) and the total number of hides in the county, it is believed, would produce enough revenue to provide troops, horses, food and other provisions for the county town or *burh*. Hertford Hundred formed a neat area around the county town but, to achieve the required total of hides, other hundreds were given some very odd shapes in order to make up the hundred hides. Ware found itself in a different, horseshoe-shaped hundred centred on Braughing, with the rivers Lea and Stort as its west and eastern boundaries – though, later, as it was the largest town in the hundred, the hundred court tended to be held in Ware. It must have been about this time that the name 'Waras' was attached to the town to distinguish it from the county-town. The shire system was a hierarchy, stretching like a pyramid from the king at the top, through the officers of his government and the major landowners in the shires down to the stewards and jurors, who could swear to the ownership and obligations of everyone of significance in each manor or parish. It was such an efficient system that it functioned equally well for the rule of Duke William of Normandy in his Domesday survey of 1086 as it had for his Saxon predecessors, Edward the Confessor or King Harold Godwinson.

In Domesday Book we have a detailed picture of life in Ware at the end of the Saxon period and the beginning of Norman rule. It was a large parish and manor, accounting for 24 hides (2,880 acres or 1,165 hectares) and with a large population. The record shows 38 townspeople, a priest, a reeve, 27 smallholders, 12 cottagers and 9 slaves – apart from another 32 men under the English and Frenchmen, who clearly came over with the Conqueror.[11] This gives a total of 125 persons but, as Domesday Book lists only heads of household, it is usual to multiply the total by five (625), and then to add 20 per cent for persons missing from the Domesday count (e.g. servants). This gives a grand total of 750 people, which made it one of the largest towns immediately north of London. Ware is described as a *vill* but this is a term which can equally well describe a town as a village. St. Albans, with a much smaller population, is described as a *vill* but also said to have burgesses. The archaeological evidence too points to a sizeable urban settlement – the archaeologist, Peter Boyer, has written: "nucleated settlements of the late Saxon period are unusual in southern and eastern Herts, suggesting that, like Hertford and St. Albans, Ware may have been a trading settlement or the site of an ecclesiastical or other important residence".[12] In fact, it was both.

In 1066 its lord was Askell (Anschil or sometimes known as Aki). He was clearly resident in the town since he is usually referred to as "Askell of Ware". But who was he, what was his rank and what role did he have, if any, in the government of King Edward the Confessor? Askell is described as a 'king's thegn' which means that he was in the upper ranks of Saxon society and from the number of manors he held, in addition to Ware, he was a wealthy man. He was not the wealthiest landowner in Hertfordshire: that honour went to Asgar the Constable, whose principal Hertfordshire holding was Sawbridgeworth (the only manor in the county richer than Ware) and who held land in Hertford, Shenley and Enfield in Middlesex – he is calculated to have been the richest landowner in England, after the king and the earls. Askell of Ware was not in that league but not far from it. One contemporary source, the *Liber Eliensis*, states that the more important magnates of the period were distinguished from the lesser thegns by having incomes of more than £40 a year. Askell's income was over £100. One historian, Peter Clarke, calculated that, after the earls, Askell of Ware was the 44th richest landowner in England.[13] He may have been higher up the league table since Clarke does not include the manors in Huntingdonshire held by one Askell, where the extra title "of Ware" is omitted. Each of the eighteen manors which Askell himself controlled was as lucrative as any of Asgar the Constable. The ones nearest Ware – at Westmill, the Pelhams, Sacombe and Stanstead Abbots – were held by thegns or freemen (or in one case a woman) while Askell

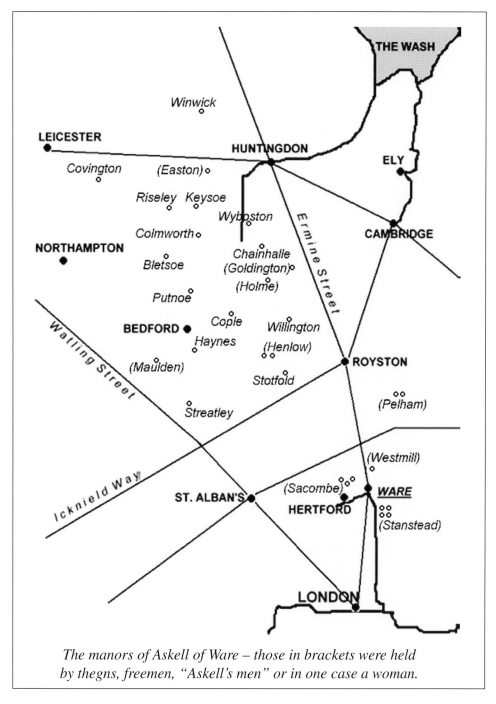

The manors of Askell of Ware – those in brackets were held by thegns, freemen, "Askell's men" or in one case a woman.

himself held most of the more distant manors. As the map shows, his manors were strategically placed near to Ermine Street and Watling Street which gives an indication of the role he played in the administration of Edward the Confessor, probably as a quarter-master to the army. Every landowner was obliged to provide men-at-arms, horses, food and money for the defence of the *burh* at his or her county-town: Askell's obligation would have been much wider since he was able to amass a large number of soldiers, horses or provisions and deliver them to the army on the move, whether it was travelling north or south on Ermine Street or Watling Street.

Another historian makes Askell of Ware even richer and important with a place – at least through his son – at the forefront of the history of the period. In his book, *Hereward: The Last Englishman*, Peter Rex identifies our Askell with Asketil Tokisune (son of Toki), who controlled a number of manors in the west of Lincolnshire, including some owned by the Abbey of Peterborough where his brother, Brand, seems to have been the abbot. Peter Rex goes on to claim that Asketil or Askell was the father of Hereward ('Hereward the Wake') who led the best known Saxon revolt against William the Conqueror and probably died in the Fens near Ely.[14] This is fascinating stuff but the identification of Askell of Ware with Asketil rests on tenuous evidence and Rex himself admits that nowhere is Asketil referred to as "of Ware".

We have spent some time discussing the possible size and importance of Saxon Ware and yet the evidence is tantalisingly scarce. It points to the need for more research and more excavations, where modern development makes them possible, in those areas of the town where the Saxons settled between the early fifth century and the Norman Conquest. The challenge is there and it has been recognised by historians like Tom Williamson:

> ... We have the case of Ware. This, as we have seen, has two spacious market places, one of them close to the church. It was a place of ancient importance, with Roman and Iron Age roots, may have formed the core of a major middle Saxon estate, was certainly an important estate centre at the time of Domesday, and had a very large recorded Domesday population (125). Did this place really only become a town and market in the late twelfth century, as the documents seem to suggest? Or had it in fact possessed some urban functions for a century or more?[15]

As suppliers of men, horses and provisions to any English army passing along Ermine and Watling streets, Askell and his people would have come into their own in the autumn of 1066. It was the first year of the new king, Harold Godwinson, who had succeeded Edward the Confessor in January and already the country was in crisis. In mid-September, a large Norwegian force under Harald Hardrada landed on the east coast and quickly defeated an English army on the road to York. The Norwegian king was joined by Tostig, the disaffected brother of Harold. King Harold had been waiting on the south coast, expecting an invasion by William Duke of Normandy. On hearing of the Norwegian victory, he dismissed part of his army and rushed north, gathering troops on the way and surprised Harald and Tostig at Stamford Bridge on 25 September. It was an unexpected and decisive victory for the English but any celebrations were cut short by news that William had landed on the Sussex coast. So Harold rushed south with what troops he could muster – probably including troops from Askell's manors – and met the Normans on 14 October at Hastings. The defeat then inflicted by William of Normandy brought to an end six hundred years of Saxon rule. What happened to Askell we do not know: he was probably killed in one of the battles of that year. Soon afterwards, Ware would have a new Norman master.

5.
Norman Lords and Monks

Engiand's new masters, the Normans, were descended from the Vikings, but they were very different from those seafarers Harold had defeated at Stamford Bridge. The name Norman was derived from Northmen or Norsemen – Danes or Norwegians who had settled in France in the early years of the tenth century. Like all Vikings they came to conquer and pillage, but instead settled and began to defend the French against attack by other Vikings. In 911 their chieftain Rollo paid allegiance to the king of France (though Rollo refused to bow to kiss the king's foot and had his servant raise the king's foot head high, which literally caused an upset) and converted to Christianity. In return he was given the area of the Upper Seine which Rollo and his warriors soon expanded into the province of Normandy. The Normans were proud warriors, ardent Catholics and highly adaptable. They gave up their own language in favour of French and readily embraced Frankish culture. So when Rollo's descendant, William the Conqueror, arrived in England in 1066, he brought with him a large number of proud barons, eager to enjoy the estates of the English nobility and church much as their ancestors had done in France a hundred and fifty years earlier. In sharing out these estates, the rough rule was that in any one shire one Norman lord would have the property of one Saxon lord. But often the Saxon estates were scattered and untidy and their Norman successors went in for deals and swaps to consolidate their gains. This led to many disputes. It was partly to resolve these, as well as to find out what every estate could produce by way of taxes, that William commissioned the Domesday survey in 1086. It is fortunate for us that he did, because it gives a detailed picture of every town and village in England (give or take a few counties) in Saxon times and in the time of the first Norman lords.

Domesday Book

Domesday Book records that Ware was the subject of one of these aristocratic swaps. It had originally been granted to Ralph Tallboys, who was married to an important lady named Azelina. Most of Azelina's new manors were in Bedfordshire and some of them had belonged to Askell of Ware, but most of Askell's Bedfordshire manors had gone to a rival lord, Hugh de Beauchamp, and more than one was claimed by both Hugh and Azelina. Besides which Ralph had been made Sheriff of Bedfordshire. So to consolidate his power base, Ralph exchanged Ware for three Bedfordshire manors owned by a lord named Hugh de Grandmesnil. Ralph did not get the best of bargains for Ware contained 24 hides of land while the three Bedfordshire manors together accounted for only 20 hides. No doubt he was satisfied (he and Azelina later married their daughter Matilda to Hugh de Beauchamp's son).

Hugh de Grandmesnil probably did not give the deal much thought. He was a more powerful lord than either Tallboys or Beauchamp. Most of his manors were in Leicester where he became sheriff and the castellan of the new Norman castle, but he did have a few interests in Hertfordshire. He owned the manor of Thundridge and his wife, Adeliza (not to be confused with Azelina Tallboys), owned Broxbourne so the acquisition of Ware was a suitable link between the two, as well as being bigger and richer than the three Bedfordshire manors he had given up. It was also an estate on the Old North Road (or Ermine Street) leading from London more or less towards Leicester. When King William left England for Normandy in 1067, Hugh de Grandmesnil was one of the barons left in charge and later had control of defences around Winchester.

Ware was merely one estate among many for Hugh – he held sixty-seven manors in Leicestershire as well as six in other counties – but it was a large and prosperous manor, with some special features to recommend it. It had five mills, two of them held by the lord of the manor – they must have included the mill on the Lea in Mill Lane (now Priory Street) and probably Westmill on the River Rib. There was a fishery which produced 375 eels (probably on the River Ash), a park for "woodland beasts" (this would have been Ware Park where the lord could hunt deer and wild boar) and four 'arpents' of vines – "just planted"[1]. The arpent was a unit of area (still used in French Quebec) equivalent to roughly 3,400 square metres. Since Roman times, the English climate had been warm enough for vineyards; it was only in the early 1200s that average temperatures fell and England began to look to France for its wines. There is an area of Ware on the south-facing slopes of Musley which has been known traditionally as 'the Vineyard'.

How big was Ware, in terms of area and population, at the time of Domesday? The area of the manor or parish is not difficult to calculate, for it did not change very much between the eleventh and the eighteenth centuries. It extended from Ware Park in the west to the borders with Widford and Stanstead Abbots in the east, including all the land lying between the rivers Rib, Lea and Ash – not counting Thundridge which Hugh de Grandmesnil also held. Domesday Book said in Ware there was land for 38 ploughs, the equivalent of 2,280 acres or 923 hectares. The town itself was quite small in area, not having as yet expanded along the river bank to the present bridge – and, of course, Ware manor and parish did not include what is now Amwell End on the south bank of the Lea. Domesday Book refers to Ware as a *villa*, which is often translated as 'village'. But Latin *villa* was the equivalent of the Anglo-Saxon 'tun' which could refer to anything from a large town to a hamlet. We have already noticed in the last chapter that Ware in 1086 had a large population of 125 identified persons, which would have amounted to a total population of 750. In terms of taxes, Ware was worth £45 and £50 before the Norman Conquest, the second highest valuation in Hertfordshire (*see Appendix One*).

There is no mention in Domesday of a church in Ware though a priest is included among the townspeople. But Ware did have a church, because there is a reference to it five years before Domesday in the writings of Orderic Vitalis. It must have been the church that most interested Hugh about Ware and it was in all probability on the site of the present Parish Church of St. Mary's. It was not usual to move the site of a church; indeed many of the earliest churches were built on sites which had been sacred before Christianity arrived. St. Mary's is built on a gravel platform, higher than the surrounding grount and the present High Street. And, in the absence of local stone, Ware's Saxon church would have been built of wood.

The Grandmesnils

The Grandmesnils were devout and active Catholics. On the death of their father in 1040, Hugh and his younger brother, Robert, founded a monastery according to the fashion then sweeping Normandy. Their first choice of a site proving unsuitable, they followed the advice of an uncle and in 1050 refounded the ancient abbey of St. Evroult, first compensating the Benedictine monks of Bec who owned the ruins. The Anglo-Norman historian Orderic Vitalis, who was a monk at St. Evroult, tells of the generous endowment of the abbey made by the brothers. In the same year Robert entered the abbey as a monk and became its abbot in 1059[2]. Orderic also tells how some of the monks of St. Evroult followed Hugh to England to seek their fortunes as chaplains to Norman families and how in 1081 the new Abbot Mainier followed them. The abbot was well received by Archbishop Lanfranc and King William, who encouraged his nobles to make grants to the abbey. Many did so. Hugh and Adeliza gave to St. Evroult the income from some of their Leicestershire manors and also 'the church of Ware'. At about the same time – the date is not very clear – Hugh founded a Benedictine priory at Ware, centred on the church, in order to administer the rents and income from the English estates of St. Evroult. The Prior of Ware became the 'proctor' of St. Evroult and was personally responsible for delivering the revenues to the mother house in Normandy. As St. Evroult acquired other churches, manors and farms either as bequests or gifts, the Alien (i.e. foreign-owned) Benedictine Priory at Ware became immensely rich and its monks influential. On the local scene, the Prior and monks became major players in the life of Ware.

For the rest of his life, Hugh played a prominent role in national affairs while precariously trying to keep the family's fortunes intact. Two of his sons, Ivo and Aubrey, earned their father's disapproval by joining the revolt of King William's oldest son, Robert Curthose, in 1078 and Hugh was among those who helped to effect a reconciliation between William and Robert in 1079. Robert became Duke of Normandy on the death of the Conqueror and then claimed the English throne. Hugh supported him against William II (William Rufus) in 1087–8 and, when this second rebellion also failed, yet managed to retain his offices under the new king. Hugh made a number of visits himself to Normandy but was back in Leicester when he died, on 22 February 1093. A few days earlier he had become a monk of St Evroult, whose habit had previously been sent to him for that purpose. Orderic records that Hugh's body, preserved in salt and sewn up in an ox skin, was conveyed to Normandy by Bernard and David, two monks of St. Evroult (probably from Ware Priory) and honourably interred by the abbot and convent, on the south side of the chapter house, near the tomb of Abbot Mainier. In the 1970s, Lady Pauline Chapman, who lived at the Manor House in Ware, was visiting Normandy and observed an archaeological dig on the site of the Abbey of St. Evroult in which was discovered a skeleton with pieces of leather clinging to it. This may well have been the last sighting of Ware's Norman lord.

Hugh and Adeliza had five sons and five daughters. The rebellious son Ivo, who had acted as his father's steward, acquired his English estates, while the Norman lands went to another son. However, for supporting Robert Curthose in his second rebellion – even though Robert and William Rufus were reconciled – Ivo de Grandmesnil was forced to mortgage his estates and go on a pilgrimage. He died *en route* to the Holy Land. His son, also named Ivo, failed to regain the family estates and witnessed the humiliation of seeing one of his family's great rivals, Robert de Beaumont, Count of Meulen, being made Sheriff of Leicester and then in 1107 first Earl of Leicester. But all was not lost for the Grandmesnils. Hugh's oldest son, Robert, who had succeeded to his father's Norman estates, remained a supporter of the dynasty of William II and Henry I and lived to a grand age, dying thirty-eight years after his father, in 1136. He was buried next to two of his three wives. Orderic wrote: "All the sons of Hugh de Grandmesnil were in person tall and handsome, as well as of great courage; but fortune persecuted them and none of them, except Robert, enjoyed a long life, nor a continuance of peace and prosperity."[3]

Petronilla

It was Robert's grand-daughter, Petronilla (or Parnel) de Grandmesnil – that is probably the descent though some sources say she was Ivo's grand-daughter[4] – who revived the family tradition of strong-willed, political leadership. She also spent the last years of her life in Ware – the first lord or lady to do so since the Saxon Askell – and oversaw some fundamental changes in the town. She was a formidable lady in every respect. She was brought up in Normandy where she was the sole heir to the Grandmesnil estates and was given in marriage by Henry II to Robert de Beaumont, only son of the second Earl of Leicester. Robert duly inherited his father's title and in due course fell out with Henry II – most people did, including Henry's wife, Eleanor of Castile, his three sons and most famously Archbishop Thomas à Becket. Three years after the murder of Becket, in 1173, Robert de Beaumont invaded England with a mercenary army to overthrow Henry. One of the chroniclers reported that Petronilla accompanied him and was obliged by the earl to dress in armour and carry a lance and shield – one historian described her as the "amazon wife"[5]. She rode with her husband as he marched to meet the royal army near Bury St Edmunds. During the battle she was unhorsed, thrown into a ditch and captured by the royalists, causing her husband to panic and lose the battle. She was imprisoned with the earl in Portchester Castle and spent the next four years in captivity in England or Normandy. The couple lost all their estates and things did not improve until Henry died in 1189 and was succeeded by Richard the Lionheart. Robert and his son, another Robert, 'took the Cross' as the saying goes and accompanied Richard on the Third Crusade, but he died on the way to the Holy Land in 1190. His widow, Petronilla, then came under the protection of her son, Robert, the fourth Earl of Leicester – but he held his mother in such high honour that he changed his surname from Breteuil or de Beaumont to *filius Petronillae* (son of Petronilla) or in English 'FitzParnel'.

6.
The 1200s: A Growing Town

The thirteenth century was a turbulent period in English politics. It began with King John, who soon faced a barons' revolt which resulted in the signing of Magna Carta. He was succeeded by his son, Henry III, who was also embroiled in civil war with a group of barons which resulted in the first parliament; then came Henry's son, Edward I – handsome and tall and known as 'Longshanks' – who defeated the barons before venting his anger on the Welsh and Scots. Since some of the rebellious barons were the lords of Ware, these national events left a clear mark on the town. There can have been few years in the 1200s when some army or group of barons and knights was not passing down Ware High Street.

It was a century in which the town took on its present shape, when some of our present buildings were erected and when Ware grew considerably in economic stature – to the detriment of neighbouring Hertford. Many of these changes were helped by having the lord or lady of the manor in residence – more often than not the lady or the widow of a former lord. Such was the position of Petronilla de Grandmesnil, after the death of her husband and even more after the death of her son, Robert Fitzparnel, Earl of Leicester, in 1204. It was then that the pace of change in Ware really quickened. The family estates now passed to Petronilla's two oldest daughters and their husbands. Amicia, the elder daughter, was married to Simon de Montfort, who became Earl of Leicester and was grandfather of another Simon, the parliamentary reformer in the reign of Henry III. The next daughter, Margaret, was married to Saer de Quincy, a formidable soldier who became Earl of Winchester as well as Chief Justiciar (the equivalent of a modern Prime Minister). These were the early years of King John's reign and Petronilla and her family were able to exert enormous influence over local and national affairs.

When Petronilla came into the Grandmesnil estates in England, she also inherited a 'hall' in Ware, attached to the Benedictine Priory. This hall would have included a large open space for public gatherings and courts, situated between the accommodation for the lord and his family (the solar wing) and that for the servants (the service wing). She lived there from before the death of her husband in 1190 until her own death in 1212. When Richard the Lionheart became king in 1189, the Earl of Leicester carried a sword at the coronation and accompanied the king's progress around England and into Normandy. Petronilla seized the opportunity of royal favour and began to redesign the town of Ware.

Her first act was to divert the Old North Road (Ermine Street) so that, instead of continuing south-west to the ancient ford, it now turned towards the east and headed along a new high street parallel with the river before crossing the Lea by a bridge. Her motive clearly was to create a market place, which would increase her own revenue and also those of the Benedictine monks among whom she now lived. She was described by the monk Orderic as "a great benefactress of St. Evroult". In 1199 King John granted Robert Fitzparnel, Earl of Leicester, the charter for a market to be held weekly on a Tuesday, and on 10 March 1207 the sheriff of Hertfordshire was informed that King John had granted Petronilla, countess of Leicester, the market of Ware for her life, just as Robert, Earl of Leicester, her son, had held it.

All of this was very much in the fashion of the time: the twelfth and thirteenth centuries were a great era of town planning. Towns like Baldock (created by the Knights Templar) and Marlborough in Wiltshire were established or rebuilt with wide market streets and narrow burgage plots running off on each side. Burgage plots were fields which had been enclosed by the lord of the manor in imitation of boroughs ('burgs') to extend the confines of medieval towns. They were invariably – as at Ware where they were created on land reclaimed from the river – long and thin and at right angles to the main street. The 'burgesses' to whom these plots were allotted were tenants; they paid a cash rent instead of occupying land by virtue of having given the lord feudal service. They had to be Freemen and entitled to practise a trade within the town, then they could participate in electing members of any council or local jury. And in the Middle Ages these burgage plots were busy commercial properties with goods being manufactured and sold there, or loaded on to barges at the riverside – it was only much later that the frontages on to the Lea became leisure areas with gardens and summer houses. What Petronilla and her successors laid out in Ware was a classic medieval town plan. The landscape historian, W.G. Hoskins, described "the huge V-shaped market-place running up to the church, and the long, narrow burgage tenements running southward from the market-place to the river-bank" at Ware as "one of the historic town centres of England, [which should be] protected from the acids of modern development."[1] Fortunately, and due partly to the campaigns of the Ware Society, the medieval layout has survived. The burgage tenements were formally authorised by Roger de Quincy in the reign of Henry III and confirmed in 1297 and again in 1447.

But none of this happened without protest and opposition – from Hertford, of course. The men of the county town claimed that they had suffered on a number of counts by the action of Petronilla and her family. They complained that the lady of Ware and her bailiffs had unlawfully neglected the weirs of Ware so that boats could not pass, and that "the said bailiffs and men of Ware diverted the King's highway which used to be through the town of Hertford and into Ware to the detriment of the same town of Hertford."[2] Of course, the old road, Ermine Street, never passed "through the town of Hertford" although the southern bank of the ford was in the parish of St. John, Hertford. All the same, they claimed ownership of the river crossing at the ford. At first, there was little that the men of Hertford could do about the new Ware market: King John had granted Petronilla the market for life, just as her son, Robert Earl of Leicester, had held it. In 1224 the Hertford men succeeded in getting Ware market closed[3] but their victory was short-lived for Ware market soon reopened and increased in size. There were similar complaints against Ware's annual fair, which according to a charter of 1254 was to be held on the eve of the Nativity of the Virgin Mary and the three days following. As part of their great airing of local grievances to the county assize, set up in 1275 by the new king, Edward I, the Hertford men said "that the lady and bailiffs of Ware have a fair in the town of Ware twice or three times in September to the great harm of the borough of Hertford."[4] But nothing seems to have come of that. The annual September fair continued in Ware until 1936.

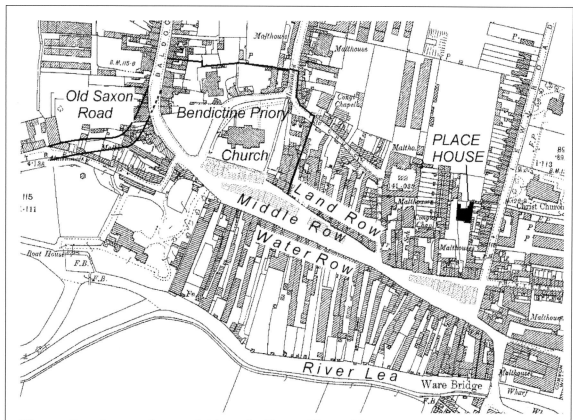

The medieval town plan, as laid out by Petronilla and her successors (superimposed on an 1897 Ordnance Survey map). The High Street would have been wide enough to hold a market and fairs – the market stalls later became permanent and were known as Middle Row. There was a second market place at the eastern end of the High Street. 'Water Row' then referred to the whole south side of the High Street, not just to one wagon-way. Note the long burgage plots going down to the river. The Benedictine Priory occupied a large site at the western end of the new High Street. After the Prior had expelled the lady of the manor, the new manor house he was obliged to build (Place House) was well outside the boundaries of the Priory.

Trouble at the Bridge

There was far more serious trouble over the bridge. As early as 1191, the men of Hertford were fined 60 shillings "because they broke down the bridge of Ware without authority". The records say that a year later the fine had been paid and "the matter was settled".[5] But it was not settled and trouble broke out again in 1217. Petronilla had died and was succeeded by her daughter and son-in-law, Saer de Quincy, Earl of Winchester. Saer was a major power in the land: he had been Justiciar of England and was one of the leaders of the barons who forced John to sign Magna Carta in 1215 – indeed, some historians state that the barons stopped at Ware on their way south and received there a delegation from the City of London. Saer subsequently found himself briefly imprisoned but on his release turned his attention to affairs in Ware. In 1217 the bailiff of Hertford (an officer of the Crown) put "a great chain" across the bridge and a barrier across the old ford, and demanded a toll for the upkeep of the Hertford Castle from any one using the bridge. This was outright provocation. Saer de Quincy broke off his struggle with King John to confront the Hertford bailiff. "He did not trouble to test the bailiff's right in a court of law, but adopted the far more expeditious plan of breaking the chain, and throwing it over the bridge, at the same time informing the bailiff that if he were dissatisfied with this proceeding, and raised any objection thereto, he should follow the chain."[6] That is how it was described by a Victorian historian, quoting an eighteenth century writer. A medieval scribe put it more starkly: "the men of Ware always used to give the crossing tolls of the bridge of Ware to the bailiff of the lord King and by force and their lord they withdrew it after the disputed inheritance of the kingdom."[7] The complaints here and throughout the Middle Ages allegedly come from "the men of Hertford" but there is no evidence of communal animosity between the two towns. It was the bailiff of Hertford Castle and, later, the castle governor, who fomented trouble with their neighbour. The issue of the bridge should have been settled once and for all when, according to the court of Braughing Hundred, "the king's highway is over the bridge and that was demonstrated in the presence of King Henry (III) and twenty-four knights in the time of Roger de Quincy, Earl of Winchester." That agreement was proof of the better relations that Roger had with his king than his father ever had with King John. The agreement sanctioned the bridge at Ware but kept the bridge tolls for the king for the upkeep of Hertford Castle – it remained a toll bridge until 1899.[8] The arrival of the king with twenty-four knights must have been a splendid sight – it was just one of the grand royal and military occasions Ware witnessed in the Middle Ages.

The Alien Benedictine Priory

While the town and the manor grew in importance, so did the Benedictine Priory. Hugh gave Ware church to the Norman Abbey of St. Evroult in 1081 and the priory must have been founded at about the same time to manage the abbey's English possessions. The first specific mention of the Priory is in a charter of the Bishop of Lincoln (1203-6) who ratified a grant to Hubert Prior of Ware of a gift that Petronilla had made to St. Evroult. The Prior was the abbey's 'proctor' – in other words, legally, he owned the Norman abbey's English possessions though, in fact, it was his job to transmit all revenues to France. An earlier proctor, named Richard in 1174, must have been Prior of Ware though he was not identified as such. As more noble families gave possessions to St. Evroult, the Prior became immensely powerful. The *English Monastic Archives* database at University College, London, records that by 1206 the priory controlled fourteen manors and 25 churches and chapels, apart from smaller farms and estates. The Prior collected the rents and tithes and had the right to present vicars or curates to the churches and chapels for which, of course, he received further revenue. So rich was the Priory that in due course the Crown would siphon off some, or even all, of the revenues destined for Normandy.

We have no record of what Ware's Benedictine Priory looked like or the area it covered. The religious house was suppressed in 1414 and all its buildings demolished or rebuilt. However, we can make an educated guess at its extent. It included the church (apart from other chapels or altars), the monks' quarters probably including a cloister, various outbuildings associated with the production of food and drink – and maybe a priory farm – quite apart from the many buildings which various lords and ladies erected within the priory perimeter. We know that Petronilla and her husband maintained a hall there, while her daughter Margaret, widow of Saer de Quincy (according to an Assize Roll of 1256) built herself a great hall, a large chamber and a chapel for her own convenience and also held the manorial courts within the bounds of the Priory. Her sons, Roger and Robert, made use of their mother's accommodation when they were in Ware. These semi-public halls must have been very inconvenient for the monks for, when Margaret's grand-daughter, Joan, the wife of Humphrey de Bohun, inherited the manor, the Prior built a small hall for her use. However, after her husband's death, Joan added yet another chamber to give herself better accommodation. This seems to have been the last straw for the Prior. When Joan died in 1283, the Prior barred entrance to the royal officials (called escheators) who came to assess her possessions – with the help of the Earl of Gloucester's men, a forcible entrance was made but in the meantime the Prior had had Joan's new chamber pulled down. As a result, the Prior was sued by the heiress, Joan's sister, Hawise Wake. Shortly afterwards the funds of the Priory were seized by Edward I and it was then by royal command that a replacement manor house was built outside the boundaries of the Priory. Another way of assessing the extent of the Benedictine priory is to see what land has been owned by the priory's successors, notably Trinity College, Cambridge – this included St. Mary's Church, the Manor House and cottages in Church Street, and the old burial ground and first four buildings on the east side of Baldock Street. When we carried out an archaeological dig in what is now called Tudor Square, we found various chunks of carved clunch, the stone of which the windows of the church are made – so this area too may have been part of the Priory.

The establishment of monks appears to have been fairly large. When the Prior went on a journey to France in 1343, he was accompanied by ten of his household.[9] The Prior was much taken up with managing the estates of St. Evroult and collecting revenues and it was left to other monks to perform the duties expected of Benedictines (in 1410 a monk was brought over from St. Evroult, with his servant, to sing the services). And the Prior, important as he was, was subject to ecclesiastical authority. Prior William was excommunicated by the Archbishop of Canterbury (we don't know why) but absolved in 1279 by the next archbishop – with a penance that on every sixth day to a total of forty days he had to fast on bread, fish and ale, feed ten people and on that day and the following one say fifty psalms. Fasting on bread, fish and ale cannot have been too great a hardship! The middle of the thirteenth century was the high point of the priory's fortunes; after that wars between England and France led to increasing interference and confiscations by the Crown. In 1231, there is mention of an interesting monk, known as "Richard de Ware Senior". Twenty-six years later he appeared at Westminster Abbey and was elected abbot in 1258, though he appears to have been a compromise candidate. For the rest of his life, he was heavily involved in Henry III's ambitious rebuilding of the abbey, travelling to Italy on a number of occasions to purchase special mosaics and marbles – he died in 1283.

As politics made life difficult for the Prior of Ware, his popularity in the town began to plummet. In 1231, Prior William attempted to increase his revenues by imposing an annual 'pension' or service charge of 10 marks on the Vicar of St. Mary's. The vicar, Nicholas Speleman, with the backing of influential parishioners objected, and took their case to Rome. The Pope passed the case back to the Bishop of London and the Dean of St. Paul's who quashed the pension payment and awarded the vicar a stable income, consisting of the tithes (a tenth of the value) of all mills in the town, the tithes of Ware Park, plus the tithes of 56 acres of arable land, 40 acres of corn, 8 acres of meadow, the hay from the Meads south of Ware and, in addition, tithes of flax, hemp, yards, fruit, wool, lambs, pigs, geese, swans, calves, cheese, butter, milk, harts, conies (rabbits), fish and fowls in the parishes of Ware and Thundridge. The vicar and his supporters must have held a party on the day they received the news. What is particularly interesting about the award is that it gives a detailed topography as good as any thirteenth-century town guide. The vicar's tithes from the arable land were from Warymo Cros (the top of Watton Road) to Baldoke Lane which abutted the Benedictine Priory, then in a straight line from Warymo Cros to Ware Mill (now part of GlaxoSmithKline), then down river to Waterlanend (the bottom of the modern Library Car Park), up Water Lane and a part of the High Street till it joined up again with Baldock Street. The area of tithes on the corn and meadow was between Cripestre (Crib Street) in the west and Whytberwe Cros (Widbury Crossroads) in the east with Popes Lane (Collett Road and Musley Lane) to the north and Gerneslane (Church Street?) to the south. And the Meads included such familiar names as Berymede, Chaldwellmede and Millemede. And the witnesses to the award had equally familiar names – Robert de Parco (of Ware Park), Silvester de Aqua (Waters Place) Osbert de Fanham, Robert Whitberwe and William Halfhide (after the subsidiary manor of Halfhide or Westmill). However, this medieval award would not have survived had it not been for a dispute in 1603 when some Thundridge farmers refused to pay tithes to the Parish of Ware, and Trinity College, Cambridge, produced the 1231 document to show why they should. The pursuit of money is the best preservative ever of ancient documents!

The next two major events brought the clash of arms to Ware, and not in any show of chivalry. In 1241 a tournament was held in defiance of Henry III's ban on tournaments. One account, by the St. Albans monk, Matthew Paris, said the "tilting march" took place "about a cross-bow shot from Hertford" but two other medieval chroniclers and most later historians put the tournament in Ware. At any event, it was a sorry business. The instigator of the event, Gilbert Marshall, Earl of Pembroke, was thrown from his horse when the stirrup broke and fatally injured. When the jousting did begin, one of the earl's followers was killed and others were badly wounded "because the jealousy of many of the parties concerned had converted the sport into a battle". Matthew Paris said the injured earl was taken to St. Mary's Priory, Hertford, but other sources say it was Ware – that seems more likely since Marshall was related to the Clares, who were lords of the manor of Standon and had property in Ware. All the sources stress the bloody nature of the tournament: it was left to later writers to give it pageantry. John Scott, the eighteenth-century Quaker poet, wrote of the tournament's "proud pomp" (in the poem *Amwell*). James Smith, a nineteenth-century writer who later went to Australia, added a more fanciful tale. On his way to the tournament, wrote Smith, the Earl of Pembroke was cursed by an old hag who prophesied that his body would lie that night on a cold pillow with God's saints looking down. In due course, the earl is wounded and taken to Ware Parish Church where he is put in the Lady Chapel under the ceiling then (in the 1830s) painted with saints – he is convinced the curse has come true. It is an entertaining tale but the tournament took place in 1241 and the Lady Chapel of St. Mary's in Ware was not built until the late 1400s.[10]

The next clash of arms involved another Earl of Pembroke – one of Gilbert Marshall's in-laws. He was William de Valence, one of the four 'Lusignan' brothers who were sons of King John's second wife, Isabella of Angoulême, and therefore Henry III's half-brothers. Henry had invited the brothers to England in 1247 to strengthen the royal family against the barons and bishops who opposed him. Immediately on arrival, William married Joan, daughter and heir of the late William the Marshall, and therefore became Earl of Pembroke in the right of his wife. Probably as part of the marriage contract, Henry granted him Hertford Castle and a double money fee: 500 marks a year for life, with an additional £500, the latter eventually to be replaced by lands. So financially William de Valence did not need to take any action against Ware over the bridge, but it was in his character to do so. The St. Albans chronicler Matthew Paris accused him of "homicide, rapine and great oppression". In 1258 on the orders of William de Valence, a crowd of armed men came from Hertford, broke down the bridge, dug a dyke in the river bed next to where the communal crossing (the ford) used to be so that no one could cross there either on horseback or foot, and afterwards made a ditch in the king's highway half a mile outside the town of Ware in the direction of London and then obstructed the highway with that ditch. The leaders of this armed band were Simon le Ferun, David le Marshall, who was then the reeve of Hertford, and others. "It was well known that they came on the very same day to the said bridge" (it was claimed at the Assizes) "and this was on the orders of their lord William of Valence who said that the Lord King by his writ had commanded the said Lord William to erect there a barrier and chain across the ford to impede the crossing there so that these same men together with others often from the town of Hertford on the orders of the bailiff there of William were accomplices in putting up the aforesaid barrier and chain." The men of Ware, who made the complaint, said that they had offered no resistance. Simon, David le Marshall and the other Hertford ringleaders were sentenced to imprisonment but William de Valence escaped censure – except in Ware.

These events took place during the lordship of Saer de Quincy's second son, Roger de Quincy (c. 1195–1264). Through his first wife Roger had inherited large estates in Scotland and was made constable of Scotland. He accompanied Henry III on his wars in France, which left him with little time to enjoy his estates in Ware or the changes made by his grandmother, Petronilla. In 1253 Roger granted a tenancy in the manor of Ware to his brother, Robert, who had also fought in the French wars. It was Robert who in 1254

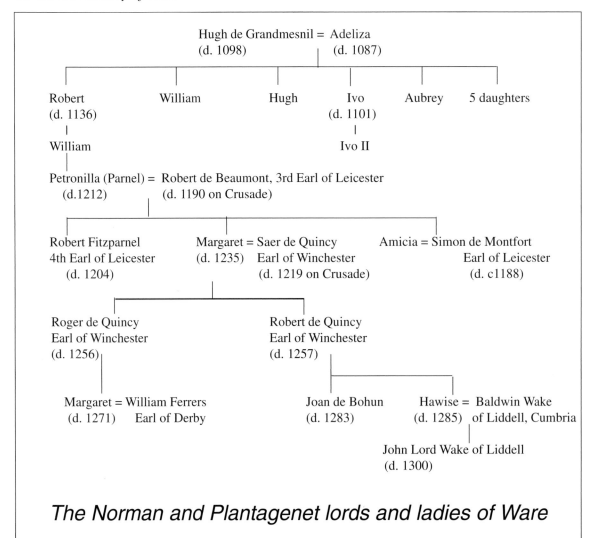

Hugh de Grandmesnil = Adeliza
(d. 1098)   (d. 1087)

Robert   William   Hugh   Ivo   Aubrey   5 daughters
(d. 1136)   (d. 1101)

William   Ivo II

Petronilla (Parnel) = Robert de Beaumont, 3rd Earl of Leicester
     (d.1212)   (d. 1190 on Crusade)

Robert Fitzparnel   Margaret = Saer de Quincy   Amicia = Simon de Montfort
4th Earl of Leicester   (d. 1235)   Earl of Winchester   Earl of Leicester
     (d. 1204)   (d. 1219 on Crusade)   (d. c1188)

Roger de Quincy   Robert de Quincy
Earl of Winchester   Earl of Winchester
   (d. 1256)   (d. 1257)

Margaret = William Ferrers   Joan de Bohun   Hawise = Baldwin Wake
(d. 1271)   Earl of Derby   (d. 1283)   (d. 1285) of Liddell, Cumbria

                                                        John Lord Wake of Liddell
                                                              (d. 1300)

The Norman and Plantagenet lords and ladies of Ware

gained from Henry III at Bordeaux the charter for Ware's annual September fair. But he lived only for three years more. After that – and with the older brother, Roger, dying soon afterwards – the manor of Ware seems to have been alternately shared and disputed among four Quincy women. They were Roger's three daughters – Margaret, wife of William Ferrers, sixth Earl of Derby, Elizabeth Comyn, wife of the Earl of Buchan, Helen, wife of Alan la Zouche of Ashby-de-la-Zouche – and the elder of Robert's two daughters, Joan de Bohun, widow of Humphrey de Bohun. Whoever was the rightful heir to the manor, it was Joan who was in possession for she was living in Ware at the time of her death in November 1283. It was following her death that the Prior of Ware demolished her residence and denied entrance to the king's assessors (escheators). As a result, the Prior was sued by the heiress, Joan's sister, Hawise Wake. Shortly afterwards the funds of the Priory were seized by Edward I and it was then by royal command that a replacement manor house was built outside the boundaries of the Priory.

Place House

The new hall, built by the Prior, is believed to be this splendid Listed Grade I building in Bluecoat Yard – Place House. Behind the seventeenth-century facade is a timber-frame of appropriately high quality and it has long been recognised that Place House was the medieval manor house of Ware. But why 'Place House'? It was known at one time as Braughing Place, indicating that that was where the courts of Braughing Hundred were held, as well as the manorial courts of Ware.

It is, in fact, what remains of a timber-framed aisled hall – consisting of the open hall itself and a service wing, separated from the hall by a cross wing which runs from the entrance, seen on the right. The solar wing where the Lord or Lady or their steward had their apartment was demolished in the seventeenth century – unless it had already fallen down. If it is the case that Place House was built on the orders of the king to replace the hall demolished by the Prior, then that explains the very high standard of carpentry. The expert on medieval carpentry, Cecil A. Hewett, described it thus: "The frame of the house is among the most sophisticated and finely wrought known, and comprises a two-bay open hall with aisles, a cross entry, and a jettied service wing."[11] On stylistic grounds, he concluded that it was built in about 1295 (dendrochronolgy – tree-ring dating – was tried in the 1980s but the results were inconclusive). Hewett illustrated the framing of Place House, the sections and profiles of the roll mouldings running around all of the principal wall plates and a section of the stout crown post in the centre of the frame.

However, he reserved his greatest praise for a 'scarf joint' (i.e. a joint holding two timbers end to end) which he described as "the apogee of English scarfing" found only in the final decade of the thirteenth century. He gave comparable

Place House

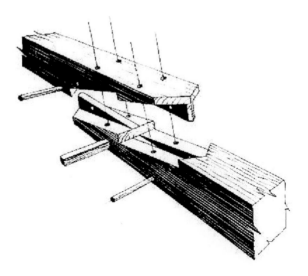

The Place House scarf joint: Cecil Hewett described it as "a stop-splayed and tabled scarf with sallied and under-squinted abutments, a transverse key, counter tongued-and-grooved tables, four face pegs and two edge pegs".

examples at Chichester, St. Etheldreda's church, London and in Suffolk, but added "these are simplified, and mechanically inferior". A mark of the sophistication of this particular joint is that it has not twisted or separated in 700 years and is held so tight it is difficult to spot it from below. Adrian Gibson, another enthusiast for timber-framed buildings, made a replica of the Place House scarf for teaching purposes; his mistake was to make it in green oak which when assembled was absolutely impossible to pull apart!

The later history of Place House is interesting but can only be sketched in here. By 1575 when the Fanshawes became lords of the manor, the hall was in such a poor state that Thomas Fanshawe sold it and built a new manor house at Ware Park. It was in private hands until 1685, when Christ's Hospital acquired it as a Bluecoat School – encasing the outside in brick and building the nurses' cottages in the yard opposite. The Bluecoat children were moved to Hertford in 1761 and the hall became a private school. It fell into disrepair again in the twentieth century, was bought by John Whitfield, who cared deeply about Ware buildings but died before he could restore it. It was then gifted to the Hertfordshire Building Preservation Trust who restored it with grants from the Ware War Memorial Fund and the Historic Buildings Council and became a village hall for the town. It was reopened in 1977 by Queen Elizabeth, the Queen Mother, and is now in the care of the Hertfordshire Building Preservation Trust. Place House contains an intriguing Tudor screen – but that is for a later chapter.

Place House is not the oldest timber structure in Ware. In 1978 part of a building some forty-five years older was discovered – almost by chance (it was an event in which the author played a small part). This was the rear portion of No.2 West Street which was revealed during the construction of the new Tesco supermarket next door. From the street the building looks like an 18th century shop, but students from the North London Polytechnic discovered that the rear two bays were thirteenth-century and incorporated the remains of scissor-bracing and even 'secret notched lap joints'. The author informed Adrian Gibson, who with Cecil Hewett made a thorough survey of the building. They concluded that this was the surviving service wing of an aisled hall – above is Adrian Gibson's reconstruction of how it would have looked when in use. With no chimney, cooking would have been on an open hearth, with the smoke exiting from an opening in the roof. It was in these two bays that archaeologists found evidence of an open hearth and an ash pit in which the Anglo-Saxon coin (*sceat*) was found along with a scatter of Roman pottery. There is a fuller description of the building and the archaeological dig in *Hertfordshire Archaeology 8*.[12]

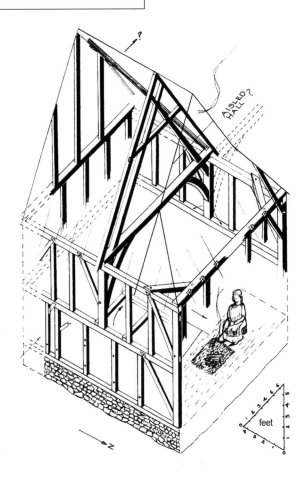

The discovery of a medieval wing behind an 18th century shop shows how Ware – in common with other towns of similar antiquity – grew piecemeal and organically, without resort to the modern practice of total demolition and clearance of a site before anything new is built. Many of the medieval timber-framed buildings on the south side of the High Street (Water Row) were given red brick frontages in the eighteenth century. To see their true age, one must view them from the back. Other buildings in the row have been blessed with an additional floor. The oldest buildings here are those which are sideways on to the street, while the those with gable ends tend to be later.

7.
1300s: the Wake family

Just as the thirteenth century had given Ware the basic physical shape it has today, so the fourteenth century began to shape the town's character as an open, commercial centre with a reputation for rebelliousness. At the turn of the centuries, Ware also acquired a new dynasty of lords and ladies – the Wake family. The dynasty was founded by Hawise de Quincy, who married Baldwin Wake of Liddell in Cumbria.

However, before we turn to the Wakes, let us look at the manor that Hawise inherited in 1284 from her sister, Joan de Bohun, for it gives a detailed picture as good as any modern town guide. The royal official (escheator) held his inquisition or enquiry on the Friday before the Feast of St. Vincent (22 January 1284) taking evidence from, among others, Adam Wytheberwe (Widbury), Hamilin de Ware, John Pastor (Shepherd), Edward the son of Robert, Philip the son of William, Geoffrey Spileman and Ernaldus de Paviner.[1] They said on oath that the next heir to the manor was Joan's sister, Hawise, the wife of Baldewyn Wake, and she was then 32 years of age. The jurors were required to put a value on everything Hawise now owned. There was a manor house with a pigeon coop, worth 5s. a year in rent, 536 acres of arable land (worth almost £9), 56 acres of meadow (£7), a park for hunting, enclosed within a three-mile boundary (£1), 30 acres of wood, worth nothing apart from the value of firewood and pasture; in addition there was a water-mill (for flour) and a fulling mill (for the beating and cleaning of cloth) with a bakehouse (all worth £10). The tolls of the market were worth 6s. per annum; the thrice yearly rents from tenants amounted to £29, feudal work for the manor by 'villanes' (feudal servants rather than 'villains') was worth £5 and rents from customary tenants (i.e. freeholders) was 43s. 6d. Hawise could expect some of the rents in kind – 20 hens at Easter, six cocks, eight score and four (164) eggs and one single lamb. The manorial courts which oversaw the transfer of properties brought in another £4. Altogether the annual income from Ware manor was £68. 18s. 4½d. part of which would naturally go to the king in taxes. It was a useful and no doubt welcome inheritance.

Hawise de Quincy was the second wife of Baldwin Wake. The Wakes were minor lords from Cumbria where they guarded the wild border and competed for control with the Scottish Graham clan. The family had the title 'Lords of Bourne', from Bourne in Lincolnshire, and there was a fanciful tale that they were descended from Hereward the Wake, who held out against William the Conqueror in the Fens – but that tale only emerged later. Baldwin was much older than the 32-year old Hawise; in fact, she was a widow by the time she inherited Ware manor and she herself died a year later in 1285. That left the manor in the hands of their son, John, who was a teenager and in the custody of Queen Eleanor, but he also died in his early thirties in 1300. Ware Manor descended to his son, Thomas Wake, Lord of Liddell, and for a few decades at least there was no change of lord or lady of the manor. The notable event in the tenure of Thomas (1300-1349) was his grant of land to the Friars Minor or Franciscan Greyfriars to establish a house in Ware. Permission was given by King Edward III on 18 February 1338 and confirmed by the

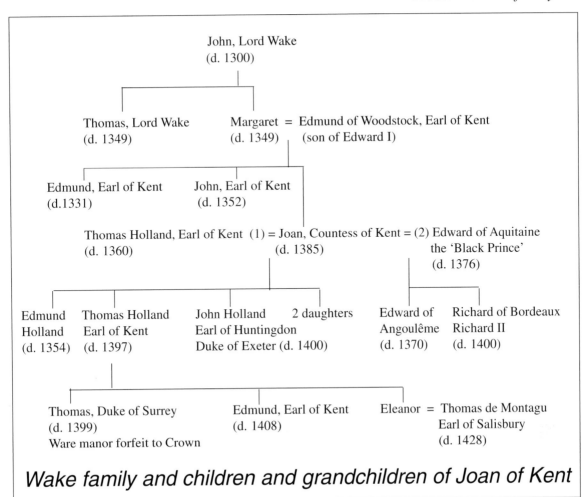

Wake family and children and grandchildren of Joan of Kent

Pope in 1350. The land was opposite the church and Benedictine Priory and consisted of seven acres extending down to the river and an existing house (or 'messuage') standing on a small platform of gravel. Later in 1372 the Greyfriars were given a further four acres of land by Thomas's widow, Blanche, and later still in 1400 they received an acre of woodland and fishery rights along the whole length of their property. In due course, the Greyfriars house in Ware would become a large complex of buildings and an important religious and political establishment – but not yet. It will be described later. For the remainder of the fourteenth century it remained a small community of poor friars, dependent for their livelihood on begging. In 1395 the Greyfriars in Cambridge complained to the Pope that "a certain small house of the Order" founded in Ware was begging on their traditional territory: the Ware friars were ordered to limit their begging to Ware and also Puckeridge.[2] Why Puckeridge is not explained.

Ware was a prosperous town. Its prosperity came partly from agriculture – Ware was a large manor with good farm land – and partly from trade through its market. Its comparative prosperity can be judged from the table: *Taxes in the Principal Towns of Hertfordshire (Appendix 1)*. Ware was not always the most prosperous town in the county. In the earlier centuries it had been outperformed by Sawbridgeworth, the manor of Geoffrey de Mandeville, and in later centuries by St. Albans with its large and growing abbey. But for five hundred years Ware was among the leaders. The spread of its wealth can be seen from the Lay Subsidy Roll of 1307.[3] This 'subsidy' was granted to the new King, Edward II, by parliament to meet the expenses of his father's funeral and his own coronation – it was 'lay' because it did not apply to the church. It was a variable tax on moveables – one fifteenth in the case of boroughs, which at that time applied only to Hertford, St. Albans and Stortford – and one twentieth for all other towns and villages. Although Ware was sometimes regarded as a borough, it was not in this case and so its prosperity was greater than the table seems to show. The biggest tax bill (40s.1¾d) was for Joan Wake, widow of John Lord of Liddell – she was lady of the manor during the minority of her nine-year old son, Thomas, but was probably not living in Ware at the time. After Joan, the biggest bills fell on the other major landowners like Gamelo or Hamilin of Ware, Richard of Ware, Stephen le Blake (of Blakesware), Thomas of Widbury and Peter of Halfhide (or Westmill). Hamilin and Richard may have been merchants as were some big taxpayers identified only by their places of origin – William of Fotheringhay (Northants) and Adam of Swillington (Yorkshire). Not all the people were taxed, only the gentry, landowners and better off tradesmen: two-thirds of the population were exempt on grounds of poverty. In Ware the tradesmen included two millers, two fullers of cloth, two smiths, a shipman (or barge owner), a carter, three coopers (makers of barrels and buckets), a mason, maltster, ropemaker, shepherd, cowman, fisherman and a forester. There were also professional people – Prior Hugh and two clergy, a steward, the town reeve's son, a butler who looked after the lord's or prior's wine cellar and a moneylender (*Robert le Fenere*). There was also *Reginald le Ballede*, in other words 'Reggie the Bald'!

Many of these men and women were involved in the weekly market and the annual fair or fairs at Ware. These were events of regional or even national importance, far more wide-ranging than our modern produce markets. In 1339 a royal writ was issued to the bailiffs of Ware ordering the restitution of 12 quarters of malt seized from an Italian merchant, a Master Peregrine. The main commerce was in malt and grain bound for London. Ware was one of the five principal markets for this trade (along with Henley, Faversham, High Wycombe and St. Albans) and in 1295 a cornmonger named William de Ware was controlling one of the syndicates buying grain for the Crown.[4] The will of another cornmonger in 1351 and a regulation order of 1374 show that Ware merchants brought their grain into the city at Bishopsgate to market at Gracechurch.[5] But it was cheaper to bring the grain by water. The monks of Westminster calculated that it cost sixpence a quarter to bring wheat from their manor at Ashwell to Ware and then a further ten pence to ship it down the Lea and up the Thames to Westminster. But many other goods were traded at Ware. In 1393 John Draper of Huntingdon, supported by two London merchants, complained that his son Thomas had taken five dozen woollen cloths to Ware market, as he had done many times before, and they had been seized by the serjeant-at-arms, who supposed them to be stolen. The king ordered them to be restored to Thomas.[6] The problem was that Ware ran a tightly controlled market under the control of 'a court of pie powder' (a court for itinerant traders from the French *pieds poudreux*, meaning dusty feet). Regulation was necessary as shown by the case of John Reynolds, of Hereford, who in 1385 confessed to housebreaking and thefts at St. Bartholomew's Fair in London, Newmarket Fair, Windsor, St. Edmundsbury, Deptford and finally Ware. Here he had met a man, who was kept busy in a tavern by Reynolds's confederates, while he stole a case full of towels, board cloths and sheets and a pound of pepper, also a knife with a pouch, belt, cloak and sword, all worth 16s. with another 7s. in the purse.[7]

The market grew steadily without interruption but control of the manor had its setbacks. If the Ware bailiff had tried to arrest a miscreant trader in early 1353, the conversation could well have gone something like this:

Serjeant: *I arrest you in the name of the lord – or er ... lady – of the manor of Ware.*

Trader: *All very well, but who is "the lord or er .. lady of the manor of Ware"?*

Serjeant: *Interesting point! Up to the 31 May 1349, it would have been Thomas Wake, 2nd Lord of Liddell, but he died of the plague. Then it was his sister Margaret Plantagenet, who became Baroness Wake of Liddell, but she died on the following 29 September also of the plague. She should have been succeeded by her oldest son, Edmund, but he died as a child, and her older daughter, Margaret, is also dead as well as the other son, John, who had the title Earl of Kent. He died on St. Stephen's Day last year (26 December 1352). This plague has certainly decimated the aristocracy. So I suppose the lady of the manor now is Baroness Margaret's other daughter, the amorous one, Joan de Holland.*

The plague of 1348-49 was bubonic, spread by rats, and known ever since as the Black Death. It came from continental Europe and it is thought to have wiped out a fifth of the population and half the clergy. Some sources say the Prior of Ware was one of its victims. There was a less severe outbreak in 1361-2, a third in 1369, and a fourth ten years later in the north. The Black Death was one of the defining events of the Middle Ages, not least in its effect on the economy and the government. Its immediate effect was to raise wages to make up for the shortage of labourers in agriculture. To counter that in 1351 the government of Edward III brought in the Statute of Labourers "to curb the malice of servants who after the pestilence were idle and unwilling to serve without securing excessive wages." In 1356 a vicar and a hermit were prosecuted for 'vigorously preaching' in Ware that the Statutes of Labourers were wicked, and there was nothing to prevent workmen from taking what wages they pleased.[8] The government's attempts to reverse the economic effects of the Black Death set off a chain of events that culminated in the bitterly resented Poll Tax of 1380 and the Peasants' Revolt of the following year.

The Wake family's first two plague victims – Thomas and his sister, Margaret – had looked set for long and influential lives, for both had married into junior branches of the Royal Family. Thomas married Blanche Plantagenet, daughter of Henry of Lancaster, a grandson of Henry III, and once King Edward II had got over his anger at not arranging the marriage himself, Thomas Wake prospered in the royal favour. He was astute enough to change sides when Queen Isabella and her lover, Roger Mortimer, invaded England to overthrow Edward II, and prospered even further. In 1326, he became keeper of the Tower of London and Hertford Castle. At the time of his death, Thomas stood high in the favour of the new king, Edward III, and Edward gave strong support to Thomas's widow, Blanche, when she was engaged in a property dispute with the Bishop of Ely. Blanche lived on until 1381 and in 1372 gave the Ware Friary her husband had established an additional four acres of land, she had specifically bought for the purpose.

Thomas's sister, Margaret, had married Edmund of Woodstock, Earl of Kent, the half-brother of Edward II – hence her married name was Plantagenet. Edmund was close to his brother-in-law, Thomas Wake, and the two sided with Queen Isabella against Edward II, but after that the earl's luck ran out. In 1330 he was found guilty of trying to overthrow the new king, Edward III, and executed at Winchester. His title passed to his older son, another Edmund, and after his death in 1331 to the younger son, John, the one who died on Boxing Day 1352.

Joan of Kent

The surviving member of the family, Joan of Kent, would have been remarkable in any age, not just the fourteenth century. As a young woman, her three marriages raised eyebrows among the prudish, though they gained her the affection of the common people; as an old woman, she used her influence with great skill to contain any rebellion against her son, Richard II. She did not live in Ware – she was far too grand for that – but her influence on the town and particularly on St. Mary's Church was extensive. One of the chroniclers, Froissart, described Joan as *la plus belle de tout la roiaulme d'Engleterre et la plus amoureuse*. She was certainly 'amorous' and local opinion called her, sarcastically, 'the Virgin of Kent'.

Joan spent much of her childhood in the royal household and in 1340, when she was twelve or thirteen, she attracted the attention of Sir Thomas de Holland, a knight of the royal household, who persuaded her to marry him. It was a secret pact without benefit of clergy and, soon after, Holland went off to fight in Prussia and France, distinguishing himself at the Battle of Crécy in 1347. Meanwhile, Joan's mother, Margaret Plantagenet, had ambitions for her daughter and, knowing nothing about the liaison with Holland, she married Joan to William Montague, son of the Earl of Salisbury. That was in the winter of 1340-41 and on that occasion everything was done properly with clergy and witnesses. Then, by one of history's ironies, Holland returned to England and became steward to Montague, who by now had succeeded his father as Earl of Salisbury. In 1347, when he had enough money to carry it through, Thomas de Holland began legal proceedings to reclaim his bride. He did this through the Vatican, knowing that Joan's mother would block any case in the English courts – and the Pope upheld his claim, on the grounds that he and Joan had sealed their marriage by cohabiting. Joan at the time had been thirteen years old, but it was clearly a love match. She bore Thomas three sons and two daughters, and conferred on him her father's title of Earl of Kent. Thomas died in 1360.

Joan's widowhood was brief. At some time in the spring or early summer of 1361, Edward, Prince of Wales (the Black Prince) asked for her hand in marriage. The betrothal seems to have been an entirely private affair unknown to Edward III, and both in view of Joan's previous marital history and her status, this was a surprising turn of events. In addition, the pair were related within the prohibited degrees: they were cousins, and the prince was godfather to Joan's eldest son. However, the couple received the king's blessing, the marriage went ahead with great ceremony at Windsor, and she duly bore the Prince of Wales two sons – Edward of Aquitaine (named after the place where he was born) who died aged five in 1370, and Richard of Bordeaux, born in January 1367, the future King Richard II. Again it appears to have been a love match. In the next ten years, Joan took on the heavy responsibility of being Princess of Wales during the illnesses of her husband and his father and of bringing up the young Richard who succeeded to the throne in 1377 at the age of ten. Joan's titles were now Baroness Wake, Countess of Kent, Princess of Wales and the mother of the king.

Among her Wake estates, Ware was ranked first and she came into possession of the manor in July 1381 on the death of her aunt, Blanche. The manor was a prosperous one and when the escheator carried out his inventory he found all the assets that featured in the 1284 inquisition after Joan de Bohun had died – the arable land, meadows, park, woods, flour mill and fulling-mill, as well as extensive fisheries. It now brought in a yearly income of £58. 2s. 8d. by contrast with the 1284 figure of £68.18s.4½d.[9] The Black Death had played havoc with property values! There was also a tiresome little sum to be paid each year to a distant Quincy relative, Henry Ferrers, lord of Groby, who had a feudal interest in the Ware manor. But that would not have bothered Joan. She was engaged in the affairs of state. She had one son who was King of England, though still only 14 years old, two other sons who were rising stars in government circles and two daughters who had made glittering marriages.

1381 was an auspicious year for Joan. On May 20 she also obtained a grant from the king defining how the assets of Ware's Benedictine Priory were to be managed. For decades the Priory's rents and other income had been in royal hands "during the war with France" (it was said, though that still applied when there was no war) and this income had been used for public expenditure. Now, at Joan's insistence, William Herbert, the Prior of Ware, was to be allowed "to farm" the income and, although he had to pay £2,451 a year for the privilege, at least he and the priory could keep a percentage.

The Peasants' Revolt

1381 was also the year of the Peasants' Revolt when Joan's popularity proved absolutely vital. When the mob invaded the Tower of London, they were determined to have some blood. It was said that they wanted the head of John of Gaunt, Duke of Lancaster and the king's oldest uncle. Gaunt was not in London but the rebels vented their anger against him by burning down the Savoy Palace, one of his residences, in the Strand. Sympathisers let the rebels into the Tower of London where they found the Chancellor (the Archbishop of Canterbury) and the Lord Treasurer whom they blamed for the Poll Tax. Both were quickly beheaded. When the ringleaders discovered Joan in another part of the Tower, 'they invited the king's mother to kiss them'.[10] Other sources say that the rebels made lewd comments to the Queen Mother. At any rate, she escaped with her life. 1381 was definitely an auspicious year for her.

The Poll Tax introduced in the previous year was different from all the earlier 'subsidies' and from the previous Poll Taxes of 1377 and 1379. It was not geared to income or the value of land or 'movable' goods. It was a tax of one shilling (1s.) to be levied on every adult man and woman, whatever their circumstances, and when the average income for a family was less than 20s. that meant that more than five per cent was being seized by the government. Parliament was aware of the hardship this would cause but thought the rich would help the poor to pay. But under a system where tax-collectors kept back a percentage for themselves, there were heavy-handed attempts to gather the Poll Tax. Trouble first erupted in villages near Stanford-le-Hope in Essex and then spread across the Thames to Kent. Meanwhile, the citizens of St. Albans, joined by others from Barnet and the vicinity, rose up against the Abbot with whom they had had a long dispute about freedoms and the use of mill wheels. Thus the rebels converged on London from three directions and for some weeks the government was in danger of being toppled. This was averted by Richard II at first being conciliatory, then the rebels overreaching themselves, and finally the authorities clamping down with the utmost harshness. If you read old histories of Hertfordshire, you would assume that Ware and Hertford were a little oasis of calm while St. Albans and district resounded with the clamour for justice. The *Victoria County History of Hertfordshire* devoted ten pages to the revolt of the St. Albans burgesses and the reprisals exacted on them; it mentioned unrest in Cheshunt and the beheading of a man in Waltham Cross. But of Ware and Hertford not a mention.

Then in 1383, a claim appeared in the Court of Common Pleas brought by John of Gaunt through his attorney Hugh Wombwell. This surprising document alleged that a crowd of 103 – 42 of them from Ware, 13 from Thaxted in Essex, five from Saffron Walden and smaller numbers from almost every town and village in between – had broken into Hertford Castle and by force of arms stolen goods and chattels worth a thousand pounds.[11] The defendants included some interesting men, but we will come to them a little later. The day before Attorney Wombwell had issued another claim, alleging that roughly the same crowd of men had broken into the Savoy Palace "in the parish of the Blessed Virgin Mary outside the Temple Bar in London" and stolen goods and chattels worth – you guessed it, one thousand pounds.[12] There is no evidence Attorney Wombwell proceeded with either case and, as far as one can tell, there were no arrests, fines or imprisonments. In any case, John of Gaunt was the richest man in England and known to be running down the Savoy Palace at the time in order to refurbish his other property at Hertford Castle. He was a man who would be king, if not of England then in Europe – he appeared in the two claims as "John King of Castile and León Duke of Lancaster". But there may be more to the events than Gaunt and his attorney trying it on. A few days later there was a case brought by the Abbot of Westminster over damage to his estate at Harpenden; the defendants included the bailiff of the manor of Halfwyke in Hatfield and four men from Ware.

The point has been made that it was craftsmen and professional men, not peasants, who dominated the Peasants' Revolt (a point made by Dr. Andrew Prescott whose research into John of Gaunt's legal proceedings led me to the events described above). The Ware defendants to Gaunt's actions included drapers, tailors, clerks, tanners, carpenters, a fletcher, a fuller, a saddler and "John the long butcher". Thomas Cook, described as a cordwainer, could well have made the fourteenth-century lady's slipper and the soles of other shoes, found by archaeologists at the end of one of the burgage plots in 1987 and now in Ware Museum. As for the Vicar, he was Philip of Hertford who had come to Ware from Aspenden in 1374 and in 1384 exchanged parishes with Nicholas de Drayton, Vicar of St. Peter's, Marlborough. Another defendant, Walter Leche died in 1388 and his widow assigned all of her property in Ware, Stanstead Abbots, Thele (St. Margaret's) and Widford, which she had inherited from her brother, to three trustees – Thomas Tonewell, William atte Water and Nicholas Blake. We know these names for they appear as witnesses or trustees on other property deeds of the period. They were probably members of the Guild of Corpus Christi which owned property in the town, including the old Saracen's Head Inn in Water Row. In 1377, the inn had been assigned to Giles Draper, possibly a relative of the John Draper, one of the defendants cited by John of Gaunt. The witnesses then included Thomas Tonewell, Nicholas Blake, Alexander Halfhide, Hugh Mice, Walter Leche, Roger Marchal and Roger Siward.[13] Blake, Leche, Marchal and Siward all appeared in Gaunt's claim as well as two other members of the Mice family. When he sued the men of Ware, Thaxted and Walden, Gaunt was not taking on peasants, but the new minor landowners and tradesmen who were prepared to demonstrate for their freedoms and privileges.

Joan's major achievements was to forge an alliance with her brother-in-law, John of Gaunt, Duke of Lancaster, to protect the Crown. It was an important protection for Richard II who had come to the throne at the age of eleven amid the jealousies and claims for wealth and status of his four uncles. The one who posed the greatest threat was Thomas of Woodstock, the nearest in age to the young king and eventually to try to overthrow him. On the eve of his coronation Richard had made Thomas Earl of Buckingham, with an income of £1000 a year to maintain his estate. This income was not deived from land, but from the revenues of alien priories, which were in the king's hands during the war with France including £206.13 .4d (the second highest amount) from Ware Priory. Thomas thus had a vested interest in the continuation of the war which was to cause friction between him and Richard later. Raphael Holinshed, the Tudor historian who had access to records that have since disappeared, wrote: *"Through the earnest labour of the King's mother, that (notwithstanding her indisposition of body to travel, by reason of her corpulence) riding to and fro betwixt them, made an agreement betwixt the King her son and the duke, to her great comfort and contentation of mind, and no less surety of quietness to the whole realm."* [14] Another of Joan's concerns was to maintain peace between Richard and his half-brothers, the sons from her first marriage to Thomas de Holland. One chronicler said her failure to resolve a quarrel between the king and her second son, John, was a cause of her death although it was almost certainly the result of illness. She died on 14 August at Wallingford Castle beside the Thames and was buried, as she had asked, not with the Black Prince at Canterbury, but next to her first husband, Thomas de Holland, at the Greyfriars' church at Stamford, Lincolnshire. The burial was delayed until 27 January 1386 for King Richard to return from the war in Scotland.

Joan's funeral was an occasion of great ceremony – "magnificent and agreeable to the grandeur of so great a king," said one source, "love, grief, pity, every tender affection

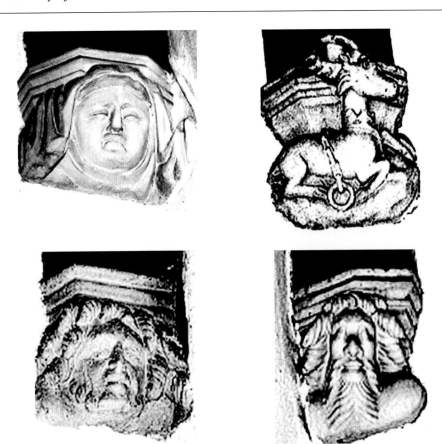

Four of the ten corbels in the aisles of Ware Church. Clockwise from top left: the death mask of Joan of Kent, the hart chained at the neck (the badge of Joan and Richard II) – these are in both the aisles – the head of a man in the South Aisle (Thomas de Holland?) and the head of a bearded man in the North Aisle (the Black Prince?).

would allow him to do no less." The cortege would have passed through Ware en route from Wallingford and then up the Old North Road to Stamford. It is known that funerals at that time included the display of an effigy of the deceased, carved in wood and using a plaster funeral mask as the model. The funeral effigies of Edward III and Anne of Bohemia – Joan's father-in-law and daughter-in-law – are preserved in Westminster Abbey. Joan's funeral too must have included a funeral mask. Her lead coffin and the accompanying effigy would have been laid out in state for public grief in the principal manor of her Wake inheritance, Ware church. There have been many ceremonial funerals in St. Mary's but this must have been the grandest. Some of her sons would have been present – at least the eldest, Thomas de Holland, third Earl of Kent – along with the foremost citizens of the town, and the Vicar and Prior in their vestments. And there must have been a mason copying Joan's effigy in stone. That would account for two of the corbels (the carved projections which hold up the roof) in the north and south aisles of St. Mary's Church. There are five in each aisle. The most easterly ones show the head of a fat old lady with her eyes closed – Holinshed mentioned her "corpulence". The next three are of harts, the central ones having a crown and chain around their necks. This is "the hart gorged and chained", the personal badge of Joan and of King Richard. There are no fewer than 83 corbels with the hart gorged and chained under the roof of Westminster Hall which Richard II rebuilt. Then at the western end of each aisle in St. Mary's is a man's head – a man with a great deal of hair in the south aisle (possibly her first husband, Thomas de Holland) and a bearded man in the north aisle (the Black Prince?). Who put them there and when? It would have been Thomas de Holland, Joan's eldest son. He retired from public life after his mother's death, devoting himself to his estates, it is said. The rebuilding of St. Mary's was taking place at this time – by Joan herself, according to local tradition. The chancel was the responsibility of the monks but the rest depended on the generosity of the lord

The font in St. Mary's with the figure of St. George slaying the dragon.

or lady and the people. In the 1380s two aisles were added to the nave and later a clerestory built above them to give the church more light. I believe that Thomas took this opportunity to make the church a memorial to his mother and her family.

There are other clues to this apart from the corbels. On the octagonal font (one of the church's treasures) are eight saints all associated with baptism and the history of the church – St. Christopher (carrying the Christ child), St. Margaret (patron of women in childbirth) the Angel Gabriel, the Virgin Mary, John the Baptist, St. George, St. Catherine of Alexandria (patron of learning) and St. James (patron of pilgrims, for Ware was on a pilgrimage route). The one facing down the nave is St. George killing the dragon and wearing armour which is a near replica of the armour worn by the Black Prince on his tomb in Canterbury Cathedral. But there is one other icon of Joan's family. Over the south door is the head of a king, rather weather-worn from the period before the porch was built: he is a beardless king, which is unusual, and he has his hair in large bunches on either side of his head, a fashion adopted by Richard II and shown in every portrait of him. Any medieval visitor or pilgrim entering St. Mary's would have been able to read these symbols and know this was a building commemorating the life of Joan of Kent and her family.

After Joan's death, the remainder of Richard's reign became bogged down in bitter rivalries and hasty attempts to head off the inevitable tragedy. He quarrelled with his half-brother, John de Holland, ill-advisedly he moved against his uncle, Thomas of

The crowned head of Richard II above the south door of the church – much weathered before the porch was built.

Woodstock, and had him killed, then foolishly banished his three most powerful rivals all at the same time – Thomas Arundel, Archbishop of Canterbury, Thomas Mowbray, Earl of Nottingham, and Henry Bolingbroke, Earl of Derby. Was Richard a "megalomaniac" as some historians have called him? He was certainly badly advised and was far more interested in art and literature than in power games. Unlike his predecessors, he wished for peace with France rather than war. In 1399 Richard went off to quell rebellion in Ireland, leaving England in the care of his one faithful uncle, Edmund of Langley, Duke of York. The Duke learned that Bolingbroke in France was assembling a formidable army to invade England and ordered every town and county in England to send soldiers to a muster at Ware.[15] In July 1399, the sheriffs of the City of York protested that if they sent their 60 armed knights and squires and 100 archers, as ordered, they would lay the county open to attack from Scotland. They were excused but many others assembled at Ware, just as Bolingbroke invaded. Lack of coordination and loss of heart by Richard gave Bolingbroke an easy victory. Richard surrendered the crown to Henry at Chester and, despite an assurance of safe conduct, was imprisoned first in the Tower of London, then in Pontefract Castle. There he died or was murdered. Henry rode in triumph to London where he was crowned as Henry IV by Thomas Arundel, the Archbishop.

But that is not the end of the story as far as Ware is concerned. In his last years, Richard had been reconciled to his half-brother, John de Holland, and made him Duke of Exeter, and his nephew Thomas, Duke of Surrey. Immediately he came to the throne Henry IV stripped them of those titles and of a great deal of their wealth. The two Hollands thereupon rose in rebellion against the new king and were defeated and killed. This had severe repercussions in Ware: a number of the townsmen, preeminently Walter Parker, the keeper of Ware Park, had joined their lord of the manor and paid for it with their lives and property. Even then, it was not the end of the story. At Whitsun in 1402 there was a conspiracy against the new king and a certain priest from Ware was arrested for writing a list of those who were likely to join the conspiracy.[16] He was hauled before a judge and confessed that he had added some of the names on his own initiative. The chronicler Thomas Walsingham, a monk at St. Albans, said that many of the suspects were set free but the Ware priest was hung, drawn and quartered. But who was he? He was certainly not the vicar who continued in post for four years afterwards, and he was probably not a Franciscan friar from the Friary across the road, for the friars who were in rebellion were all named. It is probable that he was a disgruntled monk from Ware Priory. Perhaps he had been inspired by the effigies of the late king's mother and that of Richard himself above the south door.

St. Mary's Church

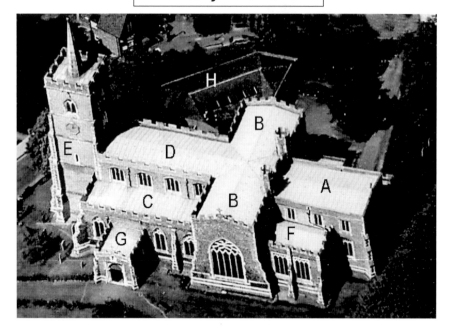

Local tradition has it that St. Mary's was built or rebuilt in the 1380s by Joan of Kent but, like other buildings in Ware, it grew over the centuries – as shown by the letters on the aerial view of the church.

A   The oldest part of the church is the Chancel, formerly the place where the monks of the Benedictine Priory worshipped. It is mainly 13th century (1200s) but with part of a window frame which may be older. It is the only section of the church which is not castellated (with decorative battlements). Trinity College, Cambridge (successor of the Priory) is responsible for the Chancel.

B   In the early 1300s the layout of the church would have had the form of a cross. The North and South transepts – the arms of the cross – are 13th century.

C   The North and South Aisles are 14th century. On the evidence of the corbels (mentioned earlier) the aisles were the work of the family of Joan of Kent.

D   Because a single storey church with aisles alongside the nave would have been very dark, a clerestory (upper level of windows) was built. Note that the clerestory windows are 'Perpendicular' while the aisle windows have the 'Early English' or 'Decorated' shape.

E   The tower was added in the 14th century.

F   The Lady Chapel was built in the 15th century, as shown by the wills of Ware men and women who left money for its construction. There was another north chapel, which now houses the organ. A vestry was also added to the east of the north chapel and has a fine oak door leading into the Chancel.

G   The Porch was also added in the 15th century.

H   The Extension which provides a large meeting room – with modern facilities like an office, kitchen and choir vestry – was built in 1982.

8.
1400s: Ware governs itself

For the people of Ware the major event of the fifteenth century was the suppression of the Benedictine Priory. It was a more momentous event than all the battles and manoeuvrings of the Wars of the Roses which did not directly touch the town. In 1414, on the eve of his invasion of France and the great victory at Agincourt, King Henry V decided to do away with all the alien priories whose finances, in any case, had been in the hands of the Crown for most of the past century. Some of the French-owned priories and convents hastened to become English but those that remained 'alien' were closed down. The most prominent were at Wareham, Carisbrooke, Hayling, Lewisham and Ware. In the case of Ware, all of the churches and manors which the Prior had administered on behalf of the Abbey of St. Evroult, along with all the rents, fees, and other income from them, were transferred to a new priory of Cistercian monks which Henry V had founded at Sheen, next to Richmond in Surrey. There were protests from St. Evroult but these fell on deaf ears as there was no one of importance, like Joan of Kent, left to plead its case.

The Prior and the Benedictine monks dispersed to find new homes and new employment but there were few tears shed in the town at their departure. The dispute between the Prior and the parish in 1231 had not been forgotten, because the Prior would not let it be forgotten. As recently as 1405, Prior William Herbert petitioned the lords of the exchequer to make the Vicar of Ware pay 200 marks – the arrears of a 'pension' of ten marks a year over 20 years – to which the Priory was allegedly entitled even though it was in the king's hands on account of the war with France.[1] After 1414, the quarrel of the Vicar and parish was with the Prior of Sheen – no doubt, he was just as demanding but at least they did not have to meet him in the High Street.

One result of the suppression of the Priory was a great expansion of the Franciscan Friary on the other side of the street. Until then it had been a small community of Franciscans living in a house, probably just one storey, given to them by Thomas Wake. It now began to expand into a range of three two-storey buildings with an attached cloister and a large friary church. The expansion did not happen all at once but there is scientific evidence that it began to happen in the years following 1414. In 1997 three scientists from Nottingham University took dendrochronological samples (for tree-ring dating) from the principal timbers of the Hadsley Room in what is now erroneously known as 'the Priory', the home of Ware Town Council. The Hadsley Room is the jewel in the crown, an upstairs hall with three massive oak cross beams and a sturdy carved crown post, above which is the scissor-braced roof. Three of the samples had the sapwood complete and these all gave the date 1416 for when the trees were felled; most of the other samples were consistent with this though four showed earlier felling dates of 1391-1410 – perhaps trees felled earlier and stored for future use. From this it can be deduced that the Hadsley Room began to be built in 1416, using newly felled and some seasoned oaks, and stonework reused from the demolished Benedictine Priory. Archaeological investigation revealed stone door posts and other features which had been adapted to new uses; there was even

Franciscan Friary

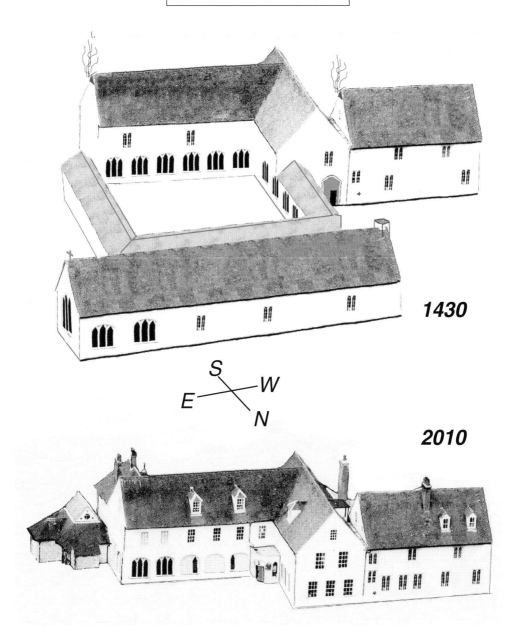

1430

S — W
E — N

2010

From a single small building (the west wing on the right), the Franciscan Friary was enlarged from 1416 onwards, using stone from the demolished Benedictine Priory and new timbers. We know the friars built a church, because its foundations were revealed when a sewer pipe was laid across the grounds. A cloister joined the church to the east wing or 'frater' where the friars lived. The west wing then became a 'refectory' where visitors stayed. The Friary was dissolved in 1538. It then became a private house and the cloister and church were demolished. Chimneys and new windows were added in the 18th and 19th centuries, when the old friary became known by the more up-market name of 'The Priory'.

Franciscan Friary

Left: the 1526 seal of the Warden of the Ware Greyfriars. St. Francis of Assisi is on the left, looking up at the vision of an angel; on the right is the friary's founder, Thomas, 2nd Lord Wake with his coat of arms. The (damaged) inscription says "the Warden of the Friars Minor of Ware". On the right is a corbel in the entrance of the Priory, showing Lord Wake in chain mail.

part of an oriel window used to fill in a hole in a wall. Ware Town Council, as the trustees of the Priory, had carried out a full-scale restoration in 1994, which revealed further medieval features, including the painting of a rose in what would have been 'the frater' or friars' quarters. As the Priory is a Scheduled Ancient Monument, archaeological exaction in the grounds is not possible, but some idea of the original layout of the building can be guessed from the trenches for sewers cut across the grounds. There is also evidence of burials, possibly of the Greyfriars, alongside the walls of their church.

The other important development of the fifteenth century was the growth of a form of self-government for the town. Although Ware was sometimes known as a borough, it was never 'incorporated' with a borough charter granted by the king. There was never a borough corporation in Ware as there were in Hertford or Bishop's Stortford. The town's affairs were managed either by the manor, through the manorial courts and officers like the steward and bailiff, or by the officers of the parish Vestry, principally the churchwardens. In the Middle Ages, there were three churchwardens – two for Ware and one for Thundridge which was treated as a chapel of the Parish Church (there are still three churchwardens at St. Mary's Church). However, manorial records for the fifteenth century show that the stewards concerned themselves solely with property transfers – from which there were fees, of course – and hardly ever with town improvements.

The manor and the town became more remote. Because of their opposition to Henry IV, the Holland family lost control of their estates and, even when they were restored to Edmund de Holland, seventh Earl of Kent, the king retained a part of the estate and among Edmund's aunts and cousins there were four dowager countesses of Kent all competing for a share in the revenues. Edmund died in 1408 fighting pirates off the coast of Brittany. The manor then passed to his niece, Eleanor, who married Thomas Montagu, Earl of Salisbury, and through their daughter Alice it then passed to the Neville family. These were powerful magnates for whom Ware was a small part of their inheritance, especially after Alice's death when the manor passed to Richard Neville, Earl of Warwick – 'Warwick the Kingmaker'. When he was killed at the Battle of Barnet, the manor passed to his daughter who married into the royal family, eventually becoming the wife of Richard III. For the remainder of the fifteenth century the manor of Ware was controlled by the Crown.

Into this vacuum came the Guild of Corpus Christi. Guilds were common in the fifteenth century – as the historian Susan Reynolds has observed:

> In the Middle Ages almost any voluntary association or club might be called a guild and its members – whether united for trading, political, religious, or any other purpose – would bind themselves together by the characteristic methods of feasting, religious ceremonies, and perhaps oath-taking. Guilds were in G.H. Martin's excellent phrase, 'a form of association as unselfconscious as the committee is today.'[2]

There was more than one guild in Ware – there was a small guild of men and women who lit candles in the church and, if one includes the various chantries and 'obits' left by people in their wills for a priest to say a mass for their soul, then Ware was awash with guilds or similar bodies. There was, for example, the Chantry of Helen Bramble whose brass is on the wall of the North Transept in St. Mary's: she left money, partly from the rent of an inn called the Cardinal's Hat, to establish a chantry in 1474 for a chaplain and preacher to say a mass for the souls of King Edward IV, the queen, Prince of Wales and Helen and her two husbands – William Bramble and Richard Warbulton.[3]

The main one was the Guild of Corpus Christi, which employed priests, provided money for the poor, owned and managed important properties like inns and carried out a number of public works. Much later – in the reign of Edward VI when it was under investigation – the guild claimed that it maintained the bridge (because the King took the tolls and gave nothing back for repairs), looked after a beacon on the outskirts of the town and used the guild's profits to relieve the town of occasional taxes. But their most important function was looking after the welfare of their members – the guild's other name was the Corpus Christi Brotherhood. Strictly speaking, the guild was illegal for it was a perpetual trust that offended against the Statute of Mortmain (designed to stop the 'hand of the dead' robbing the living of their inheritance) and should therefore have been 'incorporated' with a charter from the king. The way of getting round this important law was to use the fiction that a property was being sold to a group of individuals who would later invest it in another group of individuals. These individuals were usually the guild's officers, but they had to be careful to choose younger officers otherwise the old trustees would die off before the property could be re-assigned. Later, sixteenth-century deeds show properties being invested in the whole of the guild's membership, in one case 90 men. By looking at a series of deeds for one property – such as the old Saracen's Head Inn which used to be opposite the bottom of New Road – one can trace the leading members of the Ware guild for almost the whole of the 1400s and 1500s. In the Hertfordshire Archives and Local Studies (HALS), there are about 70 of the guild's documents with dates before 1600, some of which the present author had a hand in rescuing after a friend, Des Chappell, brought them to his house in a cardboard box. Des had been working in the cellars of solicitors' offices in Baldock Street. The solicitors had them because

Helen Bramble's brass

they acted for the Ware Charities which was the successor to the guild – indeed there was a deed of 1426 concerning the White Hart Inn which is now the local branch of HSBC Bank at 75 High Street, where the freehold is still owned by the Ware Charities. The charity deeds with earlier deposits from the trustees at HALS form a substantial record of medieval Ware and an unrivalled collection of medieval family names.

A charter concerning the Saracen's Head Inn in 1476 transferred it into the ownership of 54 people, with the rank, occupation and relationship given for each of them.[4] Another charter for the Saracen's Head in 1521 went further, transferring the ownership to 90 men, adding their rank, occupations, relationships and positions in the guild.[5] But even earlier, we are on firm ground for deducing that the guild existed. A charter of 1425, again for the Saracen's Head, transfered the inn's ownership from Ellen, the widow of Walter Mice of Ware, to John Wodele described as 'master', John Aylington 'chaplain' and Richard Greteham and John Takele, all of Ware.[6] The existence of a 'master' and a 'chaplain' can be taken as evidence for the existence of a guild. On the earlier deeds, the same names occur again and again. William atte Water was one of the parties giving up ownership of the Saracen's Head in 1391 and a witness to the transfer of the tenement in Mill Lane in 1407. Thomas Tonewell witnessed the transfer of the Saracen's Head in 1365, 1377 and 1396. Walter Mice (probably pronounced 'meece'), mentioned above as the late husband of Ellen in 1425, acted as a witness for the transfer of the Mill Lane property in 1407 while Hugh Mice (perhaps his father) was a witness to two property transfers in 1377 and 1391. Incidentally, two members of the Mice family – Richard and another Walter (or perhaps the same one) – were among the rebels indicted by John of

Gaunt in the 1380s.

Ware in the 15th century was an important stopping place on the Old North Road to and from London. It was a convenient one day's journey from the capital as Chaucer showed in the Prologue to *The Canterbury Tales,* when he wrote of the length of England as "from Berwick down to Ware". Among the travellers using the road through Ware were pilgrims on their way to Our Lady's shrine at Walsingham, which rivalled that of Thomas à Becket at Canterbury. The historian Holinshed wrote: "The waie to Walsingham was through Waltham, Ware and Royston. Those townes that we call thorowfares have great and sumptuous innes builded in them, for the receiving of such travellers and strangers as passe to and fro." To use the description given at the end of the 16th century by its home-grown poet, William Vallans, it was "the guested town of Ware". Two of the major inns were owned by the guild. But the deeds also give the names of adjoining properties. The White Hart Inn (referred to in the deeds as "le Whight hert" or "the Hert") was situated between the Katherine Wheel to the east and the Bell to the west. At the other end of the town, the Saracen's Head (called 'le Sarasyneshede' and later 'the Sarsons Hed') was flanked on the east by the Cardinal's Hat. These inns were on the south side of the present High Street, then known as Water Row. A hundred years or so later – in the Jacobean period – inns would form a continuous row from the Friary to the bridge. Even in the fifteenth century they included – from west to east – the Griffin (first mentioned in 1439), Star (1479), Bell (1479), White Hart (1426), Catherine Wheel (1470), Christopher (fifteenth-century according to the *Victoria County History*), Ram (1499), Bear (1494), Horn (1439), George (1439), Saracen's Head (1365) and Cardinal's Hat (1476). If the poet Chaucer was any guide, then you could expect good food in the inns of Water Row, provided you were not too squeamish about the person who prepared it. In *The Canterbury Tales*, the cook "could roast, and boil, and broil and fry, make thick soup and well bake a pie" but he had a gangrenous sore on his leg and was usually drunk – scholars believe he was based on a real person and Chaucer named him "Roger Hogg of Ware".[7]

A fascinating agreement was drawn up between neighbouring inn owners in 1507. William Berley, who rented the White Hart from the guild, had built "a siege-house" (meaning literally a sitting-down house, or privy) against the outside wall of the great chamber of the White Hart where it joined a barn. To repair the privy and the barn, William had to have the agreement of Thomas Nelson, a farmer who owned the Bell Inn next door. In order that he should "have and peaceably enjoye" his siege-house, William agreed to make and keep in good repair a 31½ feet long fence on the south side of the barn, between his ground and that of Thomas.[8] Berley and Nelson were both churchwardens: one wonders if they ever discussed William's "siege-house" while in church.

The charity deeds tell us a great deal about the inhabitants of Ware. On the evidence of their surnames, many of them were from local families, like John Hoddesdon, Thomas Tonewell, Richard Fanham and Thomas Braughyng. And they followed a variety of trades: yeomen, innholders and 'beerbruers', grocers, bakers, butchers, drapers, mercers, a glover, a pewterer, a tallow-chandler, a barber and a schoolmaster. The clergy included John Aylington, Robert Dorrys, Ralph Risley and Robert Lawe, while Thomas Bele, John Birch and Gilbert Rookys or Rook are described as 'bailiffs'. The townspeople of 15th century

England were highly mobile and there is plentiful evidence in the deeds of people who had moved on from Ware as they prospered or retired to the town with their wealth. John Asshewell, a grocer, was a former Mayor of Cambridge and Hugh Chapman, who owned property in Ware parish, became a burgess and later an Alderman of Cambridge. The largest group of guild members with distant trading interests are those described as Citizens of London. Their trades are also given, indicating membership of one of the London guilds, such as Robert Handford, John Marchall and John Shelley, merchants, and Nicholas Warley, goldsmith.

The Ware guild, like many others, included women among its members. When Edward VI's Commissioners came to Ware, one of the witnesses spoke of prayers being offered in St Mary's for "the sowles of all the brothers and sisters of the seid fraternytie".[9] As married women could not own property, it is mainly widows whose names appear on the deeds, like Ellen the widow of Hugh Mice. The practice of the guild seems to have been to give a member's widow a life interest in a property which would revert to the guild after her death. Sometimes the widow would sell her interest to another tenant in exchange for a pension in money. Agnes Asshewell, the widow of John Asshewell, in 1503 sold her tenancy of the White Hart to William Berley for £100 and a series of receipts record the payments by instalments between 1503 and 1510.[10] If the widow remarried or had children by a previous marriage, then there were additional problems of inheritance that could only be sorted out by a complex series of legal documents. Ellen, the wife of William Berley (of "siege-house" fame), had previously been married to Lawrence Pillye, a London merchant, by whom she had a son, Henry. After William's death in 1507, she married as her third husband Henry Risley. It took five separate deeds dated 1510-1511 for Ellen Risley's rights to the White Hart to be made fully legal.[11] The name of another property-owning woman stands out from the manorial records: she is Petronilla Myller alias Petronilla Rede, perhaps named after the great Petronilla Grandmesnil who refashioned the town in the thirteenth century.[12]

As well as owning property and using the rents to further the town's interests – and their own – the Ware guild also wielded political influence. To be a member of the guild gave a person status in the town and 'brotherhood' with other townspeople who were prospering. If some of the evidence to Edward VI's commissioners is to be believed, the guild also protected its members against lawsuits and made loans available to them. On the other hand, there was also the need for powerful patrons who would protect the guild and its members. This was especially necessary for guilds like that in Ware which had no legal protection through incorporation. One of the longest deeds is that which conveyed the Saracen's Head to new trustees in February 1476. The last battles between the Royal Houses of York and Lancaster – at Barnet and Tewkesbury – had been fought just five years before and the deed reads like a celebration of the new reign of Edward IV. At the head of the list of fresh trustees is Sir John Say of Broxbourne, Member of Parliament for Hertfordshire, and three times Speaker of the House of Commons. Then come five esquires, including Ralph Bawde of Little Hadham, who like Sir John Say was a JP for the county, William Say, the son of Sir John, and John Boteler, a member of the powerful Watton Woodhall family. After the esquires come two Yeomen of the Crown, two citizens of

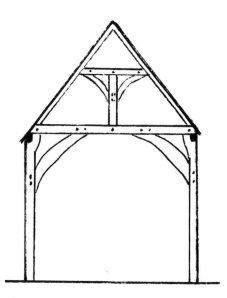

Crown post roofs were used in timber-framed buildings from the 13th to the 16th centuries – mainly in south-east England – to give a strong and stable construction. The crown post (sometimes known as a 'king post') stands in the centre of a crossbeam and supports a collar beam, often by means of curved braces (*see right*). Some crown posts are plain, others have a cross-shaped section and others are carved or moulded to resemble a stone column. The crown post roof became a feature to be seen and admired, and often the post and collar purlin were painted in bright colours.

There are many crown posts in the roofs of Ware's rich heritage of timber-framed buildings. Moulded crown posts exist in Place House, the Hadsley Room of the Priory, Westgate House and Churchgate House (Jacoby's), both in West Street, and in No. 35 High Street (Cheltenham and Gloucester Building Society). There is a cruciform crown post in Nos. 37-39 High Street and plain crown posts exist in a dozen or so buildings in the High Street, Baldock Street and East Street. Below are two fine examples.

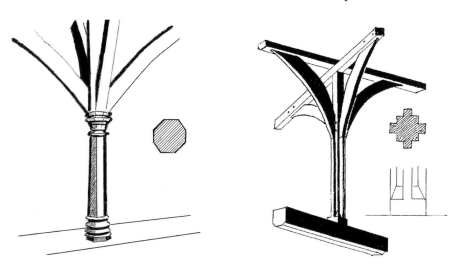

Left: the moulded crown post in the Hadsley Room of the Priory – formerly a room for honoured guests. Right: the cruciform crown post in the roof of 37-39 High Street, formerly the Horn Inn. There was a similarly shaped crown post, though much stouter, in the old Saracen's Head Inn which stood opposite the end of New Road and was demolished in 1957.

London, and six members of the landed gentry, four from Ware parish and two from elsewhere. Then come two interesting groups: three men described as "servants of Edward, Prince of Wales" and one described as "servant of the Duke of Clarence". This was the high point of the Yorkist dynasty and its darker side did not come till later. Edward Prince of Wales was to be one of the princes murdered in the Tower and the Duke of Clarence was murdered two years after this deed was drawn up, as tradition has it, in a butt of Malmsey wine. Then there are the guildsmen of Ware itself and finally their sons, a total of 54 people.[13]

Important people stayed at the Ware inns but others gravitated towards the Friary, which had replaced the Benedictine Priory as favoured accommodation for the aristocracy. Following the first Battle of St. Albans in May 1455, the defeated Henry VI with his queen and baby Prince Edward stayed at Hertford Castle but the Duke of York – afterwards King Edward IV – prudently stayed in Ware. "Mine lord York to the Friars at Ware", according to the Paston Letters.[13] It is reported that the former Minister Provincial of the Greyfriars, Dr. Roger Donwe, came to Ware in 1430 to end his days.[14] But it was not only the rich and famous who were attracted to the Franciscan house in Ware. In 1479 Pope Sixtus IV, himself a Franciscan – and famous for commissioning the Sistine Chapel – instituted a year of indulgences for friars and lay people associated with them. In October 1479, John Aleby and his wife Alice, who had no doubt supported Ware Friary with money, were welcomed into the confraternity by Brother John, the Warden,[16] and the following January John and Edmund Davenport were similarly admitted.[17] The Alebys and Davenports were guaranteed absolution of all their sins at the time of their deaths; others went further, like Thomas Hyde, who in 1525 reached an agreement with the Warden of the Ware friars for a weekly mass for himself and his wife Joan, his two previous wives, his parents and "for alle the fryndes and benefactores of the forsayd Thomas".[18] A number of wills indicate that couples left instructions to be buried in the friars' church and, when a huge cedar tree fell down in the garden of what is now known confusingly as 'The Priory', there was archaeological evidence of burials inside and against the walls of the former church. This seems to indicate that there was a degree of rivalry between the friars and the Parish Church of St. Mary across the street. Most Ware people asked to be buried in St. Mary's and left money to the church or the Guild of Corpus Christi. But one Ware family had a much grander memorial – in the Vintners' Company in London is a magnificent tapestry, depicting St. Martin dividing his cloak for a beggar and St. Dunstan celebrating Mass, with the date 1466 and the inscription in Latin: "Pray for the souls of John Bate and his wife of the town of Ware and for Walter Hertford their son a monk of this church".[19] The church may have been Canterbury Cathedral.

The parish church was still being enlarged in the fifteenth century. A will of 1416 left money for the repair and amendment of the nave, as well as a "great new bell". The bell tower had been added in the previous century and two chapels built in the 15th century, the Lady Chapel first and then the north chapel in which the Guild of Corpus Christi maintained an altar. In addition, there were the chantries, in particular the Chantry of Helen Bramble which had its own altar in one of the transepts where her brass was originally placed. It was endowed with rents from the Cardinal's Hat and Bull's Head inns as well as other properties and employed a chantry priest. The chantry priest had an apartment nearby and probably added to his income by teaching. It is believed that the Free Grammar School which existed in the churchyard in 1612 was originally a chantry school.

An illustration of how the wealthiest in Ware lived and died is contained in the will of Sir Thomas Bourchier in 1491. Sir Thomas was the nephew of Cardinal Bourchier, who had crowned Richard III, and was the hereditary Constable of Windsor Castle. But he rebelled against the Yorkists and fought alongside Henry Tudor at the Battle of Bosworth Field in 1485, after which he retired to his manor at Watersplace. The old farmhouse beside the road to Wareside was one of the subsidiary manors of Ware, the home of the "atte Water" family, and still has a moulded crownpost in the main roof. Sir Thomas's will is long and immensely colourful. He asked to be buried in Ware church and for the bones of his first wife, Lady Isabel, to be laid beside him and for this task he bequeathed "twenty pounds for their costs and ten marks for their labour". He also willed that "my best chalice, a suit of vestments of white baldric (studded with precious gems) and gold, altar clothes of the same, a vestment of black velvet, my best pax of silver, my best cruets of silver, my best mass-book, a pair of candlesticks of silver for an altar, a censor with a strap of silver, my best antiphons, my best grail, three processionaries, a manual, a book I bought of Mr William Pykenham called a lectionary, a cross of silver and gilt with a foot, and an image of Our Lady of silver and gilt be delivered to the churchwardens of the said church to be safely kept and used at times of Divine Service in such manner as is thought convenient." Among numerous bequests to churches, priories, clergy and friends, he left to his nephew, Henry Earl of Essex, "a bed of blue damask with [the pattern of] a gentlewoman playing the harp with the counterpanes and counterpoint of the same, and my cushions of blue damask – two short and one long – one of my best featherbeds, two carpets and my gown of purple velvet edged in pure white fur". Finally, "I require and pray my executors that they will order 24 torches to burn at my requiem mass and burial and that eight of them shall remain in the church and the remainder to be divided at their discretion to eight other churches nearby; And that every priest at my requiem and burial and who says mass shall have twelve pence and every other deacon or subdeacon there shall have eight pence; And every other man being there and having a surplice (i.e. as a server) shall have sixpence; And every child there and having a surplice shall have four pence."[20] It must have been an impressive farewell to an important man. There used to be a brass commemorating Sir Thomas and Lady Isabel Bourchier but it was one of those pillaged in the nineteenth century "by a knavish Sexton" – however, the stone matrix of the brasses is still there near the pews in the South Transept.

9.
Life under the Early Tudors

In earlier histories, the first Tudor lady of Ware is portrayed as a gracious friend of the town. Edith Hunt wrote that Henry VII granted Ware to his mother, Margaret Beaufort, Countess of Richmond, for her life and added that it was "part of the town tradition that the beautiful old Tudor house, sometimes called Gilpin House … was built by Henry VII for his mother".[1] Other historians have seen the countess in a less favourable light. Her most recent biographers accuse her of "unprincipled greed" adding that she had her eye on the "rich manor of Ware" and secured the right to appoint a steward there in September 1485, a full month before her son's coronation.[2] She was granted the manor in 1487, thus pre-empting any claim from the young Edward Plantagenet, Earl of Warwick, who was put in her charge. The unfortunate earl, whose claim to Ware came through his mother Isabel Neville, also had a blood claim to the throne (he was the son of the Duke of Clarence) and thus spent most of his life in custody until beheaded in 1499.

As for the tradition that Gilpin House (No. 84 High Street) was built for her by the king, the house is miniscule compared with the palaces the countess and her large household inhabited at Croydon (borrowed from the Archbishop of Canterbury), Collyweston near Stamford, and Hatfield (borrowed from the Bishop of Ely). There is no evidence that she ever visited Ware. However, Gilpin House may have been built or enlarged for her bailiff, to whom she wrote in 1506 concerning the "divising" of victuals to ensure the speedy delivery of market produce to Hatfield. One of her bailiffs was Richard Shirley who was certainly close to the life of the town. His will of December 1509 revealed that he had been buying land to support Ellen Bramble's Chantry in St. Mary's and was leaving money for candles on all three main altars – the Lady Chapel, the Rood or High Altar and that in the North Chapel maintained by the guild – as well as to the friars across the road. To his wife Joan, he left the Raven Inn which he had bought from two brothers, William and John Wengehoo.[3] No. 53 High Street (now a florist's) still has the fine roof timbers of the Raven Inn, as well as a magnificent parlour with moulded beams and fireplace: the waggonway was refurbished in the seventeenth century with stone sets, bricks in between and stone guiding blocks for carriages. The nineteenth-century malthouse behind has now been adapted for housing and is known as 'Water Row', the former name of the whole south side of the High Street.

Richard Shirley was succeeded as bailiff by William Compton, a former royal page: as well as being bailiff of the town and manor, William was designated "keeper of the fishery, truncagium (the carting of logs), two mills and the park and meadows, which were kept for the use of Margaret, Countess of Richmond, for livery of her horses".[4] But Margaret herself had died in June 1509 at Westminster after witnessing the marriage of her grandson, King Henry VIII, to Catherine of Aragon.

In his will, Richard Shirley referred to the guild not as Corpus Christi but as "the Brotherhood of Jesus". This may well have been a feature of the town's life where Margaret

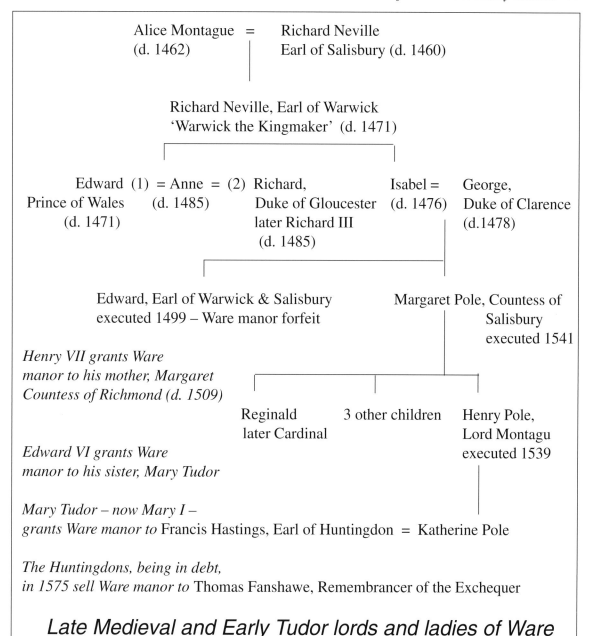

Alice Montague = Richard Neville
(d. 1462)   Earl of Salisbury (d. 1460)

Richard Neville, Earl of Warwick
'Warwick the Kingmaker' (d. 1471)

Edward (1) = Anne = (2) Richard,   Isabel = George,
Prince of Wales   (d. 1485)   Duke of Gloucester (d. 1476) Duke of Clarence
(d. 1471)   later Richard III   (d.1478)
                               (d. 1485)

Edward, Earl of Warwick & Salisbury   Margaret Pole, Countess of
executed 1499 – Ware manor forfeit   Salisbury
                                                         executed 1541

Henry VII grants Ware
manor to his mother, Margaret
Countess of Richmond (d. 1509)

                              Reginald   3 other children   Henry Pole,
                              later Cardinal   Lord Montagu
                                                               executed 1539
Edward VI grants Ware
manor to his sister, Mary Tudor

Mary Tudor – now Mary I –
grants Ware manor to Francis Hastings, Earl of Huntingdon = Katherine Pole

The Huntingdons, being in debt,
in 1575 sell Ware manor to Thomas Fanshawe, Remembrancer of the Exchequer

Late Medieval and Early Tudor lords and ladies of Ware

made her influence felt. The Feast of Corpus Christi was old-medieval, as it were, founded in the thirteenth century as a summer festival to highlight the incarnation element in the Christmas story – it was held on the first Thursday after Trinity Sunday, a good time for processions and festivities, like the mystery plays in York and Coventry. By the sixteenth century, there was a feeling that Corpus Christi celebrations had lost sight of the real Jesus. There thus arose a cult of Jesus which emphasised the benefits to Christians of invoking his Holy Name, and in this Countess Margaret Beaufort played a prominent role. In 1494 Margaret was recognized by the Pope as the chief promoter in England of the feast of the Name of Jesus, working in collaboration with monks of the Carthusian order, particularly those at Sheen near Richmond, who were of course the patrons of St. Mary's Church, Ware. At some time in the early years of the sixteenth century, the Brotherhood or Fraternity of Jesus became the dominant body in Ware – either replacing the old Guild of Corpus Christi or existing in parallel with it. The evidence is unclear. Before the will of Thomas Clarke in 1505 there is no mention of the Jesus Brotherhood and after 1505 there is no mention of the Corpus Christi Guild.[5] It may well be that the members decided it was politic to keep ownership of important inns like the Saracen's Head and the White Hart quite separate.

The only deed that mentions the Brotherhood of Jesus by name is one made in March 1521, referring to: *Gilde, ffraternitatis Jhs nuper edite et ffundat in parochiali ecclia de Ware* ("the Guild or Fraternity of Jesus recently set up and founded in the ecclesiastical parish of Ware").[6] It is a long and important document, because it shows the guild's determination to win influential friends in the reign of Henry VIII. The list of new trustees begins with three very powerful people indeed – Richard Fox, Bishop of Winchester, John Longland, Bishop of Lincoln and Henry Bouchier, Earl of Essex. Of these, only the earl had any apparent connection with Ware, his uncle Sir Thomas having owned property at Watersplace. The two bishops had probably been solicited with a letter and a gift or two – in fact the scribe was so confused he described Richard Fox as Bishop of Worcester instead of Winchester. After this eminent trio, a knight, five squires and two others are also made aldermen of the brotherhood. Then follows the list of officers – Henry Spencer, Thomas Hide, Blase Lothon and John Apdale, "at that time masters of the said venerable Guild", Gilbert Rook, the bailiff, and Thomas White, the head constable. The officers are followed by the ordinary brethren, beginning with the gentry and older men whose occupations are given – "Richard Brawghyng gentleman, William Kyng groom, William Gelden beerbrewer, John Craynfield pewterer, Robert Crosse innholder, Robert Handford Citizen and Merchant of London and John Handford baker" – and ending with their sons, a total of 92 new trustees. Mention of a 'beerbrewer' is interesting because this refers to hopped beer, recently introduced from the Low Countries: Gelden may well have been Dutch – there was a will for a Dutch beer brewer in Ware in 1504.[7] The property being conveyed by this deed is the Saracen's Head (*Le Sarysyne hed*), with a pasture for one cow "in Nethynhoomarsh in the parish of Ampwell" and two acres of meadowland. The men doing the conveying are William Say and Nicholas Parterige, the only survivors of the conveyance of 1476 in the reign of Edward IV, which is specifically mentioned here. Sir William Say, of Broxbourne, was the father-in-law of the Earl of Essex.

We know from the later enquiry in the reign of Edward VI that the Brotherhood of Jesus held a banquet on the feast of the Name of Jesus (2 January), when the four masters presented their accounts and new masters and aldermen were chosen and that it owned "a greate charger of pewter and one greate brasse pott", probably passed round as a loving cup. But where did this banquet take place? Where was the guildhall? There is no definite evidence but it was probably No. 35 High Street, a double-jettied building with gable end on to the road, which shows that it is later than its medieval neighbours. The ground floor has been cleared for modern use (now a building society) but the first floor has a heavy timber ceiling, a seven light casement window containing some ovolo moulded mullions and also, but only exposed internally, a timber window with moulded cinquefoil cusped head. This may have been the room where the commercial business of the brotherhood was done. Above that is a room with more refined timberwork and a moulded crown post – where the brotherhood may have held their annual feast – though now the room has been truncated by a nineteenth-century chimney.

Here we ought to note some of the guildhall's neighbours and contemporaries. To the east, No.33 is a squat seventeenth-century building (now a shop) and beyond that is a range of buildings which were once the George Inn. To the west, Nos.37-39 are a former hall house, probably dating from the fifteenth century with a cruciform crown post roof and curved braces to a collar purlin; the waggonway below has exposed timber-framing and two blocked ogee headed

No. 35 High Street and Nos. 37-39

doors, probably originally the doors from the hall or crosswing into the buttery and pantry. This building may well have been the Horn Inn, not to be confused with the former French Horn on the opposite side of the High Street: later in life it became a grocer's shop, the electricity showroom and is now a card shop.

On the death of Margaret Beaufort, the injustice of her seizure of Ware manor was put right. Margaret Pole, sister and heir of the unfortunate Edward, Earl of Warwick, was created Countess of Salisbury in 1513 and Ware manor was restored to her as part of that honour.[8] Margaret Pole held Ware manor for 28 years and the first twenty passed calmly enough. As a member of the former royal family, she enjoyed the favour of Henry and his queen, Catherine of Aragon, and was appointed governess of the young Princess Mary in 1520. In her many properties, including Ware, she was an active landlord and employer, appointing her officers, several of whom were women, wisely. There were some areas in which her gender proved a barrier and it was here that she utilized the services of her sons, particularly Henry, Lord Montagu. Under her lordship, the court leet for Ware or 'view of frank-pledge' which dealt with administration and customs in the manor, including the assize of bread and ale, was held regularly in April before her steward – in the later years, John Sewster, of Ashwell.[9] The other type of manorial court, the 'court baron' for the transfer of properties, was held more often. In 1515, the countess held four courts, which showed that much of the lordship was let out to tenants – the fishery called the 'truncage' along with Ware Park were let out for £8.13s.4d and the mill for £26.13s.4d. It

Trying to understand the old buildings, or any town of similar age, involves documentary research, willingness to crawl around in the dark, a knowledge of timber framing and then bags of intuition. Nowhere was this more the case than at Churchgate House in West Street, now Jacoby's restaurant. It has been explored by the author over many years and notably by Mike Dunn of BEAMS (part of the Hertford-shire Building Preservation Trust) during the latest restoration in 1999.[11] Some parts of it are older than the Tudor period but it was at that time that they began to be joined together to form a central courtyard. The earliest part is the imposing jettied façade on to Tudor Square (*the top right-hand range in Michael Dunn's drawing*): this has heavy jowelled timbers at first-floor level and a

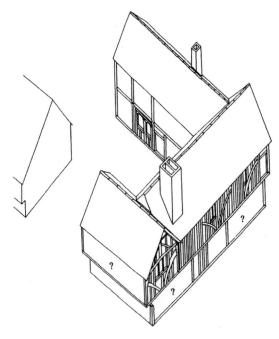

Churchgate House as it may have looked in 1580

crown post roof. Soon after 1500 another building, also jettied and with a crown post, was added to the south – lower and undersailing the existing range. Where the two ranges meet there is a moulded dragon (i.e. dragging) post. During the restoration, traces of the original red ochre paint could be seen on the crown post of this second range. Later in the sixteenth century, the north range was added – really as a commercial enterprise. At ground level this north range has the remains of two four-centred arched shop window openings; above them are a number of rooms below a roof with side purlins and curved wind braces, which may have been apartments for widows or church pensioners. Later in the seventeenth or eighteenth centuries, the gap in the West Street frontage was filled in and a cross wing was added to form the fourth side of a courtyard. At that time Churchgate House was the Eagle and Child Inn (associated with the Stanley family, Earls of Derby), later it became the Eight Bells and later still a bakery – it is still remembered by older inhabitants as Jaggs and Edwards, bakers until just after the Second World War. Since the Churchgate House range was flanked on the east by the similar Westgate House (also with a crown post roof), this complex near the church must have housed some interesting people.

is interesting that the court of pie-powder, the old market court, was still in existence and brought in 14s.2d. It is also interesting that among the strangely-named properties in the lordship – such as a wood called Wulkechyn, Goodyersmede and Cheldwellmead (Chadwellmead) – is Burymead (Buryfield) probably named, not after any plague burials, but because of the Roman graves habitually being found there.[10]

The watershed for Margaret (and many others) was Henry's decision in 1533 to divorce Catherine of Aragon, who had failed to give him a living male heir, and to marry Anne Boleyn who was already pregnant. A substantial section of the nobility and the Church opposed the move and refused to swear allegiance to the new queen. Margaret Pole as governess of Catherine's daughter refused Henry's request to surrender the princess's jewels and plate and, when Mary's household was dissolved in December 1533, offered to serve the princess at her own expense. This was firmly refused and then she was implicated in the outcry over a nun in Kent who had condemned the king's marriage as being against the will of God. Her relationship with the King was deteriorating fast and she was obliged to leave the court.

Prominent among the churchmen opposed to the king's divorce were the 'Friars Observant', a reformed branch of the Franciscan Order who had been introduced into England in 1499. Henry was initially very much in favour of them and their piety but took against them when the Friars Observant came out in public against his divorce of Catherine of Aragon – or, technically, the annulment of the marriage. When the former queen was dispossessed of her household and sent into the oblivion of various country houses, two of the Friars Observant from Greenwich accompanied her. On 23 July 1533 the spies of the king's chief minister, Thomas Cromwell, discovered these two Friars Observant were staying at Ware Friary and then followed them all the way to London. Whatever the mission of the two was, on 5 May 1534 the Ware friars made a "Declaration of Obedience to Henry VIII and Queen Anne, and of the lawfulness of their marriage, with repudiation of the Bishop of Rome's authority, and acknowledgement of the King as Supreme Head of the Church".[12]

Margaret's return to court in 1536 following the fall of Anne Boleyn was swiftly curtailed by the arrival of the letter, *De unitate*, to Henry VIII, in which Margaret's son, the exiled churchman Reginald Pole, declared his strong opposition to the royal supremacy of the church. Margaret wrote to her son admonishing him for his 'folly' but the damage was done. In 1538 another of her sons, Geoffrey, was arrested and then Margaret herself, both accused of being involved with Reginald, now made a cardinal by the Pope, in planning an invasion to restore papal control. She remained in the Tower of London as various other rebellions against the royal supremacy took place: her estates on the south coast made her vulnerable to the charge that she was involved in a possible Catholic invasion. On the morning of 27 May 1541, she was taken out and after commending her soul to God, asking the small group present to pray for the royal family and requesting to be remembered to Princess Mary, Margaret Pole, Countess of Salisbury and Lady of the Manor of Ware, was beheaded. In 1886 she was beatified by Pope Leo XIII as one of the martyrs who died "for the truth of the orthodox Faith". Poles, the former name of the large house at Thundridge (now called Hanbury Manor), is said to be named after her.

The friars had declared their allegiance to Henry as Head of the Church and to his second wife, Anne Boleyn, in May 1534. The declaration was signed by Thomas Chapman, their Warden – one of the few whose name we know (another was Paul who was in trouble in 1525 for his almost Protestant views). However, in 1538 Ware Friary was dissolved along with other friaries, convents and smaller priories and within a year or so larger monasteries like Westminster. It was part of Henry VIII's campaign to curb the power of the Church and win over the property-owning nobility and gentry. Ware Friary which in 1538 was valued at only 29s. 8d. a year was bought by Robert Byrch.[13] This may have been a temporary arrangement, for in 1544 the site and 'osier hope' (reed beds) which brought in 20s. a year, were granted to Thomas Byrch, his heirs and assigns.[14] Thomas Byrch, possibly Robert's son, was described as a yeoman of the crown but elsewhere as a 'scrivener' or moneylender and it may have been in that capacity that he served Henry VIII. He also owned the Bear and Checker inns in Water Row.

One other aspect of the Dissolution of the Monasteries affected Ware. The Priory at Sheen, near Richmond, which Henry V had endowed with all the properties of the Benedictine Priory at Ware when he dissolved it in 1414, was now itself dissolved by Henry VIII. As far as they affected Ware itself, these properties were known as the Rectory Manor – as distinct from the Town Manor. The king gave Ware Rectory Manor in 1546 to the new college he had founded at Cambridge, Trinity College, as part of its Charter of Endowment. Nowadays – in the twenty-first century – Ware's association with Trinity is limited to the appointment of the Vicar of St. Mary's, in collaboration with the parish and the diocese, and responsibility for the chancel. Thus, in 2005, Trinity College was involved in the installation of the Revd. Derrick Peel and in repainting the chancel. But in the sixteenth century the college's writ ran much wider. It owned substantial properties in the town, like the Manor House in Church Street (sometimes known as the Rectory Manor), Trinity Farm which stood on the crown of Musley Hill and also Prior's Wood. In addition, Trinity took one-tenth of the annual rents (or tithes) on many properties and most fields in the parish. In 1582 there was a legal dispute brought by some of the farmers in Thundridge whether they should be paying tithes to Trinity. That dispute was the reason why the college now holds a wealth of historical documents about Ware and Thundridge, including copies of the pope's 1291 judgement about the Vicar of Ware – all of which might have been lost if it had not been for the complaint of the farmers in Thundridge. Following the death of Margaret Pole, Ware manor again reverted to the Crown. Thomas Wrothe was appointed bailiff and keeper of the park in place of Oliver Frankleyn, who held those posts under the countess.[15] In May 1542, the steward of the Crown held a court baron and listed the main properties paying rents, most of them inns. Down the side of the manuscript were listed: "Crowne & Cock, Horshowe, Cheker, Kybeslane, Christopher, Bullhedde, Cardinals Hatt, George, Greyhounde, Grymbnalls, Kerswellmill, Whitehart, Sarasens hed, Swatries, Bell."

The inns of Ware were now known throughout the land for their hospitality and specialities, but not everyone thought they gave value for money. The Earl and Countess of Rutland often stayed at Ware, in either the Crown or the White Hart inns. In 1539, the Countess of Rutland and her retinue made a slow progress from London to Belvoir Castle, staying one night in Waltham Cross, the next in Ware (the inn is not named) and the following night in Royston. The details of their meals are given in the Rutland papers.[16] Prodigious quantities of meat were eaten at all three inns – beef, mutton, both boiled and roast, lamb, chicken and capons, though at Ware they also ate five rabbits. Interestingly, their bread cost 12d. for a dozen loaves at all three inns. The main difference in the bills – 19s.2d. at Waltham, 40s.2d. at Ware and 38s.11d. at Royston – was accounted for by delicacies and drink. At Waltham, they had plain fare, apart from a pig's foot ('pygges petytoe'), and paid for eight gallons of ale and a quart of wine "for one of the Prince's servants". At Ware, they had calves' feet, crayfish for breakfast the next day, and drank a 'kylderkyne' of beer (about 18 gallons), "a single beer for my Lady", a pint of white wine, a bottle of claret and a pint of sack. At Royston, the delicacies were six quails but here they again resorted to ale, the traditional English drink rather than the new hopped beer which had

No. 1 West Street with its upper floor timbers exposed – the curved braces were clearly intended to be seen from the street. This was probably a shop in the 15th or early 16th century (photo: Adrian Grover).

recently been introduced from the Continent. There is a hint that the countess's party felt they had been overcharged at Ware: against 17s.6d for horse fodder, the countess's clerk wrote "as aperthy by a byll".

After the Dissolution of the Monasteries, the remaining eight years of Henry's reign were devoted to increasingly desperate attempts to produce another son and to the diversions of war. Marriage to Anne of Cleves (1540 – divorced six months later), Catherine Howard (1540 – beheaded 1542) and Catherine Parr (1543 – survived) all failed to produce children. There was war with Scotland in 1542, then in 1544 Henry invaded France but the only territory he secured was Boulogne. When the French counter-invaded in 1545, Henry's pride and joy, the warship Mary Rose, sank in Portsmouth Sound in sight of the king. Since the money received from the Dissolution of the Monasteries had already been spent, Henry's government in 1525 revived the Lay Subsidies of the fourteenth century (*see Appendix 1*). When Henry VIII died in 1547, Ware Manor was still held by the Crown.

10.
Weathering Two Extremes

Henry VIII's religious policy was not so much Protestant as anti-papal. His policy of giving the Crown supreme authority over the Church reflected the ambitions of medieval kings to govern their own Church, though in a more extreme form. Under Henry there were many sudden shocks and changes of policy, but they all happened in the span of Henry's 38 year reign. His two successors together reigned for only eleven years and during that time swung the nation from extreme Protestantism to strict Roman Catholicism.

Edward VI succeeded to the throne in 1547 at the age of ten. The following year he granted the manor of Ware to his older half-sister, Mary – Catherine of Aragon's daughter. It was a move with long-term implications. But for the time being, Ware and other towns were subject to the Protestant policies of the lords around Edward to take the Dissolution of the Monasteries a step further and suppress further signs of "papal superstition" as well as their equally strong desire to replenish the government's empty coffers. They had in their sights "all Colleges Frechappelles Chauntres Fraternyties Brotherheddes Gildes Stipendaries Obites Annyversaries Lyghtes and other lyke". Henry VIII's government had already made a valuation of these bodies in 1545 when he appropriated the tenths of all ecclesiastical revenues previously paid to the Pope. Now his son did another valuation with the object of selling off the property of the colleges, freechapels and chantries.

The main chantry in Ware was that of Ellen Bramble, established in 1474. It owned a considerable number of properties in the town – the Cardinal's Hat Inn in Water Row with its barn, yard and garden, as well as 14 acres of meadow in Amwell parish which went with it, an acre of arable land in the Amwell common field, a pasture or cow-lease in 'Nedenhoo Marsh' and another in 'Little Grove'; the Bull's Head Inn (not the present pub in Baldock Street, but probably what became The Bull, now a building society on the south side of the High Street) with which went a house in Middle Row, a garden in Kibes Lane together with an adjoining oven (a bakery), three and a half acres in the common field, two acres known as Sower Croft and a garden in Gardyner Lane – and finally the chantry priest's chamber. In 1545 these properties had been valued at £7.11s.4d. but the value had increased to £9.14s.8d. in 1547 when they were bought by two Hertfordshire speculators, Sir John Perien of Digswell and Thomas Reve. The enquiry reported that the priest's chamber was in the hands of William Dosen, the former vicar who was aged 57 and of honest fame with no other income except payment from the chantry.[1] The chantries report also gave an estimation of the town's population, or at least of the people that "done receyve the Blessed Comunyon" i.e. adults. The figures for the main Hertfordshire towns were:

Aldenham	500	Stortford	500
Ashwell	520	Baldock	400
St. Peter's at St. Albans	1,000	Ware	1,000
Hitchin	1,000	Royston	100
Hatfield	600	Tring	100

There was additional mention of a small 'obit' in Ware established by William King – it owned a tenement, paying 10s. of which 6s. went to the poor, but it did not say where it was.[2]

The 1547 commissioners took evidence from a number of guilds or fraternities – at Ashwell, Baldock, Barnet, Hitchin and St. Albans, the latter being a "Charnell Brotherhedde" or burial club – oddly, there was no mention of a guild or fraternity in Hertford. Nor was there mention of the Ware guild. Since it was unincorporated it fell outside the scope of the 1547 enquiry but it could not escape scrutiny for long. On 22 December 1549, one of the same commissioners, Frances Southwell, Auditor of the Court of Surveyors under Henry VIII, together with Robert Chester, one of the gentlemen of Henry's privy chamber and knighted by Edward VI in 1552, took evidence from a number of witnesses about the "brotherhood commonly called the Jesus Brotherhood." The two commissioners were relatively junior and the government must have regretted not sending more senior officials.

The hearing, probably in an inn or even the nave of St. Mary's, heard evidence in the form of answers to specific questions (*interrogatories*). The first witness was William Spencer, a farmer (yeoman) aged 58 years, who said he had been an alderman of the Fraternity or Brotherhood of Jesus. He gave evidence of the brotherhood's annual feast, of the property it owned (the White Hart and Saracen's Head inns, etc) and of how they employed a "Jesus priest" for a wage of 54s.4d. a year. Spencer said he was the last alderman after which no others had been appointed and that was nine or ten years past. He then described how they had disposed of the brotherhood's goods, including the great brass pot and silver cups, to members including one John Marsh. All well and good: the brotherhood had ceased to exist and its silverware had been sold.[3]

Then John Marsh gave his evidence. Marsh, another farmer aged 60, was clearly a Protestant radical and determined to wash the brotherhood's dirty linen in public. He began by declaring that, at the annual feast, the masters would lend out some of the brotherhood's funds, as much as 40s. at a time, charging interest of 10d. or 12d. a year for every pound (five per cent). This was 'usury' and against the law. William Spencer was called back and admitted that the masters lent money, but said he knew nothing of interest. Marsh continued and said there had been a book of the brotherhood's constitution, by which if any brother sued another brother without a licence from the aldermen and masters that member would forfeit a pound. The book of constitution used to be in the custody of Oliver Franklyn when he was bailiff. Then Marsh dropped the first of his bombshells, that the 'Jesus priest' employed by the brotherhood used to turn to the congregation during mass and invite them to pray for the souls of all the brothers and sisters of the said fraternity. To this William Spencer disagreed strongly. Then Marsh went on to state that the brotherhood maintained an altar in St. Mary's, where there was a garland garnished with priceless jewels and the name of Jesus in silver and gilt, and also three coats of velvet whereof some were embroidered with gold, all "for the unseemly fornyture of the Image of Jhus which stode in the parishe churche uppon the Jhus Alter". After Marsh, Thomas Byrche, aged 54, the one who had bought the former friary, said he agreed with William Spencer and as for what Marsh had said he knew nothing and could not say.

Finally, William Dowsing, the former chantry priest of Ellen Bramble's Chantry, aged 59, agreed with all that William Spencer had said. He denied that the brotherhood had taken any interest on loans and said the last Jesus priest had left a year before.

This was all very embarrassing and potentially damaging to the Hertfordshire gentry and traders who had been associated with the Jesus Brotherhood. Particularly embarrassing were the charge that the brotherhood had prayed for the souls of the dead, which would have made it an illegal chantry, and the description of the Jesus Altar, which would have seemed particularly scandalous to the Protestant lords who surrounded Edward VI. The way the authorities dealt with it was to hold another hearing, as soon as possible – on 31 March 1550. Two senior commissioners, Sir Ralph Sadler and Sir Henry Parker, then took evidence on oath from twenty former members of the Jesus Brotherhood, including William Spencer and Thomas Byrche – but not John Marsh! They stated that the property of the brotherhood was held "for the use and utility" of all the inhabitants of Ware, and no other use: this included relieving the inhabitants of certain taxes and common charges, of maintaining a beacon outside the town and repairing the bridge, to which the king contributes nothing although his bailiff (at Hertford) takes 40 marks a year in tolls. They went on to say that, indeed, there had been a body called the Jesus Brotherhood but this had been founded a long time ago, kept in being by the charity of strangers as well as Ware people and that it had ceased to exist 12 years before. They then explained that employing a "morrowemass prest" had been necessary for the profit of the town as a whole and his wage had been paid from the townspeople's contributions "some giving iid., some iiiid., some viiid. and some more and some lesse as their devocion was". He also received gifts from "strangers" (probably pilgrims) and any deficit in his wages was made up from the town's common funds. As for the properties – the inns, meadowland, etc. – this was held at the will and pleasure of the town and no member of the brotherhood received any benefit from them. Everyone must have heaved a huge sigh of relief. All the scandals laid bare by John Marsh had been glossed over. None of the brotherhood's properties had been put up for sale or confiscated. A high level whitewash job had been done and the twenty former fraternity members duly put their initials or crosses at the foot of the document.[4] The book of constitutions, said to have been held by Oliver Franklyn, was not mentioned – it was probably destroyed between the first and second hearings.

The final visit to Ware by Edward VI's commissioners did not allow of any evidence or argument. In 1550, the Privy Council decreed that all churches should prepare a list of their valuables and this was done in 1553 by John Inglis or Ynglyshe. Each chalice, cross or other piece of silver or gilt was written in the return along with its weight. The heaviest pieces were a cross with images of the Virgin Mary and St. John, four staves of silver for carrying crosses, and a pair of incense censors.[5] At least six of the pieces seem to have been those given to the churchwardens by Sir Thomas Bourchier in his will of 1491. Almost all of them were taken away to be melted down for the royal coffers. At about the same time, workmen were sent into St. Mary's to destroy the 'idolatrous' stained glass windows and the heads of any images of saints. Fortunately, this latter task was done by someone who did the minimum damage consistent with his task (or his wage) – he smashed

The moveable Tudor screen in Place House

only those heads of saints on the font which could be seen from the south or west doors, thus preserving six out of the eight. Most of the gargoyles survived, also the figures of the sun, moon and creatures like rats around the external windows of the Lady Chapel, and all of the corbels associated with Joan of Kent's family.

One other item stands out from the reign of Edward VI and that is a rather splendid one. Edward gave the manor of Ware to his half-sister, Mary Tudor, who during his reign lived in seclusion in the royal palace at Hunsdon. At some time she must have visited Ware and that visit is commemorated in the fine timber screen in Place House. Despite the painted dates 1629 and 1657, put there with their initials by two later owners, Humfrey Packer and William Collett – the screen is clearly Tudor both in style and content. It is made of oak with eight panels and is carved in the parchmin style, i.e. representing not linen-folds but the turned-up corners of parchment. In the top four panels are carvings of two ornate cups, a pomegranate joined with a rose and a coat of arms with the initials RW which also appear on two of the lower panels. The conjoined pomegranate and rose was the badge of Mary Tudor, representing her mother's device, the pomegranate of Aragon, and the Tudor rose of her father; the pomegranate and rose appear alternately on the edges of the screen. The puzzles of the piece have always been the initials RW and the coat of arms which incorporates three objects which at various times have been thought to be ale tankards, milk-churns or saddle pommels. But close scrutiny reveals they are scribed to resemble brickwork and were clearly three well-heads. This was the badge of Richard Wells, a prominent Catholic landowner who may have been Mary Tudor's steward in Ware. Whether Mary did come to Ware when she was lady of the manor is a mystery. She was closely watched by the government's Protestant spies who suspected her of plotting with Catholic lords for an invasion by Spain. One of these spies was named Benet of Ware.[6]

Mary Tudor, the Catholic Queen

Edward VI died of consumption (tuberculosis) on 6 July 1553. He was never very robust in health or in personality and some historians have regarded him as a pawn in the hands of the Protestant lords who dominated the court. Under their influence Edward had named Lady Jane Grey, a niece of Henry VIII, as his successor, thus passing over the claims of his half-sisters, Mary and Elizabeth. As the king's health began to fail, the powerful Duke of Northumberland, John Dudley, moved to consolidate his own position by marrying his son, Lord Guilford Dudley, to Lady Jane. On the king's death, Northumberland had her proclaimed queen. It is sometimes said that Lady Jane was proclaimed queen in Ware; so she was but she was proclaimed in many other towns, particularly in East Anglia. What distinguished our town from others was that a small army of "500 persons in warlike manner" was assembled in Ware by William Parr, Marquess of Northampton, who declared that Mary Tudor was a bastard and Lady Jane the "undoubted and true Queen" and the Duke of Northumberland the lieutenant-general.[7] It continued the tradition of mustering troops at Ware, begun in the reign of Richard II – the town had plenty of inns and open spaces – but William Parr also owned property here, inherited from his wife, Lady Anne Bourchier, even though he had just divorced her. In the event, Lady Jane, the duke and the marquess were quickly defeated and all were sent to the Tower of London where Lady Jane, her husband and father-in-law were all beheaded. William Parr somehow survived, though stripped of all his titles by Mary (and with his divorce from Lady Anne Bourchier revoked – she was made a lady-in-waiting by the Queen). Interestingly, the indictment of William Parr was taken by Sir John Butler, a leading figure in the town's Brotherhood of Jesus in 1544 and again in 1551 when the brotherhood had recreated itself as the "co-feoffees of an inn called the Whyte Hart" on behalf of the townspeople.

On her succession, Mary Tudor set about re-establishing the authority of the Roman Catholic Church, with the strong support of Cardinal Reginald Pole, the Countess of Salisbury's son, who became Archbishop of Canterbury in succession to Henry VIII's archbishop, Thomas Cranmer, who was burned at the stake as a heretic in 1556. A similar fate was in store for hundreds of others who refused to renounce their Protestant beliefs and return to Rome. Among them was Thomas Fust, a London hosier, burned in the market place at Ware on 30 August 1554. Fust had no connection with Ware but was one of many evangelicals who refused to recant and were sent to be burned in the main towns of his diocese by Edmund Bonner, Bishop of London. It is recorded that Bonner came over from his palace at Much Hadham to watch the Ware burning and emphasise the warning to all Protestants. The London diocese which included the whole of Essex and part of Hertfordshire, had been the main centre of the Lollards who followed the radical teaching of the fourteenth century reformer John Wycliff, and had embraced the reforms of Edward VI. Ware was certainly heavily influenced by both the Lollards and Protestantism. The martyrdom of Thomas Fust was written down by John Foxe, who was keen to show the bishop living up to his reputation as "Bloody Bonner". He wrote that Fust had refused to recant his beliefs, saying to Bonner: "No, my lord, for no truth cometh out of your mouth but all lies".[8] On another occasion, according to Foxe, the bishop in a fit of temper had struck a knight standing next to him and then in a contrary mood, leaving his dinner, had taken horse and ridden with a small company to Ware, even though he had previously intended to stay three or four days at Hadham and had made provision in the palace to do so. Bishop Bonner had been deprived of his bishopric and put in the Marshalsea Prison during the reign of Edward VI and was to suffer a similar fate under Queen Elizabeth.

As far as Ware was concerned, the major event of Mary Tudor's reign was the gift of the manor of which she had been the lady to Francis Hastings, Second Earl of Huntingdon, and his wife, Katherine.[9] The earl was just the right lord for Mary's reign and an example of how to survive the extremes of religion. He had attended the coronations of Anne Boleyn and Jane Seymour and his son, Henry Hastings, was educated with the young Prince Edward. During the latter's reign as Edward VI, Huntingdon aligned himself with the Duke of Northumberland and supported the claim of Lady Jane Grey. He was put in the Tower of London in 1553 and yet, only a year later, he was restored to his honours and received the personal gift of Ware manor from the Catholic Queen. The main reason was that his wife, Katherine Pole, was the daughter and coheir of Lord Montagu, the niece of Cardinal Pole and granddaughter of Ware's last non-royal lady, Lady Margaret Pole, Countess of Salisbury. It is no wonder that, on the death of Mary Tudor in 1558, the Earl and Countess of Huntingdon had no difficulty whatever in adapting to yet another change of regime and religion. He had been lord lieutenant of Leicestershire under Edward, lost the office under Mary but received some honours there, and was again created lord lieutenant by Elizabeth. To a lesser extent, his tenants and fellow citizens in Ware had similar experiences. These included the vicar, Robert Kynsey, who had received a Protestant ordination under Edward VI and a Roman Cathlic one from Bishop Bonner. He obviously thought better of changing yet again in 1558 when Elizabeth became Queen, for he was succeeded briefly by William Dowsing, the former chantry priest, now well into his seventies.

With the death of Mary Tudor in 1558 and the accession of her half-sister, Elizabeth, the success of the Protestant Reformation was sealed. Many people in Ware were glad, particularly those like Thomas Byrche who had gained from the dispersal of church property. But there was also nostalgia for what had been lost, such as the gorgeous pageantry and the music of the old religion. The parish church lost the silver plate and the bright vestments worn by priests at mass, including two copes of crimson velvet, two others of tawny and blue and one of white Damask – and a pair of organs. There were no longer processions around the parish, like the one recalled by Dominic Jacson who had been the parish clerk for 33 years since the 1540s, when in Rogation Week they processed

Gilpin House

Gilpin House (No. 84 High Street) is a fascinating building and was probably the "house on the market place", owned by Anne Bourchier and her husband, William Parr, Marquess of Northampton. It may have been from its windows that the Marquess proclaimed Lady Jane Grey queen (the name 'Gilpin House' is much later and derived from a painting of William Cowper's poem about John Gilpin's ride to Ware).

Houses had been encroaching on the market place since the early Middle Ages. They were probably market stalls which took root: they had no yards or gardens and became known as Middle Row. Many of them were rebuilt but there is an original at No. 94 High Street, now a clothing shop ('The Closet') – it was described by the buildings historian, J.T. Smith: "although narrow, being slightly less than 12ft (3.7m) wide, it is of two storeys with cellar and of two bays with a bold jetty to the south".[10]

Gilpin House is much grander and is in two parts. The eastern (right-hand) wing is part of a fifteenth-century building, of which the remainder has been demolished – perhaps to make way for Rankin Square at some time in the eighteenth-century. This wing has a crown-post roof, a deep cellar lined with flint and some fine old timbers, including an old doorway, illustrated right. At some time in the seventeeth-century the other wing was added, with its roof over-sailing the older part. The newer part has a dining room on the first floor and a parlour above, both with elaborate plasterwork (shown on the facing page). It also has a brick-lined cellar, which was probably the kitchen for the dining room.

Gilpin House

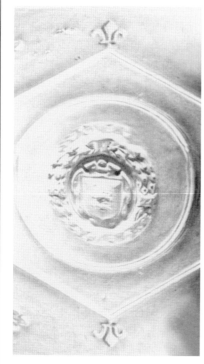

Some of the seventeenth-century plaster work on the walls and the ceilings of the west wing of Gilpin House. The coat of arms – showing two lions one above the other – clearly meant something. They appear to be the arms of the Gough family, but research has failed to find any Gough connection with Ware. The photographs were taken when this was Tarling's do-it-yourself shop. It is now a hairdressers.

from St. Mary's to Wadesmill, where the Gospel was sung, and then to the old parish church of Thundridge, where mass was sung – "that doone, as the custome then was, there we drank".[11]

More serious was the loss of Ware's considerable trade from 'strangers' or pilgrims journeying to the shrine of the Virgin Mary in Walsingham, Norfolk. Thomas Hassall, vicar of neighbouring Great Amwell, wrote: "it is not yet forgotten how frequent a pilgrimage the Lady of Walsingham drew along these parts, which made our neighbour towne of Ware so full .. more than at this present and better".[12] The poet William Warner, who lived in Amwell, said that Ware High Street was then known as Walsingham Way. It must have been partly for the passing pilgrimage trade that the Brotherhood of Jesus maintained such a richly decorated image of Jesus in the parish church. A pilgrimage badge thought to have come from Walsingham was found when an old cottage was demolished in 1979 opposite the church – as well as a cellar with one wall made of oxen bones. The inns of Water Row must have been crowded with pilgrims at certain times of the year. But all that had passed: Elizabethan England was a new country.

11.
'The Guested Town of Ware'

There is no doubt that Ware enjoyed the 43-year long reign of Elizabeth I. There was no rebellion here, no substantial body of unhappy Catholics as there was in the north of England and no threat from Spanish invaders – the days of invaders coming up the Thames and the Lea were past. During her reign, Ware lost one lord who was so poor he was forced to sell the manor and gained a new one who spent money on new buildings and even a stone bridge. Elizabeth presided over a great cultural renaissance in the theatre, literature, art and music, and Ware participated in it to the full, in the process getting its name attached to the most famous piece of furniture in the world.

The town's first Elizabethan lord was Francis Hastings, second Earl of Huntingdon. Despite receiving Ware manor from the Catholic Mary Tudor, Huntingdon successfully negotiated a place in the new religion and received a summons to the House of Lords in Elizabeth's first parliament. Here Francis and his oldest son, Henry, attended every session, including the 1559 Acts of Supremacy and Uniformity, which established the Protestant Church of England with Elizabeth as 'Supreme Governor'. But Francis died in 1560 and his titles and estates passed to his 24-year old son, Henry, who found himself responsible for a widowed mother and ten brothers and sisters. Since he was married to a sister of the Queen's favourite, Robert Dudley, Earl of Leicester, Henry might have expected some favours. But it was not to be and throughout his life he worked hard for Elizabeth, particularly in Leicestershire and Yorkshire, ending up by his own reckoning £100,000 in debt. Yet he was a fair man and a good administrator, determined to get his just deserts but unwilling to squeeze his estates dry. On 15 February 1569, a court was held in Ware, presided over by the earl's oldest brother, Sir George Hastings of Loughborough. He issued the following orders:

> Item: any horse laden with fresh water fish or eels or pike shall pay to the manor 1d. (one penny) for trunkage.

> Item: any foreign musician resorting to the town shall not be suffered to tarry or play in any Inn or usual resorting place within the said town on one night and one day upon pain of being treated as a common vagabond by the officers of the said town.[1]

In 1575, the earl sold Ware manor to Thomas Fanshawe, the Queen's Remembrancer of the Exchequer. This office, which Thomas inherited from his uncle, was one of the key administrative offices under the Crown and also a very ancient one: it involved oversight of the receipt of customs, taxes and the Crown's returns on land and adjudicating any disputes about them. The contrast with the Earl of Huntingdon, always slightly suspect because of his wife's connections with the Yorkist royal family and Mary Tudor, could not have been greater. Fanshawe's family were minor landowners in Derbyshire and, on arriving in London, he had worked his way up from auditing accounts as a sworn clerk.

He seems to have been trusted by absolutely everybody. Queen Elizabeth (according to Ann Fanshawe) was reported to have said "he was the best officer of accounts she had and a person of great integrity".[2] He was also a member of most of Elizabeth's parliaments. Fanshawe was in every respect a good lord of the manor but initially he faced opposition from a member of the prominent Harvye family, who owned the Bull and Horseshoe inns among other properties. Stephen Harvye objected to Fanshawe's purchase and had gone around London uttering "false slanderous words" that the manor had been promised to various junior members of the Hastings family by their mother, the Countess of Huntingdon — clearly the new earl's sale had caused fury among his siblings and their children.[3] To remove any legal obstacles to his title, Fanshawe took a case in the Chancery

Thomas Fanshawe

court against Sir George and Lady Mary Hastings, proving that their mother had also been party to the sale of the manor.[4]

That dispute out of the way, Thomas Fanshawe took the important decision to relinquish Place House, the old and probably tumbling down manor house in the town, and build a new manor at Ware Park. No trace and, sadly, no illustrations survive of Fanshawe's new house but it must have been a splendid Elizabethan structure. In the next century, his son's garden there was admired by everyone, including James I. The poet, William Vallans, wrote about "the parke of *Ware,* / Where *Fanshawe* buildes for his succeeding race." That is from Vallans' poem *The Tale of Two Swannes*, thought to have been written in about 1590. He also revealed in notes for the poem that "the diligence of the Townesmen who, with helpe of *M.Fanshawe,* have erected a new markette house, with entent to procure certaine Fayres to be helde there yeerely. The Bridge was reedified lately, and the arches made of stone at the charges *viz* 140 poundes geven by her Majestie". The market house was on the site of what is now the 'Town Hall', built in 1826 and now inhabited by estate agents. An old print of the High Street in 1811 shows Fanshawe's market house really on its last legs – the wattle and daub walls reduced to a few timber uprights – standing opposite the Bull Inn in Water Row. William Vallans was clearly a Ware man and his poem celebrates the town in many different ways, not least in the fantasy tale of the goddess Venus bringing from Italy to Ware a pair of swans, from which every other swan in England is descended – "yea, the verie Thames / Shall be replenisht with their princely race". Swans have always gathered on the Lea by Ware Bridge and still do.

Vallans also noted that "by means of the Lord Treasurer the river is made passable for boates and barges". The Lord Treasurer was William Cecil, Lord Burghley, and making the Lea passable to London for Ware barges carrying malt and grain was a personal mission for him. But that was achieved only with great difficulty and a number of bruised heads.

The reason for Burghley's concern was the need to feed the rapidly expanding population of London, which had doubled from 60,000 in 1524 to 120,000 in 1582 and was set to double again to 250,000 by 1605. The bakers of London were working flat out to cope with the demand for bread and now there were 'common brewers', brewing the new hopped beer for delivery to a number of inns and alehouses and demanding an assured supply of cheap malt from East Anglia. Malt and grain from Hertfordshire and farther afield had always been delivered to London by two means, road and river: the monks of Westminster had demonstrated that back in the 1370s. The River Lea was easily the cheaper of the two but at the beginning of Elizabeth's reign it was full of obstacles. There were low bridges, there were stakes driven into the river bed for fishing nets and wide beds of commercially grown osiers or reeds, worst of all there were millers channelling the river off into the mill races which drove their millwheels. A survey of the river was carried out in 1561 by two Dutchmen, commissioned by the Court of Aldermen of the City of London, but that came to nothing. It was only in 1567 that the Council demanded the business be pursued with urgency. The result was an Act of Parliament passed in 1571 which ordered that the River Lea be made navigable as far as Ware. During the next ten years, the stakes and reed beds were cleared away and many bridges rebuilt to allow barges to pass underneath. A new pound lock was constructed at Waltham Abbey in 1577, with two sets of mitred gates – a revolutionary improvement on the old flash locks which depended on a local miller giving a flash of water to drive a barge downstream. The work took ten years and cost £80,000. But there were objections, and not only from millers, fishermen and landowners who were now made responsible for the river's embankments, but also from a very powerful group of traders.

The badgers of Enfield

Behind the objections made to the Privy Council in March 1580 were the maltmen or 'badgers' of Enfield. For much of the sixteenth century, Enfield traders had controlled the delivery of malt and grain to London. They went out to the markets of Hertfordshire and made private purchases, outside the rules of the local markets, advancing credit to maltmakers to make sure they could not sell elsewhere. Then – so the accusation went – these traders held back the grain from London until they were able to drive up prices. This was known as 'badging' (probably derived from 'bagging', since all food then came in bags, though licensed badgers may also have worn badges). The Enfield badgers had sewn up the trade in grain to such an extent that Hertfordshire resembled a funnel with the narrow neck carrying all the trade through Cheshunt and Enfield. Sir Thomas Wroth was said to have counted 2,200 pack horses in one morning on the road between Enfield and Shoreditch.[5] Another witness, who claimed that Enfield traders had forced up prices in London, said they held back four thousand horseloads in one week – four thousand quarters. The bill of complaint from the loaders and carriers of grain to London was answered by Lord Burghley himself. He produced the evidence of London bakers and even the carriers themselves to show that river transport was cheaper. A witness pointed out that it took sixty horses to carry sixty quarters of malt, and twelve men to drive them, whereas the same amount of malt could be carried in one boat manned by only four or five men. There was also the advantage of the 'back carriage' of coal and iron from London which could be distributed to the smiths of Hertfordshire. The money on these return journeys, it was claimed, could compensate for the expense of building barges which could be up to £40. The larger barges could carry up to 42 quarters of malt, slightly less of wheat: carriage of a quarter of malt from Ware to London cost 8d., a quarter of wheat 12d. and a passenger 6d. If a barge was loaded at Ware on Saturday, it could go down to Bow Creek on Monday in ten to twelve hours, then wait for a flood tide, on which it could be rowed up to the Port of London in another four hours – longer than carriage by packhorse or cart but much cheaper.

A campaign of sabotage began in the summer of 1580 when it was discovered that part of the river was being diverted at Ponders End in "a great flood of water" into two previously dried up streams. The following year, there were concerted efforts to breach the embankments next to Enfield Lock. This was carried out by eight or nine men who were the servants or relatives of some of Enfield's wealthiest maltmen. One man, John Lucke, boasted that he would "go by water, and have an augur (drill) to bore holes in the barges".[6] Another said he would gladly put a barrel of gunpowder at the bottom of the lock and another in the bottom of a barge, provided the boatmen were not in it. Demands for a commission to be set up to hinder damage to the river were set out in a petition sent to Lord Burghley in 1583, supposedly by the inhabitants of Ware but in fact signed by four barge owners. The situation was grave enough for Burghley to appoint three grandees, all from Hertfordshire to the commission. Thomas Fanshawe of Ware Park was the chairman, with Sir Henry Cocke of Broxbourne (a court official like Fanshawe) and Henry Baeshe of Stanstead Abbots, at one time surveyor-general of the Navy. But the sabotage went on even as the commission was taking evidence. It was suggested that someone more important, like Lord Hunsdon, the Queen's cousin, should take charge. Hunsdon came on to the scene and, realising that the Enfield dispute could easily turn into full rebellion, suggested that it should be turned over to the Commission of Sewers for the River Lea, under the chairmanship of a judge. This stratagem worked for, under questioning, some of the conspirators confessed and implicated others, with the result that a number of Enfield men were committed to prison.

The trouble seemed to be over. The number of barges using the river had risen to thirty by 1591 and it was estimated that a thousand quarters of corn and malt were being carried to London each week. So much had the trade transferred from road to river that a commission was set up to examine the loss of tolls on the bridges of Hertford, Ware and Stanstead Abbots, which had fallen on average by £16 a year. But then in 1592 trouble again broke out, more seriously than before. At the end of May, a large party of men, armed with swords, pitchforks, mattocks and shovels, gathered at the High Bridge at Waltham Abbey, where they were joined by some of the servants of Sir Edward Denny, who owned a mill – though Sir Edward was probably in Ireland and not involved. At any rate, the enlarged gang worked through the night to tear down Waltham Bridge and rebuild it lower, so that barges could not pass underneath. In July, the bargemen retaliated, smashing Sir Edward Denny's millrace to open up a new channel for their boats. Then, on 19 July, a large party of men from Enfield and Cheshunt gathered to prevent any boats from passing up or down the river. Stones and timber were put in the river and boats were again held up. On the 24 July, a party of 24 armed ruffians assembled at the same spot and attacked the bargemen as they were towing their vessels, so that the bargees were forced to run into the water to escape. One bargeman was wounded in the shoulder by a pikestaff. There was further violence on 7 August, when some of Sir Edward Denny's servants used bows and arrows to drive the boatmen away. In November, Enfield men came with carts loaded with tree trunks which they laid across the river. And in December there were a number of attacks on the barges by armed men, throwing crews and sacks of malt and corn into the river and even sinking one barge. Despite complaints from the barge owners, the boatmen and the City of London that local landowners and Justices of the Peace were in league with the rioters, only seven men were eventually brought to trial. In November 1594 the Court of Star Chamber declared that passage on the river was, and had always been, free. In a move to appease the Enfield men, the court gave as its opinion that the carriage of malt and corn by river was cheaper, but carriage by road would employ more men and therefore should also be used. It also ordered the construction of a proper tow-path.[7]

There were still a great many Enfield badgers operating in Hertfordshire – 54 were licensed by the Middlesex Sessions in 1609[8] – but the river transport of malt into London was now established. Thirty-four barges now worked the Lea, with capacities ranging from twenty-six to forty-two quarters. There were twenty-two different barge owners – three from Hertford, three from Waltham, one of Braughing, two of Stanstead Abbots, two of Broxbourne, six of Ware, two of Enfield and three of London. They maintained over a hundred men "strong and skilled to do the Queen good service by land or sea".[9] The Ware owners were Robert Leonard, John Mathyson, John Whiskhood, John Spencer, Richard Cibborne and Richard Brooke. Brooke owned two barges, the *Great Blue Lion* carrying 42 qtrs. and worked with five men, and the *Little Blue Lion* carrying 28 qtrs. with three men. Lord Burghley, who lived at Theobalds in Cheshunt, was so taken with river transport that he commissioned a pictorial map of the Lea – measuring almost two metres in length, it shows one barge under sail near Tottenham and two at Enfield being pulled by bargees with a rope from the top of the mast looped over one shoulder.

One result of the disputes of the 1580s and 1590s was a determination by the London brewers to exclude the Enfield badgers – or 'higglers', as they were also known – from their malt supply chain. It did not happen immediately but gradually the major brewers began to buy huge quantities of malt on their own account, often privately and by giving credit to tie down the suppliers. Since the badgers were now obliged by law to buy only in local markets, the London brewers had them at a disadvantage for they could use their traditional London freedoms to buy where the best prices and quality could be obtained. To do this the brewers used their own agents, known later as 'maltfactors', and in time these factors became the crucial link between Hertfordshire maltsters and their London customers. Hertfordshire malt, particularly that coming down the Old North Road from Royston and Ware, was now vital to the economy of London. It was also psychologically important and vital to the popularity of the government. In 1588, following the defeat of

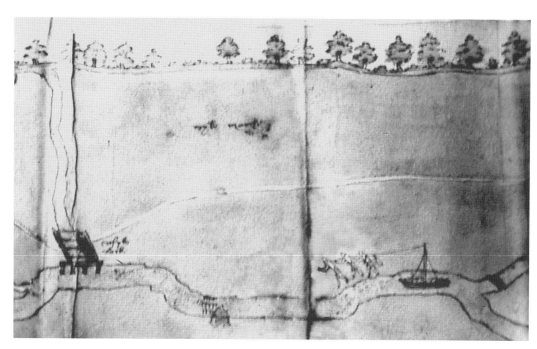

A map of the River Lea, made for Lord Burghley and showing men pulling a barge by a rope attached to the mast. Enfield Lock is on the left. (Hatfield House Collection).

the Armada, the Queen was warned that the Spaniards would no longer supply England with sack or sherry. "A figge for Spaine," Elizabeth replied, "so long as Royston will afford such plenty of good malts".[10]

One reason why these local disputes on the Lea were taken so seriously was that they coincided with a national emergency. In May 1588 King Philip of Spain sent an Armada of 130 ships and 19,000 men to rendezvous with the Spanish army of Flanders, under the Duke of Parma, to invade England and restore the Catholic faith. As everyone knows, the rendezvous never took place and the Armada was defeated and scattered around the coasts of Scotland and Ireland. England's naval strength, under Charles Lord Howard and Sir Francis Drake, was much more credible than the land army. In 1588, Trained Bands from the Hertfordshire militias were sent to London to guard the Queen and to Tilbury to be prepared to repel invaders. Men from the county militia had already seen action as volunteers against the Spaniards, in the Earl of Leicester's campaign in the Low Countries in 1586.[11] Ware men must have been involved in both of these musters of the militia. The aftermath of the Armada lingered on towards the end of the century. In 1597, Sir Robert Cecil (Lord Burghley's son) reported on a meeting with Spanish hostages from the Low Countries, being held captive in Ware, and on their efforts to buy their freedom.[12] Where in the town they were held was not revealed, nor why they were being held here rather than in Hertford Castle.

But Hertford was undergoing fundamental change, which eventually saw its emergence from the shadow that Ware had cast over it during the Middle Ages. In 1582 urgent

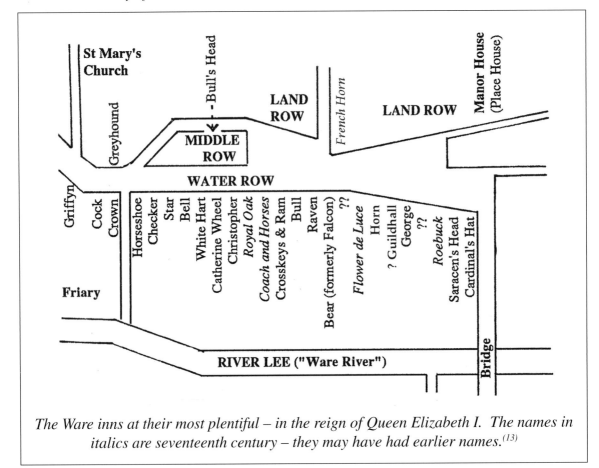

The Ware inns at their most plentiful – in the reign of Queen Elizabeth I. The names in italics are seventeenth century – they may have had earlier names.[13]

repairs were made to Hertford Castle before the visit of Queen Elizabeth and the Court and in 1589, following the defeat of the Armada, she had granted Hertford a Borough Charter.[14] The Court and Parliament – though not the Queen – came to Hertford again when they were forced out of London in 1593 by the plague. But members were looking anxiously down the river at the neighbouring town. On 5 November 1593, a correspondent told Sir William More, Member of Parliament for Surrey, that he did not know how long the session could continue at Hertford, because more than 300 people had died of the plague in Ware and that had caused the price of lodgings (presumably in Hertford) to rise alarmingly – a chamber could not be had, even if one offered five pounds a week.[15]

The Great Bed of Ware

In *The Tale of Two Swannes*, William Vallans described his home town as "the guested towne of Ware". It had certainly been that in Chaucer's time and since then the number of inns up and down the High Street had grown. The Old North Road was still a major artery, linking London with York and Scotland. There was no shortage of guests – officials and churchmen from the North on their way to conventions in London, foreign envoys *en route* to Scotland (still a separate country), spies and agitators, traders coming to Ware market to purchase malt, grain or cloth, soldiers from various militias, Spanish prisoners, and so on. In addition, Ware had been declared a 'post town' as far back as 1536 along with Waltham Cross and Royston, its distant neighbours on the Old North Road. Forty years later Lord Burghley and other members of the Privy Council were taking a special interest in the posts at Ware. In 1565 – four years after the Catholic Mary Queen of Scots had returned there from France – an order was given to the constables, officers and post of Ware that no man should be allowed to pass with dispatches for Scotland without a specific licence from the Queen or the government. They were to send weekly reports.[16] In 1578, the Ware postmaster, Richard Swynsted who was landlord of the Horseshoe Inn (now the Tap Bar) wrote personally to Lord Burghley, asking for arrears in his pay. He had not received anything for nine months, he said, "which is very long for a poor man to forbear" and yet letters and packets were arriving at more than 300 a month.[16] The "guested towne of Ware" was a crowded, bustling, prosperous place, seemingly without a care in the world about how to keep the guests coming. Or was it?

In fact, the inns had still not recovered from the end of the pilgrimages to Walsingham. In 1557 Holinshed had written that "the waie to Walsingham was through Waltham, Ware and Royston" all of which had "great and sumptuous innes builded in them, for the receiving of such travellers and strangers as passe to and fro." Catholic pilgrims were more lavish with their tips than Protestant clerks and surveyors, and probably stayed longer. Something had to be done to make sure Ware remained a guested town. A device or "advertising gimmick" was needed with a public relations campaign to back it up. Well, that gimmick was the Great Bed of Ware. That is the most likely explanation of its origin, the one that fits the earliest references to this strange piece of furniture – and the one favoured by experts at the Victoria and Albert Museum in Kensington, where the bed now resides.[17]

The first reference to the bed – presumably just after it had been bought and installed – was in 1596, when a German visitor, Prince Ludwig of Anhalt-Köhten, recorded in his verse diary that he had been to *"Wahr"* and seen a bed in which "four couples might comfortably lie side by side". Obviously, the innkeeper went for tourists first, before approaching the playwrights. Then in 1601 came the most famous literary reference to the bed in Shakespeare's *Twelfth Night*. In Act III, Scene 2, Sir Toby Belch advises Sir Andrew Aguecheek on writing a love letter and says he should employ "as many lies as will lie in thy sheet of paper, although the sheet were big enough for the *Bed of Ware*". It is a tame reference and perhaps not what the Ware publicists had in mind, but Shakespeare was certainly a good name to have associated with Ware. Equally famous was Ben Jonson, who in 1609 wrote *Epicoene: or the Silent Woman*, in which Morose, a gentleman who hates noise is persuaded to marry Epicoene, the Silent Woman who turns out to be a high-pitched scold. It is an amusing satire (Dryden especially liked it) and there are a number of references to Ware and the Great Bed, into which two lecherous knights, Sir John Daw and Sir Amorous La-Foole, try to inveigle young ladies. That was much more what the Ware publicists had in mind – *Come to Ware for a Romantic Weekend* – though Jonson also has Sir Amorous saying "Our bath cost us fifteen pound when we came home".

The playwright who really punched the message home with relish was Thomas Dekker

The Great Bed of Ware

The Great Bed (right in a print of 1878) is an English four-poster bed of unusually large proportions. It measures 10ft.10ins (330.2 cms) in length, 10ft.7ins (322.6 cms) in width and the height is 8ft.9ins (266.7 cms). There is reason to believe it was cut down in height when it was moved from one inn to another. It is made of oak (wainscot) with boldly carved posts and headboard, and in the headboard are two inlaid or marquetry panels depicting castles and swans in the river, probably the work of foreign cabinet makers from Germany or Holland, who had settled in Southwark. Because it is so impressive, people have assumed it was made for a stately home or someone important. There is a date 1463 painted on the headboard so it has been suggested it was made by Jonas Fosbrooke, a journeyman carpenter, who presented it to Edward IV or even Warwick the Kingmaker in 1463. But the style is late Tudor not fifteenth century. The date was probably added, along with a great deal of graffiti when the bed stood in the Crown Inn – demolished in 1765 and replaced with the building which is now Ware Library. Indeed, the bed has always been associated with inns. In 1610, Prince Ludwig Friedrich of Württemberg slept in a bed "eight feet wide" in a Ware inn which his secretary said was called the Stag. There has never been an inn of that name in the town and it is assumed this was the White Hart.

The tale that the Great Bed originally resided in The Crown Inn derives from the historian Cussans and is incorporated in the blue plaque over the Library door – and is almost certainly wrong. The bed stayed in the White Hart until 1706, when it was transferred to The George; it then moved to The Crown, demolished in 1765, to The Bull, demolished in 1848, and finally to the old Saracen's Head from which it was sold in 1870 and removed to the Rye House Hotel at Hoddesdon. While in Ware, the bed was always the property of innkeepers, never of the inns' owners.

in *Northward Ho*, which he co-authored in 1607 with John Webster (and which was a reply to Ben Jonson's *Eastward Ho* which was a reply to Dekker's *Westward Ho* – there's nothing new in sequels). Here Ware is mentioned on every other page. The main characters are a London merchant named Mayberry and two adventurers, Greenshield and Fetherstone, who try to out-cuckold each other by enticing the others' wives into bed and it is set mainly in Ware. Perhaps in a reference to William Vallans's poem, a prostitute named Doll confesses that she has been "an inn for any guest" but promises her lover to be "as true to thee as Ware and Wades-mill are one to another". The picture Dekker paints of Ware is interesting because it has many references to food, including crayfish, spitchcocks and fat trout, but he also says Ware is a town "where Hosts will be familiar, and Tapsters saucie, and Chamberlaines worse than the eves' intelligencers" (i.e. evesdroppers). Dekker who was known to be chronically in debt may well have been paid for the copious mentions of Ware in *Northward Ho*. He certainly fulfilled his brief, for the play ends with the couplet:

> This night let's banquet freely: come, we'll dare
> Our wives to combat ith' greate bed in Ware.[18]

The Great Bed went on collecting literary references – Edward Ward's pamphlet *A Step to Stirbitch Fair* (1700) George Farquahar's play *The Recruiting Officer* (1706), Lord Byron's *Don Juan* (1819), the pantomime *Harlequin and the Merrie Devil of Edmonton, or the Great Bed of Ware* (1839), Djuna Barnes's novel *Nightwood* (1936) and even a poem by the former Poet Laureate, Andrew Motion, in 2001.

The portrayal of the bed by Jonson and Dekker may well have influenced a ceremony associated with the bed in a number of Ware inns. This was the 'Swearing of the Horns', when for a not-so-small payment the landlord and some of the chambermaids preceded by a pair of antlers (the symbol of cuckolds) would lead a couple to the bed, reciting as they climbed the stairs:

> Take care thou do'st thyself no wrong,
> Drink no Small Beer if thou hast Strong;
> And farther do thyself this Right,
> Eat no Brown Bread if thou hast White;
> And if the Mistress can be Laid
> Be sure thou dost not Kiss the Maid.
> Show not thy Wife thy utmost Strength,
> Nor let her know the Purse's length;
> Never be bound for any Friend,
> But rather far thy Money lend;
> For thou wilt find 'tis better he
> Should break or be undone than thee;
> Trust no Man that is Proud and Poor,
> Unless thou wilt forgive the Score;
> For he will never pay or own
> The Kindness thou to him hast shown;

Be Just and Grateful to thy Friend
'Twill make thee Happy in the end;
But if thyself and thine Thou'd save,
Take care thou deal'st not with a Knave;
Trust not thy Wife, tho' ne'er so good,
With no Man but thyself Abroad.
For if thou do'st, e'er she returns,
Thy Forehead may be deck'd with Horns;
What I have said do thou retain,
So kiss the Horns and say: Amen.

The Great Bed is more folk-lore than furniture. Over the centuries the stories about the bed became more and more fanciful. A writer in 1732 claimed it could hold twenty couples, another in 1736 spoke of "26 butchers and their wives" who slept in it on the night William III was crowned – in order not to bring down the curse on anyone sleeping with a member of the opposite sex to whom they were not married, the arrangement was butcher-butcher, wife-wife, butcher-butcher … In 1706 it was claimed that the bed could "lodge a troop of soldiers, with the assistance of a trundle-bed". To prevent it being taken to America, the Great Bed was purchased in 1931 by the Victoria and Albert Museum with help from the National Art-Collections Fund. It is now the centre-piece of the V&A's English Galleries – although almost hidden beneath elaborate drapes.

A Walk around Elizabethan Ware

Before we leave the reign of Elizabeth I, let us walk around – or as they would have said perambulate – the town and see what strikes us as different. First, it was a much smaller town, confined to the river valley and not climbing the hills to the north and west. We begin with the mill at the end of Mill Lane (now Priory Street). In fact there are two mills here, a large and rambling corn mill across the millstream and a fulling mill for processing cloth located on the opposite bank, both in the possession of Thomas Lennard on a long lease from the Lord of the Manor. The Lennards are a prominent family with property in Crib Street and one had been churchwarden earlier in the century. There is also a flash lock to carry barges over the weir but there will not be much barge traffic between Ware and Hertford until a pound lock is built here by Sir Thomas Fanshawe in the seventeenth century. Opposite the mill where the GlaxoSmithKline factory stands in the twenty-first century, there is a large area of grazing land known as Berycose, Buryclose or Le Bury: most of it belongs to the Lord of the Manor but two strips are held by the churchwardens for the benefit of the poor. Part of the Buryclose is used for archery practice. Next to it is the Bell Close (now known as Buryfield Recreation Ground) owned by the Feoffees of the Town Lands (formerly the Corpus Christi Guild and the Brotherhood of Jesus).

We proceed up Mill Lane to the corner with Baldocklane: on the corner is an inn described as *Le Dolphyne agaynst the fryars crosse*. The junction was given that name because the entrance to the friary (now Thomas Byrche's private house) was then in Mill

Lane. Opposite us are the Parish Church of St. Mary on the right and the Vicarage on the left. There are only two turnings off Baldocklane, the one on the left leading to Parklane and Thomas Fanshawe's new house at Ware Park and farther up a narrow lane leading to Le Burne (now the Bourne and Collett Road).

We go down Le Burne and see Clopt Hall (Collett Hall) on the left, beside a track leading up hill to the Highland and Fanmanshall (Fanhams Hall). From this point Le Burne opens into a wider road known as Popislane (Collett Road) and if we go straight ahead we will come eventually to Hollycrop Lane (Hollycross Road). But we turn right into Cripstrete or Cryb Street, an uninterrupted row of wattle and daub houses, many with overhanging jetties: there are no turnings off Cripstrete, for Princes Street, Francis Road and Coronation Road are all 19th/20th creations. There are some important houses here including one called Disneys, named after the family who were lords of the manor of Ware Extra and Thundridge until 1543 – this is possibly No. 40, which has a fine interior doorway. At the bottom of Cripstrete, we turn left into Dedlane (we cannot turn right because Steeple End does not link up with the High Street). In Dedlane is the Corpus Christi Barn and at the end of the churchyard opposite is the small Free Grammar School.

We come out of Dedlane into the High Street, with Mr. Fanshawe's new market hall on our right in Middle Row. Opposite is Water Row with a continuous row of inns – from west to east: the Cock, Crown, Horseshoe, Checker, Star, Bell, White Hart, Catherine Wheel, Christopher, Cross Keys, Ram, Bull, Raven, Bear, Horn, George, Roebuck, Saracen's Head and Cardinal's Hat. Between the Crown and the Horseshoe is Waterlane which leads down to a communal wharf on the river – there is another Common Wharf behind Bridgefoot at the other end of the High Street. What in the twenty-first century is known as New Road only leads as far as the corner of Kibuslane, beyond that is a field with malthouses. Kibuslane or Kybeslayne is a crowded street of overhanging jetties; it eventually leads down to the River Lea near the dockyard where barges are built. Kibuslane may have got its name from 'kipes', osiers or reeds used for making baskets to catch fish.

We return again to the High Street. On our left is a group of modest tenements running into Starlane, a very narrow lane prone to flooding. The Saracen's Head Inn is opposite us: it is an ancient inn, probably founded in the thirteenth century during the Crusades (Saracens was the name the crusaders gave to the Arabs who fought under Saladin). Next door is the Cardinal's Hat, once owned by Ellen Bramble's Chantry but now an inn with an unsavoury reputation. There is a sharp right turn into Bridgefoot and the toll bridge which Mr. Fanshawe has recently had rebuilt in stone. On the other side of the bridge is Ware End in Amwell parish (now Amwell End in Ware). Many of the poorest people of the Ware township – the porters and men who load the barges – actually live in Ware End, Amwell. At the beginning of the seventeenth century, the vicar of Amwell, Thomas Hassall, will accuse the churchwardens of Ware of pushing people who have the plague over the bridge so that they die in Ware End, Amwell.[19] There is little love lost between Ware and its poor neighbour in the reign of Queen Elizabeth..

12.
James I and VI

Queen Elizabeth died on 24 March 1603 and was succeeded by James I.   James Stuart was the son of Mary Queen of Scots and, for 38 years in theory and 20 years in fact, King James VI of Scotland. The succession had been agreed by the old queen after secret negotiations by Robert Cecil, son of Lord Burghley. The cipher messages between London, Theobalds and Edinburgh were carried through Ware by special messenger, and not always smoothly. On 6 June 1601 a certain Captain Skynner, who was on an urgent errand for Cecil, tried to get a new horse and was set upon by the crowd and wounded in three or four places.[1]

Ware saw a great deal of the new king in the early years of his reign. His initial progress south had brought him to Royston, where he stayed with Robert Chester and hired his mansion for a year while he reconstructed other properties in the town for use as a hunting lodge. James then moved to Sir Thomas Sadleir's mansion at Standon, leaving on 2 May 1603 for Sir Henry Cocke's house at Broxbourne and then on 3 May moving on to Cecil's house at Theobalds where he stayed four days. As the historian Alan Thomson put it, Hertfordshire was "an early or final stage in royal progresses to other parts of the kingdom, during which the king could show himself to his subjects, live at their expense, and enjoy the hunting and other pleasurable activities which they laid on for his benefit".[2] As he moved south through the county, James gave knighthoods to local gentlemen, including Henry Fanshawe of Ware Park.

James liked large country houses, preferably with hunting parks attached, but he had nothing against the hospitality of inns. At Royston he commandeered a number of inns for his hunting lodge and stables. In December 1606 he was at an inn at Ware, "with his hawks" and was going on to Knebworth for Christmas.[3] He had stopped at a Ware inn the year before, when he was presented with a pamphlet by Thomas Bywater, a Puritan preacher and chaplain to Lord Hunsdon; Bywater wrote that the birds of the air were created by God for man's delight, not for royal falconry. The pamphlet touched a popular nerve, a number of hunting peers were jostled and Bywater was accused of publishing a seditious libel. The king was again in Ware in 1619 after the death of Anne of Denmark, when his grief was compounded by an attack of gout. "The king removed from Royston to Ware, being carried part of the way by the guard in a Neopolitan portative chair, given to him by Lady Hatton, and the rest in a litter".[4] He went on to Theobalds the next day and, weak as he was, insisted on having all his deer mustered before him. Lady Hatton, owner of the portative chair, was Sir Henry Fanshawe's sister.

The king came more and more to Hertfordshire for his hunting – particularly after 1607 when he persuaded Cecil to do an exchange of properties. Cecil took the old Hatfield Palace and other properties while the king got Theobalds which had good hunting access to Enfield Chase, Hoddesdon Woods and the Lea Valley. Royal attention then turned to the poor state of the roads. In 1605 the Privy Council told the Hertfordshire justices that the king had found great fault with the county's highways and "in riding to and fro in his pastimes hath found hard and dangerous passage". The Council suggested they levy a local rate and hire vagrants to fill in the potholes. It also complained of the great malt-wagons, drawn by teams of horses, which made deep ruts in the Old North Road every autumn as the barley harvest was brought to the malthouses. "Whereas we have formerly written letters and given directions for the amendment of highways," wrote the Privy Council in October 1623 in some exasperation, "these are to will you to see the passage betweene Ware and Royston to be presently amended before his Majesty have cause to come that way again by all the means that may be". The king himself had noticed that the highway at Collins Inn (Colliers End), near Ware, was hardly passable.[5]

Apart from the roads and royal hunting, the other aspect of Hertfordshire which received national attention was its 'sweet waters'. The growth of London had far outstripped its water supply and bringing drinking water into the City from Hertfordshire and Middlesex had been proposed as far back as 1580. It was proposed again in 1600 by Captain Edmund Colthurst of Bath. The City's Common Council took up his proposal and in 1606 sponsored through Parliament 'An Acte for the Bringing in a fresh Streame of running Water to the Northe parts of the City of London'. This granted the City the power to make a 'New River for bringing Waters to London from Chadwell and Amwell in Hertfordshire'. After a great deal of argument, it was not Colthurst who undertook to construct the New River but Hugh Myddelton, goldsmith, Citizen of London, MP for Denbigh and a member of the Merchant Venturers. With Colthurst as his overseer, Myddelton undertook to complete the work in four years. But he and the City ran into opposition in Parliament and from the owners of land through which the New River was intended to pass. They argued that floods or overflowing might create quagmires that could trap livestock, while others were concerned at disruption to road transport networks between Hertfordshire and the capital. A crisis point was reached in early 1611, when attempts were made to stop the work which had then reached Cheshunt. Realising that even with assistance from the Merchant Venturers the project was beyond his financial resources, Myddelton went to the king. James I had observed the progress of the work from his palace at Theobalds and agreed to provide half the cost of the work, in return for half the profits. With royal backing, work went ahead at full steam.

The New River relied on gravity to flow from Ware to its destination roughly 20 miles away – the new Round Pond, next to Sadlers Wells in Islington. The conduit (it was not really a 'river') followed the contour on the west side of the Lea Valley, dropping around five inches per mile (approx 8cm per kilometre). The work employed up to 200 labourers, who earned 10d a day and an extra 2d if they worked in water, as well as an army of skilled carpenters and bricklayers to wharf the banks and construct bridges for the 'waies' from east to west. The Round Pond at what became known as the New River Head was reached in April 1613. From there a network of elm pipes took the water all over the City, for those prepared to pay for it. A formal opening ceremony was held on Michaelmas Day, 29 September, in the presence of the Lord Mayor (who happened to be Myddelton's elder brother) with a pageant, and trumpets and drums. Myddelton and his partners were incorporated by charter in 1619 as 'The Company of the New River brought from Chadwell and Amwell to London', each of them allotted a share of the cost and possible profits.

The total cost had been £18,000 and the work was not at first a financial success. In 1631, King Charles I, always short of money, sold the 'Royal Moiety' as it was called and this was divided into 36 further shares, which were put up for sale. Thus the New River Company became one of the world's first joint stock companies.

The New River was hailed for centuries as a success and a remarkable piece of engineering. But not in Ware. Although Chadwell Spring provided most of the water, Ware and Amwell received none of the profits. In 1628 a commission on the state of the charitable properties held by the 'Ware Feoffees' (the former Corpus Christi Guild) commented on the damage done by the New River: in the meadow known as the Dew Rod Acre, there was an area of chalk 95 poles long and 7½ feet wide (roughly 478m x 2.25m) alongside the river "very much trodden and damaged by carts and horses". Consequently Sir Hugh Myddelton ought to make a yearly payment of 6s.8d. to the town of Ware.[6] It is likely the damage had to be repaired by the Ware trustees themselves for little maintenance or repairs were carried out until the appointment of the engineer Robert Mylne as assistant surveyor of the New River Company (NRC) in 1767 and surveyor in 1771. The banks of the New River often collapsed, as it ran through Ware End in Amwell parish, flooding neighbouring roads and meadows. There were continual complaints to the Hertford Quarter Sessions of the want of repair to the banks, particularly at the bottom of Limekiln Hill, near Chadwell – in 1722 waggons, carts and horses fell into the flooded river and some men were drowned.[7] The poet John Scott, who lived at Amwell House, was scathing about the commercialisation of the local water by the New River Company which sold 'the purchas'd wave' to London consumers. It was only in the nineteenth century, when William Chadwell Mylne was the surveyor, that the embankments in Amwell End were made secure with wrought-iron fencing – now the longest continuous line of listed railings in Britain, but often damaged by road accidents.

Jacobean Ware was getting its affairs in order. In 1612, a deed was drawn up to appoint new 'feoffees' or trustees to control the properties they owned for the "use & behoofe of the Inhabitants of the Towne & parish of Ware".[8] These included all the properties they had inherited from the Brotherhood of Jesus – the White Hart and Saracen's Head inns, the Bell Close to the east of "the field there called the Bury field", the Dewrod Acre, another acre at Ware Park, the 'cowleases' in Nethinghoo Marsh in Amwell parish, and the Corpus Christi barn in Dead Lane. But new properties were added. There were cottages for widows in Mill Lane, "one Brickhouse Commonly Called the Almeshouse ... in Cribstreete" and another communal building, the "Townehowse otherwise the Schoolehowse" on the south side of the churchyard (on the edge of what is now Tudor Square). The trustees were at last living up to their claim that they owned property for the benefit of the town. The old trustees, giving up the properties, were Humfrey Spencer of Ware, "Gent Citizen & Haberdasher of London" and John Thorowgood of Ware, yeoman. There were 81 new trustees, many of them with their sons to ensure continuity. The Spencer family were clearly prominent in the town. Apart from Humfrey, others mentioned included Robert Spencer of Babbs Green, Robert Spencer the younger, baker, and John Spencer, wheelwright. We learn more about the school or schools from Humfrey Spencer's will of 1633. He gave £100 to the trustees of the schoolhouse at Ware Upland (Wareside) to provide for a schoolmaster "to teach four of the poorest sort of the children of the Inhabitants of Ware Upland … to write and read, freely and for nothing". Humfrey added that the school should not fall into the hands of Mr. Edward Bromley, who owed him money. He then left another £100 to the Ware Town Schoolhouse, for the Vicar and Ware trustees to provide for a master to "teach and instruct so many of the children of the poorest sort of the Inhabitants of the town of Ware to write and read, freely and for nothing". Humfrey's intentions were clearly to fund elementary education, but both schools became known as grammar schools.[9]

While researching sources, historians are tempted to shout for joy when, among the wills and dry legal documents, they discover letters of the period, especially if they are colourful and gossipy. Here I can shout in praise of John Chamberlain, a wealthy London bachelor, who kept up a correspondence with Dudley Carleton, one of James I's ambassadors, often writing from the country houses of his friends. A particular friend was Sir Henry Fanshawe of Ware Park, who had inherited the new house and the post of Queen's Remembrancer of the Exchequer on the death of his father in 1601. Ware Park was convenient when the exchequer moved to Hertford because of plague in London, and also for its proximity to Robert Cecil's new Hatfield House and the king's palace at Theobalds. John Chamberlain stayed at Ware Park on and off from 1606 to 1609. It was the time when Sir Henry was laying out the gardens of the new manor house – "I should tell you of paling or ditching, plashing of hedges, stocking of trees, catching of moles, or such other exercise that is all our country husbandry".[10] Initially the gardens included a flower bed, shaped like a Renaissance fortress with ramparts and bulwarks, in which the darkest flowers at the centre gradually shaded to lighter blooms at the edge. Chamberlain admired these creations but was put out when a real gardening expert, Sir Henry Wotton, came to Ware Park and tried to take over the work. Nonetheless, Ware Park gardens were praised by Wotton as 'a delicate and diligent curiosity, surely without parallel among foreign nations'.[11] When Chamberlain returned to Ware Park in 1613, he found the whole concept of the garden had changed, with a fine fountain and pond in the upper garden and a running stream, fed from the River Rib, in the lower garden "between the knots and the rancks of trees in the brode walke or alley, wherein we hop to have plentie of troubes fed by hand".[12] Others admired the Ware Park garden: Camden said there was "none excelling it in flowers, physic herbs and fruit".[13] Chamberlain described how the Earl of Arundel and the architect, Inigo Jones, had paid a visit in 1618 and were so pleased with the grapes and peaches that the king had sent for them twice a week ever since.[14] It is from Chamberlain that we know when James I stayed in Ware. He was a prolific letter writer on all the major happenings, from the marriage of Princess Elizabeth, to the execution of Sir Walter Ralegh and Queen Anne's funeral. At Ware Park, he described preparations for May Day, 1606, hoping perhaps that his correspondent, Dudley Carleton, would come a-Maying with all the other guests, who included Sir Christopher Hatton, the son of Queen Elizabeth's Lord Chancellor, and his lady, Henry Fanshawe's sister.

According to his daughter-in-law, Sir Henry Fanshawe was a skilled breeder of horses, a great lover of music and retained an ensemble of gentlemen well qualified in music and the Italian tongue.[15] She said he was also a favourite of James's elder son, Prince Henry,

Nos.61-63 High Street (formerly Woollatt & Coggins' chemist shop and the 'Doctors' House' across the waggonway) was refashioned in the later years of James I's reign. There must have been a hall house here in the Middle Ages, probably standing sideways to the street – a pair of ogee-shaped timber arches is incorporated into one of the walls of the waggonway and on the upper floor there are jowled posts, supporting thick cross beams. But there the medieval features end, for examination of the roof shows that this was rebuilt with three gable ends facing the road. Later still the ground floor of the eastern side was refashioned as a shop, with iron posts supporting the upper floor. Much more interesting, however, is the large chamber on the first floor of the west wing. It has a barrel-vaulted ceiling and originally had filigree panelling, which was removed to the United States after the First World War. But the plaster tympanums under the vaulting remain. The north tympanum – at the High Street end – is decorated with rabbits, birds and serpents and has at its centre the date 1624. The south tympanum (*illustrated below*) has the initials I H S, the first three letters of the name of Jesus in Greek and a familiar Catholic symbol, adopted as the emblem of the Jesuits. Was this a secret Catholic chapel, for the convenience of Catholic peers and foreign ambassadors? The property was for a time the Royal Oak Inn.

who might have made him a secretary of state. Sadly, Prince Henry fell ill and died in 1612 and equally unexpectedly Sir Henry Fanshawe died of an apoplexy at Ware in 1616, having been taken ill while attending Hertford Assizes. His income was said to be £4,000 per annum and his expenditure considerable both on government work and Ware Park, but he left no debts. In his will, he was able to leave £1,500 each to his five surviving daughters. His heir was his eldest child, Thomas Fanshawe, born in 1596 and later created Viscount Fanshawe of Dromore in Ireland. More famous was his sixth and youngest son, Richard Fanshawe, the poet, soldier and diplomat, who was born at Ware Park in 1608. Sir Henry was buried in the south aisle of Ware church next to his father in what was to become the Fanshawe family vault in the Lady Chapel. He asked for a simple funeral "without the usual unprofitable and vain ceremonyes and feastings, the charges whereof will be much more profitablye bestowed upon my children which are many".[16] He gave twenty pounds to the poor of Ware.

Before leaving the reign of James I, we should note important changes that were taking place in Ware's neighbour. During the Middle Ages, the importance of Hertford lay in its royal castle but the town which served the castle was of no great significance, being known at one time as 'Hertford by Ware'. Things began to change in the reign of Elizabeth I, the last monarch to stay at Hertford Castle. In 1588, she granted Hertford a new charter, greatly increasing the borough's privileges and freedom to legislate its own affairs, and during her reign Parliament frequently escaped the London plague to meet in Hertford. These privileges were considerably extended by a new charter granted by James I in 1605, really as a reward to Sir Robert Cecil, newly ennobled as Earl of Salisbury and appointed Lord Lieutenant of Hertfordshire. Salisbury from his new seat at Hatfield House was now the dominant power in Hertfordshire and his power was beginning to be shared by Hertford Borough of which he became the High Steward. In 1625, one of the earliest acts of the new King Charles was to grant Hertford Castle to William Cecil, who had succeeded as Earl of Salisbury in 1612. In the preceding year, the Corporation of Hertford had succeeded in reviving their right to elect two Members of Parliament, a right which had been in abeyance since 1420. Although one of the first to be elected was Sir Thomas Fanshawe of Ware Park (the other was Salisbury's son, Viscount Cranbourne), Ware and other towns in the county were excluded from the new privileges acquired by Hertford. In due course, this would become a subject of dispute – even of violent dispute – between the two neighbours.

13.
Religious and Political Turmoil

James I died at Theobalds on 27 March 1625, having suffered for some time from kidney problems as well as a stroke, fever and dysentery for the previous three weeks. His reign was marked by enormous personal extravagance and failure to raise enough money to govern from Parliament, but not by any religious upheavals. Despite the rise of Puritanism, the presence of secret Catholics at Court and the religious carnage of the Thirty Years War in Europe – involving his son-in-law, the Elector Palatine – in matters of religion James was a cautious moderate. On his deathbed he implored Charles to defend the Church, protect his sister, and remain loyal to the Duke of Buckingham. Charles regarded each promise as a sacred oath. His sister Elizabeth was married to Frederick, the Elector Palatine in Germany and the elected Protestant King of Bohemia, all of which had been conquered by the Catholic Hapsburgs. Charles attempted to help his brother-in-law by sending his navy into battle against Spain and France, but this brought him into conflict with Parliament and led to attempts to impeach his favourite, George Villiers, Duke of Buckingham. In 1627, three fiddlers were arrested in Ware for performing a song, based on a popular ballad tune, satirising Buckingham – they had also performed the song in Staines and Buckinghamshire and were tried and convicted of seditious libel.[1] The following year Buckingham was assassinated in Portsmouth by a disaffected sailor.

It was Charles's other promise to his father, to defend the Church which directly affected Ware. The new king had 'high church' views about ceremony and doctrine, particularly about the authority of bishops and above all of himself, as a divinely chosen and anointed ruler. Ware was in the Diocese of London, whose bishop was William Laud, a leading high churchman and an enforcer of strict discipline in liturgy and dogma. Laud's career flourished on the accession of Charles I, at whose coronation he officiated in place of the royally disliked Archbishop of Canterbury and in 1633 he himself was appointed archbishop. Puritans, including many senior figures in the Church of England, regarded Laud with the greatest suspicion and suspected him of being a secret 'papist'. In 1627 – the year before Laud became Bishop of London – a leading Puritan, Charles Chauncy, had been appointed Vicar of Ware. The Ware living was in the gift of Trinity College, Cambridge, where Chauncy was a Fellow and Professor of Greek. At Trinity, Chauncy had preached against the new high church ceremonies and been forced to recant. At Ware he soon gained a reputation as a fiery preacher whose sermons attracted many listeners, but his strong Puritan views and nonconformity caused him problems. In 1630 he was called before the High Commission to answer a series of charges, including omitting the Athanasian Creed, the Litany, and the Exhortation in marriage ceremonies, failure to wear the surplice and to use the sign of the cross in baptism. The commission referred him to Bishop Laud and Chauncy again submitted, perhaps because he was on the point of getting married. In 1633 he left Ware to become vicar of Marston St. Lawrence, Northamptonshire. But in 1635 he was again brought before the court of the High Commission, charged with opposing the erection of an altar-rail in St. Mary's Church.

The dispute is often depicted as a struggle between the haughty Bishop Laud and the rebellious Mr. Chauncy. But there were other parties involved, particularly the Ware churchwardens. "To avoid disorder at the time of the administration of Holy Communion", the churchwardens called a general meeting and put the issue of the altar-rail to the vote. The majority agreed that the communion table should be moved to the chancel and a rail set up around it with a bench for communicants to kneel on. This was done and had the approval of Bishop Laud. But to Ware's Puritans this was a red rag to a bull – they regarded the communion as the Lord's Supper for which the people could gather round the communion table, either standing or sitting, and any suggestion of kneeling was a return to the 'papist' practices of the Middle Ages. Chauncy strongly opposed the move of the communion table, saying that

The Rev. Charles Chauncy or Chauncey (both spellings exist).

the churchwardens had done it to drive him out of the parish. He therefore went off to a new parish at Marston St. Lawrence, Northants. But he was not the only one to object to the changes. A certain Humfrey Packer refused to come to communion because of the changes, went to Marston St. Lawrence and conferred with Chauncy, then brought the vicar back to Ware to stay in his house – which was, in fact, Place House.

There then followed a very public row, in which Chauncy made "reproachful speeches", saying the move of the communion table was "an innovation, a snare to men's consciences, superstitious and a breach of the second commandment" (against idolatry). Packer joined in by deriding the rail and kneeling bench, saying they would serve a better purpose in his garden – an interesting remark as we shall see later.[2] For this Chauncy and Packer were brought before the Commission, found guilty and imprisoned until they could pay their fines and costs – twenty-four pounds for Chauncy and sixteen for Packer. But the worst punishment for Chauncy was the humiliating confession he was forced to make, appearing before Laud "on bended knee" and reading a prepared statement apologising for his "invective words" and promising never again to oppose the legal rites and ceremonies of the Church.[3] He never forgave himself for this "scandalous submission". He was finally silenced in 1637 for refusing to endorse Laud's book of 'Lawful Sunday Sports'. Chauncy took refuge in New England, arriving at the colony of Plymouth in 1638 and became minister in the town of Scituate, where he insisted on baptism by full immersion and only celebrated the Lord's supper in the evening. In 1654, during the Commonwealth, the parishioners of Ware invited Chauncy to return and concerns for his rapidly growing family led him to accept. But the plan was shelved when he was offered the presidency of Harvard College. Also tried with

Chauncy and Packer, who continued living in Ware, was Isaac Heath, a harness-maker – he emigrated in 1635 and became a senior elder in the Independent Church at Roxbury, Massachusetts.

The wooden altar-rails of Chauncy's time have a story of their own. They were removed from the church during restoration work in 1848 and put into store. Later, they were acquired by a private resident who adapted them as a fence for his garden – perhaps Humfrey Packer had second sight. The rails were rediscovered in 1933 and brought back to St. Mary's where they now partition off what used to be the children's corner and is now the church information point. From the shape and style of the rails they would certainly appear to be those that Bishop Laud ordered. In the South Transept there is a square table of the same vintage, which may have been the 'communion table' of Chauncy's time. In 1907 a memorial to Charles Chauncy was unveiled in the chancel by one of his American descendants, for he is remembered there not only for the Harvard connection but also as the ancestor of many famous Puritan and Congregationalist preachers. Chauncy died in 1672. His adversary, Archbishop Laud, fell victim to the increasingly bitter struggle between King, Church and Puritan Parliament – he was put on trial charged with treason and advancing 'popery' and executed in 1645.

But Ware in the 1630s was not wholly obsessed with religious controversy. Its chief interest was making money through the malting industry and brewing and the busy commerce of its many inns. One of these, the Cross Keys, was owned by Humfrey Packer. Packer was a London brewer, who appears to have engaged in under-the-counter distribution. In 1625, he was prosecuted along with Elizabeth Armstrong, widow, for selling to William Smith and Richard Retchford, "unlicensed alehouse keepers, to each of them 20 barrels of beer, the price of each barrel being 8s." In 1633, he was prosecuted again at the Hertford Sessions for selling to "Christopher Hande, waterman, then being an unlicensed ale-house keeper, 10 barrels of ale, at 8s. a barrel. John Howe, labourer, was drunk there".[4] Packer would have shrugged off these prosecutions. He was described as a 'gentleman' and wealthy enough to own Place House, which he probably purchased from the Fanshawes. In 1635, on the marriage of his eldest son Edward to the daughter of a rich London brewer, Humfrey made over to them Place House itself, plus ten acres of freehold pasture which belonged to that property, and the Cross Keys Inn, with four acres of copyhold pasture belonging to the hostelry. Edward Packer also took possession of a further two acres of pasture which had belonged to his father and was "intermixt with and among" the other land. This was copyhold land, in other words land ultimately owned by the manor of Ware which could be passed from occupier to occupier for only three leases of three years each without the manor claiming it back. It appears that Edward Packer had acquired these two acres without the manor's knowledge. In 1639 he proceeded to plough it up to grow wheat. This was too much for father Humfrey. He had the twelve men sent to cut down the trees and plough the land arrested. He then took out Chancery proceedings against his son. We do not know the outcome of the case, but they do shed light on Place House which Humfrey Packer had formerly lived in and where he had repaired the oak panelling and also added further buildings, as well as planting fruit trees in the gardens and orchards. It is possible it was he who rebuilt the east wing of the house and commissioned the wall paintings in the parlour. Place House then was a building standing in its own grounds – Bluecoat Yard was yet to be created. Humfrey also added his initials and the date 1629 to the screen in Place House. It is an interesting little dispute between a proud father, concerned that one son was removing part of the inheritance of two younger sons, and an elder son who assumed that he was now master in his own house.[5] Humfrey Packer came into his own during the Civil War: in November 1642 he was appointed one of the four local commissioners for raising subscriptions for the war and, three months earlier, had been one of the group ordered to make safe the Hertford powder magazine so that it did not fall into the hands of the Royalists.

As the 1630s advanced, relations between King Charles and his people were becoming steadily more strained. In England there was the 'Ship Money' controversy which alienated Parliament and people – the constables in Ware in July 1638 were ordered to work harder to collect the ship rate, totalling £10.10s from thirteen farmers. And then there were Charles's ill-judged attempts to impose on Scotland his concepts of royal rule and Church government, even resorting to armed force, which ended in humiliating failure. The nation was now moving slowly but surely towards civil war and Ware, as an important post town, was in the thick of events. In March 1639, an anonymous letter to the king was put into the posts at Ware, claiming to be from his "poor, yet true and loyal subjects" and urging him to consider before he shed innocent blood and reminding him of Elijah's curse on King Ahab (that dogs would lick his blood outside the city walls).[6]

Two months later, there was a major confrontation in Ware High Street which almost became a matter of 'pistols at dawn'. Lord Ker or Carr, son of the Earl of Roxburghe, arrived in Ware carrying letters for the king from the Scottish covenanters and demanded three fresh horses. The postmaster – it is said "out of malice" but he may simply have had a hard day – tried to give the lord a cart horse which had brought corn to market. There then ensued a row between Lord Ker, the postmaster (Thomas Swynsted) and the carthorse owner, a poor countryman. This was observed from the window of an inn by three Justices of the Peace, who were also Deputy-Lieutenants of the county. Their attempt to mediate was rejected by Lord Ker who said he would take the three justices' horses instead. When this was refused, the Scottish lord – one of the Roxburghe and Ancram Kers, well known for their hot tempers and record in duels, often against each other – said that he had a case of pistols in his luggage and challenged the three justices to go into a field and settle their differences. Two of the justices, Sir John Butler and Sir John Watts, were ready to take up the challenge, but Sir Richard Lucy quickly found substitute horses for Lord Ker and avoided bloodshed. A report was made to the Lord Lieutenant, Lord Salisbury. Ten days later Thomas Swinsed or Swynsted was bonded in a hundred pounds to appear before Sir Francis Windebank, the Secretary of State.[7]

Being Ware postmaster was well-paid – Thomas received 3s. a day, not as much as the postmasters of Royston or Newmarket, but more than any others – but it could leave one perilously exposed to political events. In August 1641, the Ware postmaster and his deputy were arrested on a warrant from the Speaker of the House of Commons, presumably for not intercepting foreign letters and sending them to London.[8] The following August, a group of Ware gentlemen took the law into their own hands and arrested a messenger who was fixing a royal proclamation to posts in the town. The messenger, named Newbolton, confessed that he had already left leaflets in Lincoln, Boston and Cambridge proclaiming that the Earl of Essex, who had just been named as general of the parliamentary army, and all his followers were traitors and rebels.[9] Ware and its postmaster received more than the usual degree of attention in those anxious years.

There were still periodic 'visitations' of plague with cruel results. There was a particularly severe outbreak in Amwell End (then known as Ware End), centred on the Griffin Inn, owned by Samuel Deards. Seven residents of the Griffin, including three of Samuel's children, as well as a neighbour died in the summers of 1624 and 1625. Deards himself had brought other plague victims to Amwell Church for burial but survived. And then there was the appalling case of John Sanders, "cumming sick from London and goinge to his wife's mother's howse in Ware," wrote Thomas Hassall, vicar of Great Amwell, "was forced out of his bed by the inhabitants of Ware and sent into our parrish to Samuel Deards his howse, where he died of the plague, buried August xvijth".[10] But Ware itself did not escape.

In May 1637, the Privy Council received a letter of urgent protest from the governors of Christ's Hospital, the school in the City of London founded by Edward VI. Almost from its beginning in 1551, the school had been sending some of the younger children out of London for their health, putting them in the care of nurses. Ware, Hoddesdon and Hertford all received children who were billeted in the towns. Because of the plague in Ware, two justices – Sir Thomas Fanshawe and Sir John Watts – had now ordered 30 children to return to London, sending them in wagons with the nurses accompanying them on foot. A further 50 children were on the point of being sent. The governors protested to the Council that, in the enclosed environment of the London school, the move was likely to spread the plague and that the children would be safer in the fresh air of Hertfordshire. The Privy Council overruled the justices and ordered the children's return.[11]

Civil War

When Charles raised his standard at Nottingham on 22 August 1642 and declared war on Parliament, two local squires declared for the king – they were Sir Thomas Fanshawe of Ware Park and Sir John Watts of Mardocks (this was the third Sir John Watts to be living at the old Watersplace manor house, a mile to the east of Ware, rather than the mill later known as 'Mardocks'). Many of the gentry of Hertfordshire did the same, but not all. Fanshawe's fellow MP for Hertford Borough, Viscount Cranbourne, and his father, the Earl of Salisbury, finally joined the Parliamentary side. Lord Capel of Hadham Hall and Sir John Harrison of Balls Park, Hertford, both of whom as Members of Paliament had spoken out against Charles's arbitrary rule, declared for the king in 1642 and 1643 respectively and later joined him in Oxford after the Battle of Edgehill. The Royalist mayors of Hertford and St. Albans were both arrested on the orders of Parliament and imprisoned.

Ware had no mayor and its townspeople were solidly for Parliament, as was most of East Anglia. But they were far from complacent, in fact the local population was suffering an acute attack of the jitters. They expected an attack to come from Mardocks where John Watts – son of Sir John Watts, a Deputy-Lieutenant – had his own arsenal as a former militia officer and had not yet joined the king. On 28 August, two different forces were mobilised to meet this threat. One under the Earl of Bedford advanced from Hoddesdon and, finding no Cavaliers at Mardocks, moved on to Ware where (according to a contemporary newsletter) they had a brief, almost farcical confrontation with the other force which had come from Hertford:

> In short, they found themselves in the presence of friends instead of enemies! Headed by the sentries, the Captain with a troop of horse was escorted up the Court of the Guard at the entrance to the town, where they found 'almost five hundred men completely armed with their muskets presented against them and their pikes'.[12]

These were the local 'Trained Bands' of Hertford and Ware, some of whom carried bows and arrows. Having failed to find any enemies, "these two forces on the next day searched Ware Park and Hadham Hall, the residences of Sir Thomas Fanshawe and Lord Capel".[13] Enough arms for a thousand men were found at Hadham Hall, it was reported, but more ominous was the discovery of two pieces of ordnance, with several barrels of powder, muskets and pikes, found at Ware Park.[14] It was alleged that Fanshawe had employed two gunsmiths at Ware Park for three months to repair arms but they had not been discovered. None of this was really surprising, since Fanshawe, Capel and Watts had all been officers in the county militia. Fanshawe and others were excluded from the House of Commons on 7 September "for neglecting the Service of the House" and on 23 October he was said to have fought for the king at the Battle of Edgehill. As a consequence, Ware Park was seized by the local Parliamentary committee and the contents sold. Sir Thomas and two of his brothers had already joined the king at Oxford, where he immediately made two or three thousand pounds available to the king's cause. The Fanshawes were to spend the remainder of the civil wars in the West Country, Channel Islands or France.

Ware did not see any fighting, although there were a few skirmishes as bands of Royalist soldiers passed through the area. The main role of Ware and Hertford was to provide troops and money for the militia, the Earl of Essex's main parliamentary army and the Earl of Manchester's Eastern Association Army, which embraced all of East Anglia and was raised in haste in 1643 when the Royalists were doing well in the north. Between them, these formed the three local Hertfordshire regiments – the Black, the Orange and the Green, named after the sashes they wore (their uniforms were a blue coat with grey doublet and hose). Hertfordshire played a leading role in the Eastern Association and raised troops and arms through a Militia Committee and money through an Assessment or Subscription Committee. The latter included two Ware men, Humfrey Packer and Thomas Meade of the Manor House.[15] Humfrey Packer, whom we have met before, was one of five men ordered by Parliament to secure the armaments in the Hertford magazine on 15 August and, later with his son, another Humfrey, he became a Treasurer for the County of Hertford, responsible for debts of £5,293.[16] Another Ware man, William Love, a draper with a shop in Baldock Street, had an important role in supporting the army. By the end of 1644, Hertfordshire had three volunteer regiments in service, mainly garrisoning Bedfordshire – the Parliamentary frontline against possible attack from Royalist Oxford and Buckinghamshire – and all three regiments were in arrears of paying their men. In May, William Love was a Muster-master and paymaster of Hertfordshire's 'Black Regiment' and in November was sent to Newport Pagnell to pay the Black and Orange Regiments. The story of Love's valiant efforts to devise new ways of raising money to pay the soldiers was told in a lecture to the Hertford and Ware Local History Society by Dr. Alan Thomson, in which he also related how another Ware man, Captain James Pinkney, was accused by William Love of embezzlement, probably with some justification.[17] In 1648 William Love was one of the town constables along with Christopher Robinson and Richard Asson. Parts of the New Model Army wintered in Hertfordshire in 1643-4 and in the early summer of 1645 when the county was used as an assembly area before the Battle of Naseby. And the horse and foot regiments of General Sir Thomas Fairfax were stationed around Ware in 1646-47.[18] In June 1647, Fairfax recounted "a Business in Ware" when a guardsman was stopped on his way to Scotland with a bundle of important government letters and found to have a pass only as far as Royston.[19]

It was the so-called Ware Mutiny of 15 November 1647 which gave the town a niche in the history of the Civil War – or, rather, in the period between the First Civil War and the Second, when Charles had been defeated and the army was feeling angry at lack of pay and the indifference of Parliament. The story of the mutiny has been told by Dr. Thomson in great detail and with scrupulous reference to original documents, many of them quite new sources in *The Ware Mutiny: Order Restored or Revolution Defeated?* Suffice it here to relate how Fairfax and Cromwell, faced with dissension and agitation by officers who supported the political agenda of the Levellers, called a 'rendezvous' of seven regiments for Monday 15 November. It was not actually in Ware, but at Corkbush or Cockbush Field in Hertford – but Ware was the well-known town close at hand and the regiments had quartered there, while the senior officers spent the previous night in Hertford. The seven regiments assembled on the field above the Meads and were then joined by two other regiments, present against orders. One of these uninvited regiments had been ordered north and instead had taken part in what Dr. Thomson termed a 'Moving Mutiny' between Dunstable and St. Albans. In addition, soldiers from both regiments had copies of a rebellious agenda, called An Agreement of the People, tucked into their hatbands. What happened next is a matter of dispute among historians, but it appears that there was a confrontation with the leaders of the revolt in which Lieutenant-General Oliver Cromwell played a flamboyant role, tearing copies of the Agreement from men's hats. Three of the ringleaders were found guilty by a summary court-martial and made to draw lots: Trooper Richard Arnold lost and was then duly shot dead by the other two. Order was restored to the New Model Army which strengthened its standing vis-à-vis Parliament. Cromwell in particular enhanced his own standing as a soldier and political leader. And the Levellers, though not yet defeated, had lost what they had hoped would be a major bid for influence in the army. One of their leaders, the flamboyant John Lilburne, was reported to be staying in a Ware inn to hear the outcome of the mutiny. As the Clerk to the Army Council, William Clark, put it: "Lieut. Col. John Lilburn came this day to

Ware : but things not succeeding at the Rendezvous according to expectation, came no further".[20] It was a Ware tradition that cavalry regiments camped in the thatched sixteenth-century corn stores in Star Street, illustrated in Edith Hunt's history – they were demolished in the 1960s.

Important as it was, the Ware Mutiny was overshadowed by an event four days earlier. Charles I was under house arrest in Hampton Court – a quite comfortable house arrest where he received what visitors he liked and had his own servants – but escaped on 11 November. Although he was soon apprehended on the Isle of Wight, he went on intriguing with commissioners from Scotland to try to overthrow what he regarded as the Puritan tyranny of the army, hoping that a Scottish Presbyterian army would invade England and restore him to the throne in return for establishing a Presbyterian Church of England. The Scots did invade in August 1648 – in what became known as the Second Civil War – and were defeated by Cromwell at Preston. The king's actions were seen by his opponents as evidence of his treachery, that he was indeed the "man of blood". This led to his trial and execution in Whitehall on 30 January 1649. This Second Civil War inevitably involved the Royalist gentry of Ware. Sir John Watts of Mardocks, who had surrendered Chirk Castle in Wales on honourable terms, now joined forces with his old commander, Lord Capel, and held Colchester against Parliament but was starved into submission. Heavily in debt from the fines ('compounding') he had paid to the New Model Army, he sold Mardocks later and settled in Tewin.[21]

Sir Richard and Lady Ann Fanshawe

Among those able to visit the king while he was held at Hampton Court were Sir Richard Fanshawe and his wife, Lady Ann. She said she went "three times to pay my duty to him, both as I was the daughter of his servant and wife to his servant" (she was the daughter of Sir John Harrison and her husband, Richard, had spent the three years since their marriage in the service of the Prince of Wales). Ann wrote of "the folly (to give it no worse name)" of the king's close advisers who were "drawn in by the cursed crew of the then standing army for Parliament" and persuaded him to escape, which led to his trial and death.

Ann Fanshawe was a remarkably strong and resourceful woman and travelled everywhere with her husband – to the Channel Islands, France, Ireland, Spain – as well as being shipwrecked, robbed more than once, having twenty pregnancies with 14 children born and christened and just one son and four daughters surviving as adults, and yet capable of keeping state secrets, of forging a passport for herself to join Richard abroad and of seeking a personal interview with Oliver Cromwell and, face to face, begging him for the release of her husband from prison. Sir Richard had been captured at the Battle of Worcester in the third civil war of September 1651 and was brought to London, charged with high treason and imprisoned in Whitehall. The story of how Lady Ann secured his release is one of many amazing episodes which she related in her Memoirs:

During this time of his imprisonment I failed not constantly to go, when the clock struck

Sir Richard Fanshawe, Bart., and Lady Ann Fanshawe – painted by Sir Peter Lely reproduced in the Memoirs of Lady Ann Fanshawe.

four in the morning, with a dark lantern in my hand, all alone and on foot, from my lodging in Chancery Lane, at my cousin Young's, to Whitehall, at the entry that went out of King's Street into the bowling ground. There I would go under his window and softly call him. He that after the first time expected me never failed to put out his head at first call. Thus we talked together; and sometimes I was so wet with rain that it went in at my neck and out at my heels.[22]

Together they planned what she would say to General Cromwell and, mainly on account of Richard's sickness with scorbute (scurvy), she succeeded in obtaining his release on bail. For the next seven years, they moved around England always fearing that Richard would be re-arrested, and all the while his health was improving and she was enduring yet more confinements. They stayed at Ware Park, Bayfordbury, lived "an innocent country life" in Yorkshire, and afterwards stayed at Bengeo. Then in August 1658, they leased Ware Friary (or Priory) from Mrs Haydon for a year:

This place we accounted happy to us, because in October we heard the news of Cromwell's death; upon which my husband began to hope that he should get loose of his fetters in which he had been seven years.[23]

During the restoration of the Priory in 1993, beneath thick layers of Victorian plaster seventeenth century oak panelling was discovered in two rooms . It is pannelling that must have been known to Richard and Ann Fanshawe during their year of living there.

14.
Ware under the Commonwealth

The Commonwealth – Britain's only period of Republican rule – lasted from the death of Charles I in 1649 to the Restoration of Charles II in 1660. In those eleven years, life in Ware both went on as normal and also existed in a strange, topsy-turvy, looking-glass world. Christmas festivities were banned along with other holidays, like the May-day jollities that Sir Thomas Fanshawe had held at Ware Park, as well as all sport and games on Sundays. Cromwell was not a kill-joy but many of his supporters were. Marriages were often celebrated in Ware Market Place by a Justice of the Peace instead of the Vicar – Mr. Justice Weld (Alexander Weld of Widbury) celebrated many between 1654 and 1657. For some of the period the registers recorded births and deaths, rather than baptisms and burials, but when Ann Weld, wife of the magistrate, had a daughter in March 1659 it must have been baptised: the entry adds "borne about 2 in the morninge" indicating an emergency baptism in case the child died.

There seems to have been some continuity among the magistrates. But other leading lights in the town were people who had previously been marginalised, but even they were under attack from new people on the margins. Being a Puritan or a Calvinist Independent was acceptable – that presumably was Cromwell's position – being a Scots-influenced Presbyterian or even worse an old-fashioned Prayer Book Anglican could lead to loss of your property. But what about the Baptists, Anabaptists and the new Quakers? William Packer (who may or may not have been a relative of Humfrey Packer) was dismissed from his regiment when someone accused him of being a Baptist; he was immediately reinstated by Cromwell, rose through the ranks to be the Deputy Major General for Oxfordshire and Hertfordshire, bought part of the royal estate at Theobalds and then (according to George Fox) became a scourge of the Quakers. But it was not just a matter of theology; anyone in a position of authority had to conform. William Packer was one of the members of a curious vetting commission of laymen, called 'Triers', who decided whether clergy and schoolmasters were fit for their responsibilities or "scandalous and insufficient". Isaac Craven, who had succeeded Charles Chauncy as Vicar of Ware, was described as a person "of great piety, learning and loyalty" and was one of the 63 Hertfordshire ministers who signed the petition in favour of the Puritan Solemn League and Covenant, but he appears to have been ousted in 1650 and imprisoned. He was later installed by the 'Triers' as Vicar of Aston, and his last recorded religious act was to bury Thomas Hassall, the Vicar of neighbouring Amwell, in 1657 according to the rites of the banned Book of Common Prayer.[1] Who succeeded Craven is unclear: there seems to have been confusing succession of ministers. On the first of May 1656, there was a petition to Protector Cromwell from "divers inhabitants of Ware" concerning Richard Farrer, who had been rejected as Vicar of Ware by the Triers and ejected from the vicarage yet continued to preach as publicly as before at a place in the town called 'Fryers'. This was the old Friars' crossroads, directly opposite the church and the vicarage. The inhabitants complained that while Farrer continued preaching they were unable to get a new minister.

Their petition was supported by evidence from the Hertfordshire Triers, one of whom was Major General Packer, and it was he together with the Justices of the Peace that the government ordered to deal with Mr Farrer "as you find most conducible to the peace of the town". [2] Four months later the inhabitants again petitioned Cromwell, this time to settle the vicarage on their new minister, John Young; the government agreed and increased Mr. Young's salary by £50. This John Young may have been related to the noted Puritan scholar, Thomas Young, who in 1617-18 had been tutor to the poet John Milton and also vicar of both Rotherhithe and Ware, and later became Master of Jesus College, Cambridge. [3] And democracy suddenly flourished in place of the old top-down rule of the Lord of the Manor – on 20 April 1652, the inhabitants of Ware met "at the stone in the parish church" and elected the three churchwardens, three overseers of the poor and two surveyors of the highways.

On the other hand, some things continued much as before – or even more so. There was a surge in demand for malt and grain, caused no doubt by the large number of people converging on London. There was an increase in river traffic between Ware and London and bargemen figure prominently among the Ware bridegrooms in the registers of 1656-57. According to one historian, malt was now being made in most of the villages of north and east Hertfordshire and many people including tradesmen and servants were investing their savings in the process: "everyone who could buy a quarter of barley did so, and sent it to one of the small maltings close at hand to get it converted into malt – for which there was a ready sale both in the market and for the use of private families". [4] During the war and the Commonwealth, the ground was being laid for a radical transformation of the local economy. Malt-making rather than the inn trade was becoming the major occupation of Ware and the surrounding district.

15.
The Restoration

The Restoration of the Monarchy in the person of Charles II occurred in 1660. The king arrived back in London to great rejoicing and Parliament immediately declared that he had been king ever since the execution of his father in 1649. In other words, the past eleven years of Puritan rule had been like a bad dream. Samuel Pepys recorded in his diary on 1 June 1660:

> Parliament ordered the 29 of May, the King's birthday, to be for ever kept as a day of thanksgiving for our redemption from tyranny and the King's return to his Government, he entering London that day.[1]

This was Oak Apple Day, when people wore oak leaves in memory of Charles's escape from the Battle of Worcester by hiding in an oak tree. It was still being celebrated in Ware in 1835 "by the decoration of shop and tavern doors with large branches of oak"[2] and as early as 1664 at least one inn was renamed the Royal Oak.

Inevitably, the Restoration led to confiscations, reprisals and the settling of old scores and promises. John Young was replaced as vicar by Richard Waugh, M.A. In June 1660, when Henry Beach was dismissed as postmaster for "being disaffected to the government", Joseph Strubie or Scrubie was recommended as his replacement. Richard Goulston and two others vouched for him as "living in an ancient inn and having good accommodation." – the 'ancient inn' was probably the Crown, demolished in 1760 when it was replaced as the post inn by the Bull. The appointment did not go unopposed. Anne Packer, wife of Edward Packer a Ware butcher, was brought before the magistrates in 1660 for standing under the eaves of Strubie's house to hear what was being said by him and others and then telling the same to divers other persons "to sowe strife and dissencion" between him and his neighbours. Her son, Nicholas, was similarly convicted in 1667 of being an eavesdropper and "fomenter of quarrels amongst his neighbours." Clearly the Packers did not intend to give the new dispensation an easy time. Old Humfrey Packer and his son, another Humfrey, described as 'Treasurers for the County of Hertford', were required by the House of Commons in May 1660 to answer for £5,293 not accounted for.[3] But no serious reprisals were taken against Humfrey senior, who at his death in 1662 was still described as "gentleman". Others who escaped relatively lightly were Alexander Weld and Thomas Meade (described as of "Ware parsonage" but this must have meant the Manor House), a former treasurer of the county fund for helping wounded soldiers – both of them were allowed 'to compound' with fines.

Local parliamentarians did not suffer greatly, nor did local royalists profit greatly. Sir Thomas Fanshawe had been living quietly in Ware since 1652, having 'compounded' for £1,300 for the return of his estate. It seems that his household goods, furniture and much of the timber at Ware Park had been sold on the orders of Parliament. At the Restoration, he was elected MP for Hertfordshire in 1661 and in the same year created Viscount

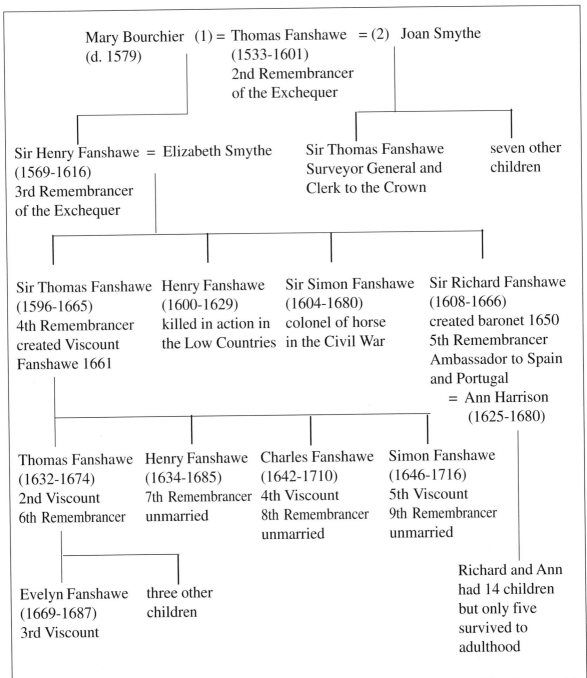

Mary Bourchier (1) = Thomas Fanshawe = (2) Joan Smythe
(d. 1579)   (1533-1601)
                         2nd Remembrancer
                         of the Exchequer

Sir Henry Fanshawe = Elizabeth Smythe   Sir Thomas Fanshawe   seven other
(1569-1616)   Surveyor General and   children
3rd Remembrancer   Clerk to the Crown
of the Exchequer

Sir Thomas Fanshawe   Henry Fanshawe   Sir Simon Fanshawe   Sir Richard Fanshawe
(1596-1665)   (1600-1629)   (1604-1680)   (1608-1666)
4th Remembrancer   killed in action in colonel of horse   created baronet 1650
created Viscount   the Low Countries   in the Civil War   5th Remembrancer
Fanshawe 1661   Ambassador to Spain
                                                                 and Portugal
                                                                     = Ann Harrison
                                                                       (1625-1680)

Thomas Fanshawe   Henry Fanshawe   Charles Fanshawe   Simon Fanshawe
(1632-1674)   (1634-1685)   (1642-1710)   (1646-1716)
2nd Viscount   7th Remembrancer   4th Viscount   5th Viscount
6th Remembrancer   unmarried   8th Remembrancer   9th Remembrancer
                                           unmarried   unmarried

                                                                 Richard and Ann
Evelyn Fanshawe   three other   had 14 children
(1669-1687)   children   but only five
3rd Viscount   survived to
                                                                 adulthood

*In 1668, because of the family's losses in the Civil War, the 2nd Viscount Fanshawe sold
Ware Park for £26,000 to Thomas Byde, a London brewer. Thus we lost the "flower of
our estates", wrote Lady Ann Fanshawe in her Memoirs.*

The Fanshawes of Ware Park

Fanshawe of Dromore which, being in the Irish peerage, did not affect his position as an MP. In the same year, he built a chapel at Ware Park which was consecrated with due ceremony by the Bishop of Durham.[4] Of more importance to him and his family, he recovered his hereditary position as Remembrancer of the Exchequer, but the office was not worth as much as it had been under Charles I and he was enormously in debt. When he had joined the late king at Oxford, like many loyal Cavaliers, Sir Thomas had lent Charles upwards of £20,000 and been granted in return certain rights over royal land in the New Forest. At the Restoration, he had been persuaded to give up these rights in return for promises of speedy repayment of the loan, if not with interest then certainly of the principal sum. Charles II endorsed these promises but, when repayments did at last begin, they were spread over three or four years, with each sum getting smaller and smaller, and there were no payments of interest.

The people who did suffer, not so much by order of the king as by the 'Cavalier Parliament' which supported him, were the Quakers. In December 1660 there was an abortive revolt by a group of religious-political radicals known as Fifth Monarchists. They were swiftly rounded up but the main reprisals fell on the Quakers, who had nothing to do with the revolt but held some beliefs that were similar. By royal proclamation, meetings of the Friends (as they called themselves) were prohibited and anyone attending them was required to swear an oath of allegiance – also a way of making the 'Friends' reveal themselves since they objected to oath-taking on principle. In January 1661 there was a wave of arrests, thirteen from Ware and even more from Hertford, which had been a major centre of the Friends ever since George Fox paid his first visit there in 1655. The following years saw the new Cavalier Parliament introducing new laws, aimed directly at stamping out the Friends, and these resulted in further arrests in both towns, followed by imprisonment, confiscation of property and an attempt at transportation. This failed because the captain of the transportation ship, the 'Ann' of London put the prisoners ashore at Deal. Persecution continued until 1672 when the king brought in a Declaration of Indulgence, but this was rejected by the Cavalier Parliament and Quakers continued to suffer until 1685. This brought Hertford and Ware Friends closer together and won them converts and admirers in both towns. To a great extent they were one community, conducting their business together as the Hertford Monthly Meeting, but worshipping separately. The Hertford Meeting House was built in 1669 and is one of the oldest in Britain still used for worship. The Ware Friends met in members' houses until 1689 when the White Hart Inn became their registered place of worship under the Act of Toleration. They finally built a meeting house on land behind Kibes Lane in 1728.[5] The Independents or Congregationalists, the dominant religious group during the Commonwealth, did not suffer as much – having been ousted from the parish church, they built their own chapel in what was then Dead Lane in 1662 – it was rebuilt in 1778 and still stands as a print works.

The persecution of the Friends threw up some important figures – on both sides. Prominent among the prisoners were maltsters from both towns, including William Adams of Ware who was trustee of the Hertford Meeting House and Thomas Docwra, who ironically operated a malthouse behind the Royal Oak Inn (65 High Street). Also involved were the maltster William Burr, one of those sent to prison in 1661, and his brother Thomas, another maltster. The Burr family originated in Baldock and must have come to Ware under the Commonwealth: later generations of the family built the fine Queen Anne house at Bridgefoot, which later became the Coop and is now 'Belgique'. The Quakers' involvement in the malting industry and in brewing was due to a number of factors. For one thing, they were disbarred from any public office, such as magistrates, and thus channelled their energies into commerce. As a persecuted minority, they stuck together and the brewers of Shoreditch and Southwark had family and friendship links with the maltsters of Ware and Hertford. These links became even more important in the eighteenth century.

On the other side were the magistrates, sitting as the Hertford Sessions. In 1664 they sat with a jury packed with anti-Quakers to try four Friends under the new Conventicle Act, which made it illegal for five or more persons to attend a meeting of worship without the use of the Church of England's *Book of Common Prayer*. The chairman was Henry Chauncey, the respected author of a book on the antiquities of Hertfordshire (and great-nephew of Ware's Charles Chauncy). Beside him on the bench sat Viscount Fanshawe of Ware Park, who angrily cross-examined the defendants. The historian of the Hertford Quakers, Dr. Vi Rowe, quoted a revealing exchange between Fanshawe and William Burr, who had said he attended the Friends' meetings because the Lord God required him to do so:

Fanshawe:	Where doth the Lord command and require you?
Burr:	In my heart and conscience.
Fanshawe:	That is the light within you, but your light is darkness, and a melancholy vapour of the brain, and leads you to one thing today and another thing tomorrow, and I know not what the third day, so you change every day.
Burr:	Thou hast not found us so changeable hitherto, neither wilt thou. [6]

Friends habitually used 'thou', the familiar form of address, rather than the polite 'you' which added to the anger of magistrates, as did their refusal to doff their hats. Burr and his fellow defendants were found guilty and put in Hertford gaol. Viscount Fanshawe, one of the members of parliament for Hertfordshire, was a particular scourge of the Quakers as a local brewer named Thomas maintained. "Richard Thomas's assertion that Viscount Fanshawe was one of the main agents behind the passing of the Conventicle Act carries conviction, and it seems that disquiet about the strength of Quakerism in Hertford, Ware and Baldock may have played a part in securing national legislation".[7] In 1675, the constables of Ware were brought before the sessions for refusing to seize goods belonging to Friends, forfeited under the Conventicle Act – unsurprising since the two constables, Henry Peach and Edward Fryer, were both maltsters.

Viscount Fanshawe died on Easter Day, 1665, without leaving a will and was buried in the family vault in St. Mary's Church, Ware. Ann Fanshawe, his sister-in-law, summed up the family's sentiments:

He did engage his person and estate for the crown, and fought in the battle of Edgehill, and thus ruined his estate, and was the cause of his son's selling Ware Park. Afterwards he tried, by the king's assistance, to be reimbursed but could not prevail. I guess his wound was too wide to be closed.[8]

In 1668, the Viscount's son, another Thomas who became the Second Viscount Fanshawe, sold Ware Park for £26,000 to Sir Thomas Byde, described by Ann Fanshawe as "a London brewer". Recognizing how shabbily the Fanshawes had been treated, Charles II said he had lost the best of men and subjects and granted his widow and her heirs an annuity of £600 for thirty-one years.

In fact, Thomas Byde was not a practising brewer – that honour went to his father, Alderman John Byde, who was Sheriff of London. His Shoreditch-brewed ale was so famous that Pepys said he went by coach to the Rose and Crown in Mile End in order to drink it. Alderman Byde and his wife were buried in St. Leonard's Church, Shoreditch, but Sir Thomas had the memorial tablet re-erected in St. Leonard's Church, Bengeo. Bengeo faces Ware Park across the valley of the River Rib and in 1601 the first Thomas Fanshawe had bought Bengeo Manor which his grandson sold to Byde along with Ware Park and the Manor of Ware. In due course, Thomas Byde demolished the Fanshawe's Elizabethan manor and built himself a large box-like mansion. He was at heart a London lawyer and a republican, but he had ambitions for a country seat. His Hertfordshire ambitions soon paid off. He was made High Sheriff of Hertfordshire in 1669, in 1672 he gave £50 to the Borough of Hertford to pay off its debts and in the same year was elected one of the MPs for the county. He died in 1704 and was buried in Ware Church, though there is no monument to him there. In her memoirs, Lady Ann Fanshawe deplored the fact that her husband's family had to sell the ancestral home at Ware Park to Sir Thomas Byde, "a London brewer". But those brewers, whether from London or home-grown, were soon to become the new aristocracy of Hertfordshire.

The Wadesmill Turnpike

In the early years of the new reign, the major event as far as Ware was concerned was the setting up of a turnpike gate at Wadesmill. With the ever increasing demand for malt and the failure of remedies like the ban on malt wagons between Michaelmas and Easter, the condition of the Old North Road was worse than when James I and Charles I complained about it. In 1648, the county magistrates heard the following complaint from the highway surveyors of Ware Extra:

The great decay of all the ways arises through the unreasonable loads of malt brought into and through Ware to Hodsdon from remote parts, and the bringing of great loads of malt from both the Hadhams, Alburie, Starford, all the Pelhams and Clavering, through Ware Extra, and the excessive loads from Norwich, Bury [St. Edmunds's] and Cambridge weekly, the teams often consisting of seven or eight horses. There is a great increase of malsters in Ware. The surveyors neglect to warn all owners of teams in the parish, and others that have draft horses, to perform their day's work, and also neglect to present defaulters in this respect.

The Canons Malting in Baldock Street – demolished by Ware Urban District Council in 1965 to make way for Lower Bourne Gardens. The oldest part was the brick building (to the left of the tree) with a mullioned stone window and one brick neatly inscribed : I C 1622. [9]

Moreover, landholders in Ware hire teams from other parishes to plough their lands, which lands are amenable to contribution towards the repair of the said ways. If the malsters would carry lighter loads with only four horses as they used to, and each person would duly perform his works, the ways could be sufficiently amended. The surveyor and inhabitants of Ware Extra are content to help the surveyors of Ware Infra on such days as may be spared, but not to neglect their own highways. [10]

With the Restoration in 1660, it was clear that drastic action needed to be taken to restrain the malting traffic and make the roads passable for other travellers. Samuel Pepys – not yet appointed Clerk of the Acts to the Navy Board – began his famous diary in 1660 and among the first entries wrote against 24 February "the way bad from Ware to Puckeridge". A year and a bit later (17 September 1661), he arrived in Ware with his wife and spent a pleasant night – but "the next morning up early and began our march; the way about Puckeridge very bad, and my wife, in the very last dirty place of all, got a fall, but no hurt, though some dirt". On 15 October 1662, he recorded that he came to Ware "about three o'clock in the afternoon, the ways being everywhere but bad." The following year the drastic action, contemplated for so long, was taken. The justices of Hertfordshire, Cambridgeshire and Huntingdonshire combined to introduce a private Act in Parliament, explaining that "the ancient highway and postroad leading from London to York and so into Scotland … by reason of the great and many loads which are weekly drawn in wagons to Ware (whence there was water-carriage to London) and the great trade in barley and

An eighteenth-century print of the Wadesmill Turnpike.

malt … is become so ruinous and almost impassable that the ordinary course appointed by all former laws and statutes of this realm is not sufficient for the effectual repairing of the same."[11] In other words, it was useless to expect the parishes to repair such a major road carrying such major loads: there had to be tollgates and the tolls would pay for the repairs and maintenance of the road. The Act of Parliament allowed the justices to set up three sets of tollgates or turnpikes, one at Stilton near Huntingdon, one at Caxton, Cambridgeshire and the third at Wadesmill, two miles to the north of Ware.[12] In fact, only the Wadesmill turnpike was effective (Stilton was never erected and Caxton could be by-passed) and it was the first in Europe. The turnpike did not lead to immediate improvements. It was not until 1733 that the Wadesmill Turnpike Trust was established with powers to raise money for real road improvements. In the meantime, the citizens of Ware gained a concession for wagons which came through the turnpike loaded and left the same day empty – and Samuel Pepys stopped coming through Ware on his way to his old college at Cambridge, preferring the Stortford route. The Old North Road was no longer the preferred route from London to the North. Many people followed Pepys's example; others used what later became known as the Great North Road through Hatfield.

The River Lea

Ware's other link with London, the River Lea, appeared in a number of different guises during the 1660s. It was then a natural, meandering river, not the canalised Lee Navigation of today – just the spot for gentlemen to take their sport in. Izaak Walton, a royalist who had kept his head down during Cromwell's rule, published *The Compleat Angler* in 1653, with many revisions after the Restoration, and identified the Lea as his favourite river.

The book consists of conversations between Piscator (a fisherman), Venator (a hunter) and Auceps (a falconer). When Piscator (Walton himself) catches up with the other two, he says: "You are well overtaken, Gentlemen, a good morning to you both; I have stretched my legs up Tottenham-hill to overtake you, hoping your business may occasion you towards Ware, whither I am going this fine fresh May morning." Later he mentions the painting of an enormous trout, which was so long and thick that its picture had been drawn and was on display " at mine host Rickabie's, at the George in Ware".[13] The George was a rambling inn, including what is now Lloyds Bank and the hairdresser's next to George Yard.

Even before the broad channels made by the Lee Navigation in 1767, the Lea was a major waterway, taking malt and corn to London and bringing back coal and iron on the return voyage. Welsh ironfounders used the Lea to set up depots in Ware and Sir Ambrose Crowley, ironmaster to the Royal Dockyards between 1689-1713, set up a warehouse at Ware for inland distribution.[14] Three events made Ware River (as the Lea was known) literally a national lifeline. One was the Great Plague in London of 1665, followed by the Great Fire of 1666. The third was the Second Anglo-Dutch War which began in 1665 and became a national calamity in early 1667 when the Dutch destroyed the English fleet at Chatham and imposed a tight blockade on the Thames Estuary. During one of these three calamities, it is said (though there is no documentary evidence for it) that Ware bargees continued to supply London with food and victuals and for this they were granted certain privileges by Charles II. It is also said – by townspeople and even some school teachers I have met – that the bargees brought back plague bodies from London and interred them in the Buryfield. This cannot be true for many reasons – here are four:

(a) plague corpses were never moved but buried immediately with quicklime to avoid spreading the infection;

(b) Londoners who escaped the plague-ridden city were shunned; even letters from the capital were treated as if they were contagious;

(c) burials of Ware's own plague victims were scrupulously recorded in the parish registers with a 'P' against them and there is no record of any London victims;

(d) the Buryfield was so called centuries before 1665 because of the Roman burials discovered there – it was known in Tudor times as 'Berrymede'.

At the height of the plague in London, there were 1,000 deaths a week. Ware did not suffer on that scale, but between July 1665 and October 1666 there were 190 plague burials, sometimes as many as seven in one day. The privileges granted by Charles II were said to be that Ware barges did not have to take on a Thames Lighterman between Bow Creek and the Port of London (quite likely because it was echoed in the Watermen on the Thames Bill of 1675) and that a Ware bargee could demand free beer at any inn on his return journey (unlikely, especially in Enfield, but a good tale to tell one's mates). It seems much more likely that these 'privileges' were granted as a result of Ware barges defeating the Dutch blockade. On 5 July 1667, the government heard of a huge fleet of colliers which were held up by the Dutch blockade – some had gone to Boston and the Humber, 100 were waiting off Yarmouth for an opportunity to get to London, while 60 had arrived at King's Lynn with more to follow – "the coals will be carried from Lynn to London: the price is 30s. a chaldron: the water carriage to Cambridge [via the Ouse] will be 4s., land carriage thence to Ware, 20s. to 25s., and water carriage from Ware to London [via the Lea] 6s. or 7s. per chaldron".[15] The Anglo-Dutch war also meant the reappearance of soldiers in the town – Sir Adrian Scrope reported that "his troop as good an one as [he] ever raised, was mustered yesterday at Ware".[16]

There was yet another use to which the Lea was put. In 1669, there was the first official mention of its waters being used to supplement the flow of the New River. The springs, first at Amwell and then at Chadwell, had begun to dry up and were apt to become swallow holes in dry summers – indeed the two springs were connected (William Vallans, in *The Tale of Two Swannes*, told of a duck which went down the latter and came up the former, completely stripped of all feathers). The New River Company gained the approval of the king and the Commissioners for Sewers of the River Lea to have two pipes taking water from the Lea near the Chalk Island in the middle of the Meads. The amount of water was measured in a crude fashion: two jetties were constructed out into the river to feed the pipes, without endangering the barge traffic or inundating the meadows. Later a marble gauge would regulate the flow into the New River and later still a New Gauge House with pontoons would be constructed on the bank of the Lea.

The 1660s saw the resumption of the manorial courts, first under Viscount Fanshawe then Sir Thomas Byde. During the Commonwealth all official documents were in English but the manorial records of Ware were again in an old-fashioned combination of medieval Latin, English and French. They were concerned mainly with property transfers in the town (Ware Infra), Wareside and the nearby hamlets (Ware Extra) and Bengeo but they also shed light on the physical state of Ware. In the High Street – called the *regiam viam*, king's highway – there was the Crown bridge where the Upper Bourne stream crossed the road next to the Crown Inn (the site of the library) and this was dangerous, especially for children, and needed repair.[17] The Market House built by the first Thomas Fanshawe (sometimes called the Townehouse) was also in a state of collapse as was the market cross, which marked the centre of the town. The market cross was used for many purposes – the main one was for the town's people to be summoned to the cross, not only on market day but also whenever it was necessary to inform the locals of various happenings, local news and political events. As in most markets, the pillory and stocks were situated next to the market cross and these too were in need of repair. Other delapidations in the town included 'Le Truncbodye', the wharf on the other side of the Ware Bridge where fish were traditionally landed – Vargus Johnson, Robert Farlowe and George Stevens were ordered to plank this wharf. Henry Pank was ordered to remove his market stall and George Stevens to remove his "house of office" (privy). The courts of 1668 and 1669 then proceeded to elect the constables, headboroughs and also Ware's two aletasters.

Many interesting characters emerge from the records of this period, some great, some decidedly less so. Edith Hunt was fascinated by famous and infamous former townspeople. Here we mention only three. On 1 July 1662 there occurred the death of Simon Ives, one of the musicians of St. Paul's Cathedral – he had been born in Ware in 1660 and was a noted composer for the viol, of which he left a whole chest "wherein are three tenors, one base, and two trebles; also another base" (now that we have begun to appreciate the viol, some of Ives's compositions are on CD).[18] In 1669, a pamphlet appeared with the title *The Hartfordshire Wonder or Strange News from Ware*, telling a story which was obviously the talk of the town – how a wheelwright had consulted a fortune-teller or 'cunning man' and accused him of being a witch, whereupon the cunning man's wife had cast a spell on Jane Stretton, the wheelwright's daughter, so that she had fits, did not eat for nine months and had flames proceeding from her mouth, one red and one blue, it was said. She was probably epileptic but, in that witchcraft obsessed age, it was taken as something more sinister. In 1676, two men and a woman in man's clothing came to Ware to tell fortunes at sixpence a time – one of them, Joseph Haynes, boasted he had "gotten five pounds and three maydenheads at Ware and a broken shinne".[19] Despite the Wadesmill turnpike, Ware was still a boisterous, open town which attracted visitors and miscreants alike.

Lady Ann as a Widow

It was a town which inspired great loyalty. When Sir Richard Fanshawe died in Spain in 1666, his widow moved heaven and earth to have him buried with his ancestors in Ware parish church. After the Restoration, Sir Richard, already a baronet, was elected MP for Cambridge University – at the same time he gained fame as a poet and translator – but the government honours he felt to be his due were not forthcoming. There were more powerful men close to the king. Instead, he was made ambassador to Spain and Portugal, where he concluded the negotiations for the marriage between Charles II and Catherine of Braganza but failed to negotiate the required commercial treaties. In June 1666, a few weeks after receiving his letters of recall, he died of a 'malignant fever' in Madrid. It then fell to Lady Ann to return to England with her husband's embalmed body, their children and servants – a party of 60 persons – together with the furniture, her husband's diplomatic and literary papers and the silver plate he had borrowed from the royal Jewel House "for the service of his chapel and household". The party travelled by coach across France to the Channel, where they embarked on a ship named 'The Victory' – a journey of six months. On her arrival, she first buried Sir Richard in All Saints' Church, Hertford – where she had rights as a Harrison from Balls Park – until she could gain permission from the Bishop of London and churchwardens to bury him in Ware church. This took more than four years, during which time she badgered the government for the £5,900 it owed her for her husband's back pay, her own travel expenses and payment for the silver plate from the Jewel House.[20] By a constant barrage of letters, she won but not before threatening a personal visit to Lord Arlington, the Secretary of State – "I would have waited on his lordship, but am ashamed to show myself, having a swelled face through the toothache".[21]

On 18 May 1671 she moved Sir Richard's body from Hertford to a vault in St. Mary's, Ware, which she had purchased for £200, and then erected a classical memorial to him inscribed in Latin on black marble. It originally covered one of the windows of the Lady Chapel, but was later moved to the South Transept. Lady Ann Fanshawe died in January 1680 and was buried in the vault she had bought for her husband. There is a postscript to the story. In 1908, a vault in the South Transept of the church was opened and a lead coffin discovered "of a very curious shape, with a window over the face of the occupant and fitted according to the Spanish custom of the time with locks and hinges". This was judged to be the coffin of Sir Richard although nothing remained of the chestnut outer coffin. The excavators, including the Vicar, Richard Benyon Croft, one of the churchwardens, and a member of the Fanshawe family, left the coffin undisturbed but placed other mortal remains near it, on the assumption that they included the remains of Ann Fanshawe who would have wanted to rest near her husband.[22] Other members of the Fanshawe family were buried in a vault below the Lady Chapel and these included Lady Katherine Ferrers, first wife of the second Viscount Fanshawe, sometimes thought erroneously to be the 'Wicked Lady' highwaywoman.

The early 1680s were politically tense. Charles II's health was failing and his brother and heir, James Duke of York, had declared that he had become a Roman Catholic – Charles was also a Catholic, but this was kept secret as was the Treaty of Dover, made with Louis XIV to restore Roman Catholicism in England. Parliament was resolutely opposed to a Catholic succession and introduced an Exclusion Bill which the king refused to sign. There were stories of 'popish' plots and, on the other side, stories of attempts on the lives of the royal family – one of them allegedly involving Richard Rumbold the owner of Rye House in Stanstead Abbots parish: the 'Rye House Plot'. On the death of Charles II in 1685 his illegitimate son, the Duke of Monmouth, organised a revolt for the Protestant cause but this was severely crushed and the Duke of York became king as James II. This national crisis had its repercussions in Hertfordshire, where the constables began a new spate of persecution of Quakers, breaking into meeting houses and sending worshippers to Hertford Gaol. For the Quakers, things improved with the accession of the Catholic James II, who ordered the release of all people in gaol because of the Conventicle Act, but others suffered.

Throughout Hertfordshire, there was a round-up of "disaffected persons" and there seem to have been more in Ware than other towns or villages. At the Hertford Sessions in June, nineteen men and one woman from Ware, including the draper Thomas Johnson and other members of his family, Mary Thornell and William Collett, were identified as persons "dissenting from the present government, who may be dangerous, especially in this time of rebellion of the Duke of Monmouth, if care be not taken to prevent them". They were ordered to appear before the town's constable and headboroughs with sufficient sureties for keeping the peace. Most of them gave sureties and were discharged, though some resisted, including John Lesteridge of Ware who was ordered to appear at the next Quarter Sessions. They were all people who had been prominent in town affairs during the Commonwealth. Collet had been a constable in 1653 and 1657 and also an overseer of the poor. He seems to have thought it advisable to leave Ware, for in 1685 he sold his property and disappeared. Collett Road is named after him and since 1821 his name has also been attached to Collett Hall, formerly known as Copt Hall. The property that Collett sold was Place House – he had bought it from Edward Packer in 1657 and painted his initials and the year over the top of Packer's on the Tudor screen. The party Collett sold Place house to was Christ's Hospital.

Christ's Hospital in Ware

Christ's Hospital was the school for orphan and one-parent children founded by Edward VI, on which Mark Twain based his story 'The Prince and the Pauper', and since 1553 it had been sending some of the younger children out of London for the good of their health. There were children (mainly boys) fostered with 'nurse families' in Hoddesdon, Ware and Hertford. In 1685 the governors had been renting Place House as a schoolroom when Collett offered to sell it to them for £400. It was hardly a bargain for Place House then was a large, rambling building with many outbuildings and extensions and the governors feared they would have to spend many hundreds more on repairs. Before making the purchase, they commissioned from their surveyor, Nathanial Bray, a survey and maps which survive in the Guildhall Library, London – one of Bray's maps is reproduced on the opposite page. The governors of Christ's Hospital beat the price down to £375.10s., demolished parts of the complex of buildings but retained the stables, and then built a line of cottages across what had been the orchard – at a total cost of £2,735.7s.7d. The stables, now No1 Bluecoat Yard, still have fourteenth-century timberwork.[23]

Place House remained the schoolroom for Christ's Hospital until 1761, when the school was closed for lack of pupils. The truncated east wing with its wall painting in the parlour became the home of the master, Samuel Hathaway, who lived there with his family for forty years. The governors had contemplated housing some of the boys with their nurses in the building but in the end put them into the cottages – each with a nurse and her family and no more than 14 boys per cottage, sleeping two to a bed if necessary. There were ten cottages with long gardens, a washhouse across a passage, and a two-hole privy in the garden. Two other cottages and the former stables had indoor privies. The rooms above the archway entrance also housed a nurse and her charges. It was a well thought out system of childcare. The governors inspected the premises every year, interviewing not only the master and nurses, but also the children. Nurse Mary Johnson, who lived in the gatehouse, was admonished in front of all the other nurses for drunkenness, swearing and neglecting her charges. Nurse Mary Boffey was a person of ill-fame who had not given the children sufficient food (two of them had died two years earlier) and she was given a month's notice, and so on. In any one year (except when the foundation was going through a financial crisis) there were on average 125 children in Ware, as well as 170 in Hertford and 550 in London.[24] In Ware the children were a well-known sight since each Sunday they processed to St. Mary's Church, where a balcony had been built for them in the North Transept.

Right: the statue of a Bluecoat Boy, which stood above the entrance to the Bluecoat Yard from 1704 to 1890, when it was taken to Hertford. It was returned to Ware in 1986 and is now inside Place House.

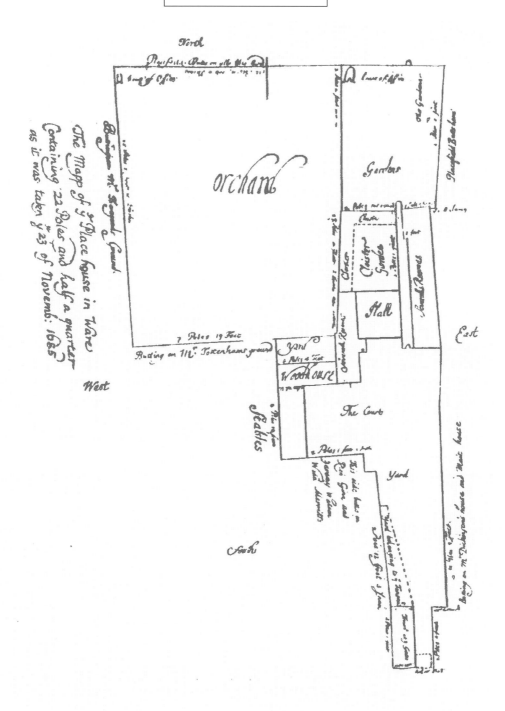

Place House in November 1685 – a contemporary copy of Nathanial Bray's survey for the governors of Christ's Hospital.
(Reproduced by permission of the Guildhall Library, London).[25]

Bluecoat Yard

Some of the nurses' cottages, built by Christ's Hospital after
1685 – now much sought after as private houses.

In Nathanial Bray's plan, the medieval hall of Place House is shown as a square shape with the long thin cross-passage to its right. On the other side of the cross-passage were "Severall Roomes" – this is the eastern wing which was probably rebuilt in the 1630s by Humfrey Packer, for in the downstairs room is a wall painting very much in the bold style of that decade. The cross-passage led to a cloister, enclosing a garden and with a long gallery above. Beyond the cloister was a larger garden and to its west a large orchard, both of them with a 'house of office' (privy) depicted in the corner. To go back to the medieval hall, to its west was a projecting block of "small rooms" and beyond that a small yard and a woodhouse, which was joined to the stables. What is striking about the map is how enclosed the Place House estate was by other buildings – "Mr Dickinson's house and malt house" to the east and numerous owners to the west – and how narrow was its entrance from what was then Upper Land Row (East Street). It shows how marginalised the former manor house of the town had become and how its neighbours crowded it in.

Right: the new Bluecoat Boy statue, carved in elm by Angela Godfrey and installed at the entrance to Bluecoat Yard in 1986. The Ware Society owns both statues.

Another prominent resident who suffered in the purge of 1685 was Alexander Mead at the Manor House in Church Street. The Mead family had rented the Rectory, as it was then called, from Trinity College, Cambridge for many years and had been leading citizens during the Commonwealth. Like William Collett, Mead appears to have thought it wise to move away from the town. According to the historian Henry Chauncy, he "assigned the lease to Sir Richard Tufton, knight, and upon his decease it came to Dame Margaret his widow who married Seymour Tredenham, Esq., the third son of Sir Joseph Tredenham of Tregonan in the county of Cornwall." That was only half the story, for Dame Margaret had a remarkable marital history. Her first husband was Sir Richard Tufton, a relative of the Earl of Thanet. When he died, she was in her mid-thirties and married Seymour Tredenham, aged 25 years, and briefly Member of Parliament for St. Mawes in Cornwall. He died in September 1696 and was buried in the chancel of St. Mary's, Ware. In 1701, she married her third husband, the Revd. Alexander Mills, vicar of St. Clement's in Sandwich in Kent. He died and she then married, fourthly, Philip Farwell or Farewell who survived her when she died in 1722, aged about 60. In her will she gave £260, the interest to be applied in coats for six poor men and gowns for six poor women once every two years, and in teaching four boys and four girls to read and write and say the catechism. She also decreed that in St. Mary's twenty loaves should be given to the poor on Christmas Day, Easter Day and Whitsunday "and so to continue to the end of the world".[26] The end of the world has not happened and, because of later reforms to charity law, Dame Margaret's will is no longer honoured. Of her four spouses, the one she loved best was "my beloved late husband Seymour Tredenham" for whom she ordered an inscribed marble memorial in Ware church.

William and Mary

National affairs moved on. In 1688 William of Orange, the Protestant ruler of the Netherlands, landed in England at the invitation of Parliament and the Catholic James II fled to France, then crossed to Ireland, where he was defeated at the Battle of the Boyne. The following year, as part of this 'Glorious Revolution' Parliament established a constitutional monarchy in Britain, barring Roman Catholics from the throne and making William III and his wife, Mary II (the elder daughter of James II) joint monarchs of England, Scotland and Ireland. The Toleration Act granted freedom of worship in England to 'Dissenters' (non Anglicans) although the Quakers were still excluded from the universities and public office because they objected to taking the oath of allegiance. Although these events would have been welcomed in Ware and Hertford, overwhelmingly Protestant and radical towns, naturally there were some who favoured the previous regime. On the 3 September 1689, two Ware men accused William Smart of Hertford, described as a 'webster', of sympathy with the Jacobites. Benjamin Patmore, a maltster, said that Smart had said King William's soldiers were oppressing the country more than those of King James. John Gillham said he had gone to save his brother, when he heard a great noise at the Saracen's Head and was told someone had drawn a sword, and there he found Smart who asked him to drink the health of King James which he refused to do.[27] Not

Dutch Summerhouses

One good thing arrived in Ware during the reign of the Dutch king, William of Orange, and that was the introduction of 'Dutch summer-houses'. They were probably built in imitation of the famous summer-houses at Edam (also known for its cheese). We now know them as 'gazebos' but that was a name given to them in the 1980s, as part of the Ware Society's fund raising for their restoration.

As the High Street became more noisy and dirty – with the malting wagons jostling with coaches and carts – the innkeepers saw the advantage of providing havens of quietness where their customers could enjoy a good view of the river and, no doubt, a drink or two. The earliest of these is the two-storey 'gazebo' behind 65 High Street which has a brick in the adjoining wall with the inscription '*MD 1697*'. The 'MD' was probably Mary Docwra, wife of the maltster John Docwra. The date would place its construction in the reign of William of Orange and that may explain the description "Dutch summerhouses" by which these structures were known in former times. They were famous enough in 1750 for Dr. Richard Pococke, a visiting Irish bishop, to note in his diary "gardens and summerhouses on the river from the houses". [28]

Writing about Ware in the 1830s, the writer James Smith said that every house on the south side of the High Street had formerly been a hostelry –

> with a large gateway giving access to a spacious courtyard, at the end of which was a pleasure-garden, terminating at the River Lea; looking out upon which was a Dutch summer-house, where in the old times, when the traffic on the road was performed by pack horses, and the place was the limit of the first day's journey to the north, weary travellers used to sit and quaff the 'old October', for which the place was celebrated, and bestow on it such endearing epithets as 'angel's food', 'merry-go-down', 'dragon's milk' or 'the balm of barleycorn'. [29]

By the end of the nineteenth century, there were twenty-five summerhouses at the end of the burgage plots between the Priory and Ware bridge.

that there was much affection for King William's Dutch soldiers. In 1690, "Mr. Wootten of London was killed at the George by five Dutch troopers and another gentleman, who wounded three of them, was sent to gaol".[30] In 1693, there was a riot in Ware when a drunk asked a Dutch dragoon from a unit quartered at Hoddesdon whether he spoke English: there was an argument, the dragoon drew his sword and was set upon by a "drunken rabble", who injured him and other soldiers and officers. Sir William Cowper, one of the justices sent to take statements, wrote that Ware was "eminently well affected to his Majesty and this difference to his soldiers proceeds principally from a roughness and barbarity peculiar to ye meaner sort of inhabitants, especially when they are drunk, who are mighty boasters of their manhood and ready to embroil themselves at any time with their neighbour towns to give demonstrations of it." So it may not have been xenophobia against the Dutch so much as rivalry with Hoddesdon which provoked the riot![31]

The burial registers (kept at HALS in Hertford) show how cosmopolitan Ware was in the last years of the seventeenth century. There were burials of the rich – Skinner Byde, who in 1685 predeceased his father Sir Thomas Byde, lord of the manor, and the third Viscount Fanshawe (son of the previous lord of Ware), who died in Aleppo, Syria, in 1687, aged 19. There were interments of the poor and those without a name – "a stranger drowned at Ware bridge", a stranger at the Flower de Luce (inn), an ostler at the Saracen's Head and "a come-by-chance traveller". Many nurse children were among the burials as well as "blewcoates" from the school in Place House and a number of French children, possibly Protestant Huguenot refugees. "Elias Twosaints, sack carrier" may have been one of these – his name was surely Toussaints (All Saints). John Bohun, "a blackamore nurse child" was buried in 1692, the year when the burial register records an earthquake. Moses Cocklie, a Bluecoat boy, was probably Jewish. Burial was a service afforded to all, whatever their religion: Joseph Burr, one of the town's leading Quakers, was buried in the churchyard of St. Mary's Parish Church in October 1695 because the Ware Quakers at that time did not have their own meeting-house or burial ground.

On 28 December, 1694, the burial register records the death of Queen Mary at Kensington. She died of the smallpox and was the best loved of all the Stuarts. The Ware register also records her funeral in March 1695, for which Purcell composed the wonderful funeral music, with drums and brass, which was played as her coffin was brought into Westminster Abbey.

16.
A Century of Commerce

The eighteenth century is – as advertising executives might say – one of history's best-kept secrets. At school I learned nothing about the 1700s, neither its politics, nor its writers and certainly not its trade and economics. It was a century when Britain was ruled by a succession of kings named George, none of whom spoke English well. Later in life, I came to appreciate the period's architecture and its music – those glorious works by Bach, Handel, Haydn, Mozart. But what else was occupying people apart from concertos, operas and oratorios? If I had been at school in the United States, I would have given a ready answer: I would have learned about the arrogant, short-sighted behaviour of George III's ministers which precipitated the American colonies into war and the famous Declaration of Independence of 1776. But school children in Ware ought to be just as proud of their eighteenth-century ancestors for it was a century when our town achieved national importance through the making of malt. In her *History of Hertford*, Dr. F.M. Page, entitled the chapter about the 1700s 'The Century of Gloom'. "The eighteenth century was throughout England a time of gloom and poverty for the ordinary citizen," she wrote. "War brings heavy taxation, high prices and scarcity, the quartering of soldiers, the call-up of bread-winners, and an increase of crime bred of sordidness and semi-starvation".[1] A bleak picture and one has to admit there is some truth in it. In some parts of Ware and Amwell End there was great poverty, although the "quartering of soldiers" mainly affected the busy and prosperous inns of Water Row, which were well able to look after themselves.

For Ware the 1700s were characterised not by gloom and poverty, but by commerce. It was a century of malt-making. The scenario outlined back in 1663 with the erection of the Wadesmill turnpike to control malting wagons moved to front stage in the eighteenth century. Slowly but surely, Ware's role was changing. No longer was it the main stopping point on the route from London to the North. The 'Old North Road' was being superseded by other roads, the one through Bishop's Stortford and especially the one through Hatfield, the 'Great North Road'. London coaches continued to stop in Ware but gradually the inns were closing or catering for mainly local customers, while in the inn yards of Water Row on the south side of the High Streeet malthouses were sprouting up. Ware was now a malting town rather than coaching stop. In the course of the eighteenth century, it would become the premier malting town in Britain. And this had a radical effect on life in the town and the countryside around.

The making of malt had been going on in Ware since 1330 or earlier. At that time maltmaking was a cottage industry. Everybody – lords and labourers, men, women and children – drank ale in the absence of any alternative beverage and to make ale you needed malt. It was an ancient procedure, probably discovered by the Pharoahs. Grain – barley was best, but other grains would do – was steeped in a water cistern and then forced to germinate under its own heat, until the germination was stopped by loading the grain on to a heated kiln. The germination had to be stopped, otherwise the grains would

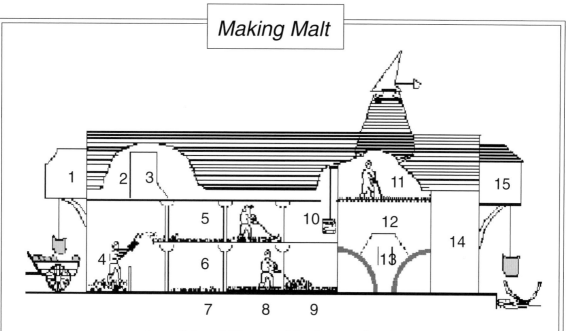

Making Malt

A traditional 'floor malting' as used in Ware.

The barley was brought by cart and loaded at the Barley Intake (1) usually via a 'lucam' or hoist, into the Barley Store (2). It was then screened (3) to remove chaff, then steeped in water in a Cistern (4). The wet barley was then laid out on the upper (5) or lower (6) working floor. There it was continually turned to help it to germinate evenly and to prevent the shoots from becoming entangled. Over the next weeks, it was moved towards the kiln – from the 'Young Piece' (7) to the 'Second Piece' (8) and finally to the 'Old Piece' (9). By then, the barley would have germinated sufficiently and the process had to be stopped – otherwise it would turn into a new plant and the sugar content would be exhausted. It was then hoisted (10) on to the kiln (11). The kiln had a wire floor or heat dispenser (12) over a furnace of oak or hornbeam, and later anthracite (13). The heat stopped the germination process and the barley was now 'cured' and made into malt. The malt was then unloaded into the Malt Store (14) where it was put into sacks. Finally, the malt was loaded from another 'lucam' (15) into carts or a barge for transport to breweries.

grow into young plants and that would use up all the sugar they were producing. It is this form of sugar, known as maltose, which is the basis of the brewing process, in which the sugar is converted into alcohol. Two things made Ware an important malting centre. One was the 1570 Act of Parliament which cleared away obstacles in the River Lea so that barges could take malt to London more cheaply than by road, with the result that much of the barley of East Anglia was brought to the malthouses of Ware then taken down river to London. The other factor was the phenomenal growth in the population of London, which became an explosion from 1650 onwards. To feed its swelling population there had to be a steady supply of bread and beer (much safer to drink than gin or polluted water). There was a new breed of wholesale or 'common brewers' in London, brewing on a large scale and supplying a great number of inns, private houses and corporations. They needed an assured supply of good malt and they found that in Ware. Malthouses sprang up all over the town, many of them small, low buildings operated by two men at the most. The local gentry, the innkeepers, landowners and ordinary folk saw what was happening and invested in the process of turning barley into malt. Fortunes were made, fortunes were lost and the town grew. Ware was not unique. Other towns and counties were pressed into supplying London's insatiable appetite for meat, bread, fruit, butter and so on, a process well observed by Daniel Defoe in his *Tour thro' the Whole Island of Great Britain* in the 1720s. Moving through Cambridgeshire, Defoe noted that most of the fields were growing barley "which is generally sold to Ware and Royston, and other great malting-towns in Hertfordshire, and is the fund from whence that vast quantity of malt, call'd Hertfordshire malt is made, which is esteem'd the best in England".

In 1722 or perhaps before, there occurred an event which changed the drinking habits of Londoners and added to the fortunes of Ware's maltsters. It was the invention or discovery of 'porter'. It is an event shrouded in mystery, and so it should be for it was the inauguration of a wonderful beverage. Before 1722 London brewers had been producing a sweetish, amber-coloured ale that quickly lost its strength, so that it became common practice for victuallers (publicans) to mix old and new ales or to draw a pint from three different casks – one of beer, another of ale and the third from more expensive pale ale, commonly known as 'two-penny'. That meant that every pint served in London consisted of at least one third flat beer. Ralph Harwood, a partner in the Bell Brewhouse in Shoreditch, overcame that problem by brewing a beer which was strong, dark and bitter and, above all, kept its strength – in fact, it was best drunk when it was several weeks or months old. Because it overcame the problem of the different casks, he called it 'Entire' or 'Entire Butt'. But because it was so popular with London's labourers it soon became known as 'porter'. Because it kept its strength, it was the first beer that was suitable for mass production by the common brewers, and soon all the major London brewers were switching from pale and amber beers to the darker porter. It was through porter that brewers like the Calverts were able to increase production to 50,000 and then 100,000 barrels a year.

What gave porter its colour and special taste was that it was brewed from a special brown malt, which was 'high dried', that is cured over a very hot kiln fire of oak or hornbeam faggots rather than coal. Whether or not brown malt was first discovered in Ware, it soon became a speciality of the Ware maltsters. It was not a particularly high quality malt, in fact it was made from poorer quality barleys and this was welcome because it gave porter a price advantage. The main features of 'Ware Brown' were its taste and its colour which gave porter its flavour – and its consistency. These features depended on the skills of the Ware maltsters. As an anonymous article in 1736 in the *London and Country Brewer* magazine, put it:

> I have heard a great Malster that lived towards Ware, say, he knew a grand Brewer, that
> wetted near two hundred Quarters a Week, was not a judge of good and bad Malts, without

which 'tis impossible to draw a true length of Ale or Beer. To do this I know but of few Ways, First, by the Bite; to break the Malt Corn across between the Teeth, in the middle of it or at both Ends, and if it tasteth mellow and sweet, has a round body, breaks soft, is full of flower all its length, smells well and has a thin skin, then it is good; Secondly, by Water; to take a Glass near full, and put in some Malt; and if it swims, it is right, but if any sinks to the bottom, then it is not true Malt, but steely and retains somewhat of its Barley nature.

It used to be said in Ware that a good maltster needed good teeth. Because the major brewers so much trusted the consistency of 'Ware Brown' malt, it acquired its own premium price at the corn market in Mark Lane, London. There were even documented instances of brown malt being brought by ship from Norfolk and then sent to Ware by barge to qualify for the Ware premium.[2]

It was not surprising that London brewers or the sons of brewers, like Sir Thomas Byde, should establish themselves as landowners in Hertfordshire. That movement would continue throughout the eighteenth century with the Hanburys at Poles, David Barclay at Youngsbury and the Buxtons at Easnye in Stanstead Abbots. But so would the movement in the opposite direction. Hertfordshire maltsters would soon become established in the major breweries of London – Edmund Halsey, Ralph and Henry Thrale (all of St. Albans), Sir William and Felix Calvert (of Furneaux Pelham), David Barclay (of Wadesmill), the Pryor family of Baldock. Ware's contribution to this traffic in maltsters and brewers was the Dickinson family. They arrived in the town in the reign of Elizabeth and after the Restoration in 1660 there were three Dickinson brothers engaged in the malt business. Rivers Dickinson in 1700 owned a house and malting at 55 High Street – between the Bull's Head and the King's Head inns – Richard Dickinson was involved in transporting malt to London and in 1694 took a lead in seeking the removal of further obstacles to navigation on the Lea, while Joseph Dickinson lived in a splendid brick house in Land Row (East Street) and had maltings directly to the north and east – *see illustrations on the following pages*. The location of Mr. Dickinson's house and malthouse is shown on a 1685 map of the Place House school for the children of Christ's Hospital. The school's records show that "the cinders from Mr. Dickinson's maltings next door blew in through the Place House windows, so that the schoolmaster asked for window shutters".[3]

The Dickinsons became London brewers in spite of themselves. In 1690, Rivers Dickinson was owed nearly £1,000 for malt by a Captain Boreham, a "'considerable brewer in Whitechapel', and to get his money he was forced to manage the brewhouse himself. He failed and lost more than £1,000 – 'from want of skill in the affairs of brewing and the failing of the victuallers he dealt with, who run away'". Yet the business survived and in 1739 a younger member of the family, Joseph (son of Joseph Dickinson of East Street), was bound apprentice to him and later set himself up at the Cannon Brewery in St. John Street, Clerkenwell.[4] For the next hundred years or so, different members of the family continued brewing in London – in Clerkenwell and in Red Lion Street, Holborn. In Ware, they carried on malting, intermarried with other malting families – Docwra and Cass – acquired more malthouses in Water Row and Crib Street and advanced up the social scale. For a while they ran the Ware Bank.

Evidence of the Dickinsons' prosperity and status can be seen in their house in Land Row (Nos. 1A, 2, 2A and 2B East Street). It is a building which in the early years of the twentieth century went rapidly down hill – at one time it was "a tramps' boarding house" – but in the early 1700s it was at the height of architectural fashion. Originally a timber-framed building (and perhaps an early Tudor guest-house for the manor at Place House), the East Street building has two main floors with attics and casement dormers above the parapet; at one time it would also have had a fine doorcase on to the street in place of the modern shop fronts. Some of the windows on the first floor are bricked up (not because of the brick tax, but because they hid staircases) and the brick lintels of alternate windows are scalloped to give a pleasing wavy pattern – a fashion also seen in Bleak House, St. Albans. Internally there is still some fine wooden panelling and there used to be a magnificent curved staircase – but I was told Drs. Moore and Sedgewick had it removed when they were fitting out their surgeries in the 1960s. At the rear is a large Palladian or Venetian window, partially bricked up now that it no longer overlooks the Dickinson malting yards. And there are dated rainwater heads – 1740 on the Bluecoat Yard side, 1742 facing New Road and, on the front, 1709 with the initials J D – Joseph Dickinson.

House in East Street

The final history of the Dickinson family is a sad one. By the late 1820s, the head of the family – John Baron Dickinson, one of the county magistrates – his wife, Martha, brother Jonathan and sister Ann were all in their seventies. To continue the family name, they put their faith in a nephew, William Dickinson, but he died aged 23 while still at university. The plaque they erected in St. Mary's recorded their grief:

> *This Tablet is erected by J.B, M and A. Dickinson, who had fondly viewed him as the Prop of their fast declining Years, but the merciful God who beheld, approved and took him to himself, will over their wounded hearts pour the soothing balm of reflecting on the bliss he now enjoys, and the cheering hope that they, ere long, shall partake therein.*

Within a few years (as another plaque records) John Baron, Martha and Jonathan were all dead.

The house in East Street was sold, the Palladian window at the back was partially bricked up and the family's malthouses were swept away. New Road was then built over their malting yard during the 1830s. But part of one timber-framed, seventeenth-century (or earlier) malthouse still survives as Nos 20 and 22 New Road. From the low sweep of the roof and the small side windows, it is obvious it was not built to be a dwelling – it must have been one of the maltings on which Joseph Dickinson built his fortune. His other maltings, in Kibes Lane, were rebuilt.

The surviving sister, Ann, moved to a house in New Road, on the site of what is now called (erroneously) 'Dickensian Way'.

Fashionable Red Brick

The Dickinson house in East Street was part of a fashion that was sweeping across the town. Every maltster, it seems, wanted a house in the latest architectural style with elegant sash windows and built of red brick. The rich deposits of brick earth, particularly in what is now the Trapstyles area, made Ware a centre for brick production from the seventeenth century onwards and brickmaking soon became the summer activity for malting workers. Iron oxide impurities in the clay produced the plum red bricks so characteristic of the reign of Queen Anne. The new houses in Ware for prosperous maltsters and maltfactors were built of this brick. It was so fashionable that many older, timber-framed buildings were given new red brick facades – among them the Christopher and Catherine Wheel inns in Water Row (67-71 High Street), a range of buildings on the market place (58-62 High Street) and a number of buildings in Baldock Street.

No. 87 High Street, built on the site of the Crown Inn. The portico and rustification were added later.

Before 1765 the Ware postmaster had been the landlord of the Crown, but in that year the inn was demolished and replaced by a handsome red brick house (the move of postal services to the Bull was accompanied by the move of the Great Bed). The house that replaced the old Crown Inn is now Ware Library (87 High Street – *above right*). It is not clear who the original owner was but towards the end of the century it became the home of Capel Hanbury III, a corn merchant and dealer in malt – and incidentally, one of the ancestors of the pharmaceutical side of the Hanbury family (viz. Allen & Hanbury). "At Ware the family had lived in some style in a large house at the top of the lane leading to the River Lea upon the banks of which Capel III had a wharf," so wrote a family historian.[5] This lane was 'Water Lane' which ran through what is now the Library carpark. Capel Hanbury did not stay long in Ware but his house passed to a succession of other maltsters – the Cass family, Edward Chuck and finally Henry Page. Edward Chuck, who was originally a plumber, made a number of changes and his initials with the date 1827 are inscribed on a lead rainwater head on the east side. The land to the rear of the house became the home malting yard of Henry Page & Company from the 1840s to 1960s.

Two other maltsters' houses face each other across the bridge and down Amwell End. At Bridgefoot (Nos 10-12 High Street) is the house that the Quaker Burr family built, with their malthouses to the rear in Kibes Lane along with the Quaker meeting house and burial ground. They were not 'plain Quakers' but enjoyed the latest building fashions, like the ornate dog-leg staircase, now running from the first floor to the attics but originally extending from the ground floor. The building suffered from conversion to the Enfield

Highway Co-operative store in the early 1900s and, even more, from neglect when the Co-op moved out in the 1970s under the threat of demolition to make way for a gyratory road scheme. But it has been restored and is now the Belgique patisserie. The building the Burrs' house faced was Amwell House, home of the Quaker maltster and poet, John Scott – *see page 146*. This is a more extensive building and has always been in good repair. After the death of Scott's daughter, Mrs. Maria Hooper, in the 1860s, it became a private house, then a grammar school and finally part of a college of further education – Hertford Regional College.

There is another red-brick maltster's house in London Road which is 'signed' but the

signature and the house itself are of a quite different scale. This is Brook House at 16 London Road, described by one architectural historian as a "mini-mansion only three windows wide but dignified by flanking pilasters".[6] This was the home of John Scott's friend, fellow Quaker and fellow maltster, William Pryor, and his initials are incised in the brickwork with the smaller initials of others, possibly the builders. You cannot mistake when this took place for the date 1737 is cut into the brick no fewer than five times.

Incidentally, the staircases mentioned above in East Street and at 12 High Street are just two examples of the craftsmanship that were hidden away behind the facades of the town centre (*see page 147*). There is another dog-leg staircase, similar to that in the Burr family home, in Nos. 37-41 High Street (formerly the Electricity Showrooms now Clinton Cards) – a jettied, medieval hall house which escaped refacing in brick and has all the eighteenth-century work at the rear. Rankin House in West Street has a very fine and spacious staircase, with moulded handrail, turned balusters and square newel posts, and also bold bolection panels on the wall – Rankin House remained a private dwelling until 1867, when a company bought it and built assembly rooms to the rear, naming the building 'The Town Hall'. There was a rival Town Hall in the Market Place, but neither truly deserved the title. On the south side of the High Street are two older staircases – a Jacobean example with carved, flat balusters at No. 79 (the convenience store) and a magnificent staircase with barleysugar twist balusters and moulded handrails, continuing up six flights at No. 63 (traditionally known as 'the Doctors' House'). But most splendid of all – and a real curiosity – is the heavy Tudor or Jacobean staircase in what was until recently the French Horn Inn, in Church Street (now residential). All the evidence points to this being a product of eighteenth-century building fashions – the wing in which the staircase is housed is clearly later than the staircase, which appears to have been crammed into a space too small for it. The clincher, perhaps, is to be found in what was once a barn in the inn yard, where a cross beam exhibits in engraved copperplate script the legend: *Jno. Clemenson May 5, 1777*, or perhaps in the carved name on a nailed-up door, found in the main building during conversion work: *THOMAS LAWRANCE, April 15 1751*. It must have been one of these gentlemen who imported the staircase from an older, larger house, perhaps demolished – records show that both of them were, of course, maltsters.[7]

The front of Amwell House. The original building – as can be seen from the outline in lighter brick – was a small, two-storey house known as The Peacock. It was purchased by Samuel Scott senior, a London linen draper, so that he could set up his two sons, Samuel junior and John, in the malting business. The family

moved in in 1740 and prospered so well in the malting business that they were soon able to transform the small house into a spacious gentleman's residence, with a large library and drawing rooms, a second storey for servants' quarters and two projecting wings (sadly cut back in the 1970s for road widening).

Behind Amwell House, John Scott laid out a large garden in the English picturesque style, with winding paths, small features like rustic seats and summer houses, and areas of wilderness. At the top of the garden, he built a grotto in imitation of Alexander Pope's grotto at Twickenham, cut deep into the chalk hillside with six underground chambers. The chambers were lined with red brick by John's father-in-law, Charles Frogley (a bricklayer) and covered with a rich decoration of shells, minerals, fossils, coal and glass. Below is the original entrance to the grotto and (right) a niche in the large 'Council Chamber'.

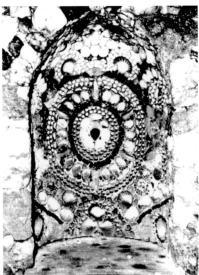

Fine Staircases

Above two 18th century staircases – left in No 12 High Street and right in Rankin House. Below left: the 17th century barley-sugar staircase at 65 High Street and right: the Tudor or 17th century staircase in the former French Horn.

Sporting Wagers

Ware's prosperous new middle classes soon embraced another fashion – that for sport and betting. Cricket became a local pastime long before other parts of the county took it up, and it was probably played on the Buryfield. That is the old Buryfield, now under the factory buildings of GlaxoSmithKline – not the Buryfield Recreation Ground, whose older name was the Bell Close. One of the earliest matches recorded in Hertfordshire took place at Ware on 12 August 1737, as recorded in the *St. James Evening Post*: "Brentwood beat Hertford by 6 notches for £200. It was generally believed that they would have beaten them at one innings had they not met with ill usage by a mob of bargemen. It is said that the bets which were laid on both sides amounted to upwards of £2000". [8] A notch was a run, recorded by the scorekeeper's knife. Even though the Ware XI was not on the field, the report gives a persuasive picture of the town at that time – elegant young men in knee-breeches with no pads or shin-guards, wielding crude curved bats, and a great deal of money changing hands, some of it obviously wagered by the disgruntled bargemen.

When Ware did field an eleven, they achieved a reputation for high standards and good scores. So much more the disappointment in September 1769, when they were playing Epping for £50 a side. The visitors had scored 95 notches and the first four Ware batsmen replied with 80 – at which the betting went to 10 to 1 against Epping. Then to everyone's astonishment, the remaining six Ware men were bowled out with the addition of just one notch. Even worse was the outcome of a needle-match in 1788 against the old rivals, Hertford. The betting was again 10 to 1 in Ware's favour for "the Town of Ware has long considered itself capable of contending with any single Town in England … and never lost a Match before the present." But Ware was beaten by an innings, which led one player "in a paroxysm of Rage and Vexation" to go home and burn his breeches.

Betting was a national pastime. The Whig politician Charles James Fox lost vast sums gambling at cards in the clubs of London, and in 1774 Lord Holland paid his son's gambling debts at a cost of £140,000. The Quaker John Scott, who thoroughly disapproved of games of chance, complained that far too many matters were settled by pulling names out of a hat, including whether he had the chance to invest in improving the turnpike roads through Ware. One can imagine his chagrin, when he discovered that horse-racing was taking place on the local turnpikes and, what was worse, there were actually Quakers engaged in it. Later in the century racing on the turnpike was recognised in one of the most famous poems in the English language – William Cowper's *The Diverting History of John Gilpin, Showing how he went farther than he intended and came home safe again*. The story concerns the vain efforts of Gilpin, a citizen of London, to get to his wedding anniversary dinner at the Bell at Edmonton when his run-away horse is determined to take him to Ware

> The dogs did bark, the children screamed,
> Up flew the windows all,
> And every soul cried out, 'Well done!'
> As loud as he could bawl.

Away went Gilpin—who but he?
His fame soon spread around—
'He carries weight!' 'He rides a race!'
''Tis for a thousand pound!'

And still, as fast as he drew near,
'Twas wonderful to view
How in a thrice the turnpike-men
Their gates wide open threw.

The poem, written in 1782, was based on a real-life story told to Cowper by his friend, Lady Austen. It is said the real Gilpin was a London linen draper named Beyer. In Ware tradition, the old shop to the west of Rankin Square was known as 'Gilpin House' and thought to have been where the owner of the horse lived – but there is no historical source for that belief.

The Lee Navigation

One tangible result of Ware's new prosperity in malt-making was the improvement of navigation on the River Lea. Earlier improvements – in the Middle Ages and the reign of Elizabeth I – had cleared away obstacles to the navigation made by millers, fishermen, osier bed proprietors, and so on. But by 1739, it was clear there was a different problem. With the failure of Amwell spring and then Chadwell for part of the year, the New River Company was increasingly taking its supply of drinking water from the River Lea. At the beginning of the century, the company had bought from Sir Thomas Byde the pound lock just above Ware Mill, so that it could control the amount of water available to barges and stop them interfering with its own intake. This lock had been built in 1658 by an agreement between the Borough of Hertford and the previous Lord of the Manor of Ware, Sir Thomas Fanshawe. To resolve the conflict between barge traffic and the New River, a petition was presented to Parliament and in 1739 an Act was passed, establishing the Lee Navigation Trustees and awarding them £350 a year from the New River Company for the water it extracted.[9] However, despite the name, the Lee Navigation (always in this context spelt 'Lee') was still basically the old River Lea and the trustees had neither the money nor the power to impose tolls so as to finance a proper navigation. And so in 1765 the trustees commissioned a survey from the engineer, John Smeaton, who recommended new straight cuts in the river and the replacement of flash locks (barriers which allowed a 'flash' of water to build up) by pound locks which could raise or lower the navigable river. A further Act in 1767 provided for these changes, together with the construction of a new stretch of canal, the Limehouse Cut to bypass the tight bends of Bow Creek near the River Thames and the long passage around the Isle of Dogs.[10] The Limehouse Cut was opened in 1770. Artificial cuts and pound locks were opened at Waltham Abbey, Edmonton and Hackney in 1769.

Above Ware Lock, which was now made toll-free, the Navigation took over the Ware Mill Stream, which was deepened and canalised. This opened up the river to barge traffic as far the Town Mill at Hertford. Another cut was made to bypass the millrace below Ware Mill and south of the town the Stanstead Cut carried the Navigation straight down to Stanstead Abbots. The Act enabled the trustees to finance this canalisation by raising loans of £35,000 and then charging tolls on all cargos carried on the navigation.

The trustees of the Lee Navigation, who now numbered more than 200, had their meetings in pubs, ranging from the Antwerp Tavern near the Royal Exchange in the City to the Rose and Crown, Enfield, or the Bull in Ware. The maltsters of Ware and Hertford were well represented among their number. It was at the Rose and Crown that John Scott sat with other trustees to cross-examine twelve Ware steersmen accused of falsifying the amount of malt they were carrying. The Bull (or the Bull's Head, as it was sometimes called) was in the centre of

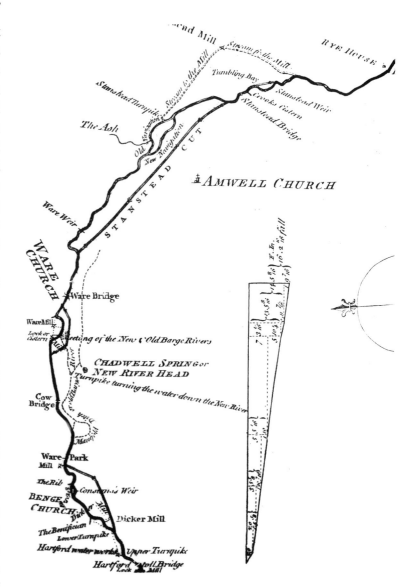

Part of John Smeaton's map of proposed alterations to the Lee Navigation, 1766. The figures in the centre triangle denote the fall in the river by "16ft. $2^{10}/_{16}$ ins." (5 metres) between Hertford Toll Bridge and Ware Bridge.[11]

Water Row and acted as the post office as well as venue for meetings of the navigation and turnpike trustees. The changes made by John Smeaton under the 1767 Act created the Lee Navigation as we know it today. Meanwhile in 1759 and 1766, two further Acts of Parliament made "the River Stort navigable ... from the New Bridge in the town of Bishop's Stortford into the River Lee, near a place called The Rye, in the County of Hertford."[12] After that Ware maltsters began to move some of their operations to Bishop's Stortford and Sawbridgeworth.

17.
Improving the Roads

The eighteenth century was a time when Britain began seriously to get to grips with its transport system. The Lee Navigation acts of 1739 and 1767 and the similar canalisation of rivers revolutionised water transport and were followed by the canals proper, beginning with the Duke of Bridgewater's Canal to take coal from his mines at Worsley to Manchester and then to the sea via Runcorn and the River Mersey. Before canalisation, work had been going on since the Middle Ages to clear rivers of obstacles to navigation. But little had been done to improve the road network.

Before 1700, the repair and maintenance of roads was the responsibility of the parishes through which they ran and much of the repair work was supposed to be done as free labour by teams from local farms. The result was that in winter almost all major roads between towns had deep, water filled ruts which spelled danger to all users. This deplorable state of affairs was remedied only by the establishment of turnpikes or toll gates, which brought in sufficient revenue for proper repairs to be carried out. The Wadesmill Turnpike, set up in 1663, was a foretaste of what was to come but it was an isolated gesture, intended to deter malting traffic rather than a serious attempt to improve the road. The first step towards a better system was an Act of Parliament in 1706 which created a turnpike trust in Buckinghamshire, not on the initiative of local justices of the peace but of private entrepreneurs. The new trustees were given powers to borrow capital for road mending against the expected income from tolls, and they used this at first to improve road alignments and ease gradients. The Bucks example was quickly followed. Between 1706 and 1750, 400 Acts of Parliament were passed setting up turnpike trusts with a further 1,600 before 1800. Turnpike mania had arrived. In 1733, an Act established the Wadesmill Turnpike Trust which took over the 1663 tollgate from the justices and administered the Old North Road as far as Royston. But already Ware had been included in a different turnpike road, that of the Cheshunt Turnpike Trust created by Act of Parliament in 1725. John Scott became a member of both these trusts, as well as a trustee and the reforming treasurer of the Watton Turnpike Trust, which managed a pair of roads running from Ware to Walkern and from Hertford to Broadwater and crossing – like a pair of scissors – at Watton-at-Stone.

In his day, Scott was highly thought of as the author of *Digests of the General Highway and Turnpike Laws* (1778), in which he drew on his experience as a turnpike trustee. But he was also an experienced road builder. His first project in 1770 was to reconstruct the road between Amwell End and Hertford, the one that was in constant danger of collapsing into the New River and which Scott described as "a Nasty and Dangerous Lane". Scott and his father used this road every week when they went to the Quaker meeting house in Hertford. To finance the road works, he laid out some of his own money (a figure of £300 was mentioned), persuaded the Great Amwell Vestry to apply the parish rates to the work, had the backing of an unnamed local philanthropist and also raised funds by a local subscription appeal.[1] Even so his first essay in road building ran into flak from some of the local gentry, led by the lord of Ware manor, Thomas Plumer Byde M.P. Undeterred, Scott went on to make further road improvements. At his own expense, in 1775 he raised the level of Amwell End by laying down tree trunks covered with gravel in order to try to stop the road flooding. Then, as a member of the Ware Committee of the Cheshunt Turnpike Trust, he introduced and supervised a scheme to clear the High Street of obstructions which made the passage of coaches and wagons almost impossible. From the Middle Ages onwards, more and more market stalls in the Market Place had been replaced by permanent structures which in turn pushed the new market stalls into the roadway. In 1778, the trustees decided to demolish four of these buildings and sweep away what they called "the shambles" of butchery and other stalls. We know who inhabited the four doomed

John Scott

shops – they were Thomas Taylor, a barber, Myhill, a feltmonger, Creed, a tailor, and Judd, a collarmaker. The total cost of the work was £370 and for this the roadway was widened and for the first time enough space found for a footpath.[1]

The road improvements brought more visitors to the area. The second half of the eighteenth century saw the arrival of "tourists" for the first time (the word was coined at that time). The smooth-surfaced turnpike roads summoned into existence a generation of new coaches and carriages – "the Machine, Fly, Dilegence, Vis-à-Vis, Curricle and Tom Whisky", according to Scott. The turnpikes also encouraged horse racing, of which Scott strongly disapproved. To provide for tourists and other visitors, Ware's innkeepers set aside some of their land as riverside gardens, each finished with a fashionable summerhouse with a view of the water and the fields beyond. Scott himself had a number of similar buildings in his garden behind Amwell House, including an octagonal belvedere.

With prosperity and the tourists came new shops. Until recently it was assumed that eighteenth-century shops – in contrast to those of the Victorians – were dark places with little interior decoration and not much effort to attract customers with window displays or the like. But recent research has shown a more complex picture with spacious interiors, in which consumers could spend time browsing, selecting and purchasing goods. The process of 'shopping' (a verb coined in the eighteenth-century) implies a much more leisurely activity than sending out a servant or child with a list of requisites. This new type of shop must have astonished some people and made them wonder if they would stay the course. In 1764 John Scott wrote to a friend: "we have Got a Bookseller come to reside at Ware; he might as well have Open'd Shop on Hartford Heath or Even in the Deserts of Arabia".[2] Booksellers were not unknown in the town: in 1742, Richard Chandler, bookseller of London and York, erected a memorial in St. Mary's to his wife, Catherine who died after just seven years of marriage (it is over the north door). But they may not have been bookshops as we know them: the Universal British Directory of 1791 lists a Mr. Macey as "bookseller and hardwareman." The most important new shop to open in the High Street was that of Robert Harradence, at No.69 in what had once been the Catherine Wheel Inn. That was in 1775 and the business at first was a haberdashery, but in time it took over four adjoining shops, expanding into dressmaking, millinery, gents' outfits, books and shoes, carpets, curtains and china. The land behind Harradence's five shops was the only area of the old burgage plots that did not have maltings built on it and remained a garden – or even a "secret garden" as some said – until Burgage Court was developed in 1997-98. Harradence's department store closed in 1971, just short of its double century – the Harradences, it appears, were intermarried with the Docwra family, which may explain why they established themselves in that part of Ware. Another business which claimed to have begun in the 1700s was the wine and spirits concern of the Ellis family, now the Punch House. Among other traders we have already met Taylor, a barber, Myhill, a feltmonger, Creed, a tailor, and Judd, a collarmaker. The Malin family were tea dealers in Back Street (East Street) and there was a Mr. Field, listed in 1791 as an apothecary.

But the prize for Georgian enterprise must surely go to another apothecary. In 1781 (according to the *Gentleman's Magazine*) a correspondent reported that a marble slab in St. Mary's churchyard bore the inscription *'William Mead, M.D., who died Oct. 28, 1652, aged 148 years and 9 months'*, and pointed out that, although the parish register for that date recorded the death of a Dr. George Mead on that date, who left £5 to the poor of Ware, there was no evidence of him living to a great age. The slab was recut many times over the years, eventually gaining a further line *'3 weekes and 4 days'* but without any explanation of the 148 years. However, in the nineteenth century a chemist in the High Street was selling "Dr. Mead's patent medicines" which guaranteed a healthy long life – so perhaps an earlier chemist added the 148 years when the trustees of Dr. Mead's charity recut the slab in the 1770s.[3] The slab used to lie flat in the churchyard and became worn and the lettering obscured, so in 2007 the Ware Society paid for it to be recut and erected vertically, beside the path leading to St. Mary's extension.

The Rich, the Middle Sort and the Poor

In 1709 Daniel Defoe identified seven distinct classes in English eighteenth-century society – and unlike medieval society or even that of the Victorians (where education and birth played their part) the classes were based wholly on money. They were: "The *great*, who live profusely. The *rich*, who live very plentifully. The *middle sort*, who live well. The *working trades*, who labour hard but feel no want. The *country people*, farmers &c., who fare indifferently. The *poor*, that fare hard. The *miserable*, that really pinch and suffer want".[4] There were no Dukes or Lords in Ware who would qualify as 'the great', but all the other classes were represented.

The rich were mainly landed gentry and brewers. Property was everything. Most maltsters and maltfactors did not qualify as "rich" until the 1800s when many of them left Ware to establish themselves in large houses in the country. Although Income Tax had not yet been invented, there was a Land Tax and to hold any sort of public office a property qualification was necessary. To become a member of the Cheshunt Turnpike

Trust, for example, a gentleman had to have money or goods in hand to the value of £1500 or a Land Tax annual assessment of £40 or more: John Scott qualified on the latter score. He owned property – estates and farms as well as maltings – in Yorkshire and Lincolnshire as well as Amwell End and at Westmill and Standon to the north of Ware. He had the wealth and it was only his beliefs as a Quaker that prevented him living "very plentifully".

Not so the residents of the Priory at the far end of Ware High Street. It had been bought in 1685 by a brewer, Robert Hadsley, who was High Sheriff of Hertfordshire. His main residence was in Great Munden and the Priory was let "to some Tradesman or other". It was common to acquire a property for its rents, both John Scott at Westmill House and the Plumer family with Fanhams Hall had done the same in the 1770s. When Robert Hadsley died, rents from the Priory provided a pension for his widow, Elizabeth, and on her death it passed to their son, another Robert. Having been abroad on the Grand Tour, Robert junior decided to take up residence in the Priory, which involved extensive rebuilding to convert the ramshackle, former Friary into a comfortable country house – or 'seat' – complete with handsome sash windows and the latest water closet with a humorous inscription: *Temple of Ease 1754*. He also tried to evict the townspeople who had built their dwellings up against the Priory wall, with "stables or brewhouses and some hogscoats, very offensive from their noisome stench". He asked a barrister at Lincoln's Inn for his (no doubt, expensive) opinion and received the reply it was better to learn to live with his neighbours than sue them. But most of his energy seems to have gone into his office, like his father, as High Sheriff. Nowadays the post is purely honorific, but that was not so in the 1740s. Here we are fortunate to have his accounts (diligently collected by the late Hugh Shayler, and now in HALS). One of his duties was to meet the Judge of Assize at the county boundary at Waltham Cross, and accompanied by the Undersheriff, the Bailiffs, 30 Javelin-men and two trumpeters (who all had to be paid and given their customary bottles of wine) lead the whole procession to the court in Hertford. This was the sort of jolly for the gentry and sons of the gentry that the eighteenth century was fond of. The High Sheriff's other main duty was gaol delivery, delivering the prisoners kept in Hertford Castle to the Assize court with details of the charges against them and their condition (many of them had smallpox or gaol fever). Then he had to see that the verdict of the court and the judge's sentence was carried out. At the summer Assize in 1741, four highwaymen – including Charles Cox, otherwise known as 'Baconface' – were sentenced to be "severally hanged by their necks until thought dead." Two felons were sentenced to be burned on the hand, two others convicted of petty larceny were openly to be whipped on their backs until their bodies were bloody, and five others convicted of stealing were sentenced to be transported to His Majesty's Colonies and Plantations in America. Then, with the Assize over, the Sheriff would escort the judge out of the county and make up his accounts. For the years 1740-1743 his expenses came to £562, for which he was reimbursed by the Exchequer.[5] No doubt he made a profit, but it was small beer compared with the higher offices of state – government ministers could make £8,000 to £9,000 a year, all in expenses of course. By comparison, a curate looking after a parish for an absent vicar or the average farmer existed on less than £100 a year.

With those figures in mind, it is interesting to look at another bill among the documents Hugh Shayler collected. It is the funeral bill of Robert Hadsley's successor, Jeremiah Rayment Hadsley.[6] He was a cousin who had inherited for the childless Robert in 1765 and had taken the surname Hadsley by Act of Parliament. Like his predecessors, he was High Sheriff and a wealthy landowner. He lived at the Priory but clearly spent much time away. He died at the beginning of March 1777 in Bath, probably while taking the waters. The funeral bill from the Bath undertaker, Mr. Pettingal, is a lengthy document for his was a funeral in the grand manner. "Item: 31 yards of fine Norwich crape – £4.5s.3d. A lead coffin – seven guineas. An outside coffin covered with fine black cloth, 4 brass chas'd gilt handles and 2000 best nails – £6.16s.6d. Bran to fill up the coffin – 5 shillings. Two women to dress the corpse – 10 shillings. 46 yards of black satin – £24.3s.0d." The total bill came to £223.13s.5d., a small fortune in the final quarter of the 18th century. It was expensive partly because the body had a journey of eight days before reaching Ware. "To a hearse and 6 and a coach and 6 horses 8 days at 42/- per day – £33.12s.0d. To 2 coachmen and 2 postillions, allowance for maintenance 8 days at 3/- per day – £4.16s.0d. To a set of feathers for the hearse and horses and bier 8 days at 21/- per day - £8.8s.0d." The feathers were more expensive than the postillions! "Turnpikes to Ware and back to Bath – £5.5s.11d. Paid 8 men for taking out the corpse on 3 nights on the road and putting it in in the morning at 1/- per night – £1.4s.0d. Paid for sitting up three nights on the road and 1 night at Ware – £1". It surely must have been the most expensive burial at St. Mary's since the funeral of Sir Thomas Bourchier in 1491.

The rich were not always good at holding on to their fortunes. Thomas Plumer Byde, the Lord of the Manor of Ware with whom Scott had clashed over the road, had a pampered childhood. As a child, his parents had his portrait done by the fashionable Polish-born painter, Enoch Seeman, who also painted George I – it shows young Thomas and his brother John, both dressed in long dresses, a fashion for children of the time. Thomas came into his fortune while still in his teens. In 1737, the family had to get a Private Act of Parliament to allow him as a minor to sell the Ware Mill to the New River Company. For that he secured an annual rent charge, as well as an income for his brother and unmarried aunt, Barbara Byde. He took up banking and became M.P. for Hertfordshire in 1761 in succession to his cousin, William Plumer. But in 1779 Thomas was declared bankrupt. It was partly the result of profligate spending and partly due to bad luck. As a banker, he had lost out when transatlantic trade was disrupted by war with the American colonies and France. He left the country to escape his creditors and settled in Italy. From Naples, he wrote an obsequious letter to the American statesman, Benjamin Franklin, pointing out that he had been M.P. for Hertfordshire in 1761 and had voted against the Stamp Act, which had provoked the American colonies into revolt. He then asked Franklin for the position of consul in one of the Italian ports.[7] He failed to get it and died in Naples in abject poverty in 1789 – *the family tree of the Bydes, as lords of the manor of Ware, is on page 156.*

In contrast there were the local poor. There had always been poverty in the town but the expanding malting industry sucked in a new population of country people, seeking work as unskilled labourers in the malthouses or loading barges. This was casual work

Ware Park in the eighteenth century, built by Sir Thomas Byde

Mary Skinner (1) =   Sir Thomas Byde   = (2) Susanna Grindall
(d. 1694)   (1628-1704)
                    MP for Hertford 1673-1690

Skinner Byde = Mary Villiers   Elizabeth Dorothy = Sir Thomas   Ralph Skinner
(d. 1685)   daughter of   Feild of   Byde of Hitchin
            Viscount Grandison   Stansteadbury

Thomas Skinner Byde = Katherine Plumer   Barbara Byde   other daughters
(d. 1732)   of Blakesware   died as infants
               (d.1749)

Thomas Plumer Byde = Eleanor Hope   John Byde
(1720-89)
MP for Hertfordshire 1761
died in Naples, bankrupt

Thomas Hope Byde = Eleanor Peacock   John Hope Byde
(d. 1830)   (d. after 1830)
                            directed in his will that
                            Ware Park should be sold

The Bydes of Ware Park

which could easily leave their families destitute for long periods. The labourers lived in yards and 'courts' at either end of the town, most of them in Amwell End (still known then as Ware End, Great Amwell) or off Baldock Streeet, including Caroline Court named after George II's queen, Caroline of Brandenburg-Ansbach. A century later these yards and courts were to be notorious as hotbeds of cholera – in the eighteenth century, the main scourge of all classes, rich and poor, was smallpox which we will come to a little later. Under the Elizabethan Poor Law it was the responsibility of the parish in which a person was born to look after them when they became ill or destitute. But the old Poor Law had long since ceased to work either efficiently or sympathetically. Commercialisation and the Enclosure Acts had disrupted the rural economy and parishes were more and more reluctant to increase their rates or taxes for the sake of the poor. A number of new acts of parliament were introduced which added to the suffering of the poor without solving the basic problem. John Scott, in a short but impassioned book of *Observations on the Poor*, pointed out the foolishness of these acts. The Vagrancy Act of 1744, which required that beggars should be flogged before being sent back to their own parishes, "defeats its purpose by the severity of its penalties." The Workhouse Act of 1723, which allowed parishes to farm out their poor to private contractors, was a "dreadful engine of oppression". The results were institutions run by petty tyrants who accumulated dishonest wealth by denying the inmates adequate food and imposing on them unreasonable labour. They were "parish prisons", Scott wrote. And without naming names, he hinted strongly that a neighbouring parish to his own at Great Amwell was a glaring example of this oppressive system of farming out its poor.

If he meant Ware, then Scott was not far from the truth. The old poorhouse was at the top of Crib Street on the right-hand side and, although officially in the care and control of the churchwardens, it was let – or farmed out – to a family named Nicholl who were manufacturers of rope and canvas. The Nicholls' ropeground was on the opposite side of Crib Street beside the Upper Bourne stream, the water source for the work. Rope-making was a labour-intensive, backbreaking industry, carried on in all weathers, using a 'rope walk'. The principle of the walk was that yarns were stretched out between revolving hooks, often 300 yards (274 metres) apart, and these hooks were then turned to twist the yarns together into rope. It was common for children to be employed turning the wheel while the adults carried the heavy, wet ropes. In the same area – and using much the same materials – they also made sack, canvas and tilt (a forerunner of tarpaulin). There was a ready market for all these products in the barge traffic between Ware and the Thames, but they were also made for sale farther afield. Pigot & Company's Directory of 1823 listed three manufacturers of rope, sack, tilt and canvas: Edward Nicoll in the Bourne and Simon Norton and Henry Whittle in Baldock Street. Commenting on the town's trade, it said: "The principal trade is in malt and corn, immense quantities of the former commodity are conveyed to London by the river and a navigable canal … considerable quantities of tilt and canvas are also manufactured here, the manufacture of these articles has long been carried on on a very extensive scale."

The major illnesses of the eighteenth century were smallpox and 'gaol fever'. The latter was a disease, often fatal, found where people lived and slept crowded together: it was particularly prevalent in prisons, hence the name. Most people thought it was due to 'bad air' passed from person to person and John Scott, a fresh air enthusiast, recommended wide open windows. In fact, gaol fever was typhus fever, caused by lice. There was no cure at that time but fresh air did help alleviate it. The other scourge was smallpox, a deadly disease which was no respecter of class or economic boundaries (Queen Anne died of it). During the eighteenth century the practice of inoculation became more common. This was not vaccination with 'cowpox', a related but weaker bacillus introduced by Edward Jenner, but injection with the actual smallpox pustules in the hope that this would produce a mild but protective infection. It was also known as 'variolation'. An exponent of variolation was Dr. Thomas Dimsdale, a Hertford physician and Quaker, most famous for injecting the Russian Empress Catherine the Great and her family. He also treated John Scott who became a keen advocate of the practice. In a magazine article, Scott said in one market town the small pox had been prevalent for the past thirty years and reached epidemic proportions every four or five years (he was referring to Ware). But since the variolation had been introduced in 1765, the annual death rate from the small pox had fallen from 80-100 a year to no more than twenty.[8] In fact, Scott's optimism was premature. In the summer of 1777 there was another serious outbreak in Ware – so reported John Coakley Lettsom, a Quaker physician and another of Scott's friends – eighty people died of it and another general inoculation was proposed which most townspeople took up. Not everyone agreed to be inoculated and in the event no one died, whether inoculated or not.[9] Dr. Dimsdale's patients were from the upper classes, for he charged a substantial fee for nursing patients to a full recovery at his inoculating house in Hertford. Scott favoured Dr. Lettsom's practice of inoculating the poor as well as the rich, but many people feared this would spread the disease even wider.

Established and Un-established

Apart from wealth, the other major division in Ware society was religion. There were four places of worship in the town, in contrast to the proliferation of churches and chapels in the following century. They were the Parish Church (of St. Mary the Virgin – Anglican), the Independent Chapel in Dead Lane or Church Street (Congregationalist), a Presbyterian Chapel which existed in Black Swan Yard, Baldock Street, from 1787 to 1807 and the Society of Friends' meetinghouse in Kibes Lane (Quaker). Attendance at the Parish Church was no longer compulsory, as it had been in the previous century, but not being present at Anglican worship had its disadvantages. To hold any major public office, like magistrate or Member of Parliament, or to be a member of one of the universities of Oxford and Cambridge, a man faced the obstacle of the Test Acts (women, of course, had even more disadvantages). These meant that a candidate had to produce a certificate, signed by a priest or parish clerk, to show that he had taken Holy Communion in the Church of England. Many Congregationalists, Baptists and Presbyterians went through the motions of taking communion in a process known as 'occasional conformity' but Quakers resolutely refused to do so. Scott complained that society did allow Quakers to perform the menial role of parish constable but never that of an M.P., sheriff or justice of the peace. However,

The Friends' meetinghouse in Kibes Lane, built in 1728.

there was one public position open to them, that of a turnpike trustee. Here it was money, not religion, that qualified them for office. Another disability faced by Quakers was church rates or taxes. Local government then was exercised by the 'Vestry' of each parish, unless it was a borough like Hertford, and it was the duty of the churchwardens to levy different rates for maintenance of the roads, the poor house and repairs to the church. It was this last one that Quakers objected to, preferring to let the bailiffs seize some of their goods rather than pay "steeple taxes."

Quakers were no longer being sent to prison for their beliefs, but the continuation of this milder persecution brought the Friends closer together. They were especially well represented in the business of brewing, malting and banking. Many Quakers came to Ware to enrol in the malting industry and many of these, like Scott and his family, hailed from Southwark, a noted brewing centre. When the Friends' meetinghouse in Kibes Lane was built in 1728, eight trustees put their names to the trust deed and five of these were maltsters, and a sixth a 'maltmeeter', someone who measured the malt before it was shipped to London. When a fresh deed was drawn up in 1750, there were five maltsters among the eleven trustees, including John Scott. The meetinghouse was a small building, tucked away behind cottages in Kibes Lane. It is possible that the land was given by the Burr family, prominent Quaker maltsters whose house was nearby in the High Street. On one side of the meetinghouse was a small garden and on the other a burial ground. Land for the garden was given by David Barclay of Youngsbury, one of the partners in the brewing firm of Barclay, Perkins & Co. The Quaker Burial Ground was acquired by Ware Urban District Council in 1934 and survives as a public garden – though in the twenty-first century the Town Council and Ware Society have had to fight off an encroachment by developers.

The Independent Chapel was the red brick building in Church Street (*illustrated on page 203*), built in 1778 on the site of a smaller chapel dating from 1662. It was a fine building with a three-decker pulpit and seats for 450 people. Its first minister was William Godwin, later to be the husband of Mary Wollstonecraft and father of Mary Shelley (author of Frankenstein). It was at Ware that Godwin met the Presbyterian minister and poet Joseph Fawcett, whom he identified as one of his four 'principal oral instructors' – and from then on Godwin turned more and more to radical politics and writing novels. Following his departure, in 1788 a dissenting group left the chapel and started Sunday Lecture Meetings in the Ware home of Richard Gridley. In 1811 successors of this group formed a Congregational Church and a Congregational Chapel was built in the High Street in 1816, and considerably rebuilt in 1859 in the Norman style (now Leaside Church). Despite the tendency of Independents to split over matters of doctrine, they remained a strong presence in Ware, supported by some important families like the Flacks who resided in the Manor House and, in the nineteenth century by Joseph Chuck of Widbury House. The original chapel in Church Street was closed in 1918 and then became, successively, a venue for private parties and pantomimes, a Masonic hall, the United Services Club, an auction room and – finally – a printing works from the 1980s on.[10]

Joseph Fawcett merits a mention in his own right for in his time he was a national celebrity. After attending Mr French's school at Ware, he entered the Daventry Theological Academy along with his schoolmaster's son, Barron French, whose sister he afterwards married. In 1785 he revived the Sunday evening lecture at the Old Jewry meeting-house in London where he became the most fashionable preacher of his day, attracting 'the largest and most genteel London audience that ever assembled in a dissenting place of worship'.[11]

Meanwhile, throughout the 1700s, St. Mary's continued as the Parish Church of Ware under a succession of mostly absentee vicars and eccentric curates. The living had been in the gift of Trinity College, Cambridge, since the time of Henry VIII and was normally bestowed upon Fellows of the college who had already developed interests outside parish affairs. Besides, the stipend was a modest one and needed to be supplemented by other occupations. David Humphreys (vicar 1730-40) had been the secretary of the Society for the Propagation of the Gospel since 1716 and worked hard to raise the society's income (he also became Vicar of Thundridge from 1732). William Webster (1740-58) was a voluminous writer, chiefly on theological subjects, but died in abject poverty, despite also being vicar of Thundridge and South Mimms. Thomas Francklin (1759-1770), playwright, poet and friend of Dr. Johnson, held Ware in conjunction with the lectureship of St Paul's, Covent Garden, and a proprietary chapel in Queen Street, London, as well as being a chaplain to the king and, through the influence of Sir Joshua Reynolds, chaplain of the Royal Academy. His successor, John White (1771-1781), was an ordinary parish priest but he was succeeded by William Hughes (1781-1790), a fine musician and canon of Worcester Cathedral. Hughes' main claim to fame was the sermon he preached in Ware in 1788, proving that there was no theological foundation for slavery and that slavery in the West Indies ought to be abolished. The anti-slavery campaigner, Thomas Clarkson, wrote that because of this sermon Hughes was enrolled as an honorary member of the Committee for the Abolition of the Slave Trade – the trade was eventually abolished in 1807.[12] The longest-serving but most absentee of all the Georgian clergy was Henry

St. Mary's in the 18th century, seen from the north and looking much as it does today, except that many of the gravestones have been moved to the edge of the churchyard.

Allen Lagden (1790-1832), vicar of both Ware and Thundridge and Rector of Weston Colville, Cambridgeshire. Apart from preaching a law-and-order sermon to the Ware Volunteers in August 1799 – in which he attacked the pacifist opinions of the Quakers – Lagden made little impression on the parish. From 1820 onwards he left the running of the parish to his curate, the Revd. James Britton (about whom more later). One other curate worth a mention is John Trusler, who leafleted every parish in England and Ireland with his offer of 150 sermons at a shilling each to save clergy the effort.

The affairs of the church were left to the churchwardens, who were usually maltsters or maltfactors. St. Mary's would have looked different from today's church. The walls and columns were not cream-coated as they have been since the 1960s and still bore evidence of painted figures and texts from the Creed and Lord's Prayer. A massive balcony covered most of the North Transept, built to accommodate the Christ's Hospital children from Bluecoat Yard. They left the town in 1761 but the balcony remained. Most work in the church concentrated on the arrangement of box pews, which were rented with the most expensive at the front near the pulpit. When a storm in November 1703 blew in the south transept window, the churchwardens took the opportunity of the repairs to construct themselves a new churchwardens' pew near the south door. The row over who should pay for this and whether a new ninepenny rate could be levied on the town rumbled on for some months.[13] Nothing much would change in the Parish Church until the beginning of Queen Victoria's reign – and then change would be fiercely resisted and argued over, including in the pages of the National Press.

18.
Malt and the Malt Tax

By the second half of the eighteenth century, Ware had become an important contributor to the British economy. It was not just that Ware was now the main supplier of pale and brown malt to the brewers of London. In fact, the town's maltsters paid more than any other town in malt tax, and the malt tax was a major source of national revenue in a period when Britain had to pay for wars against the Spanish, French and the American colonies in the War of Independence. As the historian Peter Mathias noted: "drinking to the success of British armies and navies during the eighteenth century was thus a meaningful act quite apart from the ritual of salutation.[1]

There had been a duty on beer since 1643 and its proceeds went some way to financing the Civil War. A similar duty on malt had been considered for many years and was finally introduced in 1697 at the height of war against France. Some people maintained that in the interests of social justice the beer duty should have been abolished at the same time. To avoid the problem of surveying private houses, people making malt for family consumption were allowed to compound for a modest annual figure. Commercial maltsters, like those in Ware, had to pay a duty of $6^{16}/_{21}$d. (six and sixteen-twenty-firsts pence) per bushel. As Britain found itself engaged in later wars, the malt duty was increased to 9¼d. per bushel in 1760, to 1s.4¼d. in 1780, to 1s.7¾d. in 1791 and to a phenomenal 4s.5¾d. in 1803 during the Napoleonic War, reduced to 2s.5d. in 1816 after the Battle of Waterloo. Malt and corn were always measured by their volume rather than weight – a bushel (roughly 0.036 cubic metres) was the standard measure and there were eight bushels to a quarter. A contemporary manuscript reported that in 1788 there were 33 maltings in Ware, employing 70 men and producing 1,370 quarters of malt per week during the season (October to March). That is a great deal of malt on its way to London, and represents 372,640 bushels during the season and an annual payment of malt duty by the Ware maltsters of £25,230. That was quite a considerable sum for a small town, not counting what it contributed in land tax, beer duty or duties on coal, brandy, etc. Since the total national excise revenue was only £6.75 million – there was no Income Tax until the end of the century – the Ware maltsters would have been providing something like 0.37 % of the national revenue. Every 350th frigate, or Hussite mercenary, or musket, or grenade in the war against the Americans and French was paid for by the Ware malt tax. According to the trade directories, the Ware maltsters were paying £120,000 in duty in 1838 and £200,000 in 1869.

These figures go some way to explaining the seriousness with which the Government took the events in Ware of 1787-88. Liability for the malt duty was made on the basis of measurements made by the Excise before the germination process began – excisemen would go to the malthouse of a licensed maltster and measure the piled up barley with their rules and gauges. To combat cheating, particularly hiding or compressing the barley, strict regulations were introduced throughout the century. By the end of the century there were getting on for 100 different rules and penalties, with the result that there was a continual struggle between Excise officers enforcing the law and cunning maltsters finding ways of evading the regulations to produce a proportion of duty-fee malt.

In 1787, a new Supervisor of the Excise, named Robert Grand, arrived in Ware and immediately tried to enforce the regulations by taking maltsters to court. His first efforts were a failure, because the magistrates at the Hertford Quarter Sessions (who no doubt had their own interests in the industry) threw out all of Grand's prosecutions. "This conduct of the officers made them obnoxious to the people," reported two of the local gentry, "who have hallooed and hooted them but never assaulted or obstructed them in the execution of their duty".[2] On the 24 September 1788, Grand and two of his excisemen, one of them named Veal, went to inspect the malting stock of a man called Worrall and were hooted by a crowd that had gathered. Grand took fright and called in a troop of cavalry, insisting that he should have an armed guard when he went into the Bull Inn to meet the maltsters assembled there. A commotion ensued. The town constables refused to issue warrants against the maltsters and demanded of the cavalry commander by whose authority he had come into the town. He answered that he had come at the request of Supervisor Grand. Alarm then spread throughout the town with the result that only four of the 33 maltings were in operation. The Vicar and the two Nonconformist ministers organised a petition which they passed to the county gentry and Members of Parliament. Eventually, the case came before the Chancellor of the Exchequer, William Pitt, who resolved the matter by removing Robert Grand from Ware. And no wonder. Under Pitt both as Chancellor and Prime Minister a few years later, the malt tax accounted for a quarter of the total national exchequer.

The London brewers favoured Hertfordshire malts, especially Ware Brown, and so towards the end of the eighteenth century did the Excise. In Ware, Hertford and Bishop's Stortford, the barley was steeped in a cistern and then laid on the malting floor, where it was turned but never wetted again. This method was suitable for barley grown on the light soils of Hertfordshire and East Anglia. Barleys grown from heavier soils in other parts of the country were reluctant to germinate and yield up their enzymes, with the result that the maltster would wet or sprinkle the grains after a few days on the malting floor to spur on germination. This the excisemen disliked. It made it possible for an unscrupulous maltster to add newly-sprinkled barley to the stock which had already been gauged for tax purposes. And so in 1802, an Act of Parliament was passed favouring the Hertfordshire method and prohibiting the sprinkling of barley already assessed. It caused uproar. Protest meetings and petitions were held in the West Country, the Midlands and south of the Thames. A permanent committee of maltsters from these parts lobbied Parliament, which set up its own investigation. Despite witnesses from the Excise, Hertfordshire, Cambridgeshire and Essex, the prohibition was scrapped and in 1806 sprinkling was again permitted after a certain number of days had elapsed.[3]

One great advantage the Ware and Hertfordshire maltsters had over their rivals was the friendly and family relationships they enjoyed with the major brewers of London. Many of the latter came from Hertfordshire anyway – the Dickinsons from Ware, Sir William Calvert and Felix Calvert from Furneaux Pelham, Ralph and Henry Thrale from St. Albans. When Henry Thrale died in 1771 and left the Anchor Brewery in Southwark on the verge of bankruptcy, Mrs Thrale was left to pick up the pieces with the help of Dr. Johnson. Promptly, Mrs Hankin, the mother of a Ware maltfactor, loaned Mrs Thrale the sum of £6,000. A little later, David Barclay of Youngsbury at Wadesmill, went into partnership with the brewer's manager and bought out Mrs Thrale to form the brewery company of Barclay, Perkins & Co.

One of the closest relationships was that between the brewer, Sampson Hanbury – who incidentally was married to David Barclay's granddaughter – and the Hertfordshire maltsters. Sampson Hanbury acquired an interest in the Black Eagle Brewery in Brick Lane, Spitalfields, in 1780 on the death of Sir Benjamin Truman, and in 1789 assumed full control with the Truman family as sleeping partners. In 1800, probably because of his wife's connections with the area, Sampson Hanbury took out a lease on Poles, a large country house on the Ware side of Thundridge,

Sampson Hanbury of Poles

and in 1820 bought the house and lived there until his death in 1835. Sampson and his wife had no children so the house – and a partnership in the brewery – went to his nephew, Robert Hanbury. In the meantime, in 1808 Sampson had taken into partnership another nephew, Thomas Fowell Buxton, the son of his sister Anna. This Buxton, who later became an M.P. and was associated with William Wilberforce in the campaign to abolish the slave trade, gave his name to the firm which then became known as Truman, Hanbury, Buxton & Co. His son, another Thomas Fowell Buxton, bought the Easnye estate at Stanstead Abbots while the Hanburys continued to live at Poles. The firm were mainly porter brewers and Sampson Hanbury bought his brown malt from Ware – though increasingly the pale malt came from elsewhere in East Anglia – all the while acting through the skilled intermediaries known as maltfactors.

Maltfactors were the key middlemen in the brewer/maltster relationships of the late eighteenth century. They gained an important role because the London brewers now required large quantities of malt and could not produce this themselves in London. So the factors collected samples from a number of maltings, delivered these to the brewers, held stocks of malt, distributed payment, granted credit and – in many cases – delivered the malt to London in their own barges. Sampson Hanbury employed three main factors: in Ware there was William Adams, in Bishop's Stortford John Taylor, and in Essex and the rest of East Anglia John Kemp. John Taylor was the son of Samuel Taylor, a barge-owner and maltster who had bought a small property beside Ware Bridge in 1786, about the same time John had moved to Stortford with the opening up of the Stort Navigation. These Taylors were ancestors of the prominent Sawbridgeworth firm of maltsters, H.A.& D. Taylor Ltd. The main point here is that John Taylor's relationship with Sampson Hanbury went beyond business affairs. They were close personal friends and Taylor would visit Hanbury's inlaws, the Gurney family, whenever he visited Norfolk.[4] William Adams was a member of the family which was prominent in barge-owning, malting and later banking in the town for over a hundred years. In 1809, William was the main factor for the new Meux Reid brewery and in the summer of 1814 was holding stock of malt in Ware valued at £22,000.[5]

A little later similar friendships existed between another Ware maltster, Edward Chuck, and members of the Courage and Whitbread families to whose breweries he supplied malt. Edward Chuck was godfather to Edward Courage, who joined the Courage Brewery in Southwark in 1854 and later became a partner. And when Edward Chuck died, W.H. Whitbread, head of the brewery in Chiswell Street in the City of London, came down to Ware to attend the funeral.[6] The life of Edward Chuck (1783-1852) well illustrates the steps by which many Ware maltsters rose to prominence, progressing through family links and business opportunities, some of which must have seemed dead ends at the time. His grandfather had been a publican who was engaged in maltmaking in a small way and his father a maltster. Edward's wife, Elizabeth, also came from a Ware malting family. But malting was not Edward's only or even his main occupation at first. From 1819 until 1826, he was a partner in the Ware Bank with George Cass, his father-in-law, and John Cass, his brother-in-law. For much of the same period he was a partner with Thomas Meakin and John King in a wholesale lead and glass business in London. He seems to have owned a lead mine and, in later years, he was an active farmer in the four farmsteads he owned to the north of Ware. The one in which he lived, Noah's Ark Farm, may well have been named after Edward's hobby of breeding superior livestock. Before Aline Burgess did research into her family of Collins (related to the Chuck, Page and Croft families), Edward Chuck was not fully recognised as the important maltster he was. Now it can be seen that he was a vital piece in the jigsaw of relationships between the pioneering maltsters of the eighteenth century and the large-scale, industrial maltsters of the nineteenth. The memorial in St. Mary's to his inlaws, the Cass family, shows that George Cass senior, 'Late of this Town, Maltfactor' died in 1826, aged 74 years, while Edward's successor – and relative by marriage – Henry Page, died in 1892, leaving more than a million pounds, all earned from making malt. Edward Chuck left his mark on the town in many ways, some of which will be explored later. The colourful east window of St. Mary's was a memorial to his parents while his own memorial (apart from the tomb in the old burial ground off Church Street) was the grammar school his widow built at the top of Musley Hill. He also lived in and greatly expanded No. 87 High Street (now Ware Library) which later became the home of Henry Page and his daughter, Mrs Elizabeth Page Croft.

Competition in Malt and Beer

We must interrupt the historical sequence to stay with the malting industry. As the nineteenth century progressed, the dominant position of Ware malt with the big common brewers of London was threatened from many sides. The entry for Ware in Pigot's Directory for 1832 could state "most of the London breweries are supplied from this town" but things were changing fast. There was fiercer competition from the maltsters of Norfolk and Suffolk, who took their malt to the Port of London by ship, and from those of Kingston-on-Thames and farther west, who shipped their malt to the capital by barge. Norfolk and Kingston Pale malts could now compete in both quality and price with the best Hertfordshire Pale. Matters were made worse by a rapid succession of other factors: the slump in grain prices following the end of the wars with France, the Beer Act of 1830 (which abolished the duty on beer but did not affect the malt tax) and the repeal of the Corn Laws which allowed barley imports from France, Denmark and Germany. These factors greatly increased the competition for the types of malt used in brewing pale ale, but Ware Brown malt for porter brewing was still holding its own. The reason is that the Ware maltsters and the London porter brewers had a classic symbiotic relationship. The brewers required their Hertfordshire suppliers to make malt, in which germinating barley produced an acrospire of only a half to three-quarters the length of the grain – the London brewers because of their efficient production were able to extract more sugar from this 'short-grown malt', so that is what they ordered. In Newark in the Trent Valley and other parts of Britain away from Hertfordshire, the germinating barley was allowed to develop an acrospire from three-quarters to the whole length of the grain. They achieved this by liberal sprinkling of the grains and this gave them a greater degree of modification of the starch into sugar.[7] The Ware maltsters and their backers castigated the others for 'forcing' – the Newark maltsters, on the other hand, knew a thing or two that the Ware maltsters were unaware of.

The danger came not from Newark but from farther up the valley at Burton-on-Trent. Even before the coming of the railways, the relatively small brewing industry of Burton had made its mark on the worldwide economy through its production of India Pale Ale for export via the port of Liverpool. IPA was a brew quite different from London porter: it was a heavily-hopped, strong and bitter pale ale, well able to keep its strength which was necessary in view of the long sea voyage to India. The water of Burton was found to be particularly good for IPA. There soon developed a British market for IPA which received an enormous boost with the arrival of the railways. Having a brewery only a few horse-drawn miles from its customers was no longer vital. As Burton firms, like Bass and Allsop, expanded, breweries in other parts of the country with water similar to Burton's started making their own versions of IPA. However, the London brewers did not have this advantage and so began to open their own breweries in Burton. From 1835 to 1870, most of the London porter brewers – including Truman, Hanbury and Buxton – opened their own brewhouses at Burton. But that was not the only change. As brewers around the country competed with the IPA of Burton so they produced variations of it. Pale ales became less heavily-hopped, with a lighter, brighter appearance and more sparkle. They had a shorter life and were supplied in bottles. Thus porter now had two rivals: India Pale Ale from Burton and bottled Light Ale from many different locations.[8]

These were major threats to the dominance of Ware Brown malt and they provoked widespread change. Throughout the town, older and often small, one-man malthouses were demolished and replaced with brick maltings of two or three floors, with larger kilns. Many of these new maltings were designed for the production of high quality pale malts and they had kilns fired by coal or anthracite rather than wood, but brown malt was also being produced – there was still a market for it. It was a period of technological innovation. Ware had long had a modest engineering industry: from the seventeenth century onwards Welsh ironmasters had seen the sense in having a base within easy reach of London by river. Now, in the late 1830s, with the arrival of the railways, engineering know-how was put into the service of the malting industry. One of the innovators was Charles Wells, with premises behind Nos.49-51 High Street, which in earlier times had been the Bear Inn and earlier still the Falcon. According to an illustrated feature in *The Pictorial Record* of January 1899, the Falcon Works was started by Charles Wells over a century earlier and carried on by him until his death in about 1860, when it was acquired by A.J. Goodfellow. It was an extensive works, with a large smith's shop, five fires, a farriers' shop "for shoeing horses on scientific principles", an engineering shop with steam-driven plant, a foundry and a wire-working department. The feature continued

> this latter forms one of the chief specialities of the business, and in almost every malt-producing county Messrs. A.J. Goodfellow & Co.'s malt kiln wire floors are widely used; the same applying to their own malting cowls. They have made a study of this class of work and have now a wide-spread reputation for it. In addition to the home trade, a good deal of work in this line is also done for export.

In earlier periods, kiln floors had been made of wood, of wrought-iron bars or ceramic tiles. The Wells-Goodfellow innovation was to produce floors with a fine wire mesh, suspended on wrought-iron rods running laterally across the building and held tense by wrought-iron tie-plates on the outside of the kiln. In Ware these tie-plates have the distinction of bearing the manufacturer's name, Charles Wells, the Goodfellow family and other names of smiths from Ware and Hertford. The recording and rescue of these tie-plates was a special interest of the late Michael Ottley who gave a number to the Ware Museum. Because these technologically new malt-kilns could stand very high temperatures, it was more necessary than ever that the kiln fumes and steam should be evacuated as rapidly as possible to prevent the danger of fire. Hence the work of the Falcon Works on their own malting cowls, which were of conical shape and able to swivel away from the wind and thus prevent any blow-back. A typical set of these malting cowls, and also of wire floors and tie-plates, is found in the three parallel malthouses in New Road and Kibes Lane. The new cowls were a great improvement on older ones of a 'mortar-board' design.

Malting as an Industry

The second half of the nineteenth century saw great changes in the malting industry in Ware. The prosperity of Victorian Britain and its Empire around the world meant there was a growing market for beer and ale of all varieties, and consequently for malt. New people entered the business, some with the capital and connections immediately to become maltsters, others chancing their luck and smaller resources after an apprenticeship as a steersman or barge-owner. In 1869 it was estimated that the population of the town had grown to nearly 7,000 and Ware contained "the largest malting establishments in the world" with an annual production of nearly two million bushels.[9] By 1880 there were well over a hundred malthouses in the town, many with more than one kiln. Every spare plot of land had been taken over by maltkilns, coloured as a sea of pink on one copy of the 1880 Ordnance Survey Map. Gradually these kilns were passing into the control of a handful of major malting families. The Post Office Directory of 1862 listed the main maltsters as John and Samuel Adams on Musley Hill, Charles Cass and Joseph and Silas Chuck in Baldock Street, John Cowell in Crib Street, James Collyer, William Hudson, Henry Page, George Thorowgood, Isaac Waller and Samuel Wright, all in the High Street and Henry Edward Green in Star Street. By 1882, John Adams and John Cowell were still working, joined by two other single maltsters, Caleb Hitch in Star Street and Thomas Chapman in New Road – but all the others were now malting companies – Thoday Ingle Few & Co. in Baldock Street, Chidley, Phillips & Co. in New Road, Croft & Co., Joseph Gripper & Sons, Hudson & Ward and Henry Page & Co., in High Street. The Gripper family were originally Quakers who had taken over the Dickinson family's malthouses in New Road/Kibes Lane in the 1830s. The firm of Hudson & Ward was the result of a marriage between two dynasties but sadly their offspring and hope for the future, Henry Hudson Ward, was killed fighting in the South African war as a cavalry lieutenant in February 1902 (his name is on the memorial in St. Mary's).

The greatest of these malting entrepreneurs was Henry Page. His father had been a part-time maltster, corn-dealer and baker in Churchgate House (Jacoby's Restaurant) in West Street. It was later well-known as the bakery of Jagg's and Edward's. In the 1830s, Henry married Anne Collins, the niece of maltster Edward Chuck, and on Edward's death in 1852 he acquired most of his uncle-in-law's malthouses. It was a contentious sharing out of the family assets which saw other maltings going to Joseph Chuck and his son, Silas. The dispute may have had something to do with religion, for the late Edward Chuck, his sister Susanna Collins and nephew-in-law, Henry Page (who had begun life as a Quaker) were all faithful members of St. Mary's, the Parish Church, while Joseph Chuck was a member and benefactor of the Congregational Church (Leaside).

Henry Page was a skilled maltster and a first-rate businessman. Despite losing one fortune in the collapse of Samuel Adams's Ware Bank in 1856, he went on building his business and rising up the social scale. In its heyday, the firm of Henry Page & Co. owned forty maltings in Ware and Hertford. One clue to his success is the story told in the autobiography of his grandson, Henry Page Croft (Lord Croft) – travelling up to London by train with Henry Page, a young colleague suggested he take the rugs with which they covered their knees to the left-luggage at Liverpool Street, but Page said no, they should 'pop them' in a local pawn shop because that was a few pence cheaper.[10] Henry and Anne lived first at 87 High Street, Edward Chuck's old house, with the offices of Henry Page & Co. next door at 85. Later they acquired two grander residences on the outskirts of the town – Great Cozens and nearby Fanhams Hall, which their daughter, Anne Elizabeth Croft, later enlarged into a stately home. In 1880, the Liberal government announced abolition of the malt tax which did not please Henry Page one bit. On 16 July 1880, he wrote the letter quoted opposite:

Henry Page (1813-1894)

To The Right Honourable W.E. Gladstone,
Chancellor of the Exchequer and First Lord of the Treasury

Honourable Sir,

This morning I have read in *The Times* paper "that it was for those who desired a continuance of the Duty on ready-made Malt imported into the United Kingdom, to shew cause for it, as the Duty on Malt was being abolished." May I, Sir, say a few words on this subject?

I for one, Sir, strongly object to the total withdrawal of that Import Duty. The Maltsters ought to have some security of the value of their maltings. I have under the supervision of the Excise Officers, and in entire accordance with the Law at the time, in constructing my maltings, been put to great expense which I should not have incurred had not that Law been in force. I think I ought to claim some sort of remuneration knowing as I did, that the Import Duty on foreign Malt gave me some security on building and buying Maltings to the extent of forty, which I hold in the town of Ware. I believe that single-handed I pay more Duty than any other Maltster.

I should, Sir, have applied to my friend the Honourable Henry Cowper for his assistance in this matter but did not know whether he was in England, and I feared to lose time.

I am Honoured Sir,
Always yours faithfully and obediently,
(Signed) Henry Page [11]

The reply of Mr. Gladstone is not known, but abolition of the malt tax changed the face of maltmaking in Ware. Henry Page & Co. soon closed many of their 40 malthouses and invested in larger, industrialised buildings. The biggest of these was the Victoria Malting, named after Queen Victoria's Golden Jubilee in 1887: it burned down in 1906 and was replaced a year later by a bigger Victoria Malting which survived until it too – vacant and naturally ripe for redevelopment – burned down in a spectacular blaze in 1988. Henry Page himself died in 1894, leaving to his wife and daughter personal wealth and property valued at £1,037,698. The malting company was then controlled by his son-in-law, Lieutenant Richard Benyon Croft RN (ret'd).

19.
Before the Railway came

T he first part of the nineteenth century continued the easy-going, *laissez-faire*, business-as-usual world of the eighteenth century, especially when compared with the shocks and innovations that greeted people in the 1830s. Then almost everything – religion, business, local government, fashions, shopping, education – began to change. The changes were a foretaste of the reforming age brought in with the reign of the slim young daughter of the late Duke of Kent as Queen Victoria. But to many contemporaries, the symbol of the new era of change was the coming of the railways – as James Smith put it, "at that time no railways had disturbed the even tenor of our lives". James Smith spent his childhood in Ware, progressed through the editorship of the *County Press* in Hertford to magazine contributions and literary readings in London and then emigrated to Melbourne in Australia, from where he sent back colourful reminiscences of Hertfordshire life as he remembered it. The following extracts are from "An English Country Town in 1835".[1]

A long and sinuous street, which made an abrupt turn to the westward after it had crossed the crazy old bridge, with a tollhouse upon it, connecting it with Amwell End, and then made a northerly bend near the church, constituted the backbone of the town. On the south side of it, from the Saracen's Head to the corner of the Priory grounds, abutting upon Mill-lane, every house had been formerly a hostelry, with a large gateway giving access to a spacious courtyard, at the end of which was a pleasure-garden, terminating at the River Lea; looking out upon which was a Dutch summer-house, where, in the old times, when all the traffic on the road was performed by pack horses, and the place was the limit of the first day's journey to the north, weary travellers used to sit and quaff the 'old October', for which the place was celebrated, and bestowed upon it such endearing epithets as 'angels' food', 'merry-go-down', 'dragon's milk', or 'the balm of barleycorn'. But at the time of which I speak, these inns had been transformed into private residences, and their capacious stabling into malthouses, and only one – the Bull – remained faithful to its original uses, and still retained its ancient shape, with tiers of galleries flanking the paved entrance, and a little glazed sentry-box on the right hand side of the gateway, commanding the long vista of the yard, where some scores of horses were stabled, both for coaching and posting purposes. The landlady was an institution – a strong-minded elderly spinster with a cast in her eye and the most masculine business qualifications – a capital judge of horse flesh, and gifted with an instinctive perception of the precise amount of courtesy to be exhibited to guests of all grades, from a prince of the royal blood, down to a bagman. Nobody ever spoke of her otherwise than Fanny Brown; just as nobody knew anything but the christian names of the head ostler and the head chambermaid.

Fanny Brown was the daughter of Randall Brown who had owned the Bull in 1823 and she was quite a character. Edith Hunt quoted an entertaining incident from the *Haileybury Observer*, when the young Queen Victoria passed through Ware in 1843 and expected to receive a loyal address, while the horses of her carriage were being changed at the Bull, but instead was given a basket of grapes by Miss Brown. Soon afterwards the Bull was demolished – a Victorian house in the Gothic style was built on the site with maltings in the inn-yard. This house was demolished in 1953 when a spacious, new Post Office was constructed (now a building society) with the former malting converted to a sorting office. These changes are commemorated in two plaques (*illustrated right*), one saying in Latin that the Black Bull was revived or restored in 1848 and the second that it was revived yet again in 1953. With the demolition of the Bull, its most famous artefact, the Great Bed, was sold to the landlord of the Saracen's Head where it remained until 1870. The only hostelry now on the south side of Ware High Street is the Tap Bar, which during Smith's childhood was the private residence of a curate at St. Mary's.

James Smith was an admirer of Charles Dickens (he claimed to have been the first person to give a public reading of *A Christmas Carol*) and delighted in the eccentric characters of Ware in the 1830s.

> Our school was close by the grand old church – so close that we could chivy 'Polly Gull's greyhounds' – the inmates of the female charity school inside the churchyard – round its paths, when they and we came out at 12 o'clock, to their extreme terror, and our commensurate delight. But they had a valiant protector in the person of Lawrence, the beadle, whom we hated, as in duty bound. One of his organs of vision was immovable, and had a fixed stony stare, and therefore we christened him 'Chany Eye'. We led him a miserable life, I am afraid. We waylaid him in all sorts of unsuspected ambushes. We sprang upon him from secret nooks and corners. We practised ventriloquism for the sake of calling out 'Chany Eye' from positions where no enemy was visible; and, as we were fleet of foot, and he was gouty, we provoked him to pursue us, and mocked at his discomfiture. If ever wicked young scape-graces deserved to be eaten alive by bears, I am sure we did …
>
> Every two or three years a company of strolling players visited the place, and set up their stage and paraphernalia in the long room of the French Horn – a tolerably spacious apartment, with a row of stables underneath, and pervaded occasionally by a fragrance which was neither that of new-mown hay nor of May blossoms. I have seen *Richard the Third* performed by a company of three ladies and six gentlemen, with a Richmond who squinted abominably, and a Lady Anne who was invalided – to put it delicately – three days afterwards [she was nine-months pregnant]. The leading tragedian was the stage-struck son of a London alderman, and the low comedian was addicted to convivial habits, and did not disdain to hawk tickets from door to door for his own benefit. Shall I ever forget the blood-curdling, flesh-creeping, nerve-thrilling effect of the performance of *Thirty Years of a Gambler's Life,* or the mingled feelings of awe and admiration with which I used to look up to the chief villain of the piece, when I met him in the High-street, with a blue bloom on his cheeks and chin, and a strong suspicion of ink about the seams of his threadbare frock-coat. His hat shone, and so did his hair; and if he condescended to the common custom of wearing linen, he carefully concealed it, which was not difficult when men wore flowing black-satin stocks, like that depicted by Maclise in his early portrait of Charles Dickens.[2]

The school that James Smith attended was the Free Grammar School, situated on the edge of the churchyard in what is now Tudor Square. It was a timber-framed Tudor building and the lower floor was let to a neighbouring brewer to store his beer. A later pupil, the bootmaker John Rogers, recalled that in his time the school was in such bad repair that the boys were able to pull up the floor boards of their classroom and go down to the beer cellar for a tipple. Smith wrote that his teacher was "the rector" (he meant the curate) who would leave the class every morning punctually at 11 o'clock to read the London newspapers as they were delivered to the Town Hall. This curate was the Rev. J. Britton, who ran the parish in place of the absentee vicar, Mr. Lagden. In another story – part of a novel he entitled *Ralph Penfold: An Autobiography* – Smith gave a fuller description of the curate and his household:

> Slightly bald, with bright humorous eyes, a full rich voice, a peculiarly winning smile, and a dignified yet easy carriage, he would have become a decanal stall or a bishop's throne. He had married a lady of good family, with no other portion than the extravagant habits acquired during a spoiled childhood, and an entire ignorance of household duties. At the time of which I write a large family was growing up around her; the children were as wild as colts; the household in a condition of chronic disorder, and Burly [Britton] hopelessly in debt. The Vicarage seemed to be the refuge for such slovenly, slatternly and saucy servants as were ineligible for situations elsewhere. There were no fixed hours for meals, and while breakfast might be proceeding in the study, luncheon in the dining room and dinner in the nursery, discomfort was universal. The cook was addicted to ardent spirits and to running against such solid and projecting objects as were calculated to occasion contusions of the eye; the housemaid was subject to fits, which always came on when there was company expected; and the nursery governess, having eighteen months salary in arrears, was the victim of low spirits and sullenness.[3]

The Town Hall to which the curate absconded to read the papers was of recent construction. It was built in 1827, on the site of the Tudor market-hall, as an arcaded cornmarket with assembly rooms above. It was built by public subscription on the assumption that, since Ware was the main user of wheat and barley, the corn merchants ought to sell their produce in a Ware market rather than in Hertford. But the move failed – no doubt because the Marquess of Salisbury backed Hertford's claim – and soon afterwards the cornmarket was sold as a shop. In the later part of the nineteenth century, it was the butchers' shop of the Stallabrass family and is now an estate agent.

The Great Reform Bill

In "An English Country Town in 1835" Smith wrote that Ware was solidly Whig. "We were all Radicals in those days, partly because we did not possess the franchise, and partly because the neighbouring town of Hertford, which did, was thoroughly Conservative." As well as enjoying the patronage of the Marquess of Salisbury and the Cecil family at Hatfield House, Hertford had two Members of Parliament of its own. The borough franchise had been revived in 1621 and the vote was exercised not only by Freemen of the Borough, but also by the "inhabitants". There were at most 500 electors in Hertford Borough (and slightly fewer in St. Albans, which also had a borough franchise) while in Hertfordshire as a whole there were some 4,000 voters who elected the two county MPs. 'Rotten boroughs' like Hertford would have been swept away in a Bill introduced in Parliament in 1831 by Lord John Russell, but it failed to gain a majority. The king (William IV) called an election and Hertford returned two Whigs, both in favour of reform (the county MPs were also Whigs). There was now a majority for reform in the House of Commons and the Reform Bill was passed on 4 June 1832. Another general election was called in December and this time the Tories, with the backing of the Cecil family, were determined to win back the Hertford seats. This election was described in a second article James Smith sent to the *Hertfordshire Mercury* from Australia, entitled "An English Election in the Old Times".

> I think there were only 400 or 500 voters out of a population of many thousands. Some of these enjoyed the privilege as burgesses, and others as 'pot-wallopers'. The former were, as a general rule, reputable people belonging to the trades and professions, while the latter included some of the worst elements of society, the scum and feculence of the place. They mostly inhabited a low and grimy quarter of the town, called Butchery-green [now 'Bircherley Green']. As it contained neither a slaughter-house nor a blade of grass, the appropriateness of its appellation was somewhat questionable. Chimney-sweeps, bargemen, tramps, poachers, rag and bottle gatherers, and people whose means of livelihood were as dubious as their characters, congregated in this neighbourhood, which had for one of its boundaries the river Lea. The pot-wallopers of Butchery-green were a political power in the borough. They could turn any election, and they were quite conscious of their importance.[4]

To cultivate the "pot-wallopers", the Tories laid on a sumptuous supper in a large empty granary in Butchery-green, popularly known as 'Rats' Castle'. Since voting then was not secret and took place over a number of days, drunken voters were brought from the Rats' Castle and helped to the polling station, propped up on either side, while the poll-clerks recorded their votes.

> At the close of the poll it proved that Rats' Castle had achieved the victory. The town was wild with excitement. It was once more filled, at the declaration of the poll, with the roughs from the country districts, and with the 'bargees' from Ware and Amwell End. The elation of triumph animated the former to taunt their opponents, and the exasperation of defeat provoked the latter to violent resentment, so that the place was again the scene of some hard fighting in the streets …

The two Tory candidates were elected – only to be unseated by a parliamentary inquiry in 1833 on the grounds that the result had been achieved through bribery and corruption. As a result, Hertford remained without representation in Parliament until the General Election of 1835. Then it again sent two MPs to Parliament until 1867, when its representation was reduced to one. It finally lost this right in 1885 and was included in the county constituency. Despite the Whigs' defeat, James Smith sensed there was a bigger victory.

> But throughout the length and breadth of the country, Toryism, Protection, and class legislation had received a death blow, and, not many weeks afterwards, 4,000 people sat down to dinner in the high street of a neighbouring town to celebrate the passing of the Reform Bill which changed the history of England.

An engraving of the Reform Bill dinner in Ware High Street. Despite its strange sense of perspective, the engraving shows the Market Place with all its contemporary buildings, including the 1827 cornmarket and the orginal jettied front of the French Horn Inn.

That town was Ware. The dinner held in the High Street for 4,000 people on 25 July 1832 was later celebrated in an engraving by John Stribling (*above*). One other result of the Hertford election was that one of the defeated Whig candidates, Tom Duncombe, founded a radical newspaper to agitate for an extension of the borough franchise to include Ware and Hoddesdon. The newspaper was known as *The Hertford and Ware Patriot*, and later *The Reformer*, but on the masthead of the first two editions it is called *The Ware Patriot*.

Another sign of the strong Reformist, Liberal character of Ware was the arrival in 1840 of the Oddfellows. They were a 'friendly society' combining many benefits for members, including those of sick and unemployment clubs. To give it its full name the 'Loyal Lord Brougham Lodge of the Manchester Unity Independent Order of Odd Fellows' met first at the Crown Inn in Stanstead Abbots, then in various Ware inns and after 1920 in the Priory. All of its records and the magnificent ceremonial banner (now restored) are in the Ware Museum. Incidentally, Lord Brougham was Lord Chancellor in the Whig government and played an important role in persuading the House of Lords to pass the 1832 Reform Act. The Oddfellows were followed in Ware by other friendly societies, such as the Ancient Order of Foresters (who met in the French Horn) and the Royal Antediluvian Order of Buffaloes, but the local lodges of these societies no longer function. On the other hand, the Ware Lodge of the Freemasons established in 1904 and the Rotary Club of Ware founded in the 1930s are still going strong.

Dissension in the Pews

Smith concluded his first article about Ware in the 1830s by describing unrest in the pews of the Parish Church. The "whist-playing, scholarly, easy-going rector" (Henry Allen Lagden) died and

> a Puseyite was appointed in his place, who preached in a white surplice, turned round to the Communion table when he recited the Belief, and otherwise offended the congregation, one-third of whom rose and left the church Sunday after Sunday as he ascended the pulpit stairs. Then the dissidents seceded in a body, and conducted divine service in the Town Hall; and so the town was split up into two factions.[5]

As church disputes go, this was really a long-running feud and, at one stage, it involved the Archbishop of Canterbury, the Bishop of London and the national Press. But it may not have been exactly as James Smith told it. The new vicar's "Puseyite" practices may not have offended his flock, so much as his politics and determination to enforce church law. Some people have suggested the group which left St. Mary's to worship in the Town Hall were forerunners of the High Church/Low Church split which led eventually to the founding of Christ Church in 1858 – but there is no evidence for that connection and it has to remain an open question. In trying to sort out what did happen, I am indebted to unpublished research carried out in the 1980s by the former Vicar of St. Mary's, Canon Hugh Wilcox.

In 1832 the new vicar was yet another Fellow of Trinity College, Cambridge – Rev. Henry Coddington. Born in Ireland, he was a man of many and varied accomplishments – a good linguist, an excellent musician and draughtsman, a skilled botanist, a student of church architecture and a first-rate scientist. He wrote a number of books on light and optics and his texts became standard material for Cambridge undergraduate studies. A 'Coddington lens' for microscopes was named after him, he was elected a fellow of the Royal Society of London in 1829 and was in the first published list of members of the British Association for the Advancement of Science in 1832. He became Vicar of Ware in December 1832. Although a Cambridge man, Coddington was undoubtedly aware of recent events at Oxford University. There a small group of High Churchmen had formed a loose association to demonstrate that the Church of England was a direct descendant of the Church founded by the Apostles – in other words, that it was 'Catholic'. They included Edward Pusey, Professor of Hebrew, John Keble and John Henry Newman, then Vicar of the University Church and later the Roman Catholic Cardinal Newman. The group were known as 'Tractarians' (after their publications, *Tracts for the Times*), as the Oxford Movement and, disparagingly, as 'Puseyites'. At first they did not go in for elaborate ritual or the wearing of vestments, but as soon as they did their critics accused them of trying to infect the Church of England with Roman Catholicism.

The first clashes between the new Vicar of Ware and part of his flock had nothing to do with 'Puseyite' practices. They took place in organisations outside the church. One of these was the Ware Charity Trustees, successors to the medieval Guild of Corpus Christi, who controlled a great deal of property, including the Free Grammar School, and the distribution of money to widows and the poor. As vicar, Coddington became one of the charity's two Collectors, the other being a veteran maltster, William Cobham. In April 1834 Coddington noted that there ought to have been a balance of £73.12s. but over a number of meetings Cobham was only able to come up with £45. Cobham resigned in 1839 and six meetings were held to find a replacement but without success. Eventually, the other trustees pressed him to take the post again which he did. Many of the people who later opposed Coddington in church affairs were fellow members of the Ware Charity Trustees.[6]

Disputes in another body, the Board of Poor Law Guardians, grew more bitter. The old Ware workhouse in Crib Street had been closed down with the passing of the Poor Law Amendment Act in 1834 and a new 'Ware Union' workhouse built in what is now Collett Road. The new building was a 'panopticon', a star-shaped arrangement of wards radiating from a central supervisors' station, similar to the panopticon prison layout, designed by the philosopher, Jeremy Bentham. We do not know when it was built or the name of the architect because the minute books from 1837 to 1845 are missing – once known as Western House, it is now converted to residential units and known as The Quadrant. The Ware Union included Broxbourne, Hoddesdon, Amwell, Stanstead Abbots and Hunsdon, and each parish appointed Guardians for a year. In 1835, those for Ware were Coddington, John Sworder (a churchwarden), William Flack (a nonconformist living in the Manor House) and the blacksmith Thomas Wells. The banker, Samuel Adams, was appointed treasurer and the solicitor Nathaniel Cobham (son of old William Cobham) was the clerk. In fact, there were numerous Cobhams among the Guardians and in 1835 a Thomas Cobham proposed Henry Cobham as Relieving Officer for the Hoddesdon Division, but this was defeated. In 1836, there was a dispute over who should represent Ware: one churchwarden proposed Coddington, John Sworder, William Cater and William Flack, while another proposed Sworder, Cater, Flack and Captain Ambrose Proctor – the radical sea captain who lived at Thunder Hall. Eventually others stood down and both Coddington and Proctor took their seats. The Vicar was assiduous in attending meetings of the Guardians and tried to make his influence felt – not always successfully. With the Vicar of Great Amwell, Rev. Mordaunt Barnard, Coddington tried to have a chaplain appointed to the workhouse but this was defeated. He was more successful in persuading the Guardians to buy Bibles and Prayer Books for the 'indoor poor', i.e. those inside Western House, rather than vagrants.

In 1837, the country was in a turmoil over the issue of whether church rates should be abolished – these were the portion of the local rates that went to the upkeep of church buildings, in other words the 'steeple taxes' that Quakers refused to pay. Twenty-five parishes in Hertfordshire had sent petitions to Parliament calling for abolition of church rates. At a meeting of the Ware Vestry to discuss a petition, the Vicar moved that the whole issue be dropped but was opposed by Nathaniel Cobham, Captain Proctor, the maltster John Cass and others. Captain Proctor them moved an amendment, stating that the Vicar's motion was "brought forward for political purposes". William Cobham accused the Vicar of acting on the orders of the Bishop of London which Coddington denied. When it came to the vote, the amendment was carried and the Vicar promptly left the chair. There was then a dispute over writing a minute of the meeting, with the Vicar refusing to sign unless the words "political purposes" were omitted. Again the Vicar was defeated and a further motion was passed, deploring the conduct of the Vicar – with only one vote against. The local press then took up the cudgels.

*The Ware Union Workhouse – later known as Western House and now converted into
residential units as 'The Quadrant'. The boardroom, right, is where the Board of
Guardians of the Ware Union held their meetings. The central station of the
'panopticon' is in the background with rooms for inmates radiating from it.
The carport is modern.*

The conservative *County Press* accused Ware of lacking loyalty, while *The Reformer* (successor
to the *Ware Patriot*) ran an editorial under the headline: *CLERICAL AGITATION, or the
Town of Ware versus the Rev. Mr. Coddington*. A few editions later, the *County Press* reported
under the headline *Frustration of Whig Manoeuvring* that Mr. Coddington had used his
popularity to have a loyal address sent to the Queen from Ware, despite the opposition of the
churchwardens, aided and abetted by the Cobham family. To this, Nathaniel Cobham replied
in a letter to *The Reformer*, protesting against the "unfounded insinuations" against his family
and adding:

> as to his (Coddington's) great popularity, the unanimous vote of censure passed upon his
> conduct in the chair, at one of the largest and most respectable vestries ever held in Ware,
> will abundantly show to what extent that assertion is true. In another instance, the Vicar had
> quarrelled with the Churchwardens because they temperately but firmly declined to collect
> for the Queen's letter in the precise manner he prescribed, and immediately after the service
> was over, he lectured them for not yielding implicit obedience to his wishes and actually
> threatened to report them to the Bishop, and has not from that hour spoken to or held any
> communication with his own churchwardens.[7]

The next move in the escalating row came in January 1840 when *The Reformer* reported
that the town had been "in a considerable state of excitement" at the news that the curate at St.
Mary's, Rev. Mr. Cobb, had been told by the Vicar that his services would be dispensed with
in March. It has been suggested that Mr. Cobb's preaching had been too evangelical for
Coddington's liking, but the Bishop of London agreed that Cobb should go. Next came an

article in *The Reformer*, over the name 'Ichneumon' (Greek for a mongoose), attacking the church rate set at a recent vestry meeting, and in particular the expenditure on the church clock, parish beadle, and "building a new window because the old one was insufficiently handsome." This was a reference to the new window in the South Transept, which replaced one damaged in an eighteenth-century storm. 'Ichneumon' continued:

> The attachment of the people of Ware to their Church is strong; to ensure its continuance it will be well to refrain from inculcating the pseudo-protestantism of Oxford at the expense of the Protestantism of the Reformation, and for the churchwardens to confine themselves strictly to such expenditure as the law alone will sanction.[8]

This was the first time the opposition had accused Coddington of 'Puseyism' or supporting the Oxford Movement or Tractarians and as yet they had not produced any evidence to support it. It is true that in his designs for the South Transept window, Coddington had included the symbol of Christ as a pelican feeding its young with its own blood. It is also true that in his ideas for the new chapel at Wareside (now Holy Trinity Church, designed by the architect Thomas Smith and consecrated in 1841), Coddington had included the ancient Roman feature of an apse. But these sprang from his study of church art and architecture, rather than any Romanising tendency, and they were not picked up by his opponents.

The first references to members of the congregation of St. Mary's deserting to other denominations and others walking out before the sermon came in October 1842. It was not Coddington who provoked the walk-out, but the new curate who had replaced Mr. Cobb. The Rev. W.W. Willock preached a sermon in which he attacked the previous Whig government for disestablishing the Anglican Church of Ireland, and showed his support for the new Tory administration which would protect the Church. There is little doubt that Mr. Willock was in tune with his vicar and Bishop Blomfield of London who, although he did not condone the ritualism of the Oxford Movement, was determined to restore some order and dignity to church affairs. Inevitably, Mr. Willock's sermon – preached both in Ware and Thundridge – came under attack in *The Reformer*, which attacked his "political allusions of the most offensive nature".

Then in June 1843 *The Reformer* reported meetings being held to petition the Bishop of London over "the novelties lately introduced at Ware Church". At a meeting attended by 33 people, but without the Vicar or Curate, a churchwarden had taken the chair. Captain Proctor said he had twice left the church because he was opposed to the innovations "and twice the whole congregation had been induced to quit the church for the same reason. The Church was now approaching in its forms and ceremonies to the Roman Catholic Church … these innovations originated with Dr. Pusey".

Someone else proposed that the churchwardens should go from house to house gaining signatures for a petition of protest to the bishop. Dr. Blomfield merely acknowledged the petition, which angered the protesters. When the bishop asked them to be more specific about the "innovations", the churchwardens replied that the Vicar preached the sermon in a white surplice instead of a black academic gown, he omitted some of the long prayers before the sermon and finished the sermon at the Communion Table rather than dismissing the congregation with a blessing from the pulpit. Apart from the wearing of a surplice (which was quite legal), the other matters were minor changes. Letters passed back and forth between Ware and the Bishop whose chaplain said that, as the protesters had published the correspondence without waiting for Dr. Blomfield's final answer, "the Bishop declines all further communication with you". The dispute was now becoming more widely known: national politicians took sides or tried to mediate.

In August of that year, Coddington took the chair at a meeting of ratepayers but was taken ill. In his absence it was agreed the churchwardens would write to the Archbishop of Canterbury – they did so and he replied that he would not intervene in the jurisdiction of another bishop. This correspondence was reported in *The Times* along with a resolution proposed at a subsequent meeting, that the protesters should leave St. Mary's after the Creed and before the sermon – the sermon being "the least important part of the service and in this Church indifferent and seldom worth hearing" ("Hear, Hear, Hear"). *The Reformer* reported that this brought people flocking to Ware to see if the congregation would walk out. The Curate, Mr. Willock, took the service and indeed "about 100 persons, comprising a large proportion of the most influential inhabitants of the town, rose noiselessly from their seats and quitted the Church"

The figure of 100 – or 130 according to another newspaper – was disputed by the Curate, Mr. Willock, who wrote to the *Church Intelligencer* newspaper that only 40 had left and on the following Sunday only 23 or 25. Mr. Willock also took issue with reports that the afternoon children's service, based on the Catechism, had taken place "amidst much confusion" – "on the whole, I may observe that all the symptoms of discontent which have occurred in this town, have been grossly exaggerated in several newspapers".

The dispute had now become a tit-for-tat battle between two opposing camps. The churchwardens tried, without success, to strike out from the church rate items like heating and lighting for evening services and the salary of the organist, Thomas Luppino. In January 1844, the churchwardens invoked Canon Law to criticise the Vicar's dress and vestments, to which Coddington replied that he had submitted the matter to the Bishop. At that time Coddington was in Brighton for his health. In his absence the churchwardens tried to pressure the curates, again without success. Attempts at mediation were made by neighbouring clergy, some with the backing of the Bishop, but by now the two sides were firmly entrenched and not open to persuasion. Henry Coddington, for his part, concentrated on those matters where he did not need the churchwardens' agreement – a foundation stone for new classrooms for the National Schools, behind the church, was laid on 23 May 1844 by Sarah, the wife of William Parker of Ware Park. In the same month, Coddington succeeded in his long-term plan to make Wareside a separate district within the parish, with its own church rather than a chapel of ease.

For their part, the churchwardens sought and received a mandate to take the Vicar to the ecclesiastical courts, while at the same time supporting the rival worship now taking place in the Town Hall (the former Cornmarket). There, according to *The Times* of 14 May, "the anti-Tractarian schism which has so long disturbed the ultra-orthodox party in this town, has at length assumed the more palpable character of dissent." The Town Hall had been fitted out as a place of worship, an organ had been brought down from London complete with organist, and a Wesleyan minister retained to lead the services. *The Times* clearly disliked "dissent" almost as much as it disliked "Puseyism". A quite different slant on the happenings in Ware was taken by the magazine, *John Bull,* referring to the churchwardens' letters to the Bishop of London:

> We have read the letters and think Mr. "NATH. COBHAM", whoever he may be, about as ill-conditioned a gentleman as ever obtruded impertinence and vulgarity upon a superior. But who are the 'churchwardens of Ware' in whose name, and on whose behalf, the said "NATH. COBHAM" held the pen? Are they of the Dogberry breed? Have their "reading and writing" come by nature that they do not indite their own letters? The tone of both those which have been indited for them is so utterly unbecoming when addressed to a dignitary of the Church ... that we wonder the Bishop of London deigned to reply at all.[9]

'The Dogberry breed' was a reference to the comical constable in Shakespeare's *Much Ado About Nothing* and perhaps that is what the protesters were, deep down – locals who had had the even tenor of their ways disturbed by an intellectual, new vicar foisted upon them by the church's patron, Trinity College, Cambridge.

But matters were now coming to a head. Some time in the winter of 1844/45 Coddington went abroad for his health. He probably suffered from high blood pressure, accentuated by the stress of the dispute with the churchwardens, and he had spent much of the previous winter in Brighton. In March, *The Times* reported that "the novelties" in Ware Parish Church had been discontinued and that the new curate, Mr. Collins, had preached in an academic gown rather than a surplice. In the same month, a local newspaper reported in one sentence the death of the Rev. Henry Coddington in Rome, two weeks previously, on 3 March 1845. He was in the Holy City just for his health and not for any religious reason. Later in the month, *The Times* and *Hertford Mercury* both announced that the secessionist worship in the Town Hall would now cease.

Henry Coddington passed away without ceremony or good-byes. There is a brass plaque commemorating him in Holy Trinity Church, Wareside, but nothing in St. Mary's, Ware. It is almost as if the protagonists on both sides were so relieved that the feud was at an end, they put his memory aside. And what does it tell us about Ware in the 1840s, at the very beginning of Queen Victoria's reign? Clearly, the town was caught up in the religious turmoil caused by the new ritualism and assertiveness of the Puseyites or Oxford Movement. The Victorians loved an over-the-top religious squabble, especially one that could interest the national press. Fundamentally it was not a dispute about religion, so much as the new and over-confident assertiveness of High Church clergy versus the old and obstinate Low Church views of some of the laity. It was as much Whigs versus Tories, the eighteenth century versus the nineteenth, cussedness versus arrogance, Dogberry versus the Establishment, as it was Catholics against Evangelicals. It was also a clash of personalities, especially between the Cobham family and the Vicar. It is doubtful whether the feud left any lasting impression on the town. The evangelical Anglican parish of Christ Church in New Road was not founded until 1858. However, the involvement of a Wesleyan Methodist minister, the Rev. Robert Adler, in the secessionist worship held in the Town Hall may have helped consolidate Methodist worship at the new Wesleyan chapel in New Road, founded in 1839.

McAdam versus Stephenson

Under Mr. Willock's reply to the churchwardens, *The Reformer* of 21 October 1843 carried another item about Ware with the heading, THE HERTFORD AND WARE RAILWAY. This stated that construction of the new line was progressing rapidly and should be opened on time in the first week of November. But behind this confident statement lay another dispute, more technical than that in Ware Church but equally bedevilled by clashes of personality.

Following the opening of the Stockton & Darlington Railway in 1825 and George Stephenson's success with 'Rocket' in 1830, railways had become all the rage. 'Railway mania' swept the country as thousands of the new middle classes bought shares in the railway companies and the companies put ever more bills before Parliament – there were no fewer than 272 Railway Acts in 1846 alone. It was inevitable that a line would eventually reach Ware and in 1840 there was a plan for a railway from London to Cambridge via Ware. This plan came to nothing but it did prompt the Northern & Eastern Railway to put a Bill through Parliament for a branch line to Ware and Hertford from the line they were constructing to Cambridge, via Broxbourne and Bishop's Stortford. Under this Act of 1841 (4 & 5 Vict. c. xlii) the N.&E.R. was empowered to construct

> a Branch Line of Railway, to be made in or to pass from, through, or into the several Parishes, Townships, Hamlets or Extraparochial Places of *Broxbourne, Hoddesdon, Stanstead Abbots, St. Margaret's, Great Amwell, Ware, Little Amwell and St. John's Hertford*, or some of them, all in the County of Hertford.[10]

The Act gave the company permission to put level crossings over the highway at both Stanstead Abbots and Amwell End. But at Amwell End, where the road was part of the Cheshunt Turnpike, the railway company was required to divert the turnpike by means of a viaduct and embankment and continue this new road across Crane Mead to Ware Bridge (Crane Mead was so called because the Crane Inn stood immediately next to the bridge, on the south bank). All of this work was to be carried out to the satisfaction of Sir James McAdam, Surveyor of the Cheshunt Turnpike Trust.

Here was potential for a clash between two of the most famous engineers of the day. Sir James McAdam was General Superintendent of Metropolitan Roads in England and son of the famous John Loudon McAdam, inventor of the 'macadamisation' of road surfaces with small stones and a resident of Hoddesdon. The engineer of the railway company was Robert Stephenson, son of George Stephenson, and an outstanding locomotive engineer in his own right. In his preliminary plans for the branch line, Stephenson had proposed a bridge to carry Amwell End over the railway but this would have been difficult in view of the proximity of the New River. Then – reluctantly, in view of the cost – he agreed to the turnpike road being diverted by means of a viaduct. Whatever course was taken, the railway had to cross the road if it was to go on to Hertford. As it was, construction of the line involved demolishing the original Spread Eagle Inn and left no room for access to the station from Amwell End – until 1909 passengers coming from the south side of Ware had to use a footpath from London Road and cross the line on a boardwalk. Initially, the branch line was only single track and it was constructed not to the standard gauge of 4 feet 8½ inches but to a five-feet gauge, as used by the Eastern Counties Railway (E.C.R.). This was because the N.& E.R. line used the E.C.R.'s London terminus at Shoreditch (Liverpool Street). In fact, the E.C.R. took over operation of the Northern & Eastern on a 999 year lease as from 1 January 1844.

All seemed to be going well until the weekend of 14/15 October 1843. The line was almost complete apart from the Amwell End crossing. Yet work on the viaduct had been going on for months and, even with the hundreds of labourers or 'navvies' employed, it was far from complete. Everyone was aware of the clause in the Act, stating that the line was not to cross Amwell End before the viaduct was finished. The Cheshunt Turnpike Trust was deeply suspicious and appointed a three-man team to keep an eye on the construction. On Saturday 14 October, Sir James McAdam met the railway's contractor face to face and gave him formal notice that the line was not to cross Amwell End before the viaduct was complete. But, reported *The Reformer*:

> Immediately after the interview in which this intimation was made, the sub-contractor concentrated his men, and commenced operations upon the forbidden road, which were kept up during the whole of Saturday night – and to the surprise of the inhabitants of Ware, it was discovered on Sunday morning that the road had been levelled and the rails laid down across the highway, connecting the line on the further side of Amwell End with the Hertford side of the road.[11]

The contractor, a Mr. Peto, was not just being cussed. His purpose, explained *The Reformer*, was to be able to run gravel wagons across the road rather than have to transport the gravel all the distance from Hertford.

Events moved quickly. On Monday the sixteenth, the Cheshunt Turnpike Trust took court action by means of a Bill in Chancery, demanding that the rails be taken up and the road reinstated within seven days. Mr. Peto contacted the clerk of the trust and said, yes, the rails could be lifted and the viaduct and embankment could be finished within a fortnight. However, if this was done, he would then demand Sir James's certificate of approval and, if the certificate was refused, then the rails would be put back immediately and the railway opened to the public. At this, the turnpike trustees backed down and allowed the rails to remain across the road. The line was then finished and, on Tuesday 31 October 1843, the first train left Shoreditch at 8 a.m. and reached Hertford an hour later.

Yet the viaduct was still not finished. The problem was not the slowness of the work but the connection with the turnpike at the bridge. "The crazy old bridge" (as *The Reformer* called it) was owned by the Marquess of Salisbury, whose ancestors had been collecting tolls there since 1625, and he also owned the Crane Inn. Any satisfactory diversion of the turnpike would necessitate demolition of the inn and reconstruction of the "unsightly and dangerous" wooden bridge. The Marquess had put a price on the bridge and inn, but the railway company had been unable to agree to it. The issue remained deadlocked until the chairman of the turnpike trustees, Mr. Phelps of Briggens in Stanstead Abbots, came forward with a compromise and acted as mediator between Lord Salisbury and the railway company. The Marquess agreed to accept £4,500 for the two bridges at Ware and Stanstead Abbots which he owned, this money to be paid by the railway company. Both the Lee Navigation and the Cheshunt Turkpike Trust agreed

The railway crossing Amwell End which, by the time this photograph was taken in the late 19th century, was no longer part of the Cheshunt Turnpike. The building on the left, between the railway and the New River, was at one time a Post Office.

to contribute towards the cost of a new bridge at Ware, which was to be built by the railway company. Work did not begin on the new bridge until early in 1845 and even then Sir James McAdam was voicing concern at the dimensions of the 22 foot carriageway plus a 4 foot pedestrian way (6.7m and 1.2m respectively). Eventually, the iron bridge across the Lea was completed to the design of Robert Stephenson – it remained in use until the early 1960s, when it was replaced by a wider bridge, as part of Hertfordshire County Council's re-alignment of Bridgefoot. And yet the brick foundations of Robert Stephenson's bridge remained and can still be seen at water level. One curiosity of this affair is that, although the Marquess of Salisbury sold the bridge to the railway, he retained the right to levy tolls from traffic passing over it. The tolls continued until 1899, when the new Ware Urban District Council made the bridge toll-free at a cost of £574, including fees.

Perhaps it was just as well that there was no access to the railway from Amwell End for the labourers and their families living in the yards and courts of Amwell End did not benefit from the railway. Rail travel was not cheap, even in the open sided third-class carriages. It was the better-off in the town and surrounding countryside who benefitted and one man was quick to seize the opportunity. Daniel Brown, landlord of the Saracen's Head, placed an advertisement in *The Reformer*, stating that his was the nearest inn to the station and he could provide post horses, chaises, flys, gigs, etc, ready for friends and the public at the arrival of every train. The other people to benefit were the maltsters and dealers in agricultural produce. From the beginning

Ware Station in 1910 when it was part of the Great Eastern Railway. In the 1970s there were proposals to replace it with a metal and glass box (like Rye House) but, after objections from the Ware Society, only modest alterations took place.

Ware station had a large goods shed and, a little later, a large goods yard – the delay was due to the fact that, until it could be filled in, there was a large basin used for mooring barges between the viaduct and the railway station. On the other side of the railway, adjoining London Road, there was another basin which the railway company sold to the New River Company as a reservoir. A coal yard was established beside the railway on the London side of the viaduct.

The directors of the Eastern Counties Railway, who now operated the line, were concerned that their 5 feet gauge left them isolated from other railways. So in the late summer of 1844 all their lines were converted to standard gauge 4 feet 8½ inches – the work caused no disruption on the double-track main line, but the Hertford and Ware branch line had to be closed for a week in September with a horse-drawn coach running from Hertford to Broxbourne. In 1846, the E.C.R. decided to double the branch and this was done everywhere except at Amwell End, where the railway company failed to buy any land from the New River Company. And so Ware station remained a single platform station as it is today. Things might have been different if subsequent plans for a junction had materialised. In 1846 there was a plan for a line from Ware to Cambridge, via Buntingford and Royston, and in 1857 the Ware, Hadham and Buntingford Railway was promoted. But local landowners objected, chief among them Mr. Giles-Puller of Youngsbury, and the 'Buntingford Line' was moved down the line to St. Margaret's. It was a slow and hesitant beginning, but at last the railway had arrived and the character of Ware was changed for all time.

20.
Reform and Renewal

In the 1840s, there was great talk of political and social change. Even the Tories were affected by change under their Prime Minister, Sir Robert Peel. In Ware the main advocate for change was the new Vicar, the Rev. Joseph Blakesley. Like his predecessor, Henry Coddington, he had been a Fellow of Trinity College, Cambridge, but in almost every other respect Blakesley could not have been more different. His father, who was a merchant, died before Joseph had reached the age of ten and he then went to St Paul's School in London. As a scholarship boy at Cambridge, he first entered Corpus Christi College and later transferred to Trinity where he became a member of the famous Apostles' Club. Among his many close friends was the poet Alfred Tennyson. Prevented by ill health from pursuing his ambition to take up the law, Blakesley became a college tutor in classics and mathematics. He wrote the first life of Aristotle in English. Together with other Trinity liberals he announced his opposition to university religious tests and in 1840 he acted as campaign manager to the Whig Lord Lyttelton in the election of the university high steward. Like all college fellows, he could not marry until he had given up his fellowship and this he did a few months after taking up the college living, as Vicar of Ware. His wife was Margaret Holmes, the daughter of a Norfolk vicar, and she and Joseph had seven sons and four daughters before Margaret died in 1880.

So here was a Whig vicar and one who was not afraid to speak out on social and political issues. He gained a national reputation by writing letters to *The Times*, signed a "Hertfordshire Incumbent", even contradicting bishops and Members of Parliament. These letters impressed Lord Palmerston, the Whig Foreign Secretary and later Prime Minister, who made Blakesley a canon of Canterbury Cathedral. As soon as he had settled in Ware, Blakesley took up two challenges. One was the long-overdue task of repairing and restoring the Parish Church of St. Mary the Virgin. In point of fact this was chronologically the first of the two challenges but, since it links with other Victorian restorations in the town, particularly the refurbishment of The Priory, we shall leave it until a little later. Blakesley's other challenge was to tackle the poverty and public health problems of the town.

The Local Board of Health

In 1848 in response to a major cholera epidemic, the new Whig government passed the Public Health Act.[1] This ground-breaking piece of legislation empowered any town or other populous place in England and Wales, with a few exceptions chiefly in London, to bring under the control of a single body the supply of water, sewerage, drainage, street cleansing and paving – as well as pleasure grounds, burials and slaughterhouses. This single body would be known as a Local Board of Health. Not only was this a move towards better public health, it was also an advance in democracy. Until then, most of the bodies at the local level were self-perpetuating. The trustees of the Ware Charity Estates, the Cheshunt Turnpike Trust and the Lee Navigation chose their own successors, usually with a property qualification. Boroughs like Hertford did elect a mayor and corporation, but Ware was not a borough and its Vestry was dominated by maltsters and lawyers with a vested interest in the *status quo*. Members of the Local Board of Health, on the other hand, would be elected by all ratepayers.

The General Board of Health, created by the 1848 Act, came into being in the autumn and published its regulations and directions on 3 November 1848. Yet by 15 December a public health inquiry was being opened in Ware – it was one of the first, if not the first, local health inquiries in Britain to be held under the 1848 Act. It was able to be so because the year before, the Ware Vestry, at Blakesley's instigation, had appointed a committee to do a sanitary inspection of the parish, consisting of "the Vicar, his curates, the overseers, churchwardens, medical men, surveyor and ten other persons".[2] So when the 1848 inquiry opened, most of the facts were already available from the 1847 committee. In fact, most members of the earlier committee were present. The Superintendent Inspector, Mr. William Ranger, C.E. opened his report with these words:

> In conducting this inquiry, as well as in exploring the localities of filth, overcrowded dwellings, and haunts of fever and sickness, I was most effectually assisted by the Rev. J.W. Blakesley, vicar; C.W. Pullen, Esq., magistrate and Chairman of the [Ware Poor Law] Union; Bowden, Armstrong, McNabb, Butcher and Riley, Esqrs, surgeons; J. Marchant, Esq., clerk to the River Lea Commissioners; Mr. Price, relieving officer; Mr. Wyatt, surveyor; Mr. Machon, manager of gas-works; Samuel Adams, Esq.; A.C. Bond,Esq.; – Wilkins, Esq.; and likewise by many of the poorer class, who with great readiness allowed me to inspect their habitations".[3]

The cooperation of "the poorer class" was important for the Ranger report launched straight away into a description of the yards and courts where the poor lived, and of the prevailing diseases. These diseases were typhus fever – not typhoid but that which in the previous century was known as 'gaol fever – diarrhoea amounting in many cases to cholera, and a low and intermittent fever which was endemic to the area. "Typhus fever prevailed in Caroline-court and vicinity, Blue Coat-yard, and corner of Dead-lane, as also in the various courts of Amwell, and especially Chapel-yard, Star-lane and the West Mill-road." Mr. Ranger then compared death rates in Ware with those in the most industrialised parts of Britain.

> One of the best tests of the sanitary condition of a district is furnished by the infantile mortality, which is independent of occupation, migration, or emigration, or the casualties affecting adult life. From the register of deaths in the parish of Ware in 1841 it appears that the mortality comes between the mean mortality of Lancashire (which is 2.68), the most unhealthy of all the English counties, and that of Cheshire (2.32), which stands next in order of unhealthiness. And it is found for that one year, of the children born within the years, whilst 1 in every 11 die in Ulverstone [a comparable size town in Lancashire], 1 in every 7 die in Ware; 23.9 per cent die before they pass the fifth year in the less unhealthy district, whilst at Ware 36.5 per cent of them have been swept away ... Again: the average number of years attained at Ulverstone was 41 years 8 months, at Ware it was only 32 years".[4]

The reason for this truly shocking state of affairs was the concentration of poor families in the centre of Ware, that is in the low-lying areas where open cesspools were right up against the

Caroline Court, off Baldock Street, was named after the wife of George III and was one of the largest and most notorious of the yards. This photograph was taken just before it was demolished in the 1930s and features Mrs. Skeggs, a long-time resident in Caroline Court.

houses and polluted the water supply – or even under the house (as in what is now Church Street): "*French Horn-lane.*—Three dwellings containing 19 souls; the privies situated in the cellars, with about two years' accumulation of excreta, and immediately under the living-room with a common boarded floor."

The worst sanitation – and the highest rates of disease – occurred at the two ends of the town, in the yards of Baldock Street and Amwell End – and also in Kibes Lane. *Caroline-court* was the largest of four yards on the east side of Baldock Street: there were 17 cottages inside the yard and five more on the street – offal of all descriptions was thrown into two open cesspools and these overflowed out on to the street. Amwell-end had *Chapel-yard* on the west side and six other courts on the east side, named *Cherry tree-yard, Dickenson's-yard, George-yard, Hunter's-yard* (part of which went by the name of *James's-yard*), *Horn-court*, and *Long's-yard*. These courts contained 70 tenements and a number of foul open ditches – *Dickenson's-yard* had only two privies over an open cesspool for the use of the inhabitants of 28 houses. At the bottom of *Kibes-lane* were 23 tenements close together and "not one of these miserable habitations" had any kind of convenience – all the refuse was thrown either on to a dunghill in Bowling-lane field or into the Bowling-lane open ditch, a water course that had contained minnows within living memory but was by this time "a public nuisance, as disgusting as it is noxious". Nearly half of the cholera cases in Ware in 1832 occurred in *Kibes-lane.*

Mr. Ranger then devoted paragraphs to ventilation, overcrowding, the highways, road drainage, sewers and the water supply. He also included a paragraph about baths – not baths with taps, of course, just bath tubs: "In a well-conditioned town every third house has a bath, and the proportion of private baths is increasing. But this town is entirely destitute of baths."

Everyone could agree that these conditions were deplorable, but not everyone would necessarily agree to Mr. Ranger's twelve-point plan of what was to be done about it. He proposed first that powers be taken to form Ware town and Amwell End into one district under the 1848 Public Health Act. There should be an abundant supply of pure, filtered water to go into every tenement – at a cost of 1d. per house per week. He proposed converting privies into water-closets (WCs) and, where there were none, erecting water-closets – cost £3 per closet. The town should replace open ditches by drainage pipes, there should be a daily cleansing of the carriageway and pavements – no cost given, but Ranger did recommend the rather modern scheme of paving all footways in "well-boiled gas-tar, which is called bitumen or asphalte, (which) may be done at 1s. per square yard". All blind alleys should, where practicable, be turned into thoroughfares so that currents of air flow through them; likewise all tenement rooms should be ventilated. He advocated a general system for house repairs, with wholesale contracts and a permanent force of bricklayers and plumbers. He even told employers how they should pay their workers:

> A large number of the labouring population are employed in emptying and loading barges; others are employed in manufacturing malt at 85 malthouses; the major part of these men are paid on a Saturday evening, and at public houses [of which there were no less than 30 public-houses and 19 beer-shops] … The effect of paying workmen on the Saturday night is to deprive them of the entire benefit of the Saturday's market, and frequently to encourage Sunday trading, while it makes a difference by way of loss of at least 2s. to each workman, in addition to his being compelled to attend at public-houses to receive his wages …

Although some of these individual items were uncosted, Ranger did put a figure on the cost of the major works. He estimated £7,700 would be needed for the waterworks and £4,000 for laying sewers in the streets. These were large sums but he thought Ware could afford them, either by an increase in the rates or by raising loans. With a population in 1841 of 4,653, Ware property had the rateable value of £27,137 while property in Great Amwell, where there was a population of 1,545, had a rateable value of £10,441. In the long term, he concluded, Ware would actually save money by taking action immediately.

Mr. Ranger's report was published by the General Board of Health in London in 1849. On 10 May it was considered at a special meeting of the Ware Vestry, with the Vicar in the chair. Immediately resentment at the report was apparent among the unusually large attendance of 39 men. It was moved, seconded and carried unanimously that "Mr. Ranger's report was incorrect in several important particulars". It was not expedient to carry out the provisions of the Public Health Act in Ware and "the most strenuous opposition (would) be made thereto." An amendment that a committee of five should meet with Mr. Ranger and perhaps negotiate changes to the report was soundly defeated. And that was the end of the matter as far as the Vestry was concerned, even though they continued throughout the year to debate ways of improving drainage in particular parts of the town.

Rev. Joseph W. Blakesley,
Vicar of Ware 1845-72
and later Dean of Lincoln

They had reckoned without the Vicar. On 7 August 1849, Mr. Blakesley posted a notice on the church door and the door of the Town Hall and inserted the same in *The Reformer* and *County Press*, announcing that there would be an election for members of a new Local Board of Health. As Vicar, he was the person appointed by law to call that election and he would be at the Town Hall at 11am in a week's time to meet all property-owners entitled to vote. This was not a parish priest laying down the law, but an astute politician who – with no fuss, certainly no confrontation or shouting match with the churchwardens – skilfully outmanoeuvred his opponents. Over the next month, Blakesley called for nominations, distributed voting papers and himself counted the votes – always making sure that there were two or three prominent citizens on hand to confirm that all was done legally and correctly. There were 24 nominations for the eight places on the local board, including a number of the local gentry (Robert Hanbury of Poles and Martin Hadsley Gosselin of the Priory) and known supporters of the Vicar, like the maltster Edward Chuck. In the event, the eight who were elected were long-time members of the Vestry including some who had opposed the previous vicar. The most votes went to William Parker, Esq., of Ware Park, who been a force for moderation during the Coddington dispute. Blakesley himself was not elected but that may not have bothered him. When the Ware Local Board of Health met for the first time on 1 September, Mr. Parker was elected chairman and Nathaniel Cobham, the wily radical lawyer, was appointed clerk.

The Local Board of Health remained the local government of Ware until 1894, when the Ware Urban District Council was created under the Public Health Act of the same year. In the 45 years of its existence it achieved a great deal. Gradually it carried out most of the recommendations in the Ranger report – a new cemetery at the top of West Mill (Watton) Road was acquired from the maltster Joseph Chuck in 1849, drain pipes were laid across most of the open ditches in 1850, mains drainage and a proper water supply were installed in 1869 at a cost of £20,000. Caroline Court, Chapel Yard, Dickinson's Yard, Kibes Lane and the rest were appreciably less unhealthy places in which to live after 1849, but they were not eradicated until the 1930s. And then a number of their residents did not want to move.

Renewal: St. Mary's Church

1847-50 were busy years for the Rev. Joseph Blakesley. A few months before persuading the Vestry and Board of Guardians to give attention to the sanitary conditions of Ware, he had put into motion plans to restore the parish church. The Vestry on 29 April 1847 was well attended, with Blakesley in the chair and 58 others. They agreed that the church was "dilapidated" and voted unanimously for an architect to give an estimate for renewing the timbers and lead of the roof, removing the rough cast from the outer walls, rebuilding the parapets, strengthening the walls and renewing the stone dressings around windows, doors, etc. The meeting went so well that it finished with a unanimous vote of thanks to Mr. Blakesley for his conduct as chairman (rather different from the Vestry of 1840 which strenuously criticised the previous vicar for repairs to a single window!)

Two architects were approached for plans and estimates. One was Thomas Smith of Hertford, well known locally for the designs of Hertford County Hospital (1833), the Clock House at Hoddesdon (1835) and Holy Trinity, Wareside (1841). The other was a national figure – George Godwin, editor of the influential journal, *The Builder*, already contracted to restore the magnificent church of St. Mary Redcliffe, Bristol and, incidentally, (something that recommended him to Blakesley) a campaigner for health and housing reform. The architects' estimates were put before the Vestry on 19 August when it was announced that "putting the church into thorough repair" would cost £3,653 and it was agreed they should ask for a loan of that amount from the Commissioners of Public Works. In the vote on the choice of architect, Godwin won – and Blakesley was given another vote of thanks. It was a fortuitous decision for Godwin was to have a major influence on the appearance of Ware – first at St. Mary's, then at The Priory and possibly at Thunder Hall as well.

The progress of the restoration during 1847-50 was charted in the pages of *The Builder*. First, Godwin described the church as he found it. There were two ugly wooden galleries, one built for the Christ's Hospital children in the north transept and completely blocking the large and elegant window, the other at the west end of the church – "disfigured by a similar, ugly adjunct, containing the organ". The pulpit, pews and stoves all needed restoration. The roof of the nave was acceptable and in better condition than that of the chancel which was modern, while the roofs of the aisles had been white and red and ornamented with texts. The magnificent octagonal font had been moved from the west end of the church to the north chapel (where the organ now is) and was "in a very bad condition". One window in the Lady Chapel had been blocked up by the large memorial to Sir Richard Fanshawe. But it was the exterior which needed the most urgent attention:

> The outside of the church is in a truly deplorable, and partly a dangerous condition. It is constructed of flint work, with dressings of clunch, and the whole had been covered in modern times with rough-cast, which has separated from the walls, and is now ready to fall on the heads of passers by. The stone mullions and tracery of the windows have mostly disappeared, and have been replaced by wood and cement, and all the strings and mouldings were cut off for the convenience of rough casting. The copings are loose, and the roofs decayed.[5]

Only the south transept window – the one controversially restored by Henry Coddington – was worth keeping. Not surprisingly, the first work had to be on the outside. In May 1848, it was announced in *The Builder* that Carter, a firm of builders in Holloway, had been chosen from a field of five to carry out a complete external restoration at a cost of £2,997.

By September 1849, the work was completed and drew praise from another source, *The Ecclesiologist*, the pre-eminent arbiter of good taste in Victorian church architecture. The two galleries had been removed, the journal noted, and the old box pews cut down (they were replaced in 1887). Some rebuilding had taken place and all the windows had been repaired. But what *The Ecclesiologist* liked most was the new colour everywhere:

The most striking feature in the restoration is the quantity of polychrome which has been applied. The spandrills of the nave arches, ten in number, are filled with flower-pots, from which grow lilies, each bearing a scroll, with one of the beatitudes inscribed upon it. The commandments are painted where they are ordered, on two tablets on each side of the chancel-arch. The Creed and the Lord's Prayer are on the eastern wall flanking the east window. The bosses of the nave and chancel roofs are coloured and gilt; and the architectural portions of the roof of the Lady Chapel are emblazoned.[6]

The lilies and the texts have since been white-washed over – as had been the medieval decoration of life-sized figures faintly apparent when Godwin first arrived. The decoration that was missed and regretted by all was that of the Lady Chapel roof. Here there had been 24 panels, each bearing the figure of an Apostle or a Prophet on a grey background with Latin texts around it. Apparently Godwin had promised to restore the panels but it was never done. The only criticisms by *The Ecclesiologist* were matters of detail – the new screen in front of the west door was too ornate and the corbels supporting the new nave roof which had figures of the Apostles on them were too large. But overall, the journal warmly praised Godwin and his craftsmen, and the parishioners: "with few exceptions, all the funds necessary for the restoration were raised in the parish, and contributed with most perfect good will. We most heartily congratulate the people of Ware on so good a work."

The magazine added that "a local benefactor" was about to fill the east and west windows with stained glass representing the Crucifixion and the Baptism of Jesus, designed by William Wailes. The benefactor was the maltster Edward Chuck who gave the windows in memory of his parents. Pevsner found the colour of them strident and the style of the figures too modern for a chancel of 1300.[7] However, these were the first windows in St. Mary's since the Middle Ages to be given colour.

Later in the century they were followed by more sophisticated examples of Victorian stained and painted glass, displaying the influence of the Pre-Raphaelites and William Morris.

Renewal: The Priory

Martin Hadsley Gosselin must have admired George Godwin's work at St. Mary's when he invited him in 1849 to remodel the Priory as a country house for his growing family. It was a restoration that was long overdue. Martin had inherited the Priory (the former Franciscan friary) from his spinster aunt, Maria Hadsley, who had been born there in 1777. In that same year, Maria's father, Jeremiah Rayment Hadsley, had died while taking the waters in Bath and for the next 70 years the house was the home of the women of his family. In April 1809, the older daughter, Sarah, left the Priory after her marriage to Captain Thomas Le Marchant Gosselin, who four months earlier had covered the embarkation of the Sir John Moore's army at Corunna, in Portugal – a service for which he received the thanks of both houses of parliament. Wisely Captain Gosselin never went to sea again but moved on half-pay to Bengeo Hall, Hertford, where he was steadily promoted to rear-admiral in 1814, vice-admiral in 1825 and admiral in 1841 (his family were annoyed that he never made Admiral of the Fleet). The younger Hadsley daughter was Maria who nursed her mother until her death in 1831 and then lived alone in the large house, with a host of servants and a little dog named 'Duck'. According to her diary[8] she entertained the local gentry, organised and supported a new lying-in charity and the National Schools, as well as Margaret Gull's charity school in the Priory itself, and in 1847 at the close of a long and virtuous life bequeathed the Priory to her only nephew, Martin Hadsley Gosselin. Meanwhile, Admiral Gosselin lived on at Bengeo Hall with two unmarried daughters, while a third daughter married a cavalry officer, Captain Edward Spencer Trower, and in 1853 moved to Stansteadbury at Stanstead Abbots.

The Priory that Martin Gosselin inherited was much as it had been when Robert Hadsley installed sash windows a hundred years earlier. It was heated by one massive central chimney, rising from the kitchens to the roof and only incidentally giving heat to the bedrooms. The habitable rooms were mainly in the central block; the east and west wings still looked much as they had been when the Friary was dissolved in 1538. George Godwin's task was to turn this venerable but uncomfortable old building into a family home for Martin, his young wife Frances and their growing family – their oldest child (the future diplomat, Sir Martin Le Marchant Hadsley Gosselin, KCVO, KCMG) was born in 1847 and two other sons were to follow, one of them (Hellier Robert Hadsley Gosselin-Grimshawe) destined to be five times Mayor of Hertford.

It was a formidable challenge but one that Godwin would have relished. He had a powerful historical sense and made fine detailed drawings of Gothic features; and yet he had also written an acclaimed essay on the uses of concrete. His first task was to give the Priory a new entrance which would also open up the neglected east and west wings. He abandoned the old carriage drive from Mill Lane (Priory Street) and established a new one from the High Street through the kitchen garden – and designed a lodge to give the new drive a presence in the town (in the event the lodge, now part of Ware Museum, was built to a similar design by the local builder, Walter Hitch). The new entrance was at the corner where the east wing and central block met and he cleverly made this jut out in an arc so that an entrance hall was formed. In the east wing (the old 'frater' or living quarters of the friars) he redesigned the ground floor to form three interconnecting parlours, one of which could be used as a chapel. To emphasise their medieval character, he added further Gothic windows to his own design and matching wall paintings, which were lost under later layers of paint until rediscovered and conserved in the major restoration of 1993 (*see opposite page*).

Godwin was the most considerate of architects. Among his drawings in the Hertfordshire Archives is a plan of the Priory showing the old work he retained, the old work he removed and the new work he created.[9] His major undertaking was to install new chimneys and fireplaces throughout the building and to make the building lighter by inserting new windows. In the west wing (the old refectory or guest wing of the friars), he inserted three new Gothic windows so much like the originals that, without prior knowledge, it is difficult to tell which are medieval and which Victorian. Also in this wing, where the former entrance had been, he removed the massive masonry foundations of a staircase to create "Mr. Gosselin's Room" (now the Town Clerk's office) and redesigned the kitchens and servants' area behind. The dining room remained where it was (now the Town Council office) but acquired a fine marble fireplace. On the first floor a handsome library was created (now the Council Chamber) – later one of the Gosselin family, probably Frances, painted a watercolour of children in the library and then stuck photographs of their faces on to the painting. Finally, in the garden, Godwin added a conservatory and redesigned the garden in the best Victorian style using Pulham reconstituted stone to simulate

A member of the Gosselin family in one of the parlours – part of what is now the hall of the Priory. One of the 'Gothic' changes Godwin made was to decorate the walls with medieval features. These paintings were revealed in the restoration of the building in 1993 and were conserved with a special grant from English Heritage.

natural rocks.

Godwin was fascinated by the surviving medieval features of the Priory and made a drawing of what he assumed were the roof timbers of the west wing. This drawing, published in *The Builder* in 1849,[10] accurately illustrated the scissor bracing but also showed a succession of moulded crown posts, each standing on its own cross beam. During the 1993 restoration, it became clear that there had only ever been one moulded post, which stood in the centre of the upper guest chamber, and that the posts on either side of the chamber would have been plain. This was confirmed by the late Adrian Gibson, an expert on timber-framed buildings, who also initiated the tree-ring dating or dendrochronology of this chamber, mentioned earlier in this book.

Renewal: Thunder Hall

Thunder Hall was so called because until 1827 it was held copyhold from the Manor of Ware Extra and Thundridge: it must have been Thundridge Hall at one time, possibly the house of the steward of the manor. It consists of a late 17th century three-storey house with a protruding porch for a staircase, to which in the 18th century was added a square two-storey extension. Then in the mid-19th century, the whole house was remodelled with the addition of an imposing gatehouse, a courtyard and two sides of a medieval cloister. The remodelling in the mid-19th century is the most curious feature of the house and it would be logical to assume that this was done by George Godwin, who by 1850 had already restored and remodelled St. Mary's Church and The Priory. The listing document states that the remodelling was by Godwin and that information came from this author. However, no article in *The Builder* or plans by Godwin exist as they do for St. Mary's and the Priory. Pevsner says that he heard the restoration was by Wyatt but had not been told which one (there was a whole dynasty of them in the 18th-19th centuries)[11]. Pevsner's information probably came from the Ware historian, Edith Hunt, who on 5 August 1955 wrote to the *Hertfordshire Mercury* that the remodelling was "probably the work of the architect brothers, Wyatt, who specialised in Gothic revivals, including the well-known building of Ashridge and the modern wing at Windsor Castle". That would point towards James Wyatt (1746-1813), architect of Ashridge Park at Berkhamsted, and his architect sons – Benjamin Dean Wyatt (1775-1852), Philip William Wyatt (d. 1835) and Matthew Cotes Wyatt (1777-1862 who was better known as a sculptor. James Wyatt and his sons were great users of Pulham artificial stone, invented by James Pulham I and his brother, Obadiah. Pulham stone, which was manufactured in Broxbourne from the early 1840s, was used extensively in the remodelling of Thunder Hall and also in the Gothic extensions to Benington Lordship in the late 1830s. However, the expert on Pulham stone, Claude Hitching, has said that in the early 1840s Obadiah Pulham was working with Thomas Smith, architect of the Hertford Infirmary and Holy Trinity, Wareside. So that leaves three possible architects of the makeover – Godwin, one of the Wyatts and Thomas Smith.

Both Benington Lordship and Thunder Hall were owned by the Proctor family. They were bought in 1826 and 1836 respectively as part of the rearrangement of the estate of a great uncle, Ambrose Proctor of Ware, who died in 1810, aged 95 (the rearrangment required a private Act of Parliament in 1824 and the appointment of new trustees). The oldest great-nephew, George Proctor, gained Benington Lordship for himself and family, while the trustees bought Thunder Hall for the use of George's three bachelor brothers and "each of our sisters whilst unmarried". The 1851 Census shows that living at Thunder Hall were Ambrose Frederick Proctor, aged 62, described as "an East India captain" – nothing so common as a sea captain – his brother, John aged 66, and their sister, S.M. Proctor, aged 61, who was too proud to give the census-taker her first name, plus two servants. In the 1841 Census there had been another sister, H. Proctor, and before that another bachelor brother, William Henry Proctor, but he is shown in the census of 1851 as living at Benington Lordship with his nephew, Leonard Proctor. Old Captain Ambrose Frederick Proctor was the Whig who had twice walked out of church when the vicar turned to the east to say the Creed. The family's East India Company connection obviously ran deep for a memorial in St. Mary's records the death of Ambrose Proctor Wild (maybe a cousin), who died aged 17 in 1800 aboard the East India Company's ship, the *Kent*. He was the son of John Wild of the Excise Office in London.

The work carried out on Thunder Hall – by Godwin, one of the Wyatts or Thomas Smith – was not so much a restoration as a major makeover. The original house, built in the late 17th and 18th centuries, consisted of two wings, a square redbrick north wing and a southern cross-wing with parapeted gables, both wings lit with sash windows and roofed with old-style tiles. In the makeover, the cross-wing was rendered in stucco and painted white while the north wing was embellished at two of the corners with curious, Turkish-looking pinnacles, described in the

A postcard of Thunder Hall, showing the original house and,
right, the Gothic cloister and gatehouse, added in the 1830s or 1840s.

listed buildings document as having "corbelled bases and moulded ogee caps". All the east facing windows of this wing were given dripmoulds, finishing halfway down each side with a carved head. There are twelve of these heads on this part of the building. Some of them are grotesque, others are Gothic looking and three can be identified as Chaucer, Sir Thomas More and Shakespeare. In his restoration of St. Mary's, George Godwin had the task of replacing similar dripmould heads – some of the original, medieval heads remained. Perhaps he overdid it for virtually every window and arch at the church finishes with the stone bust of a king or queen or bishop. But that was nothing compared with the proliferation of heads at Thunder Hall. Next to the house was constructed two sides of a cloister with Tudor arches, dripmoulds, buttresses and a panelled parapet. There are no fewer than 20 heads in this cloister, again varying between handsome and bearded to the grotesque: they were not carved in stone but moulded from the reconstituted stone that James Pulham and family were making at Broxbourne. The cloister finishes in a flight of steps which lead down a tall carriageway with two massive leaf panelled gates opening on to The Bourne. Again on the outer face of the carriageway there is a dripmould with two heads, of monks or friars in contemplative mood.

Inside the house, there are two staircases, one 17th century and the other 19th. And in one of the rooms on the ground floor is a Victorian arched fireplace into which is set a marble tablet with the inscription: "This marble from the room in which the Emperor Napoleon died was brought from St. Helena by Capt. Amb. Fred. Proctor, AD 1833". Thunder Hall is indeed a curious example of Victorian taste.

In the early 1970s, the grounds of Thunder Hall and the land to the north were developed as Thundercourt, a development of square redbrick houses, and Thunder Hall itself was converted into flats. The boundary wall of Thundercourt on the Wadesmill Road is constructed of red and yellow Hitch patent bricks – the interlocking bricks invented by maltster and brickmaker Caleb Hitch, Jnr, from 1827 onwards.

The Manor House

The Manor House is in the part of Church Street, once known as Steeple End. It did not connect with the High Street because until 1834 it ended at the old Vicarage, near the tower of St. Mary's Church. The house was then known as the Rectory Manor because it was owned by the Rector or patron of St. Mary's, Trinity College, Cambridge, and before them the medieval priories. The Manor House was probably the residence of the steward of the Rectory Manor.

The Manor House has two wings. The roof of the south-west wing on the Church Street frontage (*above*) has the smoke-blackened rafters with the notches that indicate a missing fifteenth-century crown post and collar beams. On the first floor is a long room with seventeenth-century panelling and an elaborately carved overmantel above the fireplace. At right angles to this wing is the long north wing (*below*) facing the garden. This wing was probably rebuilt and extended in the Regency period (1811-20) and has many elegant features of the time.

The last tenant of Trinity College, Judge Sir Stephen Chapman, bought the freehold in 1951 and became only the second owner since the Reformation. After Sir Stephen's death, the northern section of the garden was sold to a developer who built St. Evroul Court, named after the Abbey of St. Evroult in Normandy, the mother house of Ware's medieval Benedictine Priory.

Rankin Square was originally part of the Market Place. The first encroachment was the three-storey building on the right of the photo, constructed in the late eighteenth century. It contained shops and a large public house, known as the Oriental Tavern.

To the north – and dominating the square – was the Old Punch House, built as it used to say "in the glorious reign of William III" as the residence of a wine and spirit merchant, named Ellis. James Smith described it in the 1830s as one of the favourite resorts of the town:

To all outward appearance it was a substantial private residence; but it had a small bar, a miracle of neatness and elegance, at which none but the regular *habitués* of the establishment ever dreamed of asking to be served; and there was a spacious coffee-room in the rear, panelled with polished mahogany and divided into boxes, where white-headed patriarchs used to meet in the afternoon and evening, and discuss politics and local topics over their port wine negus or mulled claret.[12]

To the right of the Old Punch House were two other licensed premises – the Bell and Sun and the White Swan (now the front entrance of Tesco's). James Smith said that the White Swan was kept "by an elderly female familiarly known, both far and near, as Milly Dennis" and it was here that the prominent tradesmen and the parish clerk would gather in the evening for "pipes and gossip".

To the left of the Old Punch House was a handsome eighteenth-century house, which was acquired by a group of businessmen in 1867 and named the 'Old Town Hall' – a rival to the former Cornmarket which also had that name. The new owners constructed a corn exchange and cattle market behind the house which became the entrance to the public rooms. The fine Georgian staircase of the original house is still there (*illustrated on page 147*). In the early twentieth century, the buildings at the rear became a bus garage, operated by the National Omnibus and Transport Company, and later a depot for the vehicles of Ware Urban District Council. In 1953, the Chaseside Engineering Company moved their works into the garage and restored the house, which they renamed Rankin House.[13] Hence the present name of the square. The house is now a fashion showroom and the site to the rear became part of the Tudor Square development in the 1990s.

The Town Grows Outwards

On the opposite side of Baldock Street from Thunder Hall is the Roebuck Hotel. In the mid-nineteenth century this was a substantial house known as Canons, the home of the maltster, banker and landowner, Samuel Adams. One of the maltings which he owned was the Canons Malting, just to the north of his house, which was demolished in 1965 by Ware Urban District Council to make way for housing. This was ironic since Samuel Adams was as much interested in housing developments as he was in making malt. The Adams family had been prominent in the Ware malting industry for over a hundred years when Samuel began to buy up land in an arc to the north of the town. A sketch map in Hertfordshire Archives shows the land he had acquired by 1835.[14] Samuel's land bank consisted of a patchwork of moderate sized plots stretching from the West Mill Road (now Watton Road) through fields to the east of the Wadesmill Road to land north of Crib Street, including a field called 'Pick Purse' – a total of 269 acres. The Ware Tithe Map of 1845 shows that he had increased his holding to 387 acres (roughly 157 hectares). In April 1853, his nephew, Samuel Adams Jnr., asked permission of the Vestry to stop up Fanhams Hall Lane (the road that continued north from the top of Crib Street and is now the drive of Collett Hall) because he had already built its replacement a little to the east (the present High Oak Road).

The expansion of Ware was long overdue. New housing was needed to relieve the unhealthy, overcrowded yards and to release land in the town centre for the ever-growing malting industry. There were also the needs of the tradesmen, shopkeepers and other members of the middle classes brought in by the railway. The obvious location for this was on the slopes and hills surrounding the town centre, but the local farmers and landowners had long been opposed to housing. This opposition was overcome by successive General Enclosure Acts, passed in 1801, 1836 and 1845 which made it easier for land, especially common land, to be enclosed and to pass into private ownership. In Ware four pieces of common land were enclosed in quick succession – Wengeo Common in 1850, High Oak Common and Musley Common in 1854 and Ware Marsh (in Great Amwell Parish) in 1860.[15] Once enclosure had taken place, it was simple for landowners like Samuel Adams to lay out new roads and line them with housing. The 1851 Ordnance Survey Map of Ware shows 'model housing' on both sides of the High Oak Road – i.e. terraced two-up, two-down houses with WCs and running water.

The expansion of the town was unstoppable but the Adams family were soon ruled out of the game. Old Samuel Adams, who had amassed all the land and a fortune in his Hertford & Ware Bank, died in August 1850, aged 76, and was succeeded by his nephew. A few years later, the younger Samuel became embroiled in a scam operated by a man named Johnstone and involving a rich young man named Kaye. In 1856, Johnstone went bankrupt, Kaye sued the bank, local businesses learned of this and refused to accept the bank's notes with the result that on 22 July 1856 the Hertford & Ware Bank closed its doors and petitioned for bankruptcy.[16] The 1851 Ordnance Survey Map shows that the Adams bank had its offices at 41 High Street, opposite French Horn Lane – a building which was later Gideon Talbot's garage and is now the site of Gregg's bakery – while the London & Counties Bank (now Natwest), which was appointed by the Bank of England to sort out the Adams affairs, had its office at 46 High Street.

The malting cowls in Crib Street, Princes Street and Francis Road –
as seen in 1900 from the terrace in front of Western House

One major area of new housing was Musley Common. Before 1830 New Road and its northward continuation up Musley Hill did not exist. Where 'Back Street' (East Street) joined Kibes Lane, there was a gate and this was the entrance to the malting yard of the Dickinson family. It was only after tragedy hit the Dickinson family – as recounted earlier in this book – and the family sold their malting yard that New Road was built with 'model cottages' which, for the first time, gave the artisan classes gardens and WCs. Later and farther up New Road large detached villas were built and also a number of churches and chapels. In fact, New Road became the centre of Victorian religion in the town, as described in the following chapter.

Higher up the hill are two blocks of 'model housing' bearing plaques – one between 17 & 19 Musley Hill proclaiming "Skippers Row, Constitution Hill, Erected AD 1850", the other between 43 & 45 saying "Mount Ephraim, Erected 1849". This was housing for the better sort of workman, the skipper rather than the steersman, and because it was then the highest development in the town it was honoured with the Biblical title Mount Ephraim (where Moses first saw the Promised Land). But within a few years there were developments even higher than Mount Ephraim. Musley Villas, a group of spacious semi-detached villas, were so new that on the 1851 map the road in which they were situated did not have a name. It is now Homefield Road. Opposite in 1857 was built the Chuck Memorial School, later the Ware Grammar School, later still Musley Infants and now destined to be a community centre. Finally, over the brow of Musley Hill is Redan Road, named after one of the Russian redoubts in the Crimean War of 1854-5.

Meanwhile, one of the oldest streets in the town, Crib Street, was undergoing enormous change. It had been a street of old, jettied houses, with orchards and meadows at the top where the old workhouse was located. The demolition of the workhouse coincided with the sale in 1837 of land which had belonged to the late John Baron Dickinson.[17] The outcome was that over the next 20 years Crib Street became one of the most intensive areas of malt production in the town. Access to the new malthouses was provided by the construction of two side streets, Prince's Street (named after the Prince of Wales pub on the corner) and Francis Road, named after John Francis, who owned the White Horse public house. In Francis Road were the large Alpha and Omega Maltings – for many years afterwards, John's widow, Mrs. Francis, lived in Alpha Cottage. Alpha Cottage still exists and in the 1930s a Miss Lloyd lived there and bred 'Ware Cocker Spaniels'. So intensive was malt production here that many years later, in the 1894 obituary of Henry Page, it was stated that his malting in Crib Street was "an exceptionally large one, capable of steeping upwards of 140 quarters at a time".[18] The photograph on the previous page shows the kiln cowls of Crib Street sprouting up like a forest.

There was soon to be new housing on the other side of the town. In December 1863, Mrs. Maria De Horne Hooper of Amwell House died. She was the daughter of the Quaker poet, John Scott, and had faithfully maintained the house and garden that he had created a hundred years earlier. Some people felt that the extensive landscaped garden, with its summerhouses and grotto, should have been preserved as a public park, but it did not happen. Instead the British Land Company bought the whole estate for the large sum of £4,952 and proceeded to lay out three roads across the garden – Scott's Road and Myddleton Road running up the hill from the Hertford Road, with Warner Road running along the top. The company then sold off the 24 acre estate in separate building plots. The plot containing Scott's Grotto was bought by a Ware florist, named Nathaniel Harris – it was a speculative purchase and, before he sold it on to a builder, Harris opened the grotto to the public at sixpence a visit which included tea.[19] Other roads in the area, such as Walton Road and Little Acres, were added in the twentieth century. Amwell House itself was bought by a London banker, Mr. Arthur Tite, and later became the Ware Grammar School for Girls. The 1880 Ordnance Survey of Ware shows that many roads had been laid out but had still to be developed – these included Bowling Road and Trinity Road. Mount Street (now Gilpin Road) was developed on both sides but there were no cottages in London Road, although the Red House public house was there on the edge of the New River. In Watton Road there were small terraces of cottages, built earlier in the century by Caleb Hitch II for workers in his brickfields and using his patent bricks.

The Hitch family were prominent in many branches of the town's economy. Walter Hitch was a builder and surveyor, James Hitch a builder and lime burner, and George Hitch a builder and surveyor to the Local Board of Health. James Hitch and his son, William, were also barge builders at the Dockyard in Star Street. Caleb Hitch III concentrated on malting rather than on his father's favourite trade of making patent bricks, but he still lived in one of the semi-detached houses built by his father next to the large malthouse in Park Lane. Caleb Hitch was not the only brickmaker in the town – or even the biggest. In the late 1840s and 1850s, the brickfields between Park Lane and the river were acquired by an ambitious housebuilder, Henry Rydon. He had already built 300 or so houses in Islington adjoining the Regent's Canal and he had now gained an option to build on 121 acres to the north, on what became the "Highbury New Park Estate". Later still, he entered into a partnership with the New River Company to help develop their Islington estate.[20] The hundreds of thousands of bricks needed for these developments were shipped by barge from a cut in the River Lea (now partially filled in under the GlaxoSmithKline research buildings) to three wharves that Rydon bought in the 1860s in Hackney, Bow and Ponders End. Rydon died in 1885 at Brighton but is buried in St. Mary's Church, Ware.

As a postscript to this chapter, it is worth recording a curious episode which occured in June 1865. A general election had been called by the Liberal Prime Minister, Lord Palmerston (his name, incidentally, is commemorated on cottages in Park Road), and there was a determined effort to defeat the three Tory members for Hertfordshire – Sir Edward Bulmer-Lytton of Knebworth, Henry Surtees of Dane End House, Little Munden, and Abel Smith of Woodhall Park. The Tories gained considerable support from the county landlowners and it was taken for granted at the time, even by the Liberals, that the landowners would coerce their estate workers to vote Tory. So the electors in the towns were a prize the Liberals spent much effort in cultivating and Ware, with its long tradition of Whig politics, was near the top of the list.

Prominent among the Liberal candidates was the Hon. Henry Cowper, second son of Earl Cowper of Panshanger. Cowper's pre-election rally in Ware was arranged for 29 June, which by a happy chance was a Friday, the practice night for the bellringers of St. Mary's and they planned to give him a special peel of welcome as he entered the town. But they had reckoned without the Tory churchwardens – George Gisby who was Clerk to the Poor Law Union and a Mr. Taylor. They had the keys to the tower and refused to hand them over. So the bellringers had to greet the Liberal candidate with the church handbells but they took their revenge by telling the town what had happened in verse and printing it – in the best political tradition – as a handbill. The Hon. Henry Cowper was not only elected, but came top of the poll.

I
Said the bells of St Mary
They're growing quite chary
Of music in Ware,
And we're only to ring for the Tory.
They've locked up the belfry
And we bells are not free
(Though once free as air)
Because the churchwardens are Tory.

II
Said the bells of St Mary
Of silence we're weary,
And wont be shut up when the town is astir,
They've locked us up tight,
Being in a great fright
Lest we, like the people, should Cowper prefer.

III
There's one of the wardens,
An agent well paid,
Also Clerk of the Board
Where Surtees is First Lord,
And lest we should ring
In Cowper as king,
He sheers off with the keys,
Of our voices afraid.

IV
But if they wont let us peel,
We will certainly appeal
From G[isby] and T[aylor] the wardens I ween,
And if Ware is still Ware
It soon shall be seen
There's no vote for a Tory
Warden or Member.
Gone, gone is their glory,
And they shall remember
Who made it their care
To spite people of Ware.

V
And oh, wont we toll,
At the close of the poll,
When *one* Tory goes back,
With baggage and pack,
And we follow his track
(Peeling on till we crack
Or the belfry on Gisby doth down fall)
To Knebworth, or Munden or Woodhall.[21]

21.
An Explosion of Churches

Victorian Britain took to religion in much the same way – and with much the same motives – as twenty-first century America. The British Empire was at its height and it was almost universally believed that God had commissioned the British above other nations to take the Gospel, the rule of law and the blessings of the industrial revolution to the heathen world, especially in Africa and Asia. It was the era in which more missionaries went out than ever before. At home, it was recognised that there was poverty and inequality but it was an article of faith that Christian charity and goodwill, rather than socialism or any other political philosophy, would put this right. In many respects, the kingdom of Victoria was regarded as the Kingdom of God here on earth.

Until the 1830s, religion in Ware had been largely confined to the Parish Church of St. Mary, with a few dissenters operating on the margins. There was a long established chapel of Independents (known later as Congregationalists) in Church Street and in 1811 they were confronted by a rival Independent chapel in the High Street. There was a meeting house of the Religious Society of Friends (Quakers) in Kibes Lane. And from time to time there had been a Baptist congregation somewhere in Ware, in succession to the prominent Baptists of the seventeenth century, like the Packer family. The new chapels and churches of the nineteenth century were established mainly in New Road and Baldock Street, although a number of them had their first foothold in the town in Church Street. From time to time, there were individual Jews and Muslims visiting Ware and in 1783 a visitor to Scott's Grotto described himself as "an atheist". But religion in Ware was mainly Christianity in one of its many denominations.[1] The oldest religious building was, of course, the Parish Church of St. Mary's but we have dealt with that extensively. Here are the others in chronological order of their foundation.

Independents (Congregationalists)

Independents and Presbyterians ran the town during the Commonwealth but were at a disadvantage when Charles II came to the throne in 1660 and restored the supremacy of the Church of England. But the Act of Toleration in 1689 established freedom of worship outside the Church of England. The chapel in Church Street is probably the site of the Independents' meeting house which was known to be in the town in 1662. The present red brick building was built in 1778 and its first minister was William Godwin, who later became a radical writer and atheist and the father-in-law of the poet Shelley. The chapel had a three-decker pulpit and could accommodate 450 people. It was given a Gothic façade with a neo-Norman doorway in the nineteenth century. There was also an adjacent burial ground where many interments took place.

In 1788, a dissenting group left the chapel and started Sunday lecture meetings in the home of Richard Gridley in Ware. In 1811, a Congregational Church was formed and the first Congregational Chapel was built in the High Street in 1816. In 1859 this chapel was rebuilt in

The two Congregational churches. Left: the Independents' Chapel in Church Street, now a print works. Right: the chapel in the High Street, refaced in 1859 in the Romanesque style and now the Leaside United Reformed and Methodist Church – with the Sunday School to the right (now residential).

the Romanesque style, with the maltster Joseph Chuck of Widbury House defraying half the cost of £2,000 and building the Sunday School at his own expense. The then Lord Mayor of London, Alderman David Williams Wire, came down from London and laid the foundation stone on 25 November 1858. Another family which supported the church in the early nineteenth century were the Flacks, who lived in the Manor House and built the Non-conformist 'British School' in Church Street, which later moved to Star Lane. A new Congregational Sunday School and hall were built in 1933.

In 1918, the Independent and Congregational chapels united in the High Street. The Church Street building was closed, its pews being removed and the organ dismantled and installed in 1919 in the Methodist Church in New Road. The old Independent Chapel was used for a time for private parties and a pantomime, 'Jack and the Beanstalk', was performed there in 1925. It was used as a Masonic Hall from 1933 to 1938 and in 1964 was the United Services Club. After that it was used as an auction room by W.H. Lee, until it became a printing works in the 1980s. In 1972, the United Reformed Church was formed from the Congregational and Presbyterian churches, and in 1978 they were joined by Ware Methodists to form the Leaside Church. Some of the stained glass windows, one of them depicting the Resurrection, were brought here from the Methodist Chapel in New Road.

Between 1787 and 1807, a Presbyterian meeting house existed in Black Swan Yard off Baldock Street. In that period, over 80 baptisms took place. After the meeting house was dissolved, the Baptism Register was passed to the Independent Chapel in Church Street and in 1837 the Minister, George Pearce, sent the register to London where it is preserved. The first baptism was carried out by the Rev. Mr. Rogue of Gosport and at subsequent baptisms the Rev. M.J. Heineken of Ware officiated.

Friends' Meeting House

The Quaker meeting house in Kibes Lane was established in 1728 (*illustrated on page 159*) but the Friends had been active in Ware since 1660. Thirteen Ware Friends were among the group tried at Hertford Quarter Sessions in 1661 and imprisoned for a year in Hertford Castle, and others were among the group sentenced to be transported to America aboard the ship, the *Ann*. In 1670 Thomas Burr, a prominent maltster who lived at Bridgefoot in what is now 12 High Street, acquired a lease for a meeting house in Ware but it was never built and the town's Quakers continued to worship in Hertford. The meeting house behind Burr's house in Kibes Lane was set up at the height of the town's malting revolution and it was therefore not surprising that, of the eight trustees, five were maltsters and a sixth a maltmeeter, someone who measured the malt before it was shipped to London. The meeting house was a modest single-storey building, tucked away with an iron gate between two of the Kibes Lane houses. There was a garden, given to the Ware Friends by David Barclay of Youngsbury, and in part of the garden there was a burial ground containing over 200 graves. The last to be buried there was a surgeon, John Burr, who died in 1821 aged 76 – a descendant of Thomas Burr who founded the building. However, by 1810 numbers at the 'First Day' (Sunday) meetings did not exceed 40 and by the 1830s the Ware and Hoddesdon Friends were meeting on alternate Sundays in each others' meeting houses. The Ware meeting house was closed in 1864, shortly after the death of its last important benefactor, John Scott's daughter, Mrs. Maria Hooper. The Friends kept up the building until 1881, when the monthly meeting of the Hertford and Hoddesdon Friends was informed that it was dilapidated and beyond repair. It was then demolished and the land was eventually sold to Ware Urban District Council in 1934 on condition that the character of the burial ground was preserved. In 2006, the Ware Society saved the burial ground from being partially paved over as the outdoor drinking area of a nearby restaurant and in 2010 a commemorative plaque was unveiled by the Society.

Wesleyan Methodists

Wesleyans (the main branch of Methodism, as distinct from Primitive Methodists) were the first to open premises in New Road when it was laid out in the 1830s. John Wesley had preached in Hertford twice and visited Bishop's Stortford but there is no record of his having come to Ware. Nonetheless, Wesleyans were active in Ware as early as 1831 and in 1844 a Methodist minister, the Rev. Robert Adler, was leading worship in the Town Hall for dissident members of the Parish Church congregation. A chapel was erected in New Road in 1839 and enlarged in 1886, when it was advertised as seating 250 people. The chapel was rebuilt again in 1906. In the Second World War, the chapel was damaged when a bomb dropped on New Road and a number of windows were blown out and the organ put out of action. The Methodists stopped using the chapel in 1972 and in 1978 joined with the United Reformed Church to form Leaside Church. At that time some of the stained glass was moved from New Road to Leaside. The old chapel then became a Full Gospel Church and is now the Springs Christian Fellowship.

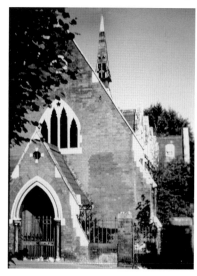

*The Wesleyan Methodist Church, left, now the Springs Christian
Fellowship. Right: the Catholic Apostolic Church before it was
refurbished, with the porch removed, as 'Chapel Mews'.*

Catholic Apostolic Church

The most mysterious denomination to move into New Road was the Catholic Apostolic
Church. It had originated in the 1830s with the fiery preaching in London of a Church of
Scotland minister, Rev. Edward Irving. His followers were at first called "Irvingites" and "spoke
with tongues". But this was soon discouraged, when the new church was founded in 1835 to
prepare the world for the Second Coming of Jesus Christ. Its leaders were 12 apostles, who
included prominent lawyers, clergy, landowners and the son of a former Prime Minister. Under
the apostles was an elaborate ministry of prophets, elders, bishops (who were also called
angels), evangelists, pastors and deacons. Each apostle was responsible for a different "Tribe
of Israel" identified with a modern state and the apostles took their Great Testimony personally
to the kings of France and Prussia, the Czar of Russia and King William IV of England. In their
worship, the Catholic Apostolics sought to recreate the wonder and mystery of the Early Church
and borrowed elements from the Greek, Roman Catholic and Anglican ministries, using many
lights, vestments and incense. The last apostle died in 1901 and "sealed the church" which
meant that no more ministers could be ordained and no new sermons written. This was in
accordance with their belief that the Catholic Apostolic Church was an emergency group which
would have its effect through other churches. Over forty years or so, the Catholic Apostolic
ministry literally died out and the remaining churches were run by lay people. Their "cathedral",
the Church of Christ the King in Gordon Square, London, was leased to the Church of England
as the Anglican chaplaincy for London University. But there is still a church in London's Little
Venice where Catholic Apostolic worship is continued by descendants of the former ministry.

The first Catholic Apostolic Church in Ware was established in 1834 in a small building in
Church Street on the site of the present Tesco superstore. In 1856, a new church was built in

New Road and dedicated on 3 August 1857 by the Rev. F. Layton – the old building being used later by the Roman Catholics. The New Road church, which seated 130 people, was a beautiful building with a highly decorated chancel and fine stained-glass windows, some of them incorporating panels of German painted glass from the 17th century (now in Ware Museum). The church's last priest was the Rev. Howard who lived at 91 New Road and his family continued to hold services, with the help of two sisters, the Misses Smith of Broxbourne, until 1952. In the following year, the church was sold to Fishpools of Waltham Cross as a furniture warehouse. In 1986 it was acquired by a developer and converted into three dwellings, known as Chapel Mews.

Zoar Baptist Chapel

Next door at No. 50 New Road was the Zoar Baptist Chapel. There had been Baptists in Ware since the seventeenth-century Civil War and it is known that a Baptist chapel existed in the town in 1715, though it is not known where. In the 1840s arising from the disputes in the Parish Church between the Vicar on the one side and the churchwardens and some of the curates on the other, a number of house churches were established. One of these was held at 1 Musley Cottages (Musley Lane – later a drovers' public house under the name of the Standard). Worship there continued into 1850 under Mr. Abraham Humphries, a missionary attached to the "Town and Country Scripture Readers", until he was forced to resign when it was known that he was holding house meetings. At about the same period, a small chapel was established at the junction of Park Lane and Watton Road. There a number of people expressed an interest in believers' baptism and two of their number went to Sutton in Bedfordshire, where they were baptised in the River Ouse by the Revd. W. Flack, one of the Flack family at the Manor House in Church Street. On 25 July 1860, the Zoar Strict Baptist Chapel was opened in New Road. It was situated behind Nos 50-52 New Road, next to the Catholic Apostolic Church, reached through an archway behind the terraced houses and could seat 200 people. The *Hertford Mercury* for the following Saturday carried the following report:

A new Baptist Chapel was opened in the town on Wednesday last, in the presence of a numerous assemblage of persons connected with nearly every religious denomination in the town and neighbourhood. A special train brought upwards of 100 persons from London. Adults were baptised and a church formed (of 21 members) according to the stricter views of this sect. Mr. John Sampford, a malt maker, who has for many years laboured with credit and usefulness amongst his fellow townsmen, was ordained pastor of the newly formed church by Mr. Flack, a native of Ware, and now a Baptist minister in London, and by Mr. Banks, minister of Unicorn Yard Chapel and editor of the *Earthen Vessel*. The chapel is situated in New Road. It is a neat and commodious building and we hear that the architect and builder (Mr. James Hitch) has given very great satisfaction by the manner in which he has carried out his contract. The expense of the building has fallen principally on those intending to worship in it, although some few others have contributed, amongst whom may be named Robert Hanbury, Esquire, who, with his accustomed liberality, sent a donation of £10.

Mr. Sampford remained the pastor for over 30 years but it seems that no-one was chosen to succeed him. Services continued under a supply ministry including Joseph Chalkley of

Braughing, who died on Bedford Railway Station on the 25 October 1926. The chapel then declined and the last member, Mrs. E. Bryant, transferrred to the Ebenezer Strict Baptist Chapel at Hertford. In 1927, the Zoar Chapel was closed. It is not known when it was demolished, but for some years afterwards the baptism tank remained and was used as a fish tank by the owners of one of the terraced houses. The name 'Zoar' came from the Book of Genesis and was the town where Lot and his daughters found refuge after the destruction of Sodom and Gomorrah. During the 1980s, a Baptist Fellowship met in Place House and Baptists are now involved (with Christ Church) in the Emmanuel Shared Church.

The foundation stone of Zoar Baptist Church, now in the Ware Museum garden

A Second Parish – Christ Church

The establishment of a second Anglican parish had little to do with the controversy of the 1840s when over half the congregation of St. Mary's walked out as the Vicar, Henry Coddington, mounted the pulpit stairs. The new parish was a product of the rapid growth of the town and the desire to give pastoral care to the labouring classes in the yards of Amwell End. The impetus came from two men. One was Robert Hanbury of Poles – a partner in the brewing firm of Truman, Hanbury and Buxton – who was both rich and ready to build new churches wherever they were needed. Already in 1853 he had provided a new parish church in Thundridge on the Cambridge road to replace the ruined Church of All Saints and Little St. Mary out in the fields of the Rib valley, and it was he who provided the funds and land for Christ Church in 1858. The other man was Alexander Gordon of Widbury Hill who apparently first proposed a new Ware chuch – but we only have Robert Hanbury's word for it since Mr. Gordon died before he could follow up his proposal with plans or money.[2]

The new church was built in 1858 of Kentish Ragstone and the architect was Nehemiah Stevens of Tunbridge Wells. The reason for the Kent connection was that from 1846-1877 there was a reorganisation of the Church of England which placed Ware in the Diocese of Rochester. It was a large church, capable of seating 700 people, built in Early English style with the walls divided into bays by projecting buttresses with pairs of lancet windows in between. The nave and the two aisles were separately roofed in Welsh slate. Thus the west elevation presents three gables as seen from New Road. The free-standing tower was built a year later than the church in 1859 and, although designed for a full peel of bells, in fact has just one three-hundredweight bell. In the chancel is a triple light east window with glass by Matthew Travers, installed in 1948 to replace windows blown out by bombing of New Road in 1940, though the circular window above dates from 1883.

Christ Church was consecrated by the Bishop of Rochester on 9 November 1858 at the

Christ Church, seen from the east, with its free-standing bell tower.

11am service of Morning Prayer. Afterwards, the bishop, clergy and guests "partook of an elegant luncheon" at Poles, the home of Mr. Robert Hanbury, who had provided the land and money for the church, as well as later paying for the Vicarage and the Mission Hall in Amwell End. The large Vicarage, also designed by Nehemiah Stevens, was demolished in 1963 when the Vicar was given a modern house at the top of Hanbury Close. There is a memorial to Robert Hanbury of Poles on the north wall of the church.

From its beginnings Christ Church was an Evangelical community and determined to tackle the major social problems of Ware, particularly poverty and drink. This was especially the case under its third incumbent, the outspoken Rev. Alfred Oates, who was Vicar from 1880 until 1914. This was a period when Ware had many pubs and ale house, and here the strong character of Mr. Oates came into its own. There was a proposal to build a new public house near the Christ Church schools' playing field, at the junction of Bowling Road and King Edward's Road, and a vote was to be taken at a meeting being held at the French Horn. Mr. Oates learned of the vote, called together his Men's Bible Class and set off for the French Horn. The people at the meeting were "presently surprised to hear the tramping upstairs ... of many feet, and Mr. Oates appeared at the head of his big body of men and the issue was, before long, settled in his favour".[3] Mr. Oates also took a personal hand in the education at the Christ Church National Schools. Each year several thousand Penny Dinners were provided for children, and education has been a continuing responsibility of Christ Church. In addition he played an important part in getting a district nurse appointed for the parish.

The Mission Hall in Amwell End was built for Christ Church by Thomas Hunt of Ware, who also built the Memorial Hall next to the church. Mr. Robert Hanbury financed building of the Mission Hall and also laid the foundation stone in 1883. It had a clock on it which was illuminated by the Ware Gas Company, and it struck the hour throughout the day. Despite the work of the Local Board of Health, there was still a large population living in appalling conditions in the yards off Amwell End. To attract people from the yards, the Mission Hall organised a Sewing and Cutting-out Class for Women, a Lending Library, Writing and Reading Room, clubs for cricket and tennis, and rooms for billiards, bagatelle, chess, ping-pong, draughts and dominoes – as well as church services and Bible reading. To counteract the influence of the many pubs in Amwell End, the teetotal Band of Hope was formed. The Mission Hall came into its own during the 1914-18 War, when it was opened daily as a club for the Forces and was

Robert Hanbury

used again as a Forces' Club during the Second World War. It was also the first headquarters of the Ware Town Nursing Association. But by this time most families had moved out of Amwell End and in 1954 it was put up for sale. It was bought by the Ware Urban District Council which had plans for widening Amwell End and demolished in 1958.

Roman Catholics

The Roman Catholics took over the chapel in Dead Lane (Church Street) after the Catholic Apostolic Church moved to New Road in 1857. This followed the re-establishment of the Catholic hierarchy in Britain in 1850 – Ware and Hertford came into the Diocese (later the Archdiocese) of Westminster in which there is now a Catholic Bishop for Hertfordshire. The small church in Church Street was dedicated to St. Joseph and served first by a priest from Hertford and then by one attached to Westminster Cathedral. Eventually, after the First World War, Ware was given its own parish priest. The longest serving priest in Ware was the Rev. Francis Macirone, who was chaplain at Hertford and parish priest in Ware from 1919 to 1945. He was a very cultured man, but an eccentric, known chiefly for riding a bicycle staring steadfastly at the ground. He was succeeded by Father Boddy (known as "Old Bodd"), and then Fr. Norman Kersey, Fr. Cathal McGonagle (known as "Father Mac") and now by Fr. John Gray.

In 1921, the building in Church Street having fallen into a dilapidated condition, the Catholic congregation moved to a temporary building erected in King Edward's Road. The foundation stone of a new church was laid in 1936 and blessed by Cardinal Hinsley. The church was opened in 1939, dedicated to the Sacred Heart of Jesus and St Joseph. It was a handsome cruciform church, built in traditional Hertfordshire flint and designed by Geoffrey Webb, nephew of the famous architect, Sir Aston Webb, and the uncle of Sir John Hanbury, who became chairman of the pharmaceutical firm of Allen and Hanbury's. The Sacred Heart JMI School at Broadmeads has links with the church.

There were other Catholic schools with connections with Ware. One was St. Edmund's College at Old Hall Green, near Puckeridge – often referred to as 'St. Edmund's College,

*The Roman Catholic Church of the Sacred Heart of Jesus and St. Joseph at
the corner of New Road and King Edward's Road.*

Ware' from its former postal address, and the oldest Catholic public school in Britain. It was a
direct descendant of the English College at Douai near Rheims in France, set up as a seminary
for Catholic priests during the reign of Queen Elizabeth I. At the time of the French Revolution,
Douai broke into two parts, one section going to Ushaw College in Durham, the other coming
to Hertfordshire in 1793. It was then housed alongside the seminary a boys' school which
Bishop Challoner had established at Standon Lordship. The seminary has now left St. Edmund's
College, being merged with the Jesuit Heythrop College as part of London University. But the
Catholic Public School, along with the St. Hugh's Preparatory School, continues to thrive at
Puckeridge. The school has a wonderful chapel designed by Augustus Welby Pugin and
completed in 1853.

The other school was closer to Ware. Poles Convent – or to give it its proper title, the
convent school run by the Faithful Companions of Jesus (FCJ) – was established at Thundridge
in the former home of the Hanbury brewing family. The Hanburys had sold the house to Mr.
H.J. King in 1913 and he sold it in 1923 to the FCJ, a teaching order of nuns founded in
Amiens, France, in 1820. The house was considerably enlarged as a boarding school for girls,
with dormitories, six classrooms, a large gymnasium, underground pottery room and a beautiful
chapel. The nuns, who at one time numbered 40 at Poles, attended chapel every day. In time,
Poles became recognised as an outstanding girls' boarding school, taking Catholic and non-
Catholic pupils. In 1974, the sixth form began to take classes at St. Edmund's College at
Puckeridge, which became fully coeducational in 1986. That was the year in which Poles Convent
and the girls' school closed, after which the buildings were converted into a luxury golfing hotel,
known as Hanbury Manor. However, the small cemetery for the nuns still exists in a corner of
the hotel grounds.

While Poles Convent and St. Edmund's were still functioning as separate Catholic schools, they were visited in turn by a small group of Carmelite sisters. The date was 25 November 1958 and the Carmelites – an 'enclosed' order of contemplative and working nuns, named after Mount Carmel in Palestine – were on their way to a new home in Ware. They had first settled in Hatfield in 1925 but in 1938, with the development nearby of the de Haviland aircraft factory, they moved to Hitchin. Again a loss of privacy in 1958 led to the move to Ware. Their monastery is across the A10 bypass, next to Ware Park, in a house built in 1930 for the Garrett milling family from Hertford. The sisters are vegetarian and self-financing, growing their own vegetables in their garden and baking altar loaves for surrounding Roman Catholic and Anglican churches.

A Disreputable Incident

When the Roman Catholic hierarchy (i.e. bishops with territorial jurisdictions in England) was re-established by Pope Pius IX in 1850, the news was greeted with a widespread display of anti-Catholic prejudice. It came to a head in November when the newly appointed Archbishop of Westminster, Cardinal Wiseman, published the papal bull and pleaded in vain for toleration. In Hertford, the Mayor and Corporation convened a public meeting to protest against what they called 'the Popish Aggression' and drew up a petition to Queen Victoria. Throughout the county, Protestant ministers announced that on the following Sunday they would preach against 'the Errors of Popery'. But in Ware something different was being planned.

The first inkling of this came in a letter from the Vicar, Rev. J.W. Blakesley, to Daniel Giles of Youngsbury, who as the High Sheriff was in charge of peacekeeping in the county. On 16 November, Mr. Blakesley wrote that Jack Dye, publican of the Union Jack [now the Rifle Volunteer] on Musley Hill, was planning a riotous assembly:

Dye, a publican at the top of New Road, with a sagacity worthy of W. Barnum the American [showman], is determined to take advantage of the last step of the Bishop of Rome, by forming an effigy of the new Cardinal Archbishop, to be burnt on Tuesday next.

As a great deal of drinking would be involved, the Vicar asked the Sheriff if something could be done to stop it. But his request was in vain – as the *Hertfordshire Mercury* reported on 23 November:

WARE

THE POPE'S EFFIGY – The effigy of the Pope, in full Papal attire, was drawn through this town on Tuesday evening, attended by the Cardinal Archbishop and seven priests, masked and habited in surplices, and smoking cigars. A band of music accompanied him. After making a tour of the town, his Holiness' effigy was taken to Musley Hill where a huge funeral pyre was erected – and having been suspended from a rope by the neck, was committed to the flames. Some thousands of persons were present, many of whom came from a great distance.

This disreputable incident is recorded here, not only as a piece of Ware history but also to show how far the town has progressed in 160 years to the present when the Catholic community with its church in King Edward's Road and primary school at Broadmeads are all accepted as integral parts of the life of Ware.[4]

The Salvation Army

Salvationists also arrived in Ware amid some controversy. The Salvation Army was founded in 1865 by William and Catherine Booth at a 'tent meeting' in Whitechapel. It was known at first as the East London Christian Mission, dedicated to individual salvation, work among the poor and destitute and a strong opposition to alcoholic drink. In 1878 it became the Salvation Army, under 'General' William Booth with the motto "Blood and Fire". From then, 'the Army' embarked on a period of unparalleled growth at home and abroad.

The Salvation Army arrived in Ware in the 1880s. They held open-air meetings, often in the middle of Ware High Street, and in 1886 sixteen members of the Ware Corps were brought before the town's magistrates court, charged with obstructing the highway. The prosecution alleged that the obstructions were caused by open-air meetings, when crowds of between 300 and 750 people gathered. When the Salvation Army band refused police orders to move on, Captain James A. Smith and some of his comrades were arrested and lodged in the Ware lock-up next to St. Mary's Church. Captain Taylor of Luton was charged in his absence and Captain Smith, in charge of the Army in Ware, was charged with five offences. The defence solicitor said that the police were trying to exterminate the Army from Ware, which was probably true since at that time Salvationists stirred up opposition even within the churches. The court was crowded and the case lasted all afternoon. At 5pm the five magistrates went into recess and on their return announced that Captains Smith and Taylor would each be fined 20 shillings and the others 10s. each, with costs. Eleven of the Salvationists refused to pay the fines and were summarily sent to prison at Holloway, then both a male and female prison. Captain Smith was in gaol for a fortnight and the remainder a week. On their release from Holloway on 19 September, over 600 London Salvationists gathered outside the prison and escorted the Ware eleven, still wearing their prison uniforms, to the Salvation Army Chalk Farm barracks where a special breakfast was laid on. There was a tumultuous reception during which the Ware eleven declared that they were prepared to go to prison again for their beliefs.[5]

The present Salvation Army Citadel in Baldock Street was built in 1907 – before that the Army used the hall in Gladstone Road, now the headquarters of the Royal British Legion. Various groups now use the Citadel and lunches are served twice a week to older residents. The Salvation Army now has good relations with all the churches in Ware and participates in many town events, including the carol singing on the Dickensian Evening on the first Friday of December.

Religion in the Twentieth Century

Since we have now strayed out of the Victorian era, this is the place to mention some of the later religious developments in the town. After the Roman Catholics had left Church Street for their new home in King Edward's Road, the small chapel was taken over by a revivalist preacher, named 'Fatty' Cutmore, who said he would found his own political party and make sure everyone had two acres of land and a cow.[6] At first Mr. Cutmore had a regular congregation of 36 or so but this declined and during the 1930s many left and formed a group called the Coronation Bethren. They were loosely affiliated to the Plymouth Brethren and met in a hall in Coronation Road, later used as a bakery and Morley Fireplaces, and then converted to housing. After the Second World War, the Coronation Road services were run by an American, Jim Taylor, who instituted a strict code of behaviour for members, forbidding them to eat or drink with non-members. With the decline in their numbers in the 1960s, the Coronation Road hall was sold and the remaining members joined the Hertford Brethren, meeting in Bengeo.

In the early 1900s a small group of Christians began worshipping together in the home of a Mr. William Radford, who held a senior position in the pharmaceutical company, Allen and Hanbury's. From there, a move was made to rented accommodation, first in the former Independent Chapel in Church Street and then to the hall in Coronation Road (later used by the Brethren). In 1920, due mainly to the generosity of the Radford family, the present Gospel Hall was built in Collett Road. The Christian group who worship there Sunday by Sunday are independent, with no administrative links with any group in Ware or elsewhere.

Pentecostalists – distinguished by worship in which people 'speak with tongues' – came to Ware in 1975 and worshipped at first in the building in Church Street which in the Middle Ages had been the site of the Corpus Christi Barn. In 1979, they moved to the former Methodist Church in New Road and founded the Full Gospel Church (Assembly of God). For twenty years the church thrived with large attendances and a vigorous outreach programme. A youth club and mother-and-baby group were popular and emergency help was sent to Protestant groups in Romania after the collapse of the Communist regime. In 2002, as a result of a split in the congregation, the community changed its name from the Ware Full Gospel Church to 'Springs Christian Fellowship'.

During the 1980s the Ware Baptist Fellowship, an extension of Hertford Baptist Church, met each Sunday in the old manor house of Ware, Place House, in Bluecoat Yard. This was discontinued in the 1990s when the Hertford Baptist Church and Christ Church entered into a partnership with further financial help from the Baptist Union of England and Wales to form the Emmanuel Shared Church. Sunday services were held, either in Tower JMI School or in private houses in the north-east of the town and a full-time worker was employed and based in a specially purchased house in King George Road.

In the early 1980s, the former Pentecostalist chapel in Church Street – before that the site of a Gospel Hall, the British School and the medieval Corpus Christi Barn – was bought by the Christadelphians. Founded in 1844 by an English doctor, John Thomas, who had travelled widely in the United States, the Christadelphians are a community of working men and women who day by day read and study the Bible. 'Christadelphians' means the brethren of Christ and in their 'ecclesia' (church) they hold lectures about all aspects of the Bible and God's plan of Salvation and the return to earth of Jesus Christ.

22.
The Schools Revolution

The nineteenth century was the period in which education in Britain took giant steps forward. Compulsory education did not come until 1870 and free education not until 1891. But much earlier in the century the government had been forced, much against its will, to take a hand in the nation's schooling and to begin providing money. As the vote was given to an ever wider section of the (male) population, so it was felt that the new voters should be given some schooling, at least to be able to read. It was one of the major turning points in British history.

Before that happened, education had been a wholly private business. The children of wealthier parents had private tutors and went to private schools or the famous and misnamed 'public schools'. It was only the cleverest children from poorer families – or those who had some influential patron to 'present' them, as with Christ's Hospital – who attended the public schools or grammar schools established in major towns. Ware had a Free Grammar School and we shall come back to that later. All the other schools in the town were privately run, as appears from the Ware entry in *Pigot's Directory for Hertfordshire 1832*:

> Miss Cates (boarding), Amwell End
> Charity school (girls), Church Lane, Mary Gull
> Susan Cobham, Baldock Street
> Ann Elizabeth Crabb, Bluecoat Yard
> Rev. Salisbury Dunn M.A. (boarding) Amwell End
> Free Grammar School, Churchyard, Rev. James Britton, Master
> Lancasterian School, Dead Lane, Joseph Dines, Master
> Susan Malin, Land Row
> Elizabeth and Martha Medcalf, Amwell End
> National School, Dead Lane, William Miller, Master
> Thomas Pavitt, Water Row
> Arthur Taylor (boarding), Star Lane
> The Misses Teed (boarding), Thunder House
> Mary Wiggens, Mill Lane.

Many of these were 'dame schools' for younger children, in effect, little better than child-minding kindergartens. But others offered a good standard of education. The girls at Mary Gull's charity school were the "Polly Gull's greyhounds" referred to in an earlier chapter by James Smith – 'greyhounds' because they wore grey cloaks. The charity reference probably referred to bequests left for schooling by Dame Margaret Tufton in 1722 and Ann Ball in 1749. Later Mary Gull moved her school to the Priory as guests of Miss Hadsley and there were schools in other mansions, such as Thunder Hall and Amwell House. The Medcalf sisters later moved their school from Amwell End to Place House, Bluecoat Yard. Such schools often ceased teaching when the owner married or moved away. But two of the schools in the above list – the Lancasterian and National schools – were to have longer lives and greater influence.

And that was partly due to government policy.

In 1833, John Roebuck, a Radical MP, introduced a resolution into the House of Commons for "a universal and national education of the whole people". The resolution was defeated, but Parliament did vote £20,000 in grants to two religious societies engaged in elementary education. This was education in the 'three Rs' – reading, writing and arithmetic – up to the age of 14, although many children continued to leave school at 11. The money was divided between the 'National Society for Promoting the Education of the Poor in the Principles of the Established Church', which ran the National schools according to the teachings of the Church of England, and the 'British and Foreign Schools Society', which ran the so-called British Schools along Nonconformist lines. Both societies arose from a system of monitorial schools, pioneered in the 1790s by Andrew Bell, an Anglican, and Joseph Lancaster, a Quaker. The idea was that a teacher would instruct the older children or monitors, who in their turn would drill the younger children. These government grants, the first of their kind in British education, were to grow to prodigious proportions before the state decided to run its own schools. In 1850 the grants to the two societies amounted to £500,000.

Both societies set up schools in Ware early in the century and both were located at first in Dead Lane (Church Street). The British School, originally called the Lancasterian School as we noted in *Pigot's Directory*, was established in 1818 on the site of the former Corpus Christi Barn owned by the Ware Charity Trustees (it is now the Christadelphian meeting hall), but on December 7 1837 it moved to new purpose-built premises in Star Lane (Star Street). The British School remained in being until 1890, when the site was sold by the trustees to the Ware Gas Company. True to the spirit of the British and Foreign Schools Society, the sale notice said that the school had been "for the education of the labouring and manufacturing classes of every religious persuasion residing in the Parish of Ware". By the time it closed, there was already a system of state education and in Ware a strongly evangelical type of education was being provided by the Christ Church schools, just 200 yards away in New Road.

Ware's first National School was established in 1820, also in Dead Lane, on another site owned by the Ware Charity Trustees opposite the British School. The National School stayed there until a new school was built in 1844, when the old schoolroom became partly a plumber's shop and partly the town's fire station, a use which lasted until well into the 20th century. On July 11 1829 a grand concert and ball were held to raise funds for the National School and the Lying-in Charities. The concert in St. Mary's Church included music by Mozart and Handel, performed by well-known soloists from London, the King's Concert of Ancient Music and the Young Gentlemen of the Chapel Royal, under the baton of Thomas Luppino, the talented organist of St. Mary's. It was held under the patronage of H.R.H. the Duke of Gloucester and many of the county nobility and gentry; a souvenir programme was printed on silk and now hangs in the Priory.

In 1844, the foundation stone for a new National School farther along Church Street opposite St. Mary's Church was laid by Mr. William Parker of Ware Park, with the Vicar, the Rev. Henry Coddington, presiding. This was one of Mr. Coddington's last duties in Ware, for he died abroad in the following year, worn out by ill health and a long dispute with his critics in the parish. The new vicar, the Rev. J.W. Blakesley, immediately took up the challenge of overseeing the building and raising money to run the school. He even wrote to Trinity College, the patrons of the living and landlords of the Rectory House (the Manor House), next door to the new school, to see if he could levy a rent on that property. He received a curt reply from the Bursar of Trinity:

> They have been lessees for a great many years (I mean the family of the Flacks); the present Mr. Flack was born in the Rectory House. They behaved exceedingly liberally in giving up the portion of their leasehold, in which the School is built; and we have no power, and I must add no wish, to constrain them to do anything against their will.[1]

The Bursar might have added that Mr. Flack was a well known Nonconformist and, indeed, a trustee of the rival British School in Star Street.

Funds continued to be a problem. As the government grant, at that time still quite small, was calculated on attendances, the Trustees reduced the charges for children to one penny a week to try to encourage more children to come. The following year, in 1846, a more ingenious scheme was tried. "When three or more children are at school from one family, payments for all above two will, if the attendance has been punctual and regular, but not otherwise, be returned to the Parents at the end of the Quarter". Apart from the government grant and payments by parents, the main source of income was subscriptions from wealthier classes in the town and surrounding country. Subscribers were invited to inspect the school at any time during school hours. They were invited to write their comments in a special book kept for the purpose and a "Timebill" was to be hung outside each of the school rooms to keep visitors informed about the classes. So far reference has been made to the National School in the singular, but by the 1840s it consisted of three schools in the one establishment – Boys, Girls and Infants. Alongside financial problems, the minutes of the Managers record their concern about the children and their teachers. Children were often absenting themselves with excuses about "nursing the baby" or "going on errands". One teacher reported: "anything unusual occurring in the town has unfortunately a decided tendency to keep the children away. At Fairtime, for instance, scarcely one-third of the boys are present."

Concern about the teachers came to a head with the inspection in December 1846 by the Rev. John Allen, a government inspector. His report was pithy but devestating:

> Discipline not satisfactory – Boys not orderly – Girls not tidy. None of the children very clean. Infants not in good order at prayers. Instruction scanty. Boys read with deliberation and some distinctions, not fluently – arithmetic, small progress in – writing, poor – spelling, poor – are not exercised in composition. Some of the upper class had learned the Gospel and Epistle for the Sunday imperfectly – also some of the Prophecies about our Saviour ....

And so on. Incidentally, no child was allowed to attend the National Schools who did not also attend Sunday School and the Infants' School Mistress was required to sit with the children in church and make sure they behaved. Mr. Allen then turned to the teachers:

> Master, as I judge, of no great capacity, perhaps he does his best – has not the faculty of quickening the sluggish intellects of his boys, or of imparting a principle of order. Mistress perhaps of more capacity, but of less training. Neither teacher is in my judgement fitted for the situation filled ....[2]

As a result of the inspection, both the Master of the boys and the Mistress of the girls were given notice to leave. The Infants' Mistress, a Miss Butcher, was to have her contract renewed if she agreed to attend the Home and Colonial Infants Training School in Gray's Inn Road, London, her expenses to be met by the Managers. But Miss Butcher declined the offer. So in 1847, the Managers set about the task of finding new teachers and this time they looked for men and women who had a certificate from a training college. But they had to pay higher salaries than before and they did not find a Certified Master until 1862. He was Archibald Bertram Bannister, who was to remain at the school until his retirement in 1906. The Managers also agreed, in 1868, to pay some of the more promising monitors among the older children.

The Infants' School journal for this period survives and is in the keeping of the present St Catherine's School. It was begun on June 27 1864 and ended on June 30 1893. The penultimate entry is a report from one of Her Majesty's Inspectors, which commended the school on the "extremely good" discipline and training of the children and the "considerable intelligence" displayed in object lessons and other occupations. The inspector therefore recommended payment of the highest variable grant without hesitation. But he added that the school needed more staff, and so two of the part-time teachers were made full-time, giving the Infants' School a staff of the Mistress, Miss Anne Wilkinson (the only certified teacher) and three other full-timers.

But a major change in the life of St. Mary's National Schools (that is what they were called by this time) had come in 1873. The 1870 Education Act, which has been described as the beginning of the modern educational system, showed that the time had now come for the state to set up its own schools and not to leave them to subsidised church bodies. The Act's most important provision was the establishment of School Boards (after which 'Board Schools' were named) with powers to levy a local rate for building new schools. On 27 August 1873, a meeting was held of the subscribers and managers of St Mary's National Schools, with the new Vicar, the Rev. E.E.W. Kirkby, in the chair. The Vicar said that they were required by the Education Department either to improve the school or to set up a School Board. Mr. Robert Hanbury and Mr. Henry Page, the town's biggest maltster, said that a School Board was unnecessary and undesirable. The meeting agreed and they immediately opened a subscription fund for a new Boys' School, which would bring the total accommodation to 1,500 children. The Hon. Secretary of the fund was Mr. Page's son-in-law, Lieutenant Richard Benyon Croft, R.N. Retired, who was to play an important role in later educational developments in the town. Henry Page promised £200 to the fund, Mr. Hanbury and Mr. Parker of Ware Park both promised £150 and many others lesser amounts. The new building, made of flint and in the Gothic style, was erected quickly and opened in 1874 at a cost of £2000. When in 1985 the disused school in Church Street was being converted into a medical centre, the builders said that the 1874 extension was shoddily built by comparison with the original 1844 school. A further classroom for the Boys' School was added in 1884 at a cost of £600, giving the school accommodation for 730 children. The decision to resist the setting up of a School Board was an important one and has influenced primary education in Ware until the present day. There is no record of the town ever having a School Board and no Board schools were established before the new Hertfordshire County Council took over education in 1906. Even in 1910, when the town's first state school was established in the former grammar school building at the

The St. Mary's National Schools, as seen from the tower of St. Mary's. The building at the back is the original 1844 school, now a medical centre. In front of it is the 1874 building, made of flint and the Master's house.

top of Musley Hill, it was to be a Church of England school, with two of the managers appointed by the Anglican parishes. The strong influence of the Church over education in the town survives to this day. One reason for that was the ability of the St. Mary's National Schools to find the funds to enlarge and modernise and thus resist setting up a School Board. But another reason was the vigorous growth of a second set of National Schools in the town.

The separate parish of Christ Church, covering the eastern half of the town, was created in 1858. The church was built on land in New Road given by Robert Hanbury and two years later he provided adjoining land for National Schools. The first public mention of them was a notice in the *Hertfordshire Mercury* on 22 September 1860 when it was announced that at the church's Sunday morning service "the Rev. Capel Molyneux will preach in aid of the Christ Church Schools". But Andrew Wang, in his book *Christ Church School, Ware, A History 1860 - 1985"* (written while teaching at the school), says that the driving force behind the establishment of the schools was Mrs. Baines, wife of the first Vicar, the Rev. F.A. Baines. They were also known as the Christ Church Day Schools, to distinguish them from the Sunday Schools, set up at about the same time.

In their early years, the Christ Church schools faced much the same problems that the St. Mary's schools had faced. Overcrowding was one of them. The maximum attendance in the 1860s and 1870s was 500 children, rising to 740 in 1878 and then falling back to around 400 for the remainder of the century. Attendances were never 100 per cent – in 1881 the average attendance was 344 children, or only 70 per cent of the pupils on the school roll. This worried

The redbrick buildings of the Christ Church National Schools. The white building on the left is part of the extension built in 1931 when the the Ware Senior and Central School moved down from Musley Hill.

the Managers because this meant a smaller income, in terms of both the children's pennies and the government grant. But at least it eased the overcrowding problem, for Christ Church Schools (Boys, Girls and Infants) then occupied only the red-brick buildings which constitute the dining room and staff area of the present school. There were also the problems of inadequate heating and noise: the partition between the boys' and girls' rooms, each accommodating 120 children, was made of wood.

We have mentioned the children's pennies. In 1877, in a remarkable spirit of cooperation, the Managers of St. Mary's and the Christ Church schools met to agree on raising the fees to three pence for each child (the schools seemed to coooperate better than their respective parishes). Free education was not introduced until 1891, when the government offered an annual grant of ten shillings for each child. The Managers of St. Mary's and Christ Church accepted the offer and then sent a typically Victorian letter to parents, suggesting that the threepenny bits they were thus saving should be spent on coal, rent, clothes or opening a savings bank account – but "might be wasted on beer and tobacco, and be a curse rather than a benefit. Which shall it be?"

At first, the Christ Church Schools, like St. Mary's before them, received severely adverse reports from government inspectors though the diocesan inspectors reported more favourably. And these reports were published in full in the parish magazine. The report in 1894 on the Boys' School found that there were "very low general standards". One class was taught by a monitor who had been "far too little supervised" and an assistant teacher was found to be "inefficient". The general work of the boys was weak, arithmetic bad and grammar "indifferent".

The girls were also criticised but not so severely. As a result, the government grant was reduced for all except the Infants' School, which had had a good report. Standards were raised but it was not until 1906 that Christ Church began to get consistently good inspectors' reports. The same adverse report in 1894 required the schools to carry out building improvements if they were to continue to attract a grant. The infants needed a larger classroom, a new cloakroom was needed, a lavatory had to be rebuilt and new flooring and furnishings were required. The enlargement was met mainly by the church giving up its parish room; it was replaced by the gift by Mrs. Page of the Memorial Room, opened in 1896. Even so the cost to the Managers of the schools was £700 and an appeal was circulated in the town. The Vicar, the Rev. Alfred Oates, wrote that the result of the appeal would "determine whether or not the New Road National Schools are to continue, or to end, their good work." Christ Church also hoped that St. Mary's would help in the fund, as Christ Church had helped when a new classroom had been added to the St. Mary's Schools in 1883.

Nineteenth-century schooling in Ware was not all problems. The Christ Church Schools held an annual concert, beginning in October 1868 with the boys singing religious and secular songs, which raised £8.11s.6d. for the Church Schoolmasters' and Mistresses' Benevolent Institution. This soon became a Christmas concert and is a forerunner of the Christmas pantomimes put on by the modern Christ Church Junior School. And in sports too, they must have enjoyed themselves though they did not always win. Christ Church's main rivals were, and still are, St. Mary's and in the first Ware schools football match to be reported in the *Hertfordshire Mercury* in 1906, the St. Mary's Boys won 3-2. But both sets of schools had entered the new century with good inspectors' reports for their education and with buildings considerably extended and improved.

The Free Grammar School

Ware's oldest school was the Free Grammar School, which probably existed in the Middle Ages. One of the deeds of properties belonging to the Guild of Corpus Christi says that in 1492 there was a schoolmaster, named Edmund Catmer, in Mill Lane (now Priory Street). Whether that was where his school was or whether he just lived there, it does not say. However, by 1612 the Ware Charity Trustees (the successors of the Guild) owned a "Towne house or schoolehouse" in the churchyard. As this building was not demolished until late in the 19th century, it can be located from Ordnance Survey maps as being just outside the south-east corner of St. Mary's churchyard, opposite Churchgate House (Jacoby's Restaurant). A Victorian schools inspector speculated that it had probably begun life as a "chantry school": the main chantry in Ware, established in 1470 to provide a priest to say Mass for the souls of Ellen Bramble and her family, was abolished in 1534. But by 1612 it was known as the Free Grammar School and it gave a free education to ten boys in writing and reading. It was endowed by a number of bequests, including £100 given in the will of Humphrey Spencer in 1633 on condition that the trustees of the town lands gave another £100, as well as by the rents of properties owned by the trustees, including the Lamb Inn at Colliers End.

There was also a grammar school in Wareside, which was then part of the parish of Ware and known as Ware Upland. As well as endowing the Free Grammar School in the town,

Humphrey Spencer's will of 1633 bequeathed £100 for the education of the poorest children in Wareside in reading and writing. Under another will of 1682, the Wareside school was given a rent-charge of £5 a year on an acre of land beside the Widford Road called Betteridge, and in 1747, the school was completely rebuilt by the squire of Blakesware, William Plumer. The Wareside Grammar School lasted until the late 19th century when it was closed as part of the scheme to reform and re-establish the Free Grammar School in Ware town. By that time, Wareside had its own National Schools for the education of children under eleven.

On 13 October 1830, the trustees admitted to the Ware Grammar School a ten-year old boy, who was later to emigrate to Australia where he became an accomplished and prolific writer. This was James Smith who had been sent first to a school run by Thomas Pavitt, mentioned in *Pigot's Directory* of 1832:

> Pavitt had been a dissenting minister originally and still adhered to the clerical garb and white neckcloth, he had a defect in his vision, which always rendered it difficult for us to determine whether he was looking at us or not; so that sometimes when we were engaged in "cribbing" from a "key", and believed that this gaze was directed elsewhere, our delinquency would be detected, and we would be called up to receive its appropriate punishment.[3]

This description comes from an autobiographical novel which James Smith began to write in Melbourne in the 1860s. In a later chapter of the same novel, he wrote:

> Some circumstance, not of sufficient importance to fasten itself firmly upon my memory, led to my removal from Pavitt's school to one conducted by the Rev. John Burly. It was an endowed Grammar School, with ten scholars on the foundation and about a score of others who paid for their education. The schoolroom occupied the south-west angle of the churchyard, and was approached by a steep flight of stairs, which seemed to be symbolical of our ascent to a good many branches of learning. A row of dormer windows, while they admitted the light, prevented our attention to our studies being distracted by the sight of external objects, and the massive beams which crossed the room were deeply indented with names or initials by bygone scholars. Every three hours the chimes in the fine old church adjacent used to execute a tune – profane ones upon week days and the 104th Psalm on Sundays; and to the thinking of us schoolboys, the twelve o'clock chime, which signalised our mid-day release from study, was fuller of gaiety and sprightliness than that which rang at any other hour.[4]

The schoolhouse itself was a tiny, two-storey building, covering an area of only 33ft. by 14ft. (10.06m x 14.26m). Charles Elton, the inspector of the government's Endowed Schools Commission, described it in 1872 as "evidently very old, perhaps older than the time of Queen Elizabeth, and constructed purely of wood". As the century wore on, the state of the Free Grammar School and the education it provided began to cause concern.

In 1866, Mr. D.R. Fearon inspected the school for the government's Schools Inquiry Commission and gave it a scathing report. There were 18 boys in the school, ten free and eight fee-paying. Five of the fee-paying boys were in a class by themselves, the remainder being in the other class. The ten free boys were the sons of a gardener, coachman, confectioner, shoemaker, farrier, wheelwright, baker, candlemaker, foreman in a malting house and a bargeowner; the three fee-paying boys in the same form were the sons of another confectioner, a butler and a foreman in a brick kiln. All quite respectable occupations, but Mr. Fearon adds this comment:

> It should be observed that the feoffees have it in their power at any moment to inundate the school with any number of children of the poorest sort. But then, on the other hand, the Master would only be bound to teach them reading and writing. Hence, a sort of tacit compromise has arisen between the Master and the feoffees, whereby they only send him ten boys, of the class which is called 'respectable', and he teaches them the usual branches of an English education.[5]

In fact, the Master left the teaching to his unqualified assistant, who gave instruction in reading, writing, dictation, arithmetic, modern geography and English grammar. No Latin, mathematics, music or French were taught, and so Mr. Fearon concluded that it was not performing any of the functions of a grammar school. To test what the boys were being taught, he gave a dictation test to the second form and found that none of them could do it without errors. One boy had 16 errors in eight lines, and he was not the worst. Mr. Fearon pronounced their English grammar "a farce". Two of the boys, the candlemaker's 15-year old son and the butler's 12-year old, could hardly read at all: "of the 13 boys in the above list I should only have passed six in the fourth standard at a National school, and I do not think any of them would have passed in the sixth standard."

What Mr. Fearon was referring to were the six "standards" or forms of the National Schools, the first three for the infants and the top three for boys and girls aged between 10 and 14. Most of the Ware Grammar School Boys, therefore, could not reach the standards of elementary school children two or three years their junior. But if the teaching was bad, the building was worse. Mr. Fearon reported that the schoolroom was small, badly lit and ill-furnished. The only privy, a small closet opening on to the public churchyard, had been locked up for some years. And then there was the matter of the lower floor being let to a brewer:

> The lower of the two rooms is let by the Master as a beer-cellar. This brewer's yard and brewhouse adjoin the school on the opposite side to that whereon the churchyard lies, and I am told that the noise and smell from this business are frequently almost intolerable in the schoolroom .... the floor is very unsound, and by inspection of the beams in the room below, I doubt if the whole school will not before long fall through into the brewer's cellar.

This is more or less what did happen. Many years later, in 1936, the octagenarian John Rogers, who had a bootmaker's shop in Baldock Street and was a great fund of local stories, sent a note to the Ware historian, Edith Hunt, in which he recounted life in the "original grammar school":

> For many, many years a brewer named Page used the lower floor to store his beer in, and as some of the boys were fairly big they managed to lift a floor board and go below for a drink. After school was over in the morning all the boys had to assemble at the Top School for afternoon education. The Rev Ch. Lilley had both schools, later on the entire school

arrangements were transferred to 193 New Road. I am the only one left in Ware who was a scholar under Mr. Lilley.[6]

The Master, the Rev. Charles Lilley, who was also the curate in charge of Stanstead St. Margaret's, was nominally in charge of two schools but spent most of his time at what John Rogers called "the Top School". Mr. Fearon's report for the government's Schools Inquiry Commission confirms this: "the Master does not in reality teach the grammar school at all. He is the Master of another school, called the Chuck Memorial School, which is more than half a mile distant, and he only comes down to the grammar school twice a week for a short time, to see how things are going."

The Rival Grammar Schools

The position of Mr. Lilley needs some explanation. On the face of it, he was being paid as the Master of the Free Grammar School but not fulfilling any of his duties. His income from the grammar school, which included the rents from the endowments, the fees from the paying pupils and the £5 a year from the brewer, totalled £75 a year, and out of this he paid £20 to his assistant and also gave him free accommodation. But the crux of the matter was that, as Mr. Fearon observed, "there has been a dispute for some years between the Master and the trustees on the liability for repairs." As far back as 1854, Mr. Lilley had complained to the Ware Charity Trustees about the state of the schoolhouse and they had written to the Charity Commissioners who advised them to borrow money for repairs. But the trustees did nothing and in December 1857 Mr. Lilley wrote again saying that, because the Free Grammar School was "untenantable" and "there is not a single article of furniture in the school which we have been able to use with any satisfaction", he had decided from Christmas to take up the kind offer of Mrs. Chuck and take all the boys to the Chuck Memorial School on Musley Hill. But the trustees refused to let him do this, so Mr. Lilley took his private pupils to the other school and left the free boys in the old building in the churchyard in the care of his assistant. But the dispute with Mr. Lilley over who should pay for repairs to the old school continued. In 1868, the trustees were still asking him to contribute – "the trustees wish to act with the spirit of liberality towards you and hope to be met in the like spirit".[7]

In the meantime, the Ware Charity Trustees had become involved in another dispute over the Chuck Memorial School on Musley Hill (the building which was until recently Musley Infants). This had been built in 1857 by Mrs. Elizabeth Moore Chuck in memory of her husband, Edward Chuck. He was a wealthy maltster whose carriage had overturned, mortally wounding him, when he was returning home to Noah's Ark Farm, next to Fanhams Hall. Mrs. Chuck described her school as being for "the education of the children of the Industrial Classes in the Town and Parish of Ware" – elsewhere it is called a "middle-class school". Soon after it was opened, Mrs. Chuck (with the backing of the Charity Commissioners in London) proposed an amalgamation of the two schools. Under the proposal, a Ware United Grammar School and Middle School would be established at Musley, with Mr. Lilley as Master, and the old schoolhouse would be sold and the proceeds invested in a repairing fund for the new school.

The Ware Charity Trustees called a special meeting to consider the matter on 25 June

1857. Only 17 of the more than 60 trustees attended, which was far more than usual, and they voted 10 to 7 against amalgamation. No reason for this refusal is stated in their minute book, but it is believed that the trustees were mainly opposed to admitting the 24 new trustees whom Mrs. Chuck proposed to nominate to the governing body of the new school. The old established Ware Charity Trustees did not wish to share any of their power, and certainly not with the representatives of the landed gentry, clergy and the new "middle classes" who were lined up behind Mrs. Chuck. A further proposal for amalgamation in 1868 was turned down by the Charity Trustees and an attempt to resolve the matter in 1872 by the Endowed Schools Commission also failed. In consequence, both schools remained in a state of limbo for 30 years, with the upkeep of both buildings suffering.

Then, in the general euphoria of Queen Victoria's Golden Jubilee in 1887, a public meeting resolved that Ware needed a "middle school" to be supported by subscriptions and a draft appeal leaflet was drawn up. With one eye on possible subscribers, the original draft said: "such a school would necessarily attract residents and improve the Retail trade of the Town by leading to the erection of a good class of houses", but someone wrote in the margin of the Chuck Trustees' Minute Book: "Don't mention this!" The sentence was left out and the appeal duly raised £982.5s. Eventually, in the summer of 1889, all the parties concerned agreed to an amalgamation scheme, drawn up by a Mr. W.C. Lefroy, an Assistant Charity Commissioner.

Under this scheme, there was to be a pooling of the resources of three schools – the Free Grammar School, the Chuck Memorial School and also the Wareside Grammar School. The Wareside school was well endowed and had a good sound schoolhouse, but its teaching was pronounced poor under its unqualified Master, Mr. W.G.E. Hobbs. Having received the consent of all the warring factions in Ware, the scheme was approved by the Queen in Council on November 28 1889. There were to be 13 governors, consisting of three representatives of the managers of the public elementary schools in Ware and Wareside, three from the Ware Vestry (forerunner of the Town Council), three from the Ware Charity Trustees, one from Trinity College, Cambridge, and three co-opted members. The Governors controlled the endowments of the three schools and in 1892 they also received a portion of the Baesh Charity at Stanstead Abbotts. The Baesh family motto "Bold in God" was adopted by the new Ware Grammar School, and later by the girls' grammar school (and is still used by its successor, Presdale School). So at long last, Ware acquired a grammar school of which it could be proud, located in the premises of the former Chuck school at the top of Musley Hill.

The Grammar School Reconstituted

The reconstituted Ware Grammar School opened, after some rebuilding, in September 1890. A notice in the *Hertfordshire Mercury* for 23 August said that "the governors feel sure that the new School will supply a much felt want in the neighbourhood of Ware." The notice also proudly introduced the new Head Master, who was Mr. Walter New, M.A., formerly Scholar of St. Peter's College, Cambridge, and late Second Master at Queen Mary's School, Walsall (the academic qualifications and teaching experience of head teachers were given great prominence in the period before County Education Committees made the appointments). Prospective parents were invited to write for a prospectus to Mr. New at the Master's Lodge

The Chuck Memorial School – later Ware Grammar School and many other forms of education before it finally closed as Musley Infants School in 2003.

in New Road, Ware. I have yet to unearth this original prospectus, but a later one of about 1899 said:

> The school accommodation has had to be extended twice since 1890, the last extension consisting of a new Class Room and Master's Room, which were added in connection with the Diamond Jubilee celebration in 1897.

By the late 1890s, the Grammar School had, in addition to Mr. New, three Assistant Masters, two of whom were London University graduates, a Music teacher, the services of the Shorthand Master at Haileybury College to teach Shorthand and Book-keeping, and Sergeant Dyer of the 4th Battalion, The Bedfordshire Regiment, to teach Drill. Seventeen subjects were offered in a curriculum "designed in preparation for the Universities, Professions and Commercial Life." All boys took Latin and French, but German, Greek, Shorthand and Book-keeping were optional for boys in the upper forms. The tuition fee for all subjects was £10 per annum, with an extra charge of 10s.6d. to boys taking up Practical Chemistry for the use of apparatus and chemicals in the Chemical Laboratory. There was also a fixed charge for stationery. Boarders could stay "under Mrs. New's personal supervision" at the Master's Lodge at 101 New Road (a house since demolished and replaced by temporary buildings for Hertfordshire Social Services). Full boarders under 13 were charged £46 per annum and older boys £49; weekly boarders were charged £38 for the under-13s and £41 for older boys; and "Day Boys living at a distance can dine with the Head Master on payment of £2.10s. per term (four days a week)." By this time, the number of governors had been extended to 15 to include the Vicars of St.

Mary's and Christ Church. All the major landowners and the worthies of the town were included.

Mr. New was clearly a successful and ambitious Head. He brought the total of boys to 40 before his departure in 1902 to become Head Master of Hertford Grammar School. His successor was Mr. G.W. Kinman, M.A. who according to another prospectus was a graduate of St John's College, Cambridge, Late Goldsmiths' Exhibitioner, and formerly Senior Resident Instructor, The Army College, Farnham, and Headmaster, Dolgelly Grammar School. This prospectus states that:

> The School buildings stand in a most bracing situation on the top of Musley Hill, 100 feet above the town of Ware. They consist of a large Schoolroom, three Class-rooms, Porch and Office, with a detached Chemical Laboratory and Balance Room. There is a good Lending Library, and adjoining are a Fives Court, gravelled Playground and an excellent Cricket and Football field with a well-equipped pavilion. The Art Classes are conducted in a specially-fitted Art Room, and the Ware Gymnasium, one of the best in the County, is reserved twice a week for the use of the Grammar School boys.

The Ware Gymnasium was the Drill Hall in Amwell End, which was later to be used extensively by the new Girls' Grammar School. Perhaps because of Mr. Kinman's army background – but perhaps too because of the growing state of military preparedness in the country with the South African War – the prospectus added the Armed Forces to the list of occupations for which the curriculum was designed:

> The older boys are instructed in Drill and Morris-Tube Shooting according to Lord Roberts' scheme for Military Training in Secondary Schools, and thus all the advantages of a Cadet Corps are secured without expense to parents.

But just over two years later, the school closed. The new Hertfordshire Education Authority, created in 1902, decided that there was not room for two boys' grammar schools in the neighbouring towns of Hertford and Ware, but there was a need for a girls' grammar school. So in January 1905 the Ware boys became part of an expanded Hertford Grammar School (later known as Richard Hale) with Mr. Kinman as Head Master and a new Ware Grammar School for Girls was opened in Amwell House, Ware, on 14 May 1906. The final act of the boys' grammar school was a Final Prize Day, held on 19 December 1904, for which a souvenir programme was printed. This included unison songs by the school choir, violin solos, a recitation in French from Victor Hugo and a "Hymn for Church Parade" specially composed by the Music Master, Mr. W.N. Govier, A.R.C.O., who was also the organist of St. Mary's.

23.
A Sense of Civic Pride

It was not until the 1890s that Ware began to gain a sense of civic pride. The opening of the new Grammar School was one sign of that, the creation of Ware Urban District Council in 1895 was another. And with the new pride in the town came a new feeling of unity. Before then the town had been split by political and social rivalries, by a carry-over of the type of bitter dispute which had plagued the Rev. Henry Coddington, by a grim concentration on the economics of the malt trade and a utilitarian, mean-minded philosophy which left little room for generosity of spirit, good taste, long-term vision or civic pride. Unless you were comfortably off, life in the town could be quite wretched.

One example of this was the offhand manner in which Ware lost its most famous artifact, the Great Bed. When the Bull Inn was demolished in 1848, the Great Bed was acquired by Daniel Brown at the Saracen's Head opposite the end of New Road – it was this Daniel Brown who had placed an advertisement in *The Reformer* immediately the railway came to Ware. The Great Bed was probably cut down to fit into a bedroom at the Saracen's Head. In 1864 Daniel died and his widow, Eliza, applied to the inn's owners for a new lease in her name – it should not have been a problem, for Daniel had been running the inn for 37 years. But the owners were the Ware Charity Trustees, not noted for their generosity or vision. They engaged in a long argument and "much turbulent discussion" with Daniel Brown's executors over who should pay for repairs to the inn. Eventually, the executors agreed to pay a repair bill of £450.9s. to clear the way for Eliza's new lease. That was a large sum to extract from the profits of an inn and the only way it could be realised was by selling the landlord's fixtures and fittings. So on Tuesday 30 August 1864, auctioneers moved into the inn and put under the hammer silver plate, prints, linen, glassware, wines and spirits, horses and carriages and at the top of their sale advertisement "the celebrated Great Bed of Ware".

There was great excitement in the national press and one newspaper reported that the bed had been bought by Mr. Charles Dickens for 100 guineas and was already at his house at Gad's Hill, Rochester. The truth emerged only much later. The Great Bed had failed to make its reserve price, had then been bought by a Hertford publican but he had failed to find the money. In 1870, it was finally purchased by William Henry Teale, who owned the King's Head Hotel at Rye House and made the bed the centre of a pleasure garden. The bed remained at Rye House until 1931 when it was purchased by the Victoria and Albert Museum.

The Ware Charity Trustees were a mean bunch – as evidenced by their refusal for almost thirty years to put the grammar school in order. Apart from the school, among their many other properties were three sets of almshouses, a number of plots of land on the Meads, the White Hart and Saracen's Head inns and the Bell Close (the present Buryfield Recreation Ground). Rents from these properties were intended to be distributed among the poor. On 5 February 1863, 219 persons lined up to receive £51.15s from the 'Town Land Money'. They received sums ranging from £2 down to half a crown (2s.6d.) with no reason given for the difference. Most had comments against their names – many were "ill", some were marked "destitute," "cripple," "imbecile". Those marked "not belong" were from outside the parish and received nothing. A Mr. Burgess was marked "impudent" and also received nothing.

This was public charity, but there was also private charity, given with more investigation and some sympathy by the ladies of the big houses in and around Ware. When Sarah Parker, the young wife of William Parker, set up house at Ware Park in 1843, up to 20 women were coming to the door with hardship tales:

> Harwood, Amble (?Amwell) End, a young woman with a baby: her husband works occasionally for Mr. Hitch, who she says will give him a good character: she has been living at Ware about two months. She begged very hard for a trifle, if it were only a penny, declaring that she had had nothing to eat that morning. I kept my resolution of giving nothing without some previous enquiry or examination and did not give her anything. If I give something to everyone who comes on the Wednesday morning that I see poor people, everyone in Ware will come up. More come up now than suits me, in consequence, I believe of my giving them 6 pence or a shilling at first. There must be some method in one's charity.[1]

For the really destitute, there was the workhouse. After it was established in 1837 in Collett Road, the records of the Ware Union Warehouse went missing – it was said later by the gossipy bootmaker, John Rogers, that this was because of a succession of scandals involving the staff. But the Census returns survive. In 1881, the Master was Thomas Phipps, with his wife Margaret as Matron and daughter Sarah as Assistant Matron. There were also a schoolmaster and schoolmistress, a female nurse and male assistant nurse, a tailor, cook and a 72-year old 'Shoemaker of Workhouse'. Among the 171 'inmates' or 'paupers', there were 44 children under 15, three deaf-and-dumb including 11-year old Annie Blackaby, one young man who was blind, four persons described as "imbecile", one "lunatic" and one "idiot". This was a Union workhouse so the inmates came from all parts of the area. In addition, there were seven "casual paupers" who had occupations and one "tramp" without an occupation – all given food and shelter strictly for one day only in the vagrants' house (until recently Social Services at the corner of High Oak Road). All were English except Sarah Stoten, an 88-year old soldier's widow from Ireland.

But things were looking up. With the railway – and later the new grammar school – came the middle classes and professional people. Villas were being built for them in New Road, West Mill (Watton) Road, Scott's Road and Myddleton Road. And there were new shops to cater for the new people. Kelly's Directory for 1882, before listing the private residents and shopkeepers, devoted four solidly-packed columns to a history of the town and description of its institutions – from the schools, places of worship, magistrates, public officers and insurance agents down to the number of 'pillar boxes' for letters. Anyone mourning the lack of retailing in the modern town would be amazed at the variety of shops in 1882 – eleven bakers, three booksellers and stationers, six butchers, two chemists, two confectioners, eight drapers as well as one "traveling draper", three dressmakers and seven tailors, three fishmongers and poulterers, six greengrocers, eight grocers, two hairdressers, one milliner, two furniture dealers, two 'fancy repositories' and seventeen 'shopkeepers' (general stores). There were fourteen boot and shoemakers (carrying on Ware's medieval tradition of 'cordwainers'), one photographer, one house agent (estate agent), five watchmakers (including three of German origin – Andrew Heitzman and Constantine and Joseph Ketterer, who served with distinction in the British Army in the First World War). But overshadowing all other trades were the 65 public houses and beer retailers catering not only for the town and passing trade, but also the thirsty maltmakers. In 1909, according to research carried out by the Campaign for Real Ale, Ware was said to be the most heavily-pubbed urban district in Hertfordshire – *see Appendix Three*. Many of the grocers considered themselves a cut above the ordinary shopkeeper. Charles Cook took an advertisement in Kelly's Directory to state that he was the "agent for W.& A. Gilby Limited, wine and spirit merchants and sole agent for Mazawattee teas". His rival in the High Street was Samuel Giffin at 37-39 High Street which remained a grocer's until after the Second World War when it was the Epicure Delicatessen, also known as Swain and Nickolds.

Good Taste in Art

Good taste in art was also showing itself in the town. And from the 1860s onwards, good taste meant the bright colours and simple lines of the 'Arts and Crafts' movement, founded by William Morris, Burne-Jones and their friends. To appreciate the textiles, furniture, wallpaper and glass being produced by Morris and Company, one needed to be young and educated, and also to have money. Who better to fulfill those conditions than Anne Elizabeth, the only child of Ware's most prominent maltster, Henry Page? In 1869 at the age of 26, Anne Page fell in love with a young naval officer, Lieutenant Richard Benyon Croft, whose family had held manors on the Welsh borders since Domesday Book. They were married in St. Mary's Church, Ware, on 22 September 1869. Two years later, in accordance with the wishes of his father-in-law, Richard retired from the Navy and joined the firm of Henry Page & Co. They set up house in Great Cozens to the north of Ware, then in 1880 or so moved across the road to Fanhams Hall, the Queen Anne house which Henry Page had bought in 1859 but never lived in himself. There they raised their eight children – the two boys, Richard and Henry, and six girls, Joyce, Maud, Anne, Helen, Mary and Grace.[2] When she had the money to do so, Mrs. Croft enlarged and rebuilt Fanhams Hall from a comfortable Queen Anne house to a stately home – we shall leave that story until a little later. She was a remarkable lady, as her younger son acknowledged:

> My mother, unlike her parents, was tall. When young she was beautiful and, indeed, remained so to the end of her life. She was of a sensitive and retiring nature and yet she inherited in a marked manner the business capabilities of Henry Page. In fact, right up to her death, she managed everything in connection with her estate, including two home farms and paid the weekly wages herself. Whilst taking an immense interest in all public affairs in the locality she was also of an extremely artistic temperament and when my grandfather made over Fanhams Hall to her in the year 1880, she proceeded to use her talents in beautifying the garden.[3]

It was not only the garden that she beautified. In June 1878, Mrs. Croft (or just possibly one of her parents) commissioned from Morris and Company a set of new windows for Fanhams Hall. There was a twelve-light window for the Library, with the figures of four medieval minstrels in the middle tier, and the other panes decorated with a lightly-coloured floral design that might have come from a wallpaper design by William Morris himself. There were also small windows for the Billiards Room and the Smoking Room. These windows were repaired or reglazed by Morris and Company when Fanhams Hall was rebuilt in 1901.[4] It must have been in 1878 that some of the surplus floral glass was used to glaze the staircase window at Henry Page's house at 87 High Street (now Ware Library).

Mrs. Croft, photographed by her husband

There were others in the town who admired the designs of William Morris and his circle. At Amwell House, the former home of the Quaker John Scott on the south side of the town, lived Arthur Tite and his family. He worked for the merchant bank of N.M. Rothschild & Son where he was a manager. His wife was French, the former Virginie Elizabeth Desportes. In 1888, they built a timber summerhouse in the garden, no doubt to complement the surviving summerhouses of Scott's time. It was a modest structure, with one window facing south – and then, perhaps as an after-thought, five of the panes were decorated with bas-relief pastoral scenes in plaster and in the central pane was the date 1888 and the initials AVT (Arthur and Virginie Tite). It is a pleasant piece of art – but nothing compared to the Tites' other investment: the 'Gilpin Window'.

By coincidence, Randolph Caldecott had also worked in a bank before moving to London to illustrate fashionable 'gift books', printed by the new colour lithographic process developed in the 1870s. One of the best known of these was Caldecott's version of William Cowper's poem about John Gilpin (1878), which was published under many titles including Randolph Caldecott's *First Book of Pictures and Songs*. It has virtually remained in print ever since. Whether Mr. and Mrs. Tite themselves designed the large window for their staircase – or had an artist or glazier do it for them – it is a magnificent example of Arts and Crafts glass (*see colour insert pages*). In the top panes are six whimsical figures, such as a frog and a hare on a bicycle, while in the bottom corners are nautical scenes, including a giant turtle with a sailing ship in the background (perhaps Darwin's *Beagle*). In between are fourteen tiers of individually painted flower and leaf designs and set in the middle two large scenes taken from Caldecott's Gilpin books. The higher one shows the turnpike gates being flung open as the bare-headed Gilpin gallops through; the lower painting shows the gentlemen chasing after him, thinking it's a race. So faithful are the glass panes to Caldecott's originals that it is possible they were painted by the artist himself and brought from London to be installed in the window at Amwell House.

To return to Mrs. Croft – in 1894 there occurred a major change to her circumstances. Her father died on the morning of Tuesday 16 January. On the Saturday the *Hertfordshire Mercury* carried an obituary which included the following:

Mr. Page, as is well-known, was originally in business as a baker, but subsequently he became a maltster, and being possessed of great shrewdness and excellent judgment, he ultimately developed a very large business. He was not only the largest maltster in Ware, but for some time he was regarded as one of the largest in the kingdom.

A few weeks later, the newspaper published details of Henry Page's will. He left £500 to his godson, George Blakesley, son of the former vicar, and £20,000 to his son-in-law and executor, Mr. R.B. Croft. A later edition of the paper reported that he had also invested £3,000 for the churchwardens of St. Mary's and put £200 into a post office savings account for the 'Ware Poor and Aged Men's Society'. All the investments in his own name with the Bank of England he left in trust to his daughter, Mrs. Croft, for life and then to her issue, including grandchildren and even "more remote issue". But what must have astonished readers of the paper was the total value of the old man's estate — £1,087,000. It was a phenomenal sum, worth at today's values using the retail price index over £100 million. And that was apart from the funds invested in Henry Page and Company. Mrs. Croft was to use her fortune for the good of her family and of the community. Some of it went on the rebuilding of Fanhams Hall, some on the purchase of the Priory in 1913 and her gift of it to the town in 1920, and yet more went on the political career of her second son, Henry Page Croft, as a Conservative MP and Secretary of State for War in the House of Lords in Winston Churchill's government from 1940-45.

The plaque recording "the ever grateful and deep appreciation of the inhabitants of Ware for the magnificent gift of the Priory" by Anne Elizabeth Croft of Fanhams Hall.

And some of her fortune, Mrs. Croft used to commission two windows for St. Mary's Church from an outstanding disciple of William Morris. The artist was Christopher Whall (not to be confused with William Wailes, who had designed the west window in memory of the parents of the maltster Edward Chuck). The first of these windows was that in the north aisle commemorating Ware men killed in the South African (or 'Boer') War. Her older son, Lieutenant-Colonel Richard Page Croft, had gone to South Africa with the Hertfordshire Militia and taken part in the relief of Mafeking, but was later shot through the chest and foot and laid out with the dead. He survived but only after a leg was amputated. The window has three panels, with the Archangel Michael flanked by two early Christian martyrs, St. George and St. Alban (one of the first representations of this saint after the foundation of the new Diocese of St. Albans). Above and below the saints are five regimental badges – the clue to them is to be found on a marble plaque at the side. It is headed: *"To the Glory of God and in Memory of those who fell in South Africa 1899-1902, This Window was erected by Anne Elizabeth Croft as a Thank Offering for the Safe Return of a Son dangerously wounded"*. It then lists with their regiments and places of death the five Ware men – Lieutenant Henry Hudson Ward (of the malting family), Sergeant Albert Albany (of the barge-owning family), Samuel Long, Driver James Walter Scales and Private John Clark. Mrs. Croft was later to incorporate regimental badges in the new Fanhams Hall windows of the billiards and smoking rooms.

Mrs. Croft's second window from Christopher Whall is one of the glories of St. Mary's Church (*see colour insert pages*). It is in the north transept and was made as a memorial to her parents – her mother had died in 1900. Pevsner dates the window to 1910 and say it is "inspired by the Pre-Raphaelites but refreshingly different from the ordinary run of early C20 windows".[2] The theme is the Te Deum hymn, and the design cascades down from the topmost light, showing the Holy Ghost as a dove, through the red-winged Cherubim and Seraphim to Christ, flanked by Angels and Archangels, to the bottom tier crowded with figures of relevance to St. Mary's Church – among them John the Baptist, St. Catherine, King David with his lyre, other kings and bishops, and Joan of Kent carrying a model of the church in her hands. The position of the window in the north transept points to a family connection. Mrs. Croft's mother was the daughter of Lieutenant Thomas Collins of the Dragoon Guards and Susanna Chuck and on an adjoining wall is a memorial to Mrs. Page's brother, Captain Thomas Chuck Collins, who was killed in 1842 "in the disastrous campaign of Afghanistan". Mrs. Croft was a patriot who strongly approved of her family's military record in defence of the British Empire.

Her most lavish creation was Fanhams Hall and its gardens. The original Queen Anne house had been partially rebuilt in the late 1870s to make a larger family home, but in 1898 Mrs. Croft had in mind something more ambitious. She commissioned a London architect, W. Wood Bethell, who increased the size of the house by some 400 per cent and encased it in Derbyshire stone. On the outside, the new Fanhams looked like a major Jacobean mansion, with its own great court reached through an arch under a clock tower. Inside, it acquired numerous suites of rooms, including a Great Hall and Minstrels' Gallery with walnut-panelling inlaid with mother-of-pearl, a first-floor Long Gallery with splendid Arts and Crafts plasterwork, a Library, Smoking Room, and cavernous kitchens to match. Throughout the house no expense was spared on fittings and their detail, whether they were beamed ceilings, doors, chimney pieces, the walnut panelling, Delft tiles or curtains made by the Royal School of Art Needlework.

Fanhams Hall and its formal gardens – the Japanese garden is lower down the extensive estate, laid out by Mrs.Croft.

As her new home took shape, Mrs. Croft turned her attention in 1900 to the gardens. She was particularly interested in Japanese culture and enlisted a Mr. Inaka to draw up designs for a traditional Japanese Garden. There were in fact three different types of Japanese Garden among which Mr. Inaka included a *Shin Garden,* an elaborate design of undulating landscape with hills, waterfalls and lakes, each physical feature having some intrinsic significance in its relationship to the others. Mr. Inaka called the garden *Koraku en* after a famous garden in Tokyo. Professor Suzuki and two professional Japanese gardeners came over and spent the summer months in each year before the First World War turning Mr. Inaka's plans into reality. Genuine Japanese tea-houses and other features were sent over and erected under their direction. These include the 'House of the Pure Heart' (*Sei-shin-tei)* and the 'Fox Shrine' (*Azuma-inari*) by the 'Fox Lake' *(Kitsune-ike*) which was crossed by a 'Spirit Bridge' (*Shin-Kyo*). There were seventeen lanterns made of Japanese grey granite. Mr. and Mrs. Croft also took part in the design of the gardens. They purchased an Austrian House at the 1900 Paris Exhibition and had it installed, and an Italian garden was planted by a well known firm of landscape gardeners in 1905.

The gardens of Fanhams Hall remain much as they were in Mrs. Croft's time but the house has gone through a number of transformations. It ceased to be a home for the Page Croft family in 1950 when it was bought as a staff training centre by Westminster Bank. The bank was succeeded as owners by the insurance industry and Sainsbury's plc, who added a modern conference wing and new entrance. Fanhams Hall is now a hotel.

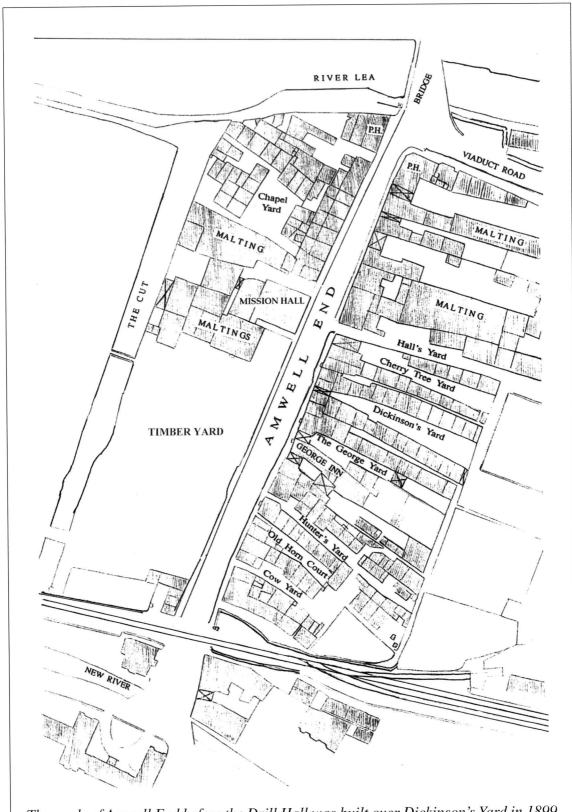

The yards of Amwell End before the Drill Hall was built over Dickinson's Yard in 1899.

The architect's drawing of what the front of the Drill Hall would look like.

Local Government and Public Buildings

In January 1895, Ware Urban District Council took over government of the town from the Local Board of Health under the Local Government Act of 1894. Under the same Act, the ancient parish was now divided into two civil parishes, Urban and Rural, each with its own council. And just a few years earlier, in 1888, there had been another tidying up of local government boundaries, when the remaining parts of Amwell End which were in the parishes of Great and Little Amwell were made part of Ware. In due course, the two councils gained their own offices – Ware Urban after 1919 in the Priory and Ware Rural in New Road – but when first set up the two councils met either in a Council Room in Rankin House or in the Boardroom of the Ware Union Workhouse in Collett Road. Until elections were held, the chairmen of the two councils were the local magistrates, chief among them being Mr. Richard Benyon Croft.

Alongside these institutional changes, Ware acquired a number of public buildings and facilities. A magistrates' court and police station was built in Watton Road in 1882 (now Powell's funeral services) and a Mission Hall in Amwell End was erected in 1883 at the expense of Robert Hanbury of Poles. Queen Victoria's Golden Jubilee in 1887 was celebrated by a carnival, sports and a public dinner in the High Street – and a subscriptions list was opened for the new boys' grammar school. The school opened in 1890 and was enlarged in 1897 in time for Victoria's Diamond Jubilee. In the 1880s both parish churches acquired parish rooms and in 1895 the Christ Church Memorial Hall was built by Mrs. Henry Page in memory of her husband.

In the summer of 1899, work began on construction of the Drill Hall in Amwell End for the 1st Hertfordshire Volunteer Battalion, the Bedfordshire Regiment. The idea of a military facility for the town came initially from Dr. A.J. Boyd, officer commanding D Company of the volunteers but Dr. Boyd, who was one of the town's GPs, had a further motive. With the Rev. Alfred Oates of Christ Church, he was concerned about the unsanitary slum conditions of the narrow

*The interior of the Drill Hall with a floor space of 108 x 52 feet (33 x 16 m)
which makes it the largest venue in the town.*

yards and courts in Amwell End and they turned to Edmund Smith Hanbury, the grandson and heir of Robert Hanbury who had financed the Mission Hall. During 1897 and the early part of 1898, Mr. E.S. Hanbury – or more probably his agent – purchased 27 cottages in Dickinson's Yard and a part of Cherry Tree Yard to the south to clear a site for the new building. The hall was built with space for drill, a gymnasium and armoury.

The scene was now set for construction of the Drill Hall. This was done in the summer of 1899 after plans had been drawn up by Mr. Vivian Young, A.R.I.B.A. of Westminster, and put out to tender. The lowest bid was £5,250 from J. Simpson and Son of Paddington. So no local firms were involved but at least the new Drill Hall was built out of local (probably Ware) red brick.

The opening was planned for October 1899 but this was cancelled because of the outbreak of hostilities with the Boers in South Africa. However, D Company of the Hertfordshire Volunteer Battalion were able to move in and begin drill and training before some of them went to war. One of the first non-military uses was for an old people's dinner in June 1902 to mark the Coronation of King Edward VII. The Drill Hall, which is now owned by East Herts District Council, remains in use and is well managed by a committee of trustees; it was made a listed building in 2006.

The Victoria Maltings, which dominated the town until 1988. The pub on the left is the Victory, usually known as 'The Ship'.

Malting and Other Industries

During the last two decades of the nineteenth century and the first decade of the twentieth, great changes took place in the malting industry in Ware. With the end of the malt tax in 1880, the way was open for competition from the Continent and the way to meet that competition was with industrial-scale production, using the latest technologies. Fortunately, the last quarter of the nineteenth century experienced an economic boom in which publicans, brewers and maltmakers all became wealthy. In Ware, a large number of small malthouses, operated by one or two men, were shut down and multi-storey maltings built in their place. In 1885, Henry Ward & Sons moved to Brewsters' Yard behind 65 High Street and built a tall malt kiln, on the bricks of which they inscribed the initials of the company's directors. Ward's went on to acquire other maltings, including the big Hope Maltings in Baldock Street. Their rivals, Henry Page & Co. built the first of their Victoria Maltings in Broadmeads in 1887. It was a large building with three storeys of malting floors but it burned down in 1906. What replaced it in 1907 was a colossus with seven storeys of malting floors from which the grain was transported to the kiln by hydraulic shafts. For a short while it was the biggest and most modern malthouse in the country, until overtaken by others at Sleaford, Lincs. It survived in Ware as a sort of commercial cathedral until sadly – and, to some townspeople, suspiciously – it was emptied of tenants and burned down one evening in 1988. Other large industrial malthouses were built in New Road, on a site which later became Kiln House Close off Musley Lane, and in Crib Street. But nothing could match the Victoria Maltings for its majestic place on the Ware skyline.

During the 1890s, Ware acquired a number of new industries which lessened the town's reliance on malt making. There were, of course, some well-established industries already – A.J. Goodfellow & Co. at the Falcon works in the High Street, brickmaking at the western end of the town, barge-building at the east and William Wickham, brewers and mineral water manufacturers, at the Star Brewery in Watton Road. In fact it was from the brewery that an important new company arose. In 1886 Dennis Wickham, a member of the brewing family, went into business as a motor car and general engineer with a special line in beer bottling equipment. His first premises were in Mill Lane (Priory Street) in a building which later became the Ware Technical Institute. In 1900, D. Wickham & Co. moved to larger premises in Viaduct Road, from where the company expanded even further, eventually taking over much of nearby Crane Mead. Dennis Wickham died in 1911 at the young age of 52 and his widow became both chairman and managing director of what was then a limited company. It was still general and motor car engineers and remained so until after the First World War, when in 1921 James Cooper became a director and Wickham of Ware embarked on its famous journey as railcar manufacturers to the world. More of that later.

Equally important at the time and very important later was the arrival in 1898 of the pharmaceutical firm of Allen and Hanbury. The company's chairman, Cornelius Hanbury, was only distantly related to his namesake, Edmund Smith Hanbury of Poles, a director of the brewing firm. Until 1898, Allenbury's had always been based in London but the directors were looking for a more appropriate site than their factory in Bethnal Green for production of dried milk products. The story goes that in 1896 director William Ralph Dodd, a keen fisherman, followed the footsteps of the seventeenth-century angler, Izaak Walton, and discovered that Ware was a pleasant, pollution-free place in which to locate the company's milk food business. Allen and Hanbury's first move was to lease the old flour mill in Mill Lane (Priory Street) along with the adjoining island known as Mill Mead at a cost of £200 a year from the New River Company. The old eighteenth-century mill buildings were demolished in 1897 and replaced by a brick building, with two water turbines producing 30 horsepower of electricity. In 1898, the firm purchased eleven acres of meadow known as Buryfield opposite the mill and constructed a brick warehouse connected to the mill by a footbridge. Dried milk and malt extract products were now being produced at Ware, followed in 1900 by pastille and capsule production. From then until 1914 and the beginning of the First World War, the whole of the Buryfield site was extensively developed with warehouses, workshops and additional power plants.[6] The Priory Street frontage – with the main entrance deliberately sited across Roman Ermine Street – took on its present form. Other buildings on the site, like Hope House in Harris's Lane, were taken over and adapted (and later demolished). The unoccupied land in a square formed by Priory Street, Harris's Lane and Park Road was used at first for growing blackcurrants – for the famous Allenbury Blackcurrant Pastilles – and later as the firm's sports field. This remained the company footprint until after the Second World War, when the acquisition of Allen and Hanbury by Glaxo led to a considerable expansion for pharmaceutical production and research – an expansion which still continues.

Mention of 'Buryfield' in connection with Allen and Hanbury's may cause some confusion for readers, since land directly to the east is now known as 'the Buryfield' or the 'Buryfield Recreation Ground'. The original Buryfield site was the meadow which Allenbury's bought and it gained its name, not from any burial of London plague victims, but from the continued discovery over the centuries of Roman burials and remains. The historian Gordon Moodey told a "harrowing tale of the 1890s, when a schoolboy whose father owned the Bury Field patiently dug the ground for coins and amassed enough to make a model engine – after the metal had been melted down".[7] The land which we now call the 'Buryfield Recreation Ground' was originally called the Bell Close, owned by the Corpus Christi Guild and their successors, the Ware Charity Trustees or feoffees, and in the 1860s it was purchased by William Parker of Ware Park. John Edwin Cussans in his *History of Hertfordshire* (1870) explained what happened next:

> There are four acres of land, called the Bell Close, belonging to the feoffees, the lease of which has just expired. William Parker, Esquire, is the owner of an adjoining piece of land, containing 1acre, 2rods, 39perches, which he has proposed to let at a nominal rent, provided the whole portion be devoted to the purpose of a public recreation ground.

This was agreed by the Local Board of Health and its successor, Ware Urban District Council, continued the lease. In 1931 the UDC purchased the recreation ground from the trustees of the late Mr. Parker and applied for grants from the National Playing Fields Association and the Carnegie Trust. Part of the land was then leased to Ware Football Club. Under the 1974 reorganisation of local government, the recreation ground and football pitch were acquired by East Herts District Council which in 1993 proposed leasing part of the land to Glaxo Manufacturing for a multi-storey carpark and new goods entrance. The present author, backed by the Ware Society, attempted to defeat this plan by applying to make the recreation ground a 'town green'. This failed but we did plant in the minds of both the council and Glaxo that it was trust land. The issue was finally decided by a High Court judge who agreed that it had been trust land but should become a carpark in the interests of the local economy.

Another important industry was displaced by the arrival of Allen and Hanbury. John Whyman French had been milling flour in Ware since 1855, first at Westmill then at the Ware Mills in Priory Street and later, operating as J.W. French & Co. Ltd., at both Ware Mills using steam and at Ware Park where the mill was an 'overshot' type with the head of water coming from above. Displaced by the lease of Ware Mills to Allenbury's, in 1897 John Whyman French constructed a new brick-built steam-driven mill in Viaduct Road. The new mill used the roller system which French had introduced at his Bow Mills in London in 1880. In 1919, the company began packing high quality self-raising flour for home baking under the registered name of Frenlite. The Ware Flour Mills were then renamed the Ware Frenlite Flour Mills. It is clear from the old maps that there was no mill here until 1897. It therefore cannot have been one of the two mills owned by the Lord of the Manor in Domesday Book, as Edith Hunt thought.[8] These were the Priory Street mill and Westmill, on the road to Tonwell and Watton-at-Stone. The other mills in the area were much later – Ware Park Mill used 'overshot' technology, not available until the 1700s, and Mardock Mill was built in the nineteenth century. There were also said to be two windmills on the edge of the town – the Peafield windmill after which Windmill Field is named, and another somewhere in the vicinity of Wadesmill Road.

24.
Before 1914

Edwardian Ware was an upbeat sort of place. Queen Victoria died on 22 January 1901 and her oldest son became King Edward VII. The South African War ended in May 1902 and the soldiers began to come home. The new king's coronation date was set for 26 June 1902, but, due to illness, it was postponed until 9 August 1902. Celebrations in Ware went ahead in June and included a dinner for old people in the new Drill Hall and a Coronation Tea, arranged by a special committee, held in Western Meadow "kindly lent for the occasion by Captain R.P. Croft". Western Meadow, also known as Deer Field, lay between New Road and Crib Street and was where the Page Croft family kept their herd of deer – not as pets but for the dinner table.

The major event of the decade was the opening of the new girls' Grammar School in Amwell House on 14 May 1906. The house had been empty for some years following the death of Mr. Tite and was bought by Hertfordshire County Council in 1905. The new school put Ware on a par with other Hertfordshire towns, like Barnet and Watford, which had acquired girls' schools. The prospectus said that the school would give a "Thorough English Education". It was founded to meet the needs of the whole neighbourhood, especially Ware and Hertford, and its organisation and aims were strongly influenced by the Girls' Public Day School Trust. At first, the Governors were those of the boys' school, including Lieut. Richard Benyon Croft, Mr. Thomas Buxton of Easneye and Mr. William Graveson of Hertford, who all gave their names to school Houses. The fourth house was later named after the first Headmistress, Miss M.E. Brough, who had been a mathematics graduate at Newnham College, Cambridge, and on the staff of Maida Vale High School.

When Miss Brough arrived, the conversion of the house had not been completed and assemblies were held in the old drawing room, which still had its walls covered with green damask. Gymnastics and even some classes had to be held in the Drill Hall in Amwell End. But as the number of girls increased, so new buildings were added. In 1908, additional classrooms and an Assembly Hall were built on the site of a stable block at the western side of Amwell House. On the other side, adjoining houses were acquired and converted, Millbrook in 1918 and then Riverside, until the Ware Grammar School took the shape familiar to generations of pupils. Miss Brough, Headmistress since 1906, retired in 1931 and St Mary's Church was crowded with pupils past and present for a farewell service. In Presdales School there still hangs the portrait of Miss Brough, painted in vigorous style in 1916 by the Australian artist, James Quinn, which was displayed at the Royal Academy and favourably reviewed by *The Times*. Miss Brough, who was the sister of the film star Mary Brough, was succeeded by Miss H. Woodhead, Headmistress from 1931 to 1956 – a remarkable achievement for a school to have just two heads in 50 years. Miss Woodhead contributed articles to the Golden Jubilee book and also to a special book of pupils' drawings of Amwell House in 1962, when she commented on the difficulties of the school's buildings: "The uncertain angle of the picturesque spiral staircase gave me from the first much anxiety, but, about 1945, I stopped worrying – if it could stand up to a war with two additional schools of evacuees, it and the house were probably

The new porch of Scott's Grotto (above) was designed by the Irish architect, James Howley, to replace one demolished in the 1960s. It is larger than the original (illustrated on page 146) and brings all the entrances to the underground chambers under one roof. There is also now a secure front door.

The Council Chamber (left) was so-called by the Victorians because it has six seats in niches, decorated with shells, rocks, coal, glass and fossils. We do not know what Scott's name for this chamber was. The pattern of the floor, in different coloured pebbles, was discovered during the restoration in 1990, when the floor was cleared of debris from the 1960s demolition.

The Gilpin Window in Amwell House (Hertford Regional College), incorporates two panels from Randolph Caldicott's illustrations for the William Cowper poem, as well as many other imaginative images – such as an owl, a frog, a giant turtle and a hare on a bicycle.

The Te Deum window in the North Transept of St. Mary's Church was commissioned by Mrs. Ann Elizabeth Croft in memory of her parents and created by the artist, Christopher Whall. The figure of Joan of Kent, holding a model of the church, was inserted at Mrs. Croft's suggestion and is in the bottom row, second light from the left.

The maltmaker statue was created by the Oxfordshire sculptor, Jill Tweed, working from old photographs of Ware malting workers. It was unveiled on 4 November 1999, to mark the Millennium and the end of 600 years of malt-making in the town.

Amwell House as the girls' Grammar School. On the right are the school hall and classrooms, added after 1906.

indestructible." But by 1962 plans were already in hand for a move to Presdales, the large house, formerly the home of the Sandeman and McMullen families, which was just half a mile to the south in Hoe Lane. These plans continued during the brief headship of Miss Barbara Robinson (1956 to 1962) who left to return to teaching at Broxbourne School. It was the next Headmistress, Miss Margaret Martin (later to become Mrs. Helmore), who saw the opening of the new school at Presdales in 1965. We shall return to Presdales later.

The 1900s was a prosperous and proud decade. It was the period when picture postcards were at their most popular and could be sent anywhere in the country with guaranteed delivery the next day, all for a halfpenny stamp. The Ware Museum has a very large collection of postcards of the town, printed between 1900 and 1914. Among them is the start of the annual Postmen's Walk in 1901, when local postmen competed to see who could do the 21-mile course to Buntingford and back in record time. Others show street scenes, with children standing in the middle of the road – photographers would give them sweets if they stood stock still to give the scene a sense of proportion. A whole succession of postcards commemorates the accession of King George V in May 1910. The king was "proclaimed" in the Market Place from a balcony outside the 'Town Hall' (then Stallabrass Brothers' butchers shop) by a crowd of local dignitaries and at the front of the crowd were the ranks of the Hertfordshire Territorials, Baden Powell Scouts (as they were then known), Boys' Brigade and girls from the Grammar School in their straw boaters. Flags were strung across the High Street and a parade and dinner were laid on. The Ware Garage stood beside Stallabrass in the Market Square (it was where Boots the

Chemist now is) and in another postcard a line of ten saloon cars is drawn up outside the garage. A few better-off Wareites owned motor vehicles, but horses were still used to deliver milk, bread, beer, coal and dozens of other necessities. Dr. W.G. Stewart still did his rounds in a horse-drawn buggy. The Ware Garage – on the site of the Lamb and Wheatsheaf public house – was founded by Mr. Arthur Davis Skipp, a member of the enterprising Skipp family who operated barges, made bricks and had a huge gravel pit in Watton Road (now Wülfrath Way). On the opposite side of the High Street was Gideon Talbot's garage with petrol pumps, and next door the 'Ware Library' and printing works of George Price, later sold to Jennings and Bewley. At one time it had been the Flower de Luce Inn.

The senior member of the Skipp family was William Skipp, brick-maker and gravel merchant, who had been born in Hope House, Harris's Lane. He founded Ware's first cinema, the 'Picture Hall' in Amwell End. It was hurriedly put up in six weeks in 1911 to compete with rival film shows in the other Town Hall's Assembly Rooms (behind Rankin Square). The Drill Hall was also licensed to show films – silent, of course – in 1913. The Picture Hall opened on Boxing Day 1911 and featured in a half-page advertisement in the following week's *Hertfordshire Mercury*. It was open every evening from 6 to 10.30pm with matinees every Thursday and Saturday and would show films which were "the finest obtainable and absolutely up-to-date including Drama, Comedy, Cowboy, Travel and Laughable Farce". The cinema was fire-proof, properly ventilated and heated, with comfortable seats and "great care is taken in selecting Pictures that will appeal to the tastes of the most fastidious".[1] In 1925 there were new owners who renamed it the Ware Cinema, and in 1948 it was thoroughly modernized and renamed yet again as the Astoria. Its owner then was Charles Ballands, who had begun as a thirteen-year old re-wind boy, becoming then chief operator, manager and finally part-owner. He was a great independent cinema proprietor and innovator, introducing live shows which included an early appearance of Cliff Richard and the Drifters. After his death in 1975 the cinema was converted into a night club and shopping arcade, Becket's Walk – it is now wholly used as a club.

One new feature of life before the First World War was the phone. Telephones had been introduced in 1878 when Alexander Graham Bell demonstrated one to Queen Victoria and by 1900 many businesses in Ware had them. The first telephone exchange, with young women operators, was at No.1 New Road on the corner with East Street. The Post Office took over the service in 1912 and in 1927-28 the telephone exchange was moved from New Road to above the main post office at 55 High Street. A new automatic exchange was built off West Street in 1962. Early telephone lines around the town were carried on huge 'telegraph poles': there was a whole line of them along the river towpath.

In winter Ware was a smoky, polluted place since the malthouses and many other buildings were heated by coal. On the railway sidings running from Ware station southwards under the viaduct stood the trucks of William Page and Son, coal and coke merchants, and others were lined up in the goods yard. Electricity had not yet arrived but the town had gas, supplied by the Ware Gas, Light and Coke Company from their works in Star Street. All of this added to the danger of fire. Ware Fire Brigade was founded originally in 1820 by the Unity Insurance Company, taken over in 1846 by the Local Board of Health and in 1898 by Ware Urban District Council. For the first 87 years of its existence the brigade used hand pumps, with three firemen on each side of the appliance pumping away furiously to produce a squirt of water. It was with one of these that they fought the disastrous fire at the old Victoria Maltings in 1906. The following year they acquired a new steam pump "with a throwing capacity of 350 gallons per minute". They also had an 'escape' ladder, stored in a tall building opposite the Independent Chapel in Church Street. However, pump and escape were still horse-drawn and there was often a delay getting to a fire while the firemen rounded up the horses grazing on the Meads.

Ware Grammar School for girls was not the only new arrival on the education scene. With the departure of the boys' grammar school in 1905, the little building at the top of Musley Hill remained empty for two years. For the second time in its history it fell into disrepair – the lead was reported to have been stripped from the roof. In 1907 it reopened as the Junior School of St. Mary's. This was a controversial decision for there were now three schools in Ware giving an education in accordance with the "doctrines of the Church of England" and none giving a non-denominational education. The controversy had been going on for a year before the announcement that the Musley School would be Anglican. A Bill introduced into the House of Commons in 1906 (but not proceeded with) had proposed the abolition of all church schools and this had been attacked by the Ware clergy in their parish magazines. The Rev. Alfred Oates, Vicar of Christ Church, wrote that non-denominational schooling might produce a headteacher who was a socialist or even a Roman Catholic. And there had been local opposition to another Anglican school from the town's Noncomformists, led by a Mr Thomas Burgess, a bootmaker in Baldock Street and preacher at the old Independent Chapel in Church Street, who wrote to the *Hertfordshire Mercury,* describing himself as a "champion of Christianity and of religious liberties". Nevertheless, Musley reopened as a Church of England aided school. Children went first to St. Mary's Infants' School in Church Street for three years, then transferred to Musley for a further three years before, at the age of eleven, attending St. Mary's Senior School back in Church Street. The school had four managers, representing the St. Mary's Schools, the Christ Church Schools, Hertfordshire County Council and Ware Urban District Council. There were places for 80 children, but in the first year only 47 were enrolled. Miss Benton was the first Headmistress, assisted by the Misses Mordick and Dimmock. During the First World War, the Northumberland Yeomanry were camped on the school's playing fields and soldiers sometimes slept in the school.

But in 1918, the school's role changed yet again. Throughout the country, central schools were being set up to cater for the more able children between the ages of 10 and 14, who did not have places at grammar schools and who until then had been taught in the senior sections of elementary schools. There was specifically a need for skilled teaching in science and crafts. And so the junior classes on Musley Hill were transferred to St Mary's School in Church Street and the Musley Central School opened catering for pupils who had passed the entrance examination, not only from Ware, but also Buntingford, Braughing, Puckeridge, Hunsdon, Widford, the Mundons and Wareside. The school opened with 60 children in three classes, under the headship of Mr Carlo C. Loretto. A fourth class was formed in the early twenties, when Mr Lorretto was succeeded by Mr A.E. Evans B.A.(Wales). Albert or "Taffy" Evans, as he was inevitably known, had been a Welsh Rugby cap and was to play an important and long role in Ware education, retiring as Head of the Ware Secondary School in 1948. When a fifth class was added a few years later, it was taught in the two top rooms of his house, opposite the school at the corner of Homefield Road. Science was also taught in the headmaster's house and later in the Priory, by then occupied by the Ware UDC As the sports fields of the old grammar school had been sold for housing, sports activities were held on Allenbury's Sports Ground in Priory Street. The town's swimming pool had not then been built so the school's swimming gala took place in the River Lea, with a barge drawn across the river by Allen and Hanbury's wharf. A Young Farmers' Club was formed and the members reared calves, pigs and chickens and received instruction from the staff of the Oaklands Institute in St. Albans. Other activities in the handicrafts and domestic sciences were provided at the Ware Technical School in Priory Street.

Then in 1932, came a further change in the role of the Musley school, the fifth in its history. The numbers of older children were outgrowing the small building. At the same time, there was a national move towards a broader education for older children and there were only two of the old, exclusively Central schools left in Hertfordshire, at Watford and Ware. The time had come to bring all of Ware's senior non-grammar school children together in one school and it had been agreed, at a public meeting held in the Drill Hall on February 28, 1930, that this should be a town affair, rather a continuance of the two parish system of education. The building chosen for this was not Musley (which was too small) but Christ Church down the road. The decision to form the Ware Senior and Central School was taken by the diocesan education authorities in 1931 and by January 1932 the ground was already being cleared at the Christ Church schools for a large extension to cater for up to 300 pupils. This was opened on July 2 1932 by the Bishop of St. Albans and on July 22 the Central School pupils marched down the hill to their new premises. On September 6 1932, the Musley school reopened as an infants school. Eighty children, aged from 5 to 7, were admitted by the Headmistress, Miss Want, assisted by Miss Stamp and Miss Hunter. In 1982, Musley celebrated the 125th anniversary of its opening as the Chuck Memorial School and the 50th of its opening as Musley Infants and entered a float in the Ware Week carnival and a commemorative mug was produced.

Two odd facts remained about this little school. Although a County infants' school, it still remained part of the endowment of the old grammar school and Hertfordshire County Council paid a small rent to Presdales, which was used for providing grants to pupils in need. The other survival of its days as a grammar school was that Musley had an Eton Fives Court – surely the only infants' school in Britain to have one. Musley Infants closed in 2003 and at the time of writing the building is boarded up, awaiting its next reincarnation as a community centre.

We end this chapter with a sad story which took place in the year before the First World War. But let us go back to 1880. In that year the Priory was owned by John Gwyn Jeffries, a world famous conchologist or expert on seashells – the story is told that he offered to sell his shell collection to the Natural History Museum who delayed an answer, hoping he would give it to them, but they delayed too long and he sold it to the Smithsonian Museum in Washington DC. Mr. Gwyn Jeffries (after whom Jeffries Road is named) and his wife Anne had their initials painted in two small windows in the main hall of the Priory. In 1881, his wife died and he sold the Priory to Robert Walters, a retired barrister, London clubman and amateur playwright. It is a tradition in the town that Mrs. Walters was an actress who had appeared in one of her husband's plays. It was Mr. Walters who in 1892 remodelled the small south-east wing, added a turret with his initials on (*on the right in the photo opposite*) and also built a Billiards Room

Mr. Walters in the garden of the Priory in 1905.

(the present Garden Room) – no doubt to entertain his Garrick Club friends. In 1905, Mr. Walters put the Priory up for sale. The sale particulars described it as "occupying a perfectly retired position on the fringe of this quiet Old World town, screened by a wealth of grand timber of ancient growth, and High Walls, Ensuring Complete Repose and Absolute Seclusion".

But it was not sold and Mr. Walters remained there until his death in 1912 when he was described as "a generous and kind-hearted man who led a very useful though unostentatious life". Eight months later, Mrs. Walters was taken ill and retired early to bed. One of the maids went to her room at 8 o'clock and found her comfortable. But when the maid returned at 9.30, she found her mistress lying in the fireplace terribly burned. Ware tradition had it that she was distraught at her husband's death and committed suicide. But the inquest returned a verdict of accidental death. This tragedy marked the end of the Priory's time as a private house. In 1913, it was bought by Mrs. Croft but, having only just completed the transformation of Fanhams Hall, she had no intention of living at the Priory.

25.
A World War and its Aftermath

The outbreak of the First World War found Ware's part-time soldiers at their annual camp. The First Battalion, the Hertfordshire Regiment (Territorial Force) had been formed in 1908 from the amalgamation of two volunteer battalions of the Bedfordshire Regiment. Various companies were spread around the county and part of C Company was based in the Drill Hall, Amwell End, with the battalion's Corps of Drums. In the weekend when the nations of Europe declared war on one another, the Ware half-company was under canvas at Ashridge Park, near Berkhamsted. They quickly returned home on the Sunday. Orders for mobilisation were received on Tuesday evening, 4 August 1914, when Britain joined its allies, France and Russia, in declaring war on Germany. The mood in the town was described in the *Hertfordshire Mercury*:

> The Territorials were seen hurrying hither and thither saying good-bye to their friends and relatives before leaving the town, the reserve men were busy making preparation for active duty in the ranks, the streets were thronged with people anxious to hear the latest news from the seat of operations, and what the latest orders were to be. Later on in the evening patriotic songs were to be heard from the young bloods of the Territorials and their immediate friends and companions, so for hours the martial element was abroad, and in not a few cases anxiety was writ large on the faces of wives and sweethearts.[1]

Early the next morning, Captain Henry Page Croft of Fanhams Hall, Commanding Officer of C Company, mounted on a fine horse from his hunting stable, led the company through the town to the railway station. The Corps of Drums struck up a march and the men, with every evidence of being ready for action, marched to the station *en route* for the barracks at Hertford. Others went to Hertford by river aboard a Ware barge, owned by the Skipp family, who had renamed it 'Our Boys'. Shortly afterwards all ranks were asked to vary their terms of service to include service overseas in a theatre of war. Some eighty percent of the Territorials agreed to serve abroad including some fifty men from Ware. The list of the Ware volunteers was drawn up by Colour Sergeant George Hart, brother of Joseph Hart who was the Captain of the Ware Fire Brigade and landlord of the Prince of Wales public house in Crib Street. On Friday 27 August Viscount Hampden, Commanding Officer of the Hertfordshire Territorial Regiment, announced officially that the regiment had volunteered for foreign service and that a few vacancies were still open for picked men. Then at the beginning of September, the first battalion moved from Hertford to Romford for intensive training. Some of their experiences were described in letters printed in the *Hertfordshire Mercury* on 19 September:

> From Hertford we went on to Romford by train, and remained there for ten days. We then left Romford in marching order for Long Melford. We did 18 miles the first day, 13 miles the second day, and a twelve mile march brought us to Long Melford on the third day. We rested for five days, and then went on to Bury St Edmunds, a distance of nine or ten miles. We were

billeted in some old maltings about a mile to the east of Bury St Edmunds, but we did not like these old buildings, and so, as the weather was fine, we soon moved out, and have since bivouacked in a field near by. The people have been kindness itself to us while on the march, and would give us anything they had in the way of butter, cheese and so on. The boys have been wonderfully well all the time, the only complaint has been blistered feet. I know some have complained of the food supply. For service conditions it has been remarkably good, but to a man used to luxuries it would be a hardship. For breakfast we have had ham and beef; certainly the ham is rather fat. There has been boiled beef for dinner and potatoes (when we could get them). The bread has been very good. For tea we have had bread and jam, and sometimes butter. Cheese is given out at the same time, and which we are supposed to keep for supper. We have had drills, route marches and so on since we have been here, and we are keeping very fit.

Another letter implied that the maltings were rat infested, but so were some of the older maltings in Ware.

Meanwhile military activity continued in and around Ware. On Friday 21 August, over 1,000 troops of the Royal Berkshire Regiment camped in Ware and Hoddesdon. A rifle range existed in Kibes Lane with a 25 yard covered section and a 50 yard open air range. It was announced that service rifles had been adapted to a small bore with ammunition available at a nominal charge and that there was the opportunity for everyone to learn how to fire a rifle.

In 1914 it was generally believed that the Territorial regiments of the British Army would need six months training before they left for France. However the 'Herts Terriers' was one of the few Territorial regiments which went to France within three months of the outbreak of war and they were probably the first to come under fire. Two trains took nearly 850 men from Bury St. Edmunds to Southampton on Thursday 5 November 1914, including nearly eighty men from Ware. They left for France on *The City of Chester* of the Ellerman Line and landed at Le Havre at midday on the sixth. Since the 1st Battalion arrived in an active area before the 22 November 1914 they were entitled to the 1914 Star and could proudly call themselves "Old Contemptibles" after the name Kaiser Wilhelm gave to the British Expeditionary Force. The 'Herts Terriers' remained in France and Flanders until 1919 and experienced with great bravery and bloodshed some of the fiercest action of the Western Front. Their story has been told with great sympathy and a wealth of detail by Derek Armes in *Our Boys: Ware Men in the First World War* (Ware Museum, 1998). Our concern here is with the Home Front.

Every man going to France made a will disposing of his estate – often this amounted only to his army back pay. As a married woman then had no legal right to her husband's property, the husband was directed to sign the appropriate form (or put his mark) in the presence of the magistrate, Mr. A.H. Rogers, who owned the newsagent's shop at the bottom of New Road. Dependants were looked after by the SSFA (Soldiers and Sailors Families' Association). Mrs. Croft of Fanhams Hall was President of the Ware Division of the Hertfordshire Branch and her daughter Ann Page Croft was the Treasurer and Hon Secretary. During the year 1914-15 the Association paid out grants of £450.19s.8d. to 78 wives, 169 children and 114 "other relatives", the money having been collected by donations. Many of the town's younger servicemen were former members of the Ware Scouts under the leadership of the Curate of St Mary's, the Rev. F.W. Farmer, who wrote and received many letters from former members of the troop.

By the end of 1915, Lieut. Colonel Henry Page Croft, as he then was, had become the regimental commander and Mrs. Henry Page Croft launched an appeal for donations to buy Christmas presents for the boys at the Front. Christmas puddings for the whole regiment were sent together with separate packages for each man containing a writing case and prayer book, a handkerchief, chocolate and bull's-eye sweets, potted meat, soup tablets and a cake of soap. This was the last Christmas that Mrs. Page Croft organised parcels for the troops at the Front. Early in 1916 a committee was formed to take charge of 'The Ware Boys at the Front Fund'. Its President was Lieut. Colonel G.R. McMullen who lived at Presdales in Hoe Lane, Dr. W.G. Stewart was its Chairman and Mr. T.W. Jennings the Secretary. Funds were raised through fêtes, one such fête held at Presdales on August Bank Holiday Monday raised £158. Initially parcels were sent throughout the year to all servicemen at the Front. Although the troops acknowledged the parcels and said nice things about them, they were not always a success. One man wrote home that the sausages were in such a state when they arrived that they put them in the trenches to scare the rats away! Shortly after this, on 7 February 1916, Lieut Colonel Henry Page Croft was promoted to command the 68th Brigade – this was a first for the battalion and for Ware since it is believed that Henry Page Croft was the first Territorial Officer to achieve the rank of Brigadier General and to lead a brigade in France.

Many servicemen were brought back home to Ware to convalesce and recuperate. Mrs. Croft, of Fanhams Hall, had bought the Priory in 1913 and in 1914 she allowed it to be used as a VAD (Voluntary Aid Detachment) convalescent hospital. Dr. Stewart was the Medical Director and his wife held the post of matron. Although it is not known if any Ware men from the Herts Terriers stayed there, one Ware man certainly did. He was Petty Officer Simpson who was seriously injured at Beaucourt sur l'Ancre in November 1916, while serving with the 63rd Naval Division which fought in close proximity to the 'Herts Terriers'. Simpson won the DCM in this action and was presented with his medal at the Priory. The use of the Priory as a convalescent hospital is commemorated by a plaque adjacent to the main entrance. The nurses and other helpers were young women from Ware and district, many of them members of the VADs which had been formed in 1909 to provide medical assistance in time of war. One of the cooks at the Priory was Edith Hitch who later married Major T.C. Hunt and, as Edith Hunt, became the town's historian. During their convalescence, some of the soldiers carved graffiti on the cloister arcades in the main hall – there is evidence of at least two Union Jacks and one name.

In the last summer of the war, the town was still doing its best to support the troops. On August Bank Holiday Monday, 1918, a fête in aid of "The Ware Boys at the Front Fund" was held at Presdales and over £200 was raised, £80 of which was taken at the gate which indicates that a considerable proportion of the town attended. The committee decided to donate £50 to 'The Prisoners of War Help Committee (Herts Branch)' for the benefit of Ware men from the Herts and Beds regiments who were prisoners. The committee felt that this Fund needed liberal support, as the men depended mainly on parcels from the Fund for their sustenance. Around this time another fund was set up in the town, when Mr. F.T. Barker of Baldock Street was appointed the secretary of the Ware fund to help blind soldiers.

Armistice and the War Memorial

The end of the war and the general Armistice was declared at 11 am on 11 November 1918, but it was weeks and even months before most of the Ware men returned home. However, in some cases men's pre-war employers successfully pressed for their early release. In addition to their discharge papers each man was given a regimental buttonhole badge and a payment on account, pending final settlement of his pay. With the war over the committee for 'The Ware Boys at the Front Fund' had surplus funds and on 29 January 1919 gave a dinner at the Drill Hall in Amwell End to commemorate the cessation of hostilities. Invitations were sent to all men whose homes were in or near the town and 171 men sat down to a meal comprising soup, roast beef, roast and boiled mutton, roast pork, baked and boiled potatoes, brussel sprouts and parsnips, followed by ginger and fruit pudding with beer, lemonade, coffee and cigarettes *ad lib*. Music throughout the evening was played by Mr. R.Langton Bones' orchestra, patriotic speeches were made and the troops were entertained by conjuring tricks, humorous ditties, clog dancing and songs. Returning servicemen set up the 'Ware and District Ex-servicemen's Association', the forerunner of the Royal British Legion, and by March 1919 it had a membership of 260 men. Further celebrations and dinners followed.

Before the war had ended a general committee had been set up by Ware Urban District Council to consider the provision of a suitable memorial to those who had laid down their lives during the conflict. A sub-committee was formed specifically to look into the proposals for the memorial. Suggestions tabled included a stone memorial with several sites suggested; the Vicar proposed seats in various parts of the town together with a garden as a pleasure resort; Mr. Albany suggested that the Council form a colony of housing and workshops together with recreational rooms for discharged soldiers. Mr. A.H. Rogers, the magistrate, proposed an Institution to comprise a free public library and rooms for recreation, while his brother, the bootmaker, John Rogers, said that he thought that no better scheme could be contemplated than to build almshouses for married couples such as those built and endowed by the Ware Charities – to be allotted in the first instance to wounded or incapacitated soldiers. The sub-committee sought the advice of Sir Reginald Bloomfield, one of four architects retained by the War Graves Commission for the design of War Memorials. He recommended that the most suitable site was in the corner of the New Burial Ground – on the north side of Church Street facing Mr. Yorke's forge. His proposal was for a 22 foot high cross with a bronze sword set in the centre to be mounted on a square platform accessed by three steps. The names of the fallen were to be carved on a tablet at the back and the whole memorial was to be in Portland stone. The cost was estimated at £1,000. The committee favoured the Cross of Sacrifice as the permanent memorial to 'Our Boys' who had laid down their lives for King and Country.

A public meeting was held in the Town Hall on Monday, 28 April 1919 when the committee described the various suggestions. Their recommendation was that the Cross of Sacrifice located in the New Burial Ground adjacent to the churchyard was the most suitable. A motion proposed by Mr. E.H. Hitch and seconded by Dr A.J. Boyd that the Committee's proposals be accepted aroused a long and heated debate. A Mr. James Relf of Musley Lane rose and said he was against the idea of spending £1,000 for public property standing on private land – the site proposed was church land. He proposed that no decision be taken that night since he had a petition containing nearly a thousand signatures addressed to Mrs. Croft of Fanhams Hall, respectfully asking her to sell or lease the Priory grounds for rest and recreational purposes. No decision about the war memorial was made that night. However, before the wrangling was resolved the Ware Scouts stole the march on everyone and erected a roll of honour painted on a board and hung on the church railings where the present memorial stands. Allen and Hanbury followed suit when Captain Capel Hanbury unveiled a brass plaque at their sports pavilion in June 1920, dedicated to the eleven colleagues who made the supreme sacrifice. A list of men who had fallen in the war was also hung in St. Mary's Church.

Mrs. Croft agreed to let the Priory to Ware Urban District Council and other groups in the town for a period of 90 years (subsequently changed to a 999 year lease) but the argument continued as to where the War Memorial should be sited. In June 1919 another public meeting was held. The committee still wanted to site the memorial in the corner of the New Burial Ground and to raise money for its construction by public subscription. This was opposed by a section of the town led by Mr. Relf who proposed that the council obtain the site of Yorke's old forge (the present Memorial Gardens) and build the war memorial there. The meeting became heated and it was even suggested that relatives of the fallen should have the final say. Needless to say, the site of the Memorial remained unresolved that night also.

In fact, the so-called New Burial Ground (which had been acquired in 1834 when the old Vicarage was demolished and not used for burials since 1854) was town property by virtue of the 1852 Burial Act. However the ground was still consecrated and could not be disturbed without the authority of the Chancellor of the Diocese. At a special Vestry meeting, the Vicar of St Mary's, Canon Martin Reed, and the churchwardens agreed to petition the Chancellor for a Faculty to erect the Memorial within the New Burial Ground. Permission was duly granted, Mr. Relf's objections were overcome and the town was not put to the additional expense of buying Mr. Yorke's forge. By November 1919 a list of names which were to be carved on the memorial had been prepared and posted in public places within the town, the public being asked to send corrections to Miss Anne Page Croft at Fanhams Hall.

On Sunday afternoon, the 30 January 1921, several thousand people gathered in the vicinity of St. Mary's Church in spite of high winds and a threatening storm to witness the unveiling of the War Memorial. An inter-denominational service was conducted in the church by Canon Reed before a congregation nearing a thousand people, mainly relatives of the fallen. The Bishop of St Albans was in attendance. Outside the church the band of the newly-formed Beds and Herts Regiment took up the music played on the organ enabling the onlookers to partake in the hymns. The regiment also provided a guard of honour. The War Memorial, draped in a huge Union Jack donated by Mrs. R B Croft, was unveiled by Viscount Hampden, the Lord Lieutenant for Hertfordshire and former Commanding Officer of the 1st Battalion of the Hertfordshire Regiment. The prayers of dedication were led by the Bishop of St. Albans and the last post played by Sergeant Carpenter, followed by an address by Viscount Hampden. A list of the 212 names of Ware men who died in the Army, Royal Navy, Merchant Marine and Royal Air Force was engraved on the plinth of the Cross of Sacrifice and published with the account of the unveiling in the *Hertfordshire Mercury*. In common with many inscriptions on memorials throughout the country the list of names was not definitive. Some Ware men were commemorated on other memorials and some names were not recorded because their relatives did not wish to

The unveiling of the War Memorial on 30 January 1921

admit their loved ones were dead. With the publication of Derek Armes's book in 1998, a further name was added and the Ware War Memorial refurbished.

The Unemployed 1920s

Anne Elizabeth Croft – mother of two brave soldiers, widow of Lieutenant Richard Benyon Croft RN and only daughter of the maltster Henry Page – died on 6 October 1921. It was almost exactly eight months since she had attended the unveiling of the War Memorial for which she provided the 26-foot long Union Jack. An obituary in the *Hertfordshire Mercury* said that Ware people owed her a deep debt of gratitude – "bazaars, sales of work, religious societies and churches of all denominations found a real friend in Mrs. Croft … and many a poor soul in distress has offered up a prayer of gratitude for the comfort afforded them at her hands". The bells of St. Mary's (which she loved) were rung at her funeral and crowds lined Watton Road as her coffin was taken to the new cemetery to be laid beside her husband, who had died in 1912.

Mrs. Croft's greatest benefaction had been the gift to the town of the Priory. In fact, she had leased it in 1919 to the Ware Urban District Council but on far more generous terms than anyone had hoped. The lease was for 999 years at an annual rent of three shillings (15p) and she gave detailed instructions for its use. The main user was to be Ware UDC, including provision for the Fire Brigade "and the Council's horses and carts"; any spare accommodation was to be used as a Library and lecture rooms for the Ware Young Men's Friendly Society, nurses associations, the armed forces or "any other public purpose for the benefit of the inhabitants of the area now or at any time comprised within the Urban District or Town of Ware". Ware UDC were to occupy the Priory for the next half century until the reorganisation of local government in 1974, when for a short period ownership was wrongly transferred to East Herts District Council. In 1979 the Priory passed back to Ware Town Council acting as the 'Ware Priory Trustees' who then acquired the freehold for a nominal sum from Mrs. Croft's grandson, Major Richard Page Croft. The UDC did very little to the building apart from removing the partition walls in the East Wing to create a large assembly hall. The inaction of Ware UDC was criticised by the same Mr. Relf who had raised problems about siting the War Memorial – in September 1921 he wrote to the *Hertfordshire Mercury* complaining that the council had done nothing to make the Priory attractive and suggesting that they should organise outdoor concerts.

Ware Urban District Council met once a fortnight throughout the 1920s under the chairmanship of Mr. H.S. Gilbert and faced difficult times. One word characterised the Twenties – unemployment. The war years and the years immediately following had produced an economic boom but that had obscured the underlying economic problem that Britain was no longer a first-rank manufacturing power, and this was one cause of the high unemployment of the 1920s. It was made worse, of course, with the collapse of world stock markets in 1929 and the Great Depression of 1929-1933. Hertfordshire did not suffer as much as other parts of the country but unemployment was still an issue. At the same time there was an increase in tension between the trades unions and employers who saw unemployment as an opportunity for holding back wages, if not actually reducing them – an issue which gave rise to deep resentment in coal-mining areas and caused the General Strike of 1926. In Ware unemployment and labour relations were already an issue in January 1921. Then the idiosyncratic MP for East Hertfordshire, Pemberton Billing, made a speech attacking the unions and blaming them for his decision to close his Ware factory. Billing, who held a pilot's licence and always wore a monocle, was a great self-publicist. The Ware factory was run by 'Pemberton Billing Economic Housing Ltd.' and he claimed that trades unionists there had threatened to down tools if he gave work to ex-servicemen in training who had not joined the union. Members of Ware UDC expressed their sympathies with Billing, but later in the year they set up their own unemployment committee and agreed to participate in public works schemes to help the unemployed.

Much of the business of Ware UDC in 1921 was granting licences for new services. This was a time of frantic competition between private bus companies. In one month alone, the UDC was asked to license a service from Waltham Abbey to Hertford via Ware by the London General Omnibus Company, from Hertford to Bishop's Stortford via Ware by the National Omnibus & General Transport Company, and local services by the Hertford & District Motor Omnibus Company. This last company was, in fact, based in Ware – it had a garage behind Rankin House (the 'Town Hall') built in 1923 and offices in Clyde House, 90 High Street. It was also known as Harvey & Burrows and offered "private saloon buses for hire day and night" and also "parties from 20 to 400 catered for". By 1924 Harvey & Burrows had about 24 buses operating a wide local network, much to the distaste of the London General. A public war was waged in the streets and in newspaper articles, and in July 1924 H&B was taken over. The operating licences were immediately transferred to the National Omnibus and Transport Company, who were the agents of the General in the northern country area. The garage behind the Town Hall was also acquired by the General and operated by the National.

But the General and the National did not enjoy their monopoly for long. In 1927 they found they had a rival in the People's Motor Services, operated by Walter L. Thurgood, from premises in Park Road (the former maltings of Caleb Hitch). Thurgood was a remarkable entrepreneur. His buses could not compete with those of the General and National on the main roads, so they operated on minor roads with fares that undercut the General's. In 1934 the People's service was compulsorily purchased by the London Passenger Transport Board. Mr. Thurgood then turned his skills to the manufacture of 'warerite', a type of laminated plastic. This company was taken over in 1940 by Bakelite Ltd. and during the remainder of the Second World War manufactured wings for Mosquito aircraft. Thurgood also founded Jersey Airways and a coach repair garage in Widbury Hill, which later became part of Plaxton's.

Another licence which would bear fruit later was the agreement which Ware UDC sealed in December 1921 with the North Metropolitan Power Distribution Company for a supply of electricity in Ware. Electricity had been known and used as a form of lighting for some years, certainly since 1883 when Thomas Edison and Joseph Swan combined forces to produce the Edison-Swan incandescent lamp. The company set up a Ware operation in August 1922 in the former Barge Inn, at Bridgefoot on the corner with Star Lane. From that base its linesmen and engineers took power to more and more buildings in the town and a widening circle of villages. Ware became in 1922 one of the first towns to have electric street lighting, replacing the cast-iron gas lamps. The first concrete lamp-stands were installed in Amwell End in 1936 supplied by Concrete Utilities of Lower Road, Great Amwell, founded by the Australian Charles Marques. St. Mary's Church was given electric lighting in 1936 (paid for by Thomas Cyril Hunt, husband of the historian Edith Hunt) and Christ Church in 1937 as part of the Coronation celebrations. In 1938 the Barge Inn was due for demolition under a plan to widen Star Street. The electricity company then built Northmet House, an imposing building with a terraced garden beside the river (later Bridge House and, at the time of writing, a public house known as The Navigator). In 1948, electricity supplies were nationalised and Ware was included in the Eastern Electricity Board which opened a consumer office at 39 High Street, formerly the grocers, Swain & Nickold.[2]

The 1920s saw great progress in modernising the utilities of Ware, what we would now call 'the infrastructure'. As the town expanded out of the valley and up the adjoining hills, a good supply of water became crucial. It was ironic – and a constant source of local criticism – that water from the Lea was not available to the town since it was used to supply London, first by the New River Company, then by the Metropolitan Water Board and later by Thames Water. The water supply for Ware came from boreholes operated by the Herts and Essex Water Company, formed in 1883 and now part of Veolia Water UK. In 1895 a pumping station was established at Musley Lane above a well 100ft (30.48m) deep and 7ft (2.13m) in diameter, and this was linked to another well on Musley Hill. In 1924 a water tower was constructed off what is now Tower Road to increase the pressure for houses built on higher ground. Drainage and sanitation were another problem with the increase in the town's population. A 'sewage farm' or treatment works was created by Ware UDC in 1928 on land they had purchased at Rye Meads, where the rivers Lea and Stort meet. It was later made available to neighbouring councils and greatly expanded in 1950 to serve the New Towns of Harlow, Stevenage and

Welwyn and Hatfield, with trunk sewers running across the Meads at Ware. In 1974 the works was transferred to the Lea Division of the Thames Water Authority. Leslie Southall, clerk of Ware UDC from 1934-74, told the present author that there had been an agreement that Ware people would not pay for their sewage treatment until the population of the town reached 20,000 – but it never did and the agreement seems to have been forgotten. In recent years Rye Meads has become an important nature reserve and bird sanctuary.

As the Twenties came to an end, Ware UDC began to think about another modernisation, that of the Fire Brigade. It was obvious that the steamer, purchased in 1907, was no longer fit for purpose. The Hertford brigade had a motorised engine and usually got to fires way ahead of the Ware men. In July 1929 the council proposed putting the steamer on a petrol-driven chassis but this was thought technically difficult. They then asked neighbouring councils to contribute to the cost of a motor engine, but only Thundridge was prepared to do so. The council asked the National Omnibus Company if they would provide a bus from their Ware depot to take the firemen to fires. The bus company said yes, but it was a short-term measure. Finally, in 1930 the UDC abandoned its obsessive caution and agreed to ask for tenders for a motor engine – provided the Ministry of Health would sanction a loan. And wonder of wonders, they actually got what everyone had longed for – a big, red 60 horse-power Merryweather Hatfield open engine with a solid base on which the firemen in buttoned tunics and brass helmets could stand, with a big bell attached to the windscreen and, at the rear, a petrol-driven pump capable of delivering 400 gallons a minute. It would have been every schoolboy's dream and that of some councillors. In an illustrated article in the *Mercury*, the chairman of the UDC, H.S. Gilbert, suggested the engine should be called 'Perseverance' because it had taken a lot of perseverance to acquire it. The newspaper gave a history of the brigade and listed all its members as well as the three surviving members of the Ware brigade in 1889 when it was re-organised.[3] The Merryweather served the town well throughout the Second World War and was retired in 1946. Its last duty was to pump out the basement of Northmet House at Bridgefoot. It was later acquired and restored by a preservation society. It was a fitting end to the modernising Twenties and a beginning for the optimistic Thirties.

But it was not the end of that story. The new engine would not fit in the Church Street fire station. A number of temporary homes were found – among the buses in the National's garage, in one of the malting yards behind 39 High Street. But then – in another fit of throwing financial caution to the wind – Ware UDC decided to buy from the Page Croft family 87 High Street (the former home of the maltster, Henry Page) and the malthouse behind it – provided again that the Ministry of Health would sanction a loan. So 87 High Street became a public building, later to be leased to the Ware Nursing Association for accommodation for District Nurses, and part of the malthouse behind was converted into a fire station and mortuary. No.87 High Street was first used as Ware Library in 1949; during the Thirties the library inhabited a room in the Priory. The purchase was further evidence of Ware's optimism about the Thirties.

26.
The Thirties

It may seem strange to link the Thirties and "optimism" in the same sentence. During the Thirties – following the Wall Street Crash of 1929 – economies were in deep trouble throughout the world, unemployment was a major problem and Fascism was on the rise in Europe. It has been called the 'Dirty Thirties', the 'Bitter Thirties' and the 'Hungry Thirties'. Indeed the Jarrow Hunger Marchers did pass through Ware on their way to London in 1932 and were warmly received. There was unemployment and poverty in Ware but it was nowhere near as serious as in the manufacturing regions of the Midlands, Wales, the North-East and Scotland, where the drying up of export markets put thousands on the dole. By comparison, Ware was still busily at work, even in the malting industry which was depressed by the drop in beer consumption. Henry Page & Co. were still Ware's biggest maltsters but in 1931-32 they made a loss and were employing only 40 per cent of the labour they had in 1930.[1] The firm's ledgers show that in 1932 they passed a significant historical milestone when they stopped dealing in Brown Malt.

Two other industries in Ware weathered the Depression with more success. Allen and Hanbury were still benefiting from the vast expansion of their works in Priory Street in the period up to the First World War when all their milk, malt and pastille production was transferred to Ware from Bethnal Green. During the Thirties they faced stiffer competition in home markets, particularly for infant foods and dried milk. But they were able to compensate with new products, like their successful halibut-oil marketed as 'Haliborange'. They expanded their facilities for manufacturing surgical instruments and also began to give more emphasis to pharmaceutical drugs, such as insulin.[2]

At the other end of the town, D. Wickham & Co. Ltd. experienced something of a boom during the Thirties. They had moved from general engineering into railway vehicles soon after James Cooper joined the company in 1921, becoming chairman a year later. In 1929 they undertook their most ambitious project to date, with an order from the Central Argentine Railway for two diesel shunting locomotives, and it was realised that the existing works in Viaduct Road were too small for producing rail vehicles of this size. The No 1 Works at the top of Crane Mead was expanded with installation of a heavy-lifting crane and this was followed by construction of No. 2 Works at the end of Crane Mead, when the company took on orders for diesel locomotives to run up the Andes in Peru. At about the same time, Wickham's began using arc-welding to produce lightweight versions of its popular gang and maintenance trolleys, which were being exported throughout the world. In 1933 the *Hertfordshire Mercury* published a feature about Wickham's under the heading 'Ware Engineering Enterprise with Worldwide Reputation':

> The more one pursues the quest of investigating the industries of Hertfordshire, the more fully it is realised that the county is gaining a commercial prestige which cannot be challenged. After motoring through several miles of country where the plough predominates the landscape, we dropped down beside the old wharf at Ware and found here a foundry and engineering

shop in full swing; lathes dealing with all sorts, shapes and sizes of castings, drilling machines humming the tune of prosperity, men in overalls pouring molten metal into moulds, smithy fires glowing and blacksmiths playing merry tunes on anvils.

When due allowance is made for the romantic view of the writer, it is obvious that he was amazed by the scale of production at Wickham's. Later in the article he described the company's success in selling to China, South Africa and South America. He also reported that the workforce included "a considerable number from Hertford, Ware and Bishop's Stortford" and that boys were being apprenticed and trained from the age of 15.[3] It is said that Allenbury's and Wickham's had a gentlemen's agreement not to poach each others workers and that was one reason for the large number of girls and young women employed by Allen and Hanbury.

Homes Fit for Heroes

It was in slum clearance and new housing that Ware's new spirit of hope and determination showed itself. During the Twenties, a good start had been made on fulfilling Lloyd George's promise of "Homes Fit for Heroes" for ex-servicemen. The Housing and Town Planning Act of 1919 provided government subsidies for council housing, and over the next ten years Ware Urban District Council constructed council houses in Croft and Canons Roads, Musley Hill and Tower Road. But that was only a beginning and the appalling conditions in the courts of Amwell End, Baldock Street and Kibes Lane remained. Although there had been improvements in sanitation since the notorious Public Health Report of 1849, there were serious problems with overcrowding, small windows which did not admit decent light and buildings which were overall in bad repair. For years it had been felt that most dwellings of this type should be demolished. Amwell End was in the parish of Christ Church and in 1928 the former vicar, the Rev. Alfred Oates, wrote:

> I shall not attempt to describe these courts, beyond saying that in not one of them was there a public lamp, and that the Drill Hall now covers one yard in which there were more than two dozen dwellings quite unfit for human habitation.

But neither the council nor the churches had the legal powers to pull down the slums nor did they have the money to compensate owners or provide new accommodation – until 1930.

In 1930 the Labour Government passed the Housing Act usually named after its main advocate, Arthur Greenwood, the Minister of Health. This act introduced a five year programme for the clearance of slums in towns with designated Improvement Areas. Local authorities were given the legal powers and the money to buy up slum properties and demolish them, on condition they provided housing for those who lost their homes at affordable rents. It was the opportunity that the more enlightened councillors and doctors in Ware had been waiting for. But there was an obstacle which first had to be removed. That was the Urban District Council's Surveyor, Albert Dickinson, who was himself a slum landlord. In May 1930 – while the Greenwood Housing Act was still before Parliament – the town's Medical Officer of Health, Dr. R.A. Dunn, manoeuvred the council into a position where they could not fail to act. Dr. Dunn proposed

The old Machine Shop in Wickham's No. 1 Works in Viaduct Road, before 1935

first, that there should be a separation of the posts of Surveyor and Sanitary Inspector, second that there should be an immediate survey of areas to be designated slum clearance or improvement areas, third that property owned by the existing Surveyor, Mr. Dickinson, should be inspected independently, and fourth that Ware UDC must take immediate action before Hertfordshire County Council moved in and acted for them. To make sure that his report was not shelved, Dr. Dunn sent copies to the Ministry of Health and the County Medical Officer. He was further supported by a letter from the chairman of the Ware Labour Party calling the council's attention to the "disgraceful condition of a great number of houses in the Ware District". Dr. Dunn's plan worked. Albert Dickinson was dismissed and in February 1931 a new Sanitary Inspector and a new Surveyor were appointed. The latter was R.W. (Robert) Grantham from Rotherham, who was to achieve great things for Ware later in the decade. In 1934, there was another change when Leslie Southall succeeded George Gisby as Town Clerk.

Clearing away the large amount of substandard housing was a time-consuming and laborious process. First the council's Public Health and Housing Committee had to designate streets or groups of houses as 'Clearance Areas' and the Medical Officer had to report on which houses were "unfit for human habitation and dangerous and injurious to the health of the inhabitants" and which could be repaired and retained. Then, with the backing of the full council, the Surveyor had to negotiate compensation with the property owners and proceed to demolition. There was at least one public inquiry in August 1933 to hear objections from property owners (including the former Surveyor, Mr. Dickinson). The new Medical Officer, Dr. Whitelaw, gave evidence and said that one clearance area, Caroline Court off Baldock Street, had a density equivalent to 60 houses to the acre, mostly with low ceilings, insufficient light from the windows and so badly arranged and congested that the free circulation of air through the court was greatly impeded. Further evidence was given in support of demolitions in Watton Road, Park Road, Cherry Tree and George Yards in Amwell End, Red Cow Yard, Crib Street and the Bourne. At the same time, the council was obliged to rehouse persons displaced by the demolitions. Most of the new council housing was provided by the Workmen's Housing Association working with local builders, but the council did construct bungalows in Bowling Road by direct labour. A second stage of clearance in 1934 included parts of the High Street and West Street, including 'Church Alley' bordering St. Mary's churchyard, Black Swan Yard off Baldock Street and houses at the top of Priory Street, backing on to the Priory grounds.

Another clearance programme was agreed for Kibes Lane between 1934 and 1936. This was a complicated affair in view of the large number of properties with different owners. One of these was a Mrs. Rayner who decided not to sell her properties but to give them to the council as a carpark "to perpetuate the memory of her father, the late Mr. John Adams". This was agreed and the council erected a plaque to John Adams which remained in the Kibes Lane carpark until the 1950s. The council also purchased the former Quaker Burial Ground in the centre of Kibes Lane – the Society of Friends sold it at a low price on the understanding that it was reserved for use as an open space or recreation ground and the council agreed that "the character of the ground would be preserved and respected".[4] As Kibes Lane was being cleared of houses, the council took the opportunity in 1937 of purchasing land from the Enfield Highway Co-operative Society so that Bowling Road could be extended to meet Star Street. By this stage, in 1936-37, the council had run out of land on which to build council houses to rehouse families displaced by the demolitions. King George Road and the Vineyard Estate had been purchased from the Fanhams Estate (the Page Croft family) and it was proposed that one of the Kibes Lane pubs, the Jolly Bargeman, should be relocated there — in fact it went to Cromwell Road, and the Harrow was built at the top of King George Road. But more land was needed, and so the council negotiated with the Fanhams Estate to buy part of Cundalls Farm.

The wisdom of appointing R.W. Grantham as Surveyor was demonstrated in July 1933 when the *Hertfordshire Mercury* ran a long article under the heading 'Ware Moving with the Times'. It concerned the plan for a swimming bath in Ware, able to accommodate 400 people and having dressing rooms, clothes lockers, showers, a sun bath, car park and café – all "in the lovely grounds of the Priory". The plan had the backing of the children of the late Mrs. Croft who had given the Priory to the town and was supported by a petition of 150 leading ratepayers. One person objected, saying that the pool should not be sited in the Priory gardens. But others pointed out that there were 1,300 children in the town with no provision for learning to swim, and many people in the town still did not have a bath or shower in their house. What the newspaper did not say was that the bath would be built by the council's direct labour, using hard core from the demolitions that had taken place. The swimming bath (later known as the Lido) was opened in May 1936 and was soon visited by delegations from other councils, as far away as Durham.

In 1936, the main drive to demolish slum properties was coming to an end. The council could give attention to other matters. "The old king" – George V – died in January and on the

27th the Prince of Wales was proclaimed king, as Edward VIII, from a platform erected outside the Town Hall (by now occupied by the Home & Colonial Stores). But the king abdicated to marry an American divorcee, Mrs. Simpson, and in May 1937 Ware celebrated the coronation of his brother as King George VI, at which the Salvation Army Band played and received six guineas from the council. Throughout the Thirties, one of the Surveyor's responsibilities was to pick the grapes growing in the conservatory at the Priory and then send some to the workhouse at Western House, and some to the TB sanatorium established at Ware Park.

Another of his responsibilities was to inspect the town's barges and ensure they had adequate cooking and sleeping facilities for the crews. These were malt and coal barges, mostly owned by Albany & Son which had been bought out by the Thames Steam Tug and Lighterage Company. They were steel barges, similar to those operating on the Thames, and their names began with a 'W' – Ware, Wargrave, Warren, Warsaw, Warwick, Watford, Woking and Windsor. Older barges like the

Mr. R.W. Grantham as a captain in the Royal Engineers – he died of malaria in Egypt in 1941.

Earl Roberts and Black Prince were still operating. Brickmaking in Ware had come to an end and the wooden barges used to transport bricks had been left to rot in a cut off the Lea above Ware Lock (later filled in when Glaxo's research buildings were built). There is a rudder and a name board from one of these barges – the *Perseverance* – in Ware Museum. The Surveyor and Sanitary Inspector were also busy checking that the remaining houses in Ware were fit for purpose and not overcrowded.

'Saracen's Head Corner'

As early as 1935 Ware Urban District Council discussed widening the High Street. Motor traffic had greatly increased since 1918 and there were frequent requests to the superintendent of police to do something about cars speeding through the town. The main problem was that, just after the junction with New Road, the High Street made a ninety-degree turn before crossing the river. This turn was known as 'Saracen's Head Corner'. In 1937 the UDC and the county council agreed to demolish four properties near the bridge and transform the 90° turn into a gentle curve – provided, of course, that the Ministry of Transport made a grant of 50 per cent of the cost. The properties to be demolished included part of a malting, the Reliance Laundry, a long jettied building which had once been the Cardinal's Hat Inn and – at No. 13 High Street – the Saracen's Head Inn. The Saracen's Head had been sold by the Ware Charity Trustees in 1921 to McMullen's and the brewery now drove a hard bargain – it agreed to sell the Saracen's Head for £1,000, provided it was given any land left over from the demolitions which was not needed for the road widening, provided also that the councils found a new home for the Jolly Bargeman, and provided that the councils would agree to purchase The Victory pub on the opposite side of the bridge. All was agreed and, in April 1939, Mr. Grantham announced that

Saracen's Head Hotel, *FAMILY & COMMERCIAL*

Telephone : Ware 118 High Street, Ware, Herts.

FRONT OF HOTEL

REAR VIEW

A postcard of the Saracen's Head – the clock with the message 'Tempus Fugit' is on the timber-framed building to the right. The reverse of the postcard says 'Can we have a lettuce, please'.

demolition of all the Bridgefoot properties would begin soon after the Easter vacation. Nos 5, 9 and 11 High Street were duly demolished. For the time being, the Saracen's Head was saved. In September 1939 – with the outbreak of the Second World War – the government decreed that demolitions must stop, since there could well be a shortage of accommodation as a result of air attacks. What local people thought of the demolitions is not recorded, but in 1937-38 the travel writer Owen Hamilton felt the pangs of regret when he stayed at the Saracen's Head:

> Although the county town of Hertford lies only a few miles off, life seems to have slipped by, leaving Ware, with its red-roofed maltings and mills, almost untouched. Surely its High Street, with John Gilpin's famous house, must have looked just so a hundred years ago! The broad doorways, needful for coaches of those days – Ware being once an important coaching-halt – are still there; also the original rough-hewn cross-beams, placed as at first, with their ends rudely projecting under the eaves. One thinks of some medieval German town of the Meistersingers' period. What a sketch Vermeer would have made of the old bridge! Yet I hear that most of the High Street is about to come down; all those lichened, gold-brown roofs I see as I write, built of tiles they cannot now copy, coming down! Below, in the courtyard, under the old clock I read the inscription *Tempus fugit*. Too true. And, as it flies, people and places change.[5]

The Saracen's Head, along with the clock in the courtyard and the motto *Tempus fugit*, was finally swept away after the war in 1957.

27.
War with Hitler's Germany

Adolf Hitler came to power in Germany in 1933 and before long it seemed likely there would be another war. In January 1936, Hertfordshire County Council called a conference of all local councils to set up a joint committee for Air-Raid Precautions (ARP). The big fear was that the enemy might use gas bombs as it had done in the trenches of the First World War and a 'gas school' was set up to which St. John Ambulance, the Red Cross and other groups from Ware were invited. In May 1936 Ware appointed its own ARP Committee with representatives from the UDC, medical services, Red Cross and St. John Ambulance. At its first meeting it decided to set up a Gas Decontamination Centre in the malting next to the fire station, behind 87 High Street, and to use the Western House laundry for cleaning contaminated clothing. At the time of the 'Munich Crisis' in September 1938, the government began issuing gas masks to everyone in the country – including for young children the 'Mickey Mouse' gas masks with red rubber pieces and bright eye piece rims – and, by the outbreak of war in September 1940, 38 million gas masks had been issued. The other main precaution for members of the public was the installation of Anderson shelters in their gardens or Morrison shelters under the stairs in their homes.

Under the emergency regulations, the council had to set up a Report and Control Centre to coordinate the work of the police, rescue services and ARP wardens in the event of enemy air-raids. The first sites proposed for this centre were the Priory Lodge or rooms in the Priory itself, but in May 1939 the Surveyor, Mr. Grantham, put forward plans for a reinforced concrete bunker in the lodge garden. Work started in the summer and the bunker was finished before the declaration of war on 3 September, at a cost of £406.18s. The centre, which was manned day and night throughout the war (including by women), was connected by telephone to the County ARP Centre at Hertford – from where the 'red alert' would be given, the signal to sound the sirens throughout the town – and also with the Fire Station, Police Station, the Priory and other civil defence posts in the town and surrounding area. There were four posts for air-raid wardens, all well manned since a large number of men and women had come forward as volunteers during the Munich Crisis. The posts were mainly Nissen huts, provided by the Nissen Company of Rye House. In addition there were a Rescue and Demolition Squad (later the Civil Defence Rescue Service), recruited mainly from St. John Ambulance, and the Ware Fire Brigade, supplemented by volunteers in the Auxiliary Fire Service (AFS).

The Home Guard (originally called the Local Defence Volunteers) was set up when the Germans began their major offensive against the Allied armies in Belgium and France in May 1940 – culminating in the Dunkirk evacuation in the week ending 3 June – and the threat of an invasion became a reality. The Home Guard recruited veterans of the First World War, too old for military service, and men who had yet to reach recruitment age; the Ware platoon was based in the Drill Hall, Amwell End, under the command of Major Ian Buxton DSO of Stanstead Abbots. This part of 'Dad's Army' received training at a special range set up by Captain Charles Marques MBE, behind his family business, Concrete Utilities, in Lower Road, Great Amwell. But everyone in Ware – man, woman, boy and girl – was in some way involved in the defence of the 'Home Front', whether in the volunteer organisations, youth groups, fund-raising for the war effort or giving accommodation to evacuee children from London and the South Coast. The full story has been skilfully told by Derek Armes in *Ware at War 1939 – 1945*. Here we will look at the changes that the war brought to the physical and organisational character of the town.

Ware was hit by a number of enemy bombs between 1939 and 1945. With the exception of a V1 Flying Bomb in 1944, most of these explosions occurred during the 'Battle of Britain' in September and October 1940. On the night of 18 September a high explosive bomb fell on New Road, demolishing Nos. 61 and 63, killing six people, injuring two others and causing considerable damage to houses, churches and the nearby Ware Central School. By a cruel irony, the dead were workers evacuated from London by the Stadium engineering firm and their relatives. Debris from the bombed houses was cleared away within a week by local builders and the site left bare – in the 1980s it formed Dickenson Way, leading to the carpark of the Tesco Superstore. The damaged windows of Christ Church were replaced with plain glass and a new east window installed in a dedication service in 1948. Parachute bombs were dropped over the area in the last days of September 1940, one causing considerable damage and killing four people in Tamworth Road, Hertford.

One of these parachute bombs became entangled in a tree, failing to explode, at the Ware Park Tuberculosis Sanatorium which was immediately evacuated while a detachment from the Royal Navy made the bomb safe. The bomb or mine was then taken into the town and displayed outside the Priory to raise money for the Ware 'Boys at the Front Fund', until a soldier on leave noticed that the mine had not been properly defused. An Army bomb disposal team was called in and took it to the Braziers' pit in Watton Road, where – despite protests from the council – it was exploded, causing considerable damage over a wide area. Ware UDC claimed the cost of repairs from the Ministry of Health and in January 1941 won their claim. On 16 October a high explosive bomb hit Thurgood's Coachworks in Park Road, causing a fire and injuring two men working in the adjoining Warerite factory. The final incident of bomb damage came in 1944 when the Germans launched their first V1 Flying Bombs – popularly known as 'doodle-bugs' because they could be heard flying in until their engines cut out and they crashed to earth – and then their V2 high explosive rockets. A Flying Bomb fell on a gravel pit in what is now the Trapstyles area of Ware, causing damage to roofs and windows throughout the west of the town, injuring one small child, and killing a large number of chickens kept by Allen and Hanbury at their premises off Park Road.

The Ware War Memorial Fund

A large number of Ware men and women served in the Armed Forces in all the theatres of war and at home and, although casualties were not on the terrible scale of the First World War, many gave their lives to secure victory. In due course their names were added to the War Memorial in the High Street, which was rededicated on Armistice Sunday, 8 November 1947. But in 1945 there was a wide feeling that there should also be a more practical reminder of the sacrifice of Ware men and women. The debate over what this should be went on for decades and was described by Derek Armes as "a saga". In length of time, it easily outdistanced the

The ARP bunker built in the garden of the Priory Lodge in 1939 – it has since been incorporated in the extension of the Ware Museum

debate after the First World War about the site for the War Memorial.

In June 1945 the British Legion proposed a War Memorial Hall. This led to a public meeting held in the Priory when a motion was proposed by Miss H. Woodhead, the long-serving head of the girls' grammar school, seconded by Mrs. Margaret Percival, wife of General Arthur Percival (former Allied commander in Singapore), that a fund be opened to engrave the names of the fallen of the last war on the present memorial and to provide a hall and, if funds were sufficient, a community centre, a recreation ground, and alterations to the existing memorial – "the various schemes to be executed in that order."

A fund raising committee was formed, with Councillor Tom Burgess as chairman, the UDC Clerk Leslie Southall as secretary, and committee members from the British Legion, Ware Football Club, Red Cross, St. John Ambulance Brigade, the town's churches, youth groups and schools. Some £750 had been raised by July 1946 when a grand fête was held in the Priory grounds featuring the Dagenham Girl Pipers. The fête was a revival of the Ware Carnival Queen's crowning, last held in June 1939, and it raised £170. The fêtes continued to be run in conjunction with a gala at the Priory Street swimming pool and until 1953 all the proceeds went to the Memorial Fund. Many of the town's businesses and banks gave donations of hundreds of pounds. Another fund raising event was the Christmas Fair in the Drill Hall, opened in 1946 by General Percival. Charlie Ballands put the Astoria Cinema at the Committee's disposal for a special children's matinee. There was great public enthusiasm for the Memorial Fund and by 1948 it had raised £3,000.

The Clerk, Leslie Southall, was always in favour of a new building. He suggested to the committee that an architect be retained to design a building capable of holding 500 people complete with a stage, a foyer and a bar. Other members of the committee realised that building costs had soared and the proposed hall would cost far more than the original estimate, yet they pressed on. By 1954 the fund stood at £7,500, still far short of the cost of any new building. However, in 1960 Ware UDC sold its water utility to Three Valleys Water and came into serious money. Southall, who by then had retired as Town Clerk, wrote to the council asking if it would give matching funds provided the Memorial Fund was reopened and raised further contributions. But the council turned this down on the grounds that the Memorial Committee would never raise sufficient money for a hall. In 1962 the council reversed its earlier decision and agreed that £52,000 of the money raised from the sale of the water utility could be spent on a new hall. They proposed to move the town depot from behind 87 High Street (by then used as Ware Library) to a site in Priory Street and build the Memorial Hall on the old site. But by the time the new depot was completed, the national economy had taken a downturn and there was a credit squeeze. Thereupon Ware UDC decided to purchase the Drill Hall in Amwell End from the Territorial Army and the Memorial Committee agreed to hand over their funds to help with the conversion, but the government would not sanction a loan for the work.

Further hopes were raised in the early Seventies. In 1971 there was the possibility of a public hall being built in Church Street, as part of the Hertfordshire County Council's 'Central Area Development Plan', but this plan eventually came to nothing. In 1973, the Age Concern building in Priory Street was being built and a number of people wrote to the *Hertfordshire Mercury* suggesting that some of the Memorial Fund be spent there, but this would have conflicted with the original aim of the fund which by now was enshrined in a charitable deed. In 1975 there was a proposal by a group, known as 'Ware 4', to establish an arts centre in one of the maltings in Kibes Lane, but the group were unable to get a lease of more than five years from the newly formed East Hertfordshire District Council. Another proposal was for the fund to take over the United Reformed Church in the High Street (the former Congregational Church) whose minister was keen to sell the building and join up with St. Mary's Church, but the minister moved on and instead the URC merged with the New Road Methodists to form the Leaside Church. The Memorial Fund appeared to be running out of possible sites and ideas – when on to the scene came Place House, the old manor house of the town in Bluecoat Yard.

Place House had been bought after the war by John Whitfield, a solicitor, who for a while was also Deputy County Archivist – he had intended to restore Place House, as he had his other Ware properties which included some of the Bluecoat Yard cottages and Churchgate House in West Street. But before he could carry out these plans, he developed Parkinson's Disease. Mr. Whitfield died in 1970, leaving Place House to the National Trust, but they would not accept it without an endowment for maintenance. So it was handed over to a judicial trustee who gifted Place House to the Hertfordshire Building Preservation Trust (HBPT), on condition it restored the building and used it for the public good. In December 1975 the seven town councillors on the Memorial Committee wrote to Leslie Southall suggesting the restoration of Place House as a fitting scheme to spend the Memorial Fund on. Much to Southall's distaste (he disliked old buildings and was still hoping for a new hall), the Charity Commissioners agreed with them, provided Place House was made available to the public of Ware under a trust deed. It was estimated by the architect, Russ Craig of the county council, that the restoration work would amount to £80,000 but this would include two residential parts of Place House and a suite of offices. Restoration of the public hall would amount to £20,000 and this was provided by £11,000 from the Ware War Memorial Fund and the rest in grants from the government's Historic Buildings Council. The Memorial Fund by then had raised a total of £19,341.67 so the remaining £8,341.67 was given to the newly created Place House Charity as an endowment. These sums of money were inscribed on two plaques put up inside the building.

The restoration complete, Place House was formally opened by the late Queen Elizabeth, the Queen Mother, on 8 July 1978. The week before, on 24 June 1978, Ware Town Council as the custodian of the Place House Charity had signed a lease for 28 years to enable Place House to become "a village hall for the use of the inhabitants of the Town of Ware in the County of Hertford … without distinction of political, religious or other opinions, including use for meetings, lectures and classes, and for forms of recreation and leisure-time occupation, with the object of improving the conditions of life for the said inhabitants." The lease and trust deed was to run for 28 years from 24th June 1978. John Bishop was the first chairman of the charity and worked hard to make sure Place House was a well-used 'village hall' for the town. The final meeting of the Ware War Memorial Committee was held at the Priory on 16 September 1980, nearly thirty-five years after its formation, and Leslie Southall received a well earned vote of thanks for his years of service.

That should have been the end of the story. After all, everyone believed that when the Queen Mother declared it open, Place House would remain for all time the 'village hall' of Ware at a very low annual rent. But in March 2006, negotiations for a new lease between the HBPT and Ware Town Council broke down. A new, commercially minded agent for the HBPT was demanding more than the old 'peppercorn rent' and Ware Town Council announced "with a heavy heart" that it was not renewing the lease. It was accused by one East Herts district councillor of "stabbing in the back" the memories of those who died in the war and their loved ones, and wishing to replace Place House with a new public hall at Fletcher's Lea. A group of citizens, including the present author, tried to restart negotiations for a long lease but without success. At the time of writing, the Hertfordshire Building Preservation Trust itself is opening Place House as a public amenity. But the fact that £11,000 from the Ware War Memorial Fund was invested in the restoration of Place House to provide a 'village hall' for the town will ensure that – for the future – the people of Ware keep a keen eye on the management of this fine old building.

28.
Post-war Progress

One might have assumed that in 1945 Ware UDC would finish the projects they had started in 1939. As the BBC announcer Leslie Mitchell was supposed to have said when the television service was resumed: "As I was saying when I was so rudely interrupted …" But it was not to be. Admittedly, in 1949 the council did flag up the proposal to demolish cottages in Monkey Row, off Baldock Street: "owing to the recent war the matter had been in abeyance" – but then it did nothing about Monkey Row until 1970. Similarly with other 1939 projects – demolishing the Saracen's Head Inn to give traffic an easier turn into the High Street did not happen until 1957, and the Jolly Bargeman pub was not relocated from Kibes Lane until 1956 – and then not to King George Road, as originally planned, but Cromwell Road. And the continuation of Bowling Road to a junction with Star Street had still not taken place in 1958.

Like all councils, Ware had other priorities. There was a Labour government in Whitehall which imposed new rules on local authorities, especially about spending money. The main post-war priority – as it had been after the First World War – was building new houses. By the end of the Fifties, Ware UDC had commissioned over 700 council houses with others still in progress, as well as about 150 built by "private enterprise", houses for the police and nurses and shops. Most of these were in the area to the east of Cromwell Road, part of which had been Cundalls Farm, but there were also new estates going up near Presdales. Flats were built in Tower Road in 1955 – the first in Ware – but others would follow in Crib Street and Kingshill, and many others from the 1980s onwards. In 1950 Wickham's asked for priority places on the council's housing list. "They stated that they were in a position to accept large orders from America, thus earning dollars for the benefit of the country, but were unable to find workmen owing to the lack of accommodation" – but the council advised them to build their own houses.

The other priority was industry. Ware had been designated an "industrial town" by the county council (Hertford was still a market town). In March 1950 there was an air of optimism as the Ware Exhibition (Trades and Hobbies) opened in the Drill Hall, jointly organised by the Rotary Club of Ware and the Ware Chamber of Commerce. Writing in the souvenir brochure, the president of the exhibition, Cyril Maplethorpe, managing director of Allen and Hanbury Ltd., described Ware as

> a closely knit centre of industry: it does not matter that in size and numbers Ware is a small industrial centre by present-day standards—what gives it its character is the fact that this is a town in which people work and play, and buy and sell in a compact and closely integrated township.

The industries featured in the exhibition included Warerite (then part of Bakelite Ltd.) whose laminated plastics were used in shops, hotels and famous ships like RMS Queen Elizabeth, the railcar manufacturers D. Wickham & Co. Ltd., Warecrete Products in Crane Mead (later in Marsh Lane) which provided pre-cast concrete blocks, fencing, lintels, etc., A.B. Swain &

Co. Ltd., envelope manufacturers at Swain's Mill in Crane Mead, the printing works of Jennings and Bewley in the High Street and the Star Press in Bowling Road, H. Wells & Son, ironmongers and smiths at 25 High Street, J.W. French's Frenlite Flour Mill then specialising in self-raising flour for home baking, the Dairy Maid Ice Cream Co. in Church Street, many retailers – and, of course, Allen and Hanbury Ltd. of Priory Street. The four surviving malting companies banded together to put on a display entitled the 'Malting Industry of Ware', featuring traditional wooden shovels, a large model of a floor malting and sacks bearing the names of the four companies – Henry Page & Co. Ltd., Henry Ward & Sons Ltd., Gripper & Wightman Ltd. and John Harrington & Son Ltd., all with malthouses in Hertford as well as Ware.

Of these, Allen and Hanbury was seen as the dynamic, science-based company of the future. Following the bombing of Allenbury's Bethnal Green factory in 1940, Ware had become the centre of all the company's manufacturing, at first in Nissen huts, later in new buildings on the Buryfield site, each given a letter – the 'P' building originally built for penicillin manufacture, the 'X' building for traditional drugs, and so on. The range of products was very wide – from fruit pastilles, health foods and traditional remedies to surgical instruments and modern pharmaceuticals. The company even owned a string of dairies and distributed milk throughout the area – a leftover from wartime. But behind the Priory Street façade things were changing fast. The challenge facing the whole of the pharmaceutical industry was the manufacture of antibiotics. The first of these was penicillin, discovered in 1928 by Alexander Fleming at St. Mary's Hospital, London, and then developed in 1938 in Oxford by Howard Florey and colleagues. But it was in America that further developments were made in penicillin, streptomycin, tetracycline and other antibiotics. And it was American companies which found the most effective and economic method of growing penicillin cultures in deep tanks, while British companies, including Allenbury's, were using the less efficient 'surface culture' method. One British company used the American method and stood out from the rest and that was Glaxo Laboratories. In 1958, faced with the daunting task of raising millions in capital for pharmaceutical research, the directors of Allen and Hanbury commended to shareholders a merger with Glaxo and the new company embarked on research and manufacture on a totally different scale. In due course, GlaxoSmithKline (GSK), as it now is, had transformed the Buryfield manufacturing site, not once but three or four times, and on the other side of Harris's Lane, in the Eighties and Nineties the research company developed many of GSK's most successful products, like Ventolin and Becotide for asthma sufferers and the anti-ulcer drug, Zantac.[1]

While the pharmaceutical industry changed and forged ahead, the malting industry in the Fifties went deper and deeper into recession. The industry had done relatively well during the war – soldiers and defence workers drink a lot of beer! In 1950 most malt was still being produced in 'floor maltings', by the old labour-intensive method of workmen turning the germinating barley with wooden shovels and then loading it manually on to a kiln. Twenty years later, 80 per cent of all malt was being made by modern, technology-based methods, with the barley steeped and turned in single vessels or by huge screws moving up and down 'a street'.[2] As a result large companies, like Associated British Maltsters, swallowed many smaller, and not so small, maltsters and it was a matter of either modernise or close down. In 1958, a Land Use map produced by Hertfordshire County Council showed only three malting sites in Ware still producing malt, with as many as twelve other sites, including the Victoria Malting in

Broadmeads and the Hope Malting in Baldock Street, used for storage. Many were storing television sets for Thorn Electrics in Enfield. In 1961-62 the four Ware and Hertford maltsters merged to form Harrington Page Ltd. and agreed to pool their resources to build a modern 'Wanderhaufen street' malting in Broadmeads, Ware, next to the Victoria Malting. Finance was arranged with an insurance company and work began, when a combination of blows – the expense of pile-driving in the marshy subsoil, a government credit squeeze and other factors – forced the Hertfordshire directors to sell out to Pauls Malt of Ipswich. Pauls took on the plant which, when completed in 1965, operated night and day throughout the year and had a capacity of 74,000 quarters – more than all the floor maltings in Ware together.[3] It was an efficient and economic although comparatively small producer of malt, until Pauls closed it in 1994 in a reorganisation which concentrated production to a handful of very large malting sites, mainly in Suffolk. By then most of the redundant floor maltings in Ware had been demolished and replaced by flats, but some remained and were converted to other uses.

The Relief Road Saga

Towards the end of the Fifties, Britain was again prosperous. "You've never had it so good" was the slogan of Harold Macmillan, who became Prime Minister in 1957. In Ware prosperity meant an increase in traffic and the problems of the High Street could no longer be ignored. For six years, at least, the UDC had been imploring the county council and Ministry of Transport to finish the 20-year old road improvements at 'Saracen's Head Corner'. The buildings between the inn and the bridge had been demolished in 1939, but the Saracen's Head still stood opposite the bottom of New Road and the original road alignment and kerb stones remained. The brewers, McMullen's, were anxious to demolish the old inn and develop the site. So, at last, in October 1957 the Saracen's Head came down watched by the historian, Gordon Moodey:

> The buildings of the inn, set around a spacious yard between the High Street and the River Lea, would have made the fortune of any town more heedful of antiquity. In character and extent they were comparable with the Sun at Hitchin, although the dinginess of recent years disguised their quality. The inn faced the High Street with a square three-storeyed front of Georgian brick; on the right an archway opened into the wide innyard, bordered by lesser, older ranges left and right and extended by diverse buildings to the river bank. A group of local residents, formed to study and survey Ware's old houses under the guidance of Mr. J.T. Smith and Mr. J.R.D. Whitfield, seized the chance that demolition gave to dissect the complex of buildings on the site. Their discoveries made the loss all the more lamentable. Kingpost roof construction was found in the High Street front of the right-hand wing, and Elizabethan wall-paintings were revealed in the range on the left. These bold floral arabesques were on the upper floor, filling the panels between the vertical studs of a partition; they had been hidden by plastering of later date, but were themselves later than the heavy tie-beam with curved braces, chamfered on their lower edges, to which the partition was attached. Buried among the miscellany of structures at the lower end of the yard was a forgotten assembly room of Regency date. The sum total of antiquity lost to the town at this one stroke is tragically high.[4]

In the 1990s, medieval deeds of the Ware Guild of Corpus Christi were discovered in a cellar in Baldock Street and they included one for the Saracen's Head dated 1365, but the inn was probably much older. Eventually 'Saracen's Head Corner' was rebuilt as an arcade of formless shops with flats above and a new Saracen's Head pub was built beside the river.

Ware's traffic problems were now high on the agenda of the county planners. In 1959 they published the Ware Draft Plan, which proposed no fewer than three new roads as well as further changes in the High Street. First, they admitted, all the town's traffic problems would be solved by the building of the Hoddesdon-Ware bypass across the Meads – but that would probably not happen for 20 years. Then there was what the planners called the 'Link Road' designed to solve the problem of the level crossing at Amwell End and the bottleneck in Hertford Road outside the Grammar School. Their solution was radical: a high-level road coming off the hill above Chadwell, crossing the New River and railway on a bridge and reaching the River Lea at the top of Amwell End. The Link Road was far too ambitious and later Hertfordshire County Council proposed to solve the bottleneck by demolishing Amwell House, the home of the Grammar School. More about that later.

The planners' third and most important proposal was for a 'Relief Road'. This would have started at Bridgefoot, which was to become a one-way system with the building of a second river bridge from Viaduct Road to the Common Wharf in Star Street. The Relief Road would then have gone through the site of the Enfield Highway Cooperative store (No.12 High Street), crossed Kibes Lane, curved west across New Road, narrowly missing Bluecoat Yard, cut across Crib Street and then joined Baldock Street opposite the junction with Watton Road. As yet, it was still the outline design of a new road to by-pass the High Street. In due course, the line of the road would be firmed up and become a dual carriageway or 'urban motorway' with pedestrian underpasses like those later built under Gascoyne Way in Hertford. And, after a few years, it would be elaborated by the planners even further into the Ware Central Area Development Plan, involving the wholescale demolition of buildings to make way for a modern shopping and civic centre. This is what happened in Hoddesdon, where an elaborate system of by-passes was built in the early 1960s and many fine buildings in the town centre demolished to make way for the Tower Shopping Centre.

But already in the Ware Draft Plan there were hints of what was to come. "The majority of buildings in the Centre are in poor condition", said the planners and Church Street and Crib Street were ripe for redevelopment. There was also the idea of a service road between the High Street and the river – the service road was never built, but its entrance from the High Street was and this led to the demolition of two majestic old buildings (one the former Fleur de Luce Inn, home of the printers Jennings and Bewley). The town's first Tesco store occupied the new brick building, with groceries on one side of the archway and Home-and-Wear on the other.

While these far-reaching proposals were being considered, the county council abandoned its plan for the Link Road. This freed up the top of Amwell End for redevelopment. The Victory public house, beside the bridge, was demolished in 1961 along with the adjoining row of old shops and the Mission Hall. In their place, the road was widened and a new shopping arcade built for Ware Properties Ltd., formerly known as the maltsters, Henry Page & Co. Ltd. A little later, the Black Bull pub on the opposite corner of Amwell End was also demolished to ease traffic turning from Viaduct Road.

The Ware Society

Reading the minutes of Ware UDC for this period, one has the impression that the elected councillors were being pulled along by forces outside their control. Some did vote against details, but mostly they accepted that something had to be done about the traffic and went along with the county plans. The driving forces were the Surveyor and Planning Officer of Hertfordshire County Council, aided and abetted by officials of the Ministry of Transport and Ware urban council's own officers, especially the Clerk, Leslie Southall, a convinced moderniser.

Opposition to the Relief Road and Central Area plans came from a new body, representing a coalition of town opinion. The Ware Society was formed at a public meeting held in the Priory on 5 May 1965 and became the amenity society for the town, affiliated to the Hertfordshire Society. Its first purpose was to defeat or at least change and mitigate the Relief Road and Central Area redevelopment. The committee inevitably included persons with a special concern in this issue. The president was Judge Sir Stephen Chapman whose Manor House garden would be on the edge of the Relief Road. Two solicitors, John Baily and Peter Mottershead, became chairman and vice-chairman, and the Honorary Secretary was Dr. Violet Rowe, head of History at the Grammar School and founder of the Amwell House Preservation Society to fight demolition of the school's buildings. There was a large and active committee, including four of the town councillors. Publicity was in the hands of Jane Evans, whose family lived in Crib Street, just north of the line of the proposed road. The society held two public meetings on the county plans, wrote numerous letters and press releases, and lobbied the UDC to arrange an exhibition of the plans in Ware

In November 1965, the secretary, Dr. Rowe, sent to Hertfordshire County Council a long critique of the Relief Road. A dual carriageway would be out of scale for a small town centre, it would sever the major residential areas to the north and east from the town centre and it would not solve the problem of through traffic:

> The road as proposed appears, both in scale and alignment, to be an unhappy short-term compromise between relief of the High Street and the indisputable ultimate necessity for construction of the proposed Cambridge Radial Road intended to by-pass the Town.[5]

The Cambridge Radial Road was the Hoddesdon and Ware by-pass. The society proposed that the Relief Road be sited south of the Lea – between the river and the railway. Dr. Rowe sent this letter to the town and county councils and the ministries of Transport and Local Government. The southern route was rejected by the Clerk to the County Council in a seven-page reply to the Ware Society in March 1966. His letter went over the whole history of the Draft Central Area Plan of 1959 and the amended version of 1965 and then came out with a surprising statement. The Ware Inner Relief Road was not designed to relieve Ware of through traffic – that would be the function of the by-pass when it was built; the Relief Road was there to redistribute traffic coming into the town for shopping or business. This was a surprising statement, given that all the county's traffic surveys failed to distinguish between through traffic and local traffic. Ultimately, the Clerk conceded, it was up to the Minister of Transport to approve the Relief Road or not.

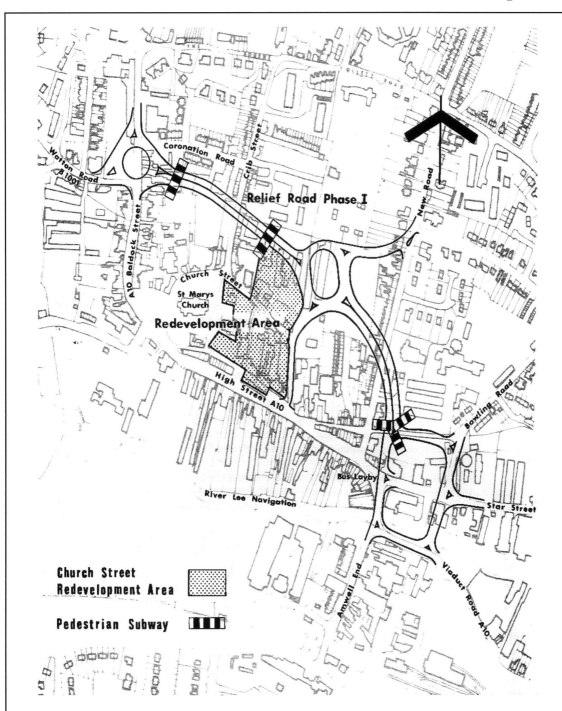

The Ware Inner Relief Road and Central Area Development plan proposed by Hertfordshire County Council in 1965.[6] *This plan does not show the service road between the High Street and the river, which had already been partially implemented with the construction of the large arch between the two parts of the Tesco store opposite the bottom of Church Street (now the separate shops of Peacock and Greggs).*

Meanwhile the county council went on purchasing property in Baldock Street, Bluecoat Yard, Church Street, Crib Street and New Road, as if the line of the Relief Road was now agreed. For its part, Ware Urban District Council began entertaining property developers interested in the Central Area Redevelopment. For three years and more, managing directors and their architects toured the town and presented their different plans to the UDC. It was pointed out that, to be viable, the Central Area should have more floor space for shops and certainly more parking. In 1970 a revised plan was published, showing an enlarged redevelopment area and a revised line of the Relief Road. But still the Minister had not given his approval. It was a stand-off and the two sides continued to argue their case through meetings, plans, correspondence and articles in the local press. In her report to the 1969 AGM, Dr. Rowe was able to write:

> It is good news indeed that the Cambridge Radial Road (the Hoddesdon-Ware Bypass) is to be built earlier than we had dared to hope, and the Ware Inner Relief Road, or at least its present proposed alignment, does not look nearly as inevitable as it did a year ago.

It was in the Seventies that the pace began to quicken and by then there were new faces in the Ware Society team. Harry Wilson, an advertising executive and amateur painter, took over from Vi Rowe as secretary and traffic surveys in the High Street were managed by John Williams, a chemical industry executive. In June 1972, a public inquiry was held into the county council's compulsory purchase orders on Nos. 8-12 High Street. A group from the society, including the present author, showed the inspector over the Enfield Co-op building including its fine eighteenth century staircase. In October the inspector reported that he could not confirm the compulsory purchase orders. In November 1972 there was a second inquiry, into the county's compulsory purchase orders on buildings in the old Market Place – Nos. 60-64 were to be demolished to create a clear vista from Tesco's through to the new shopping precinct. Again the outcome was inconclusive. A further inquiry was announced for March 1973 into the second river bridge and the gyratory system at the east end of the Relief Road, but this was postponed and reconvened in October 1973 with a broader remit. At all of these inquiries, the Ware Society team, led by Harry Wilson, presented cogent and viable alternatives to those of the county council.

In the meantime, the environment – both the natural environment and the social and built environment of towns and villages – had become an important new issue in British politics. The Conservative government under Prime Minister Edward Heath created a Department of the Environment and, in July 1972, it received a report entitled *New Roads in Towns* which recommended "a new approach to major urban road schemes" to prevent local communities being adversely affected.[7] Consequently, the Ware Inner Relief Road was virtually dead – but it took a very long time to lie down. Although Hertfordshire County Council issued a new scheme in 1975 as part of its revised County Structure Plan, it still included the line of the Relief Road. Even after the opening in 1977 of the Ware Bypass, which skirted the town by means of a long viaduct across the Meads, the county council held on to the properties it had acquired just in case the Relief Road was revived. Some properties in Crib Street and Church Street were so badly blighted by neglect that they had to be demolished and rebuilt. At one stage, the new East Hertfordshire District Council had to threaten the county council with a compulsory purchase order to make it release a building in Crib Street, which now houses a nursery school. Even today there remains a gap on both sides of the street where the Relief Road would have crossed.

The only part of the Relief Road which was actually built was the large roundabout at the junction of Baldock Street and Watton Road. And thereby hangs an interesting and very human tale. A number of buildings were demolished including the Hope Malting and the maltster's house, which had a mulberry tree in its garden (still there in the centre of the roundabout). On the opposite side of Baldock Street, however, at the entrance to Monkey Row was a large Tudor building, divided between Page's bakery and the home of Miss May Savidge. Miss Savidge had lived there for 30 years, including the wartime when she worked as a draughtswoman at De Haviland's aircraft factory in Hatfield, and she had fought hard to save the building from demolition. It was

May Savidge outside her partially rebuilt 'Ware Hall House'.[8]

acquired by compulsory purchase by Ware UDC and then in 1969 passed to Hertfordshire County Council for the Relief Road. But May Savidge refused to accept the council's compensation, instead choosing to dismantle the whole building and number all the thousand or so timbers for re-erection elsewhere. In 1970 she started rebuilding 'Ware Hall House', as she called it, at Wells-next-the-Sea in Norfolk. Sadly she would not let any craftsmen help her until she was forced to do so when a storage firm went bust and she had to store her furniture in the half-completed house. May Savidge died in 1994 with the house still unfinished.

The opening of the Ware Bypass in 1977 relieved the town of a great deal of through traffic, although the High Street remained an A Road and an alternative to the A10 in case of accidents or high winds across the viaduct. Another consequence was that in the early Eighties all the land between the town and the new bypass became scheduled for housing, mainly for what was known as the Vicarage Estate, after the Victorian vicarage for St. Mary's just off Poles Lane. Thus all the hills to the north of Ware were now to be covered with housing – the King George and Cromwell roads in the Fifties, the Kingshill Estate in the Sixties and Seventies and the Vicarage Estate in the Eighties. And with the houses went shops, pubs and schools.

Post-war education

The first new school was in fact on the level, the move of the juniors of the St. Mary's National Schools to Park Road in 1947 to form St. Catherine's. St. Mary's infants moved up to Heath Drive in 1966 as Kingshill Infants and neighbours to a new St. Mary's Junior School. At about the same time, Priors Wood JMI (Junior Mixed and Infants) was established in Cozens Road, Tower JMI in Tower Road and the Sacred Heart RC School across the river at Broadmeads. There were similar moves in secondary education. In 1962, the Ware Senior and Selective Central School in Bowling Road moved up to Fanhams Hall Road – overlooking the rolling farmland of the Rib Valley – and became the Ware Church of England Secondary School, later known as Trinity School (after the nearby Trinity Farm). Educationally and socially, Trinity was an enterprising school with a thriving Film Society and adventurous drama productions, ranging from Benjamin Britten's opera *Noyes Fludde* to Joan Littlewood's *Oh What a Lovely War* and *The Caucasian Chalk Circle* by Berthold Brecht. But falling numbers led in 1982 to a merger with the newer Fanshawe School, in Park Road, to form the Chauncy School which upholds the best traditions of its two constituents.

On the other side of the town, the hills received a similar covering of housing – from Presdales Drive across to Little Acres and Springview. It was only the East Herts Golf Club which saved the south side of Ware from bordering the bypass. Here too there was a new school, Presdales, established as a comprehensive for girls in the former Hoe Lane home of the Sandeman and McMullen families. The school opened in 1965 but even before then girls from the Grammar School had been having classes at Presdales. Their former home at Amwell House was saved from demolition but had the indignity of losing much of its projecting wings, so that traffic could pass more easily along the Hertford Road.

The truncated Amwell House became the core of what at first was Ware College of Further Education, later Hertford Regional College, Ware Centre (though many people still refer to 'Ware College'). Eleven glass-fronted teaching blocks were erected in what had been the rear gardens of Amwell House and, for 40 years, the college built its reputation on the large number of sixteen-eighteen year olds it taught. In 2006 a new facility for remedial teaching was opened, known as Millbrook, and Amwell House was refurbished as the college's administrative headquarters. Even more remarkable, in 2007 the college embarked on a £30 million programme to replace the eleven Sixties buildings with three two- and three-storey buildings around a courtyard. However, at the time of writing, only part of this ambitious programme has been completed – owing to the abrupt termination of building contracts by the former Learning and Skills Council.[9] The new buildings that do exist, including 'shop front' facilities for the college's hairdressing students, are splendid and augur well for the completion of the rebuilding, when and if it receives government funds.

29.
A Period of Restoration

What happened after the long drawn-out and damaging saga of the Relief Road deserves a chapter to itself. Ware now began to recover its self-respect, pride in its history and – dare one say it – its beauty. It was a period in which old and neglected buildings were restored, when landscaping became again something to spend money on and when art, sculpture and architecture in the town assumed a new importance.

The new era began with the restoration of Place House. The former manor house is situated in Bluecoat Yard, opposite the row of cottages which Christ's Hospital built for the children it sent down from London in the seventeenth century. Before 1978, many of these cottages had been derelict, even those which were occupied suffered from neglect and planning blight and the yard itself was a mess. When it was announced that Queen Elizabeth, the Queen Mother was coming to open Place House, everything changed. Gravel was found to cover the yard, buildings were painted and what had looked like a 1930s slum began to look like a desirable place to live. The day of the opening, 8 July 1978, was beautifully sunny, the Queen Mother wore one of her famous flowery hats and there was a carnival atmosphere. The royal car deposited the Queen Mum at the entrance to the yard in East Street, where school children, pensioners and inmates of Western House in wheelchairs were waiting. She then walked through crowds which included Scouts, Guides and other uniformed orgnisations, as well as 'the Great and the Good'. Inside Place House, a small orchestra in Tudor costume was playing in the gallery under the direction of David Freeman; the Queen Mother invited them to come down but they would not risk the descent by fireman's ladder in their doublets and hose.

More visible and in worse condition than Place House were the riverside gazebos. They had suffered badly during the Relief Road saga, for the service road behind the High Street would have cut off the gazebos from their owners. The service road was abandoned in 1969 but there was worse to come. In 1976-77, the Thames Water Authority (as it then was) began work on a flood alleviation scheme which involved dredging the River Lea and pile-driving close to the banks. The TWA offered to protect and restore the gazebos – but only on condition they could be moved back from the river by ten metres or so. Old maps had once shown 25 gazebos between the bridge and Ware Priory, but by the Seventies there were just eight, most of them in ruins. In 1978 the Ware Society carried out repairs on the gazebo behind 69 High Street, but the volunteers had to row across the river with their tools because East Herts District Council was unable to give permission for the volunteers to gain access from the High Street. Yet it was clear that repairs were not enough and a more comprehensive restoration scheme was needed. Government, county council and district council money could be available but this was held up by the unwillingness of the gazebos' private owners to put up their share. In 1981, the Ware Society made the historic decision to raise funds in place of the private owners. The society agreed to raise £4,000 as its share of the £37,000 scheme and in July 1983 work began on the two gazebos. They were the two-storey brick gazebo with its watergate behind 65 High Street – the oldest and most spectacular of the group – and the gazebo behind 51 High Street, with the white horse on the weathervane.

The gazebos were a turning point for the society, its first major conservation project after years of opposing road schemes. The Gazebos Fund increased awareness of the society and greatly swelled the membership. In the newsletter for January 1984, a list of the gazebo donors was printed, ranging from a sponsored walk by the 4th Ware (St. Mary's) Brownies, to bring-and-buy sales and dinner parties, grants from companies and other societies, the proceeds of a special advertising feature in the *Hertfordshire Mercury* and donations from hundreds of individuals, including the sculptor Henry Moore OM, CH. The restoration of the first two gazebos was followed by refurbishment of two others as part of a sheltered housing scheme and the rebuilding of a further three by private enterprise. There was again a new team running the society – Dr. Roger Lowery, a biologist, was chairman, the present author, David Perman, was secretary and one of the members, Ken Weeks, freely gave his services as a civil engineer to the gazebos project. At about the same time, the society undertook a number of small improvement schemes in the town, produced its first *Walk about Ware* guide and initiated the first of its biennial Town Award competitions for new and restored buildings, with the winners' plaques made by students of Ware College of Further Education. The first plaque was awarded to the extension of Ware Library behind No. 87 High Street.

Ware was now looking up. The first malthouse off the High Street to be converted to housing was occupied and known as Water Row, the name once given to the whole south side of the street. The former Catholic Apostolic Church in New Road became three residences known as Chapel Mews. Tesco opened a superstore behind the High Street – actually in the area earlier earmarked for the Central Area Redevelopment, with a large carpark entered from New Road. St. Mary's Church was given a modern extension, dedicated in November 1982 and paid for from the sale of a field, bequeathed by a long forgotten parish clerk, for construction of the A10 Ware By-Pass. The Ware Society helped save the railway station from demolition and replacement by a glass box – the refurbishment received a society plaque. Unfortunately, the Station Inn opposite stopped serving beer to thirsty commuters but retained its attractive facade in residential use. The Ware Conservation Area was extended and the 'Vivat Ware' consultancy of architects, Rock Townsend, continued, first by East Herts District Council and later by Ware Town Council. Rock Townsend had managed the gazebos restoration but their main contribution to the town was Wickham's Wharf, an imposing riverside development on the site of the engineering company's former offices in Viaduct Road. In 1984, the old Town Hall was restored and became the offices of estate agents and in 1985 Westgate House, at the end of West Street, was rebuilt with its fifteenth-century crown post roof retained. Its neighbour, Churchgate House, was restored in 2000 and became Jacoby's restaurant.

In 1986, the Ware Society undertook two major projects. One was the founding of Ware Museum with the beginnings of a permanent collection of archaeological and historical artefacts displayed in the Priory Lodge. The museum was set up by a small committee, including Town Councillors Dorothy Palmer and Michael Tucker, the Town Clerk John Fletcher, and Roger Lowery and David Perman from the Ware Society. The granting of a lease on the Lodge by the Town Council followed a number of successful 'Museum Afternoons' in the Priory itself. In 2002 the museum was extended with a grant from the Heritage Lottery Fund to include a new entrance, an office and stores and refurbishment of the Second World War ARP bunker as an educational activity area. It was during this work that a medieval, chalk-lined well was uncovered.

The award-winning Library extension, drawn by Harry Wilson for the Ware Society Newsletter.

At the time of writing, the museum holds all the archaeology unearthed in Ware, has been extended yet again and has gained full accreditation from the Museums, Archives and Libraries Council.[1]

The second project of 1986 concerned the two Bluecoat Boy statues. One of the statues had stood in the niche above the entrance to Bluecoat Yard from 1704 until 1894, when it was removed to the Christ's Hospital Girls School in Hertford. When the Hertford school closed in 1985 and the girls joined the boys in Horsham, the Ware Society asked for the return of the statue which in view of its age and fragility is now installed inside Place House – the former schoolroom of Christ's Hospital. The society then commissioned a new Bluecoat Boy to go in the niche in East Street. It was made by the Roydon sculptor, Angela Godfrey, who carved it in elm, using her nine-year old son, Paul, as a model. The uniform of a blue cassock and 'petticoat' (said to be yellow to deter vermin) was borrowed from the school in Horsham. Both statues are owned by the Ware Society.

In 1990 the Ware Society undertook its most ambitious project, the full restoration of the eighteenth-century shell grotto, created by the Quaker poet and reformer, John Scott. The grotto – cut into the chalk hillside on the south side of the town and consisting of six subterranean chambers – had had a chequered history since Scott's Road was built across the original estate in the 1860s. For most of that period, the grotto had been in a private garden. But in the 1960s the garden was sold and modern houses built on the site. On one side of the grotto is No. 28 Scott's Road and on the other No. 34 – the builder clearly intended to build Nos. 30 and 32 over the grotto itself. Why he desisted we do not know, but what is known is that in the Sixties the porch of the grotto was demolished and the dome of the main chamber knocked in. The grotto was acquired by the former Ware Urban District Council in 1967 and in the reorganisation of local government of 1974 passed to East Herts District Council, but neither council did more than safeguard it against further damage. When the Ware Society undertook occasional opening to the public, parts of the grotto were still inaccessible. A full restoration was first suggested in 1986 when the society received a grant of £3,000 from an unexpected source – the Pilgrim Trust, established in 1930 and set up by an American philanthropist. The Ware Society then began a long negotiation with the district council and English Heritage for funding and permission to carry out the restoration.

The design for the restoration was by James Howley, a young Irish architect working for Rock Townsend but already an expert on Irish garden buildings. Howley's design was exhibited at the Royal Academy Summer Exhibition in 1989 and involved a new secure porch, to replace the one demolished, replacement of the shells and minerals in the large 'Council Chamber', rebuilding the ruined summerhouse above the grotto and landscaping the garden. Work began in January 1990, managed by the present author who was still secretary of the Ware Society, at a total cost of £124,000. East Herts District Council contributed £60,000, English Heritage £32,000 and the remainder was raised by the society from businesses, individuals, charitable trusts, Ware Town Council and the Georgian Group. One of the interesting aspects of the work was finding replacement shells for those that had been looted or damaged or had deteriorated with exposure to the weather. The large, gold-rimmed oysters in the Council Chamber came from the South Pacific and proved too expensive to purchase, so an appeal was made to the Ryukya Pearl Company on the Japanese island of Okinawa, who donated 350 similar black-rimmed oysters. Ware people also donated shells, including some taken from the grotto in the Sixties. And in April 1990, the author took his car to Guernsey and, as the result of an appeal in the local newspaper, toured the island collecting people's collections of 'ormer' shells and scallops – the ormer (*Haliotis tuberculata*) is now a protected species which may not be taken from the sea, so the old Guernsey collections were invaluable. It is interesting to note that John Scott, and before him Alexander Pope at Twickenham, had collected their shells in a similar manner from friends and also by purchase. The restored grotto was formally opened by the chairman of English Heritage, Lord Montagu of Beaulieur, on 30 April 1991 and was later accorded the status of a Grade I Listed Building. The garden was landscaped, mainly due to the efforts of Ware Society members. The grotto continues to be opened by volunteers from the Ware Society on Saturday and Bank Holiday afternoons between April and the end of September, or by arrangement with the curator.[2]

Reminiscences of Ware's Past

Conservation needs the support of sound historical research. But history is not only the province of academics. In the early eighties, the Ware Society set up a series of meetings which garnered some fascinating reminiscences of the town's older inhabitants. Between 1981 and 1986 annual meetings were held in the main hall of the Priory, with a panel of speakers and a large audience who added their own memories and corrections. The *Reminiscences* meetings were chaired by Dr. Roger Lowery, chairman of the Ware Society, and recorded, transcribed and published as booklets by the present author, who was the Society's Hon. Secretary.

The reminiscences of those taking part ranged as far back as the 1914-18 War or earlier. At the first meeting, Sonny Sharp, a former Urban District Councillor and magistrate told how in 1915 the Northumberland Yeomanry had taken over a building in Gladstone Road (now the Royal British Legion hall) and set up their field ovens in the road to do their catering:

> As a boy, I wouldn't go to school without I went up to the Rose and Crown [now the Worppell] and had a ride on one of the horses, because there was all the Yeomanry and Artillery that was stationed in Ware.[3]

The days of horse transport were recalled at many of the meetings – from the shoeing of the horses that hauled the barges in the town's four forges to the difficulty of getting horses to pull the steamer of the Ware Fire Brigade when the same horses were also being used to pull the town dustcart. Other panelists at the first meeting were Joan Brogden, a former Ware Grammar School teacher and a founder of the Ware Society, and Elsie Barker, who became the first Town Mayor in 1974. But the contributions from members of the audience were equally memorable. Gerald Sayers, who owned the Ware Hardware Stores in East Street, told the story of a man who had drowned in the Thames and could not be identified, until someone noticed warts on his chest and identified him as a Ware man – from leaning on the iron railings of the old bridge, waiting to be employed as a casual labourer on the barges! The meeting finished with a discussion of the mysterious word 'ogies' used to describe the ditches or tips which formerly existed in Clement Street.

The second Reminiscences meeting began with a show of slides by two Ware Society veterans, Maurice Edwards and Stuart Timmons. As one of the panelists was Dr. G.W. (Bill) May, much of the proceedings was devoted to the medical history of the town. He said that the only hospital there had ever been in Ware was a TB (tuberculosis) sanatorium at the Canons Hotel (now the Roebuck) which transferred to Ware Park in 1922. Western House in Collet Road was not a hospital, he said, having been originally the Union Workhouse, though it was known as 'an infirmary'. The first motorcar in the town had been owned by Dr. Boyd – to which the builder, Frank Suckling, added that when he was a boy there were just four cars in Ware, owned by Dr. Boyd, Dr. Butcher, Mr. Parker (chauffeur to Dr. May's father, another GP) and the engineer, Mr. D. Wickham. A further medical reminiscence came in the third meeting from Fred Woodhouse, a Serving Brother of the Order of St. John. He said that before 1928, when St. John Ambulance in Ware acquired their first ambulance, they had kept a litter in a small brick building next to the Mission Hall in Amwell End. It was

> a sort of stretcher on big wheels with a big canvas canopy over the head part of it, like a pram hood. When they had an accident, they used to get this litter, go out to the accident, wheel it down to the station, wait for a train, put it in the guard's van, transport it to Hertford, take it out the other end and wheel it up to the County Hospital.[4]

Dr. May also described how, when someone was sick in one of the big houses in the High Street, straw would be put down to deaden the noise of carts rumbling on the cobble stones.

At the fourth *Reminiscences* meeting, Evelyn Bouttell recalled being apprenticed as a dressmaker in R.W. Harradence's department store. The store, which closed in 1971 after almost two hundred years of trade, occupied five shops from 65-73 High Street. After her two years' apprenticeship in the workroom, Mrs. Bouttell moved to the showroom.

> We used in those days to take a lot of the goods out on 'appro' (approval) to the big houses around. And, of course, if there was a mourning order, we used to jump for joy because we got commission on it, you see. You took it out into the country to one of the big houses, where they had staff, and everybody wore black. One day I went out and it was to the Thrifts, down London Road, to take some mourning. Well, actually I did not take it. It used to be a pony and trap and then we got a van. And they left me in this house – I had never been there before – all the blinds were drawn and it was in complete darkness. They opened the door and let me in, and it smelled completely of apples – they must have had all their apples stored on the floors. I really got frightened because nobody came and I could hear funny noises of people

walking about. And then in the end a man came – I don't know who died there, I can't remember now – and he said "nobody can see you now, we will keep the mourning clothes". And I said "all right, I will collect them another day".[5]

The town's characters were recalled in the *Reminiscences* meetings – including 'Blood' Cox, a showman who kept horses in Clement Street, 'Whistling Billy' from Bishop's Stortford who stood in pub doorways playing a tin whistle and 'Billy No Hat' who begged on market days and said he was not greedy and would always take a smaller coin (such as the 6d.) rather than the big penny. Sheep and cows were sometimes driven through the town, and milk was delivered from a churn on the back of a cart. Mrs. Grace Kay described how Christ Church had started a scheme for the town's first District Nurse and, when they became a national institution in 1919, the District Nurses lived on the top floor of what is now Ware Library. There were many memories of school days and of the rivalry between St. Mary's and Christ Church schools. Henry Vaughan, who had been head of the Art and Technical School in Priory Street, said he had wondered why there was always a yellow smear along the beams of the cookery room on the first floor – until he found out that the building had originally been an engineering workshop, belonging to D. Wickham & Co.

Many of the panelists remembered working malthouses throughout the town (the large number of rats and measures to catch them were a favourite topic). But Tom Ives, who eventually became a foreman for Henry Page & Co., gave an insight of the hard work involved.

We used to get a flat wage in those days. In 1937 it was two pounds a week – for a seven-day week. And once the [malting] season started, of course, you did not get a day off until it ended. You worked on Christmas Day and whatever. That two pounds was a flat rate. Then you got what they called 'extras'. For carrying barley, it worked out at about one penny a sack: you had to carry it up the ladder and across the floor, [each sack weighing] sixteen stones – unless you were unlucky and got Canadian barley. That was eighteen stones [114 kilos]. And yet I honestly cannot remember anyone hurting themselves.[6]

The maltmaker's day usually began at 4am – "in those days, maltmakers reckoned that one hour before breakfast was worth two after" and the malting season ran from the end of September to the end of May. In the summer, there were a variety of jobs on offer – remaining in the malthouse for 'bug-lining' (whitewashing the walls), brickmaking at Trapstyles or working in the nurseries farther down the Lee Valley.

The *Reminiscences* meetings continued until 1985 and were discontinued only because the fire officer warned that audiences of almost a hundred, many of them standing, were not permitted. Other panelists included Albert Wiggall (a former councillor who opened a hairdressing saloon in New Road), Jimmy Crane, Richard Andrews, John ('Bomber') Wells, Bill Lee and Leonard Goldstone, who worked for the National Bus Company in their garage behind Rankin House. Following the five meetings, three further booklets of written reminiscences were published – two by Henry Page, who grew up in Crib Street and worked for Ware UDC, and one by Edwin Lynch OBE, who had begun his career working for the rival Ware Rural District Council at 97 New Road.

The restored Priory and (left) Fletcher's Lea, opened in March 2007.

Restoring the Priory

In 1993-94, Ware Town Council acting in their capacity as the 'Ware Priory Trustees' carried out a major restoration of the former Franciscan Friary. It was long overdue. As the architect Peter Locke (of Donald W. Insall & Associates) wrote in an appeal booklet:

> As a result of the building's proximity to the river, the site is inherently damp, and its effect in rising within the walls has been to cause decay of ground floor timber joist ends, in contact with long stretches of the external walls. More seriously, a concentrated area of rising damp in the south wall (alongside the main staircase) has caused the establishment of a dry rot zone, with infestation permeating the core of the rubble wall.[7]

There was also structural movement in external walls, spongy internal floors and the nineteenth-century conservatory was derelict. As a result, in places the Priory was stripped back to its basic frame so that the six-hundred year old building could survive for a few hundred years more. Many surprising features were revealed, including the medieval painting of a rose, a set of Victorian 'gothic' decorations and graffiti, carved in the arcades of the former cloister – probably by soldiers recuperating in the 1914-18 War. The restored Priory was formally opened on 30 November 1994 by HRH the Duke of Gloucester, himself an architect.

In March 2007 the Duke also opened 'Fletcher's Lea', a large assembly hall built in the Priory grounds and named after the late John Fletcher – assistant surveyor of Ware UDC, Town Clerk for the town council, cricketer and historian of Ware (even though he lived in Hertford). The new building is described as providing "a fantastic, modern meeting facility, which can hold up to 220 delegates theatre style in the entire suite". The architects were Donald Insall Associates, who also oversaw the restoration of the Priory itself. But, it has to be said, that the architecture of Fletcher's Lea remains controversial in the town.

The architecture of Ware's modern buildings has varied greatly. At the indifferent end of the scale, since 1980 the town has acquired a large number of blocks of flats, mostly in yellow brick with red brick lintels and wrought-iron balconies, hardly spacious enough for a window box. They are grouped near the station and designed for commuting couples. More adventurous have been the new industrial buildings at GlaxoSmithKline in Priory Street and Park Road and the new Farecla buildings at Broadmeads. The rebuilding of the Ware Campus of Hertford Regional College, though incomplete at the time of writing, has also produced exciting architecture – especially in the new Millbrook building at the corner of Warner Road, which incorporates enhanced facilities for students with learning difficulties and disabilities.

However, in terms of public appreciation it is the refurbishment and re-use of older buildings, such as the many malthouses off the High Street and Watton Road which have gained the most plaudits. And new buildings, designed in traditional styles, have perhaps unsurprisingly proved popular. This is especially the case with Christopher Court, a cul-de-sac of 15 houses running down to the river from Burgage Lane, behind the High Street.

The last quarter of the twentieth century also brought its setbacks. In 1988, the magnificent Victoria Malting burned down suspiciously, just after its tenants, including a chandlery for narrow boats, had been given notice and moved out. East Herts District Council explored ways of retaining what was left but eventually the shell was demolished and a new factory built on the site. It was not yet the end of malting in the town, for next door Pauls Malt were still producing malt by modern methods. But in 1994 the company closed its Ware operation as part of a major reorganisation to ward off European competition. For the first time in six centuries, the scent of malt no longer hung over the town. The end of maltmaking in the town might have been expected, but the closure of Wickham's engineering works in 1991 came as a shock. In the post-war period, the company had continued to build railcars and rail trolleys but had also diversified into construction plant, particularly hoists and pumps, and filter equipment for water and sewage treatment works. James Cooper Jnr., who had been chairman since 1954 as well as the main shareholder, in 1986 moved to America. There was a management buy-out but it was under-capitalised and in 1987 the share capital was purchased by the BM Group Ltd, an acquisitive company in the engineering sector. On 7 April 1991, the company announced that it was closing the Ware factory and moving production to its other factories. The name 'Wickham of Ware' survives in museums and in the restoration of trolleys and railcars by rail enthusiasts.

It was fitting that, to mark the new Millennium, a statue should be unveiled to a Ware industry and that industry should be malting. The idea of a bronze sculpture was first mooted when the small memorial garden outside St. Mary's Church was being redesigned in the Eighties and the present author persuaded East Herts council to leave space for a statue. He then enlisted the help of two important representatives of the malting industry. Guy Horlock was chairman of the Stanstead Abbots maltsters, French and Jupp Ltd. (the only maltsters left in Hertfordshire) while Hugo Page Croft was not only the great grandson of Henry Page but also a former maltster in his own right, on the Moray Firth, and later a director of brewers Scottish & Newcastle plc. Initial funding was provided by French and Jupp who also held a competition to choose the sculptor. The winner was Jill Tweed from Oxfordshire, who had done a number of sculptures, commemorating traditional industries.

The finished sculpture was unveiled by Hugo Page Croft on 4 November 1999 before a

Above: the refurbished entrance (right) of GlaxoSmithKline's Global Manufacturing and Supply in Priory Street. The original entrance to the 1898 building (centre) still bears the name 'Allen & Hanbury Ltd.' – it stood almost exactly over the line of Roman Ermine Street.
Below: the new development of Christopher Court behind the High Street.

crowd of donors and supporters, including many retired Ware maltmakers. Jill Tweed based her design on photographs of past maltmakers but had not actually met any until that day. However, the resemblance of her sculpture to the broad-shouldered men in the audience was remarkable. The maltmaker stands with one hand resting on a large shovel, proudly looking out from his plinth towards Ware Library, No. 87 High Street, which had once been the home and headquarters of Henry Page & Co. At the maltmaker's feet is a cat – every malthouse kept a cat to keep down the rats – and the cat now has a shiny nose and ears from being stroked by admiring visitors.

30.
Epilogue

Ware can be proud of its history. It is a long history, in which certain periods and events shineout like jewels. The Roman and Saxon towns unearthed by archaeologists – the medieval and Tudor periods when large and sumptuous inns lined the High Street and the Great Bed of Ware was located in more than one of them – the nationally important malting industry and later industries, like Wickham's railcar engineering and Allenbury's (GSK) pharmaceuticals. This history deserves to be more widely known. The Ware Museum, founded as recently as 1986 and staffed by volunteers, does well in promoting the town's history but it deserves more support. The town also has a splendid built heritage, with four buildings listed Grade I – St. Mary's Church, the Priory, Place House and Scott's Grotto – fifteen listed Grade II* and 181 buildings listed Grade II. They also deserve to be better known, nurtured and carefully maintained. And for a town so close to London, Ware is located within beautiful and surely unrivalled countryside – viz. the River Lea and the Meads, Post Wood, Widbury Hill, the Amwell Nature Reserve and the Rib and Ash valleys. Again this natural heritage must be safeguarded[1].

But for those who know Ware, it is not the history nor the buildings nor the natural surroundings which makes the town special. Rather it is that much overused but in this case totally appropriate term, 'community'. Community feeling informs and guides most things which happen in Ware. It is palpable in the Carnival procession and Town Fair which inaugurate the Ware Festival during July; it is palpable in the hundreds of local groups participating in the Dickensian Evening in December. Or in the fêtes, festivals and fairs at other times of the year which – so I'm told – are the envy of other Hertfordshire towns. It is palpable in Ware in Bloom, organised by the Ware Town Partnership, which with the help of volunteers and corporate sponsors, enabled the town within two years of entering the Anglia in Bloom competition to gain a Silver-Gilt Award.

No history of Ware would be complete without recognition of the phenomenal number of its community organisations. The Ware Society remains active in guarding the town's heritage, as do the Friends of Ware Priory and the Friends of St. Mary's. There are three Rotary clubs (with breakfast, lunch and supper meetings). Women's groups are even more prolific – the Inner Wheel, Women's Institute (both the Kingshill W.I. and the weekly W.I. country market), the After Eights Club which used to meet at Chadwell Golf Club, Millbrook Women's Club, the Christ Church Ladies (formerly the Phoenix Club) and the Royal British Legion Women's Section. Youth is extensively catered for. The Ware and District Scouts, founded in 1911, have eight troops, three of them in Ware with a fourth in formation; there are also Explorers, Cubs and Beavers, as well as Girl Guide (or Girl Scout) and Brownie packs with equally long histories. The town has cadets of the Air Training Corps, the Army Cadet Force and St. John Ambulance and a number of youth clubs. Sports clubs include Angling, Bowls, Cricket, Jogging, Swimming and Ware F.C. (now at Wodson Park) as well as two youth football clubs. In the arts, there are Ware Choral and Ware Operatic, Ware Brass, the Maltings Sinfonia, Ware Poets, the Age Concern Art Group, Ware Arts Centre and a number of dance groups. There is also the Wine and Beer Circle, the Ware and District Photographic Society, Ware Cogers (dedicated to free speech) and the Ancient Order of Foresters. The Town-Twinning Association promotes links with Wülfrath in Germany and Cormeilles-en-Parisis in France. And bringing many activities together there is the University of the Third Age (U3A) with a large membership.

But it is in caring organisations that the town stands out. Ware has its own branch of the Alzheimer's Society, its own Stroke Club and two or more support groups for carers of people with learning difficulties. There is an active Christian Aid group and Ware was one of the first in Hertfordshire to become a Fairtrade town. The town also plays host to the Guideposts Trust, which provides services for people with dementia and other difficulties, the Hertfordshire Mind Network and the Samaritans. A friend who organises collections for the RNLI said that Ware's contribution is always among the most generous. And, of course, there are groups which Ware shares with its neighbour, Hertford – including the Hertford and Ware Local History Society.

Not everything in the garden is rosy. At the time of writing – at the beginning of the second decade of the Third Millennium – Ware faces problems, common to many small towns. Through traffic in the High Street, supposedly alleviated by the opening of the A10 Bypass in 1977, is heavy at certain times of the day and becomes nose-to-tail when a large truck is making deliveries. There is the problem of waste tips, and possibly incinerators, on the town's periphery. And there is a growing number of empty shops and a lack of certain retailers (no longer a DIY store or a shoe shop, for example) as a result of competition from nearby retail parks. Then there is the changing demographic character of Ware. Since the 1990s, the area near the railway station has been extensively developed with blocks of starter-home flats; there is no stopping it, since central government policy is to increase the number of new homes within easy commuting distance of London, particularly on 'brown field' sites. From Monday to Friday the occupants of these flats leave Ware early in the morning and return only after most shops have closed. They may patronise the evening, restaurant-based economy of the town but their benefit to the town's retailing is only available at weekends. When people complain about planning, the waste tips and the rest, they complain first to Ware Town Council, whose members are more available than those of the district or county councils. But the town council did not create the problems and its ability to mitigate them is limited. Initiatives to promote and improve the town's character – whether from the town council or other bodies – often suffer from lack of funds and what funds there are may already be allocated to other, centralised policies or to larger towns, like Bishop's Stortford or Hertford. It then becomes a matter of Ware being thrown back on its own resources of fundraising and ideas. There is a parallel here with the late Middle Ages, when the Crown seized the Manor of Ware and its assets and gave little to the town in return. In 1550, the complaint was made that the King took the tolls of the bridge but it was left to the people of Ware to repair and maintain it. However, in the twentyfirst century as in the sixteenth, there is a commitment in the town to get the job done and make sure it does not suffer from neglect.

Ware is not unique, of course. No doubt there are hundreds of towns and villages which can field as many or more community organisations and a similar, deep sense of community. The United Kingdom is all the richer for them and that gives one hope for our town's future. In the 1980s a slogan was coined to symbolise the town's regeneration. It is a good slogan on which to close this history. *Vivat Ware – Long Live Ware!*

Appendix 1

MEDIEVAL TAXES IN THE PRINCIPAL TOWNS OF HERTFORDSHIRE

TOWN	STATUS	PAYING	NUMBER OF BURGESSES
1086 Domesday Book			
Ashwell	'burgesses'	£2 . 9s . 4d	14
Berkhamsted	'burbium' (burgus)	£4	52
Hertford	burgus/suburbium	£20	18
St. Albans	villa with 'burgesses'	£11 . 14s	46
Sawbridgeworth	villa	£50	—
Stanstead Abbots	'burgesses'	£1 . 3s	7
Ware	villa	£45	—
1290 Lay Subsidy – *Tax of a 'fifteenth' on all movables (National Archives E179/120/2)*			
Ashwell	burgus	£48 . 13s . 2½d	156
Baldock	burgus	£33 . 13s . 10d	86
Berkhamsted	burgus	£16 . 5s . 4¼d	100
Hertford	burgus	£16 . 13s . 8¼d	103
St. Albans	burgus	£53 . 0s . 5¾d	181
Stortford	burgus	£18 . 14s . 8¼d	79
Ware	—	£54 . 12s . 4½d	164
Watford	burgus	£15 . 14s . 3¾d	77
1307 Lay Subsidy – *Tax of a fifteenth in boroughs and a twentieth elsewhere (National Archives E179/20/8)*			
Ashwell	—	£11 . 0s . 7½d	129
Baldock	—	£9 . 0s . 1¼d	90
Berkhamsted	'villata' (township)	£5 . 13s . 10d	85
Hertford	burgus	£7 . 16s . 8d	67
Hitchin	burgus	£7 . 18s . 3½d	69
Sawbridgeworth	—	£17 . 3s . 8¼d	119
St. Albans	villa	£14 . 7s . 7½d	88
Standon	—	£12 . 9s .11½d	97
Stortford	burgus	£5 . 18s . 5¼d	56
Ware	—	£14 . 4s . 5¼d	118
Watford	—	£5 . 19s .11½d	47

continued .....

TOWN	STATUS	PAYING	NUMBER OF BURGESSES

1334 Lay Subsidy *– Tax of a tenth and fifteenth on movables (E179/120/13)*

Ashwell	—	£9 . 19s . 9½d	
Baldock	—	£8 . 16s . 9¼d	
Berkhamsted	—	£10 . 6s . 6¼d	
Cheshunt	—	£10 . 12s . 0d	
Hatfield	—	£13 . 6s . 3d	
Hertford	burgus	£5 . 13s . 7½d	
Hitchin	villata	£7 . 19s . 0d	
St. Albans	villata	£17 . 13s . 11d	
Sawbridgewoth	—	£9 . 9s . 10½d	
Standon	—	£9 . 13s . 8d	
Stanstead Abbots	—	£3 . 7s . 10d	
Stortford	burgus	£9 . 12s . 5½d	
Ware	—	£12 . 17s . 4½d	
Watford	—	£6 . 15s . 3¾d	

1428 Parish Tax *(Feudal Aids, Vol II pp 452-466)*

St. Albans (St. Peter's parish)	120s.
Ware	80s.
Ashwell	53s. 4d
Berkhamsted St. Mary's and St. Peter's	48s.
Stortford	26s. 8d
Watford	23s. 4d
Stanstead Abbots	20s.
Hertford	nil

1524 Lay Subsidy Roll *(E179/120/...)*

St. Albans	*(E179/120/114)*	£70 . 5s . 11d	432
Ware	*(E179/120/118 – incomplete)*	£42 . 11s . 0d ?	256+
Ashwell	*(E179/120/115)*	£14 . 19s . 0d	118
Berkhamsted (both parishes)	*(E179/120/119)*	£12 . 18s . 4d	129

Appendix 2

VICARS OF WARE
from a list compiled by H.R. Wilton Hall from the London Episcopal Registers
(HALS D/P116 29/3) with later additions

Nicholas Speleman	1231
John de Pylardynton	1336-37
Richard de Pylardynton	1337-43
John de Colne	1343
Ralph —	d. 1371
Robert de Garton	1371-72
John Wengrave	1372 resigned
Peter de Winstead	1372-74
Philip Hertford	1374-84
Nicholas Drayton	1383-85
Henry Vyneter	1385-87
Robert Langeton	1387-1406
John Hatfield	1406-14
William Gyfford	1414
Simon Say	d. 1451
Thomas Graunger, B.D.	1451-67
John Elton, B.D.	1467-68
John Lawesby, M.A.	1468-76
John Bennet, S.T.B.	1476-80
John Foster, M.A.	1480
Robert Lawe	1506-20
Stephen Leder	1520-34
Richard Wylcockson Senior	1534 -42
John Harte	1542-52
Robert Kynsey, M.A.	1552-58
William Dowsing	1558-59
John Bendall	1559
Robert Kay	1567-1623
Thomas Young	1617-18
Robert Tyer or Tife	1623-27
Charles Chauncy, S.T.B.	1627-33
John Mountfort, S.T.B.	1633
Isaac Craven, ejected	1634 -50
Richard Farrar, ejected	1650-56
John Young	1656
Richard Waugh, M.A.	1661
Robert Bulman	1670
Samuel Scattergood, M.A.	1681
Joseph Weld, M.A.	1681

Roger Wye	1682
William Burrough, M.A.	1689
David Humphreys, S.T.B.	1730
William Webster, D.D.	1740
Thomas Franklyn, M.A.	1759
John White.	1777
William Hughes, M.A.	1781
Henry Allen Lagden, M.A.	1790
Henry Coddington, M.A.	1832
Joseph W. Blakesley, B.D.	1845
E.E.W. Kirkby, M.A.	1873
Richard Appleton, M.A.	1904
Martin Reed	1907
Noel Marsh	1924
A. Lloyd Phillips	1928
Frank Ferguson	1947
John Whitley	1961
Trevor Beeson	1971
Hugh Wilcox	1976-2003
Derrick Peel	2005

VICARS OF CHRIST CHURCH
from *Christ Church, Ware, A History 1858-1985* by Andrew Wang, with later additions

Francis A. Baines	1858
Daniel Bell Hankin	1864
Dawson Campbell	1875-79
Alfred Oates	1880
William E. Daniels	1914
John W. Fall	1917
Frank Hobson	1926
John Gilliat	1940-48
Arthur Bennett	1949-56
John C. King	1957
John Bournon	1960-85
David Wheaton	1986-96
David Proud	1997

Appendix 3

PUBLIC HOUSES IN WARE IN 1905

Ware in 1905 was – in the words of the noted beer writer, Martyn Cornell – "the most heavily-pubbed urban district in Hertfordshire. Even in 1911 – when six pubs had been closed in five years – there was one on-licence per 106 people in Ware, compared with one per 155 in Hertford, one per 251 in St. Albans and one per 660 in Watford. Perhaps it was the hot and thirsty work in the maltings ..."

    Below is a list, compiled from a survey in 1905 by the Herts Licensing Committee, with the breweries that owned them. Pubs are denoted by (p) and ale or beerhouses by (a).

AMWELL END

New Bull (p)	Christie	
Cherry Tree (a)	Holt	closed 1912
George (p)	Christie	closed 1931
Old Cock (p)	Christie	closed 1907
Old Victory (p)	McMullen	
Spread Eagle (p)	McMullen	still there

BALDOCK STREET

Black Swan (p)	Holt	closed 1912
Bull's Head (p)	Christie	still there
Fox (p)	McMullen	closed 1912
Royston Crow (p)	Phillips	closed 1912
Waggon & Horses (p)	Pryor Reid	
White Hart (p)	Christie	closed 1912

THE BOURNE

Cannon Tavern (a)	McMullen	still there

BRIDGEFOOT

Barge (p)	Pryor Reid	closed 1920
Bridge Brewery Tap (a)	Pryor Reid	closed 1912
Bird in Hand (a)	McMullen	closed 1931

CRIB STREET

Albion (a)	Phillips	still there
The Cabin (a)	McMullen	
Green Dragon (a)	Holt	closed 1912
Prince of Wales (a)	Baker	
Red Cow (p)	Christie	closed 1912
White Horse (p)	Simpson	

EAST STREET

Crown & Anchor (p)	Baker	closed 1912
Dolphin (p)	Christie	closed 1931

HIGH OAK ROAD

Windsor Castle (a)	Holt	now High Oak

HIGH STREET

Bay Horse (p)	Christie	
Bell (a)	Fordhams	now the Vine
Eagle (a)	McMullen	closed 1912
Forester's Arms (p)	McMullen	closed 1912
French Horn (p)	McMullen	
High St. Brewery Tap (a)	Holt	now Tap Bar
John Barleycorn (a)	Holt	closed 1910
Lion & Wheatsheaf (p)	Pryor Reid	closed 1909
Oriental Tavern (p)	Christie	closed 1908
Saracen's Head (p)	Holt	closed 1957
Star (p)	Christie	
Wine Lodge (p)	private	still there

KIBES LANE

Old Harrow (p)	Christie	
Jolly Bargeman (a)	Pryor Reid	now in Cromwell Rd.

LONDON ROAD

Royal Oak (p)	Watney	still there

MUSLEY HILL

Rifle Volunteer (p)	Baker	still there
Jolly Gardener (a)	McMullen	
Crooked Billet (a)	McMullen	still there
Rising Sun (p)	Christie	

MUSLEY LANE

Standard (a)	Christie	closed 1912

NEW ROAD

Red Lion (p)	McMullen
Two Brewers (a)	Silas Barker

PARK ROAD

Bricklayers Arms (a)	Pryor Reid	closed 1910

PRIORY STREET

King's Head (p)	Wrights	closed 1931
Mill Stream (a)	McMullen	

STAR STREET

Angel (p)	Christie	still there
Victoria (p)	Holt	still there

STATION ROAD

Railway Tap Hotel (p)	private	
Railway Tavern (a)	McMullen	closed 1906

WATTON ROAD

Chequers (p)	McMullen	
New Rose & Crown (a)	Simpson	now Worppell
Rose & Crown (p)	Holt	still there
Star Brewery Tap (a)	private	

WEST STREET

Bell and Sun (p)	Simpson	now part of Punch House
Punch House (p)	Mrs.Ellen Ellis	still there
White Swan (p)	Holt	now Tesco

NOTES ON WARE'S PUBS AND INNS

The above list of the pubs which existed in 1905 – and those which exist today – is not to be confused with the historic inns in the High Street *(see page 98)*. The only one of the above which was an inn is the old Saracen's Head. The Brewery Tap in the High Street (now the Tap Bar) is on the site of the Horseshoe Inn, but when it was rebuilt in the nineteenth century it became for a short period the home of the curate of St. Mary's.

Moreover, the pubs have constantly changed their names. For that reason, the hundred or so pubs listed on the wall of the Bull's Head in Baldock Street does not give a true picture of Ware's pub trade.

Notes on Sources

Printed books and booklets have their titles in italics. They can be found in the Local Studies Library at County Hall, Hertford and – if not – in the British Library. All other sources are manuscripts which are in the National Archives at Kew, unless otherwise stated. Other sources are abbreviated as follows:

BL	British Library
CLRO	City of London Record Office (The Guildhall, EC2)
CSP	Calendar of State Papers
HALS	Hertfordshire Archives and Local Studies
RCHM	Royal Commission on Historical Manuscripts
VCH	Victoria County History of Hertfordshire

Other abbreviations used: *op.cit.* – the work by the same author cited above;
Ibid. – as above, the last cited source.
passim – 'throughout' i.e. the whole work.

Introduction

(1)   Edith Hunt, *The History of Ware* (Hertford, 1946; new edition 1986).

Chapter 2 – Early Wareites

(1)   Robert Kiln and Clive Partridge, *Ware & Hertford: the story of two towns from birth to middle age* (Welwyn Garden City, 1995) 14-15.
(2)   Robert Kiln, *The Dawn of History in East Herts* (Hertford, no date) 60.
(3)   Clive Partridge, *Foxhole Farm: A Multi-Period Gravel Site* (Hertford, 1989) 15.
(4)   Clive Partridge, *Skeleton Green: A Late Iron Age and Romano-British Site* (Britannia Monograph Series, No.2, 1981) 351.

Chapter 3 – A Roman Town

(1)   Kiln and Partridge, *op.cit.*
(2)   C.R. Partridge, *Allen & Hanbury, Ware: Progress Report No. 3, September, 1977* – unpublished (Ware Museum).
(3)   HALS, Acc. 3194 – Correspondence of J. Allen Tregalles and Richard Benyon Croft.
(4)   I. Margary, *Roman Roads in Britain* (London, 1967) 196.
(5)   *Transactions of the East Herts Archaeological Society 13,* 1955, facing page 156.
(6)   M.R. Petchey and T.J. Collier, 'Excavations at Ware Lock, Ware, 1974' (*Hertfordshire Archaeology and History, Volume 14, 2004-2005,* 45).
(7)   N. Godwin, *Developer's report by Hertfordshire Archaeological Trust* – unpublished (Ware Museum).
(8)   W.C. Mylne, 'Discovery of some Roman remains at Ware in Hertfordshire', *Archaeologia, XXIV* (1832).

(9)   Kiln and Partridge, *op.cit.,* 31.
(10)   M.R. Petchey, *Excavations at Ware Lock, Ware, 1974: a Preliminary Report* – unpublished (Ware Museum), 3. Interestingly, when Petchey's report was written up for publication in *Hertfordshire Archaeology and History 14* – 30 years after the actual excavation – all discussion of a toll house was omitted. The "dense scatter of coins" from the Early Fourth Century was then described as a hoard, "suitable for a foundation deposit or votive offering" (Petchey and Collier, *op.cit.*, 49.)
(11)   Hertfordshire Archaeological Trust, *Archaeological Excavation Update*, 10/3/03, 'Roman Ermine Street found below the new canteen facility, GlaxoSmithKline, Ware' – unpublished (Ware Museum).
(12)   Kiln and Patridge, *op. cit.*, 46-47.
(13)   Kiln and Patridge, *op.cit.,* 71.

Chapter 4 – The Saxon Settlement

(1)   *Herts Archaeology and History*, Volume 7, 1979, 147.
(2)   *Herts Archaeology and History*, Volume 8, 1980-82, 141.
(3)   Hugh Borrill, *The Post-Roman Pottery from Excavations in Hertford and Ware 1973-2004* (Supplement to *Hertfordshire Archaeology and History, 15*), 58.
(4)   Bob Zeepvat, *Excavations in Ware 1979-1993: Review of Site Records and Proposals for Archive and Assessment* (Hertfordshire Archaeological Trust, 1997), 15.
(5)   "Similar [early-mid Saxon] pottery was also known to have been found at the WBS site, but the material has apparently been misplaced by the former Hertfordshire Archaeological Trust and only 'small finds' consisting of cut down bases that were reused as lids survive," Hugh Borrill, *op.cit.,*58.
(6)   Kiln & Partridge, *op. cit*, 66.
(7)   Sal Gafi in Kiln and Partridge, *op.cit.,* 116.
(8)   Nathaniel Salmon, *The History of Hertfordshire* (1728) 242.
(9)   J.E.B. Gower, Allen Mawer and F.M. Stenton, *The Place-Names of Hertfordshire* (1938) 227.
(10)   *The will of Æthelgifu : a tenth century Anglo-Saxon manuscript.* ed. and trans. by Dorothy Whitelock (Oxford, 1968), i 22.
(11)   *Domesday Book, Hertfordshire,* ed. J. Morris (Chichester, 1976) 26.
(12)   Peter Boyer, *Assessment of Archaeological Evaluation and Excavation, Yorkes Yard, Priory Street, Ware.* (CqMS Ltd., 2002) – unpublished (Ware Museum).
(13)   Peter A. Clarke, *The English Nobility under Edward the Confessor* (Oxford, 1994) 38.
(14)   Peter Rex, *Hereward: The Last Englishman* (Tempus Publishing, 2005).
(15)   Tom Williamson, 'Urban origins: location, topography and the documentary record' in *A County of Small Towns* (Hatfield, 2008) 43.

Chapter 5 – Norman Lords and Monks

(1)   *Domesday Book, op.cit.,* 26.
(2)   Ordericus Vitalis, *Historia Ecclesiastica, Vol.2, pp 253ff (Bk VI, cap. V)*
(3)   Ordericus Vitalis, *op.cit., Vol.3, pp 554-57 (Bk VIII, cap. XXVIII).*
(4)   David Crouch, *The Beaumont Twins: The Roots and Branches of Power in the Twelfth Century* (Cambridge, 1986) 96.

(5)   David Horspool, *The English Rebel, one thousand years of troublemaking from the Normans to the Nineties*, (London, 2009) 49.

Chapter 6 – The 1200s: A Growing Town

(1)   W.G. Hoskins, 'The Uniqueness of Ware' in *The Listener*, 22 July 1965.
(2)   BL: Rotuli Hundredorum (HLL941 vol. 34) pp 190, 194.
(3)   Assize Roll 313 (32 Hen III), m.6.d.
(4)   Close Roll, CRR, xi, no. 1434.
(5)   Pipe Roll (3 Ric I) m.12 d.
(6)   Cussans, *History of Hertfordshire*, 1870: Braughing Hundred, 132-33.
(7)   Rotuli Hundredorum, *op. cit.*, 194.
(8)   Charles Dawes, *Records of Ware* (Ware, 1901) 29 – Ware Urban District Council bought the tolls from the Marquess of Salisbury, whose ancestor was given them by Charles I.
(9)   BL, *Calendar of Patent Rolls 1343-5*, 35.
(10)   *A Quaint Old Fashioned Place*, Writings of James Smith edited by David Perman (Hertfordshire Publications, 1990) 55.
(11)   Cecil A. Hewett, *English Historic Carpentry* (Chichester, 1980) 123.
(12)   *Hertfordshire Archaeology and History,* Volume 8, 1980-82, 126-143.

Chapter 7 – 1300s: the Wake family

(1)   Inq. post. mort., 12 Ed. I., No.27.
(2)   BL: *Calendar of Papal Letters*, iv, 517.
(3)   E179/20/8 – see also *Hertfordshire Lay Subsidy Rolls 1307 and 1334,* ed. Janice Brooker and Susan Flood (Hertfordshire Record Society, 1998).
(4)   B.M.S. Campbell, J.A. Galloway, D. Keene and M. Murphy *A Medieval Capital and its Grain Supply: Agrarian production and distribution in the London region c.1300*, (London, 1993) 76, 109.
(5)   *ibid.*, 46, 101.
(6)   BL, *Calendar of Close Rolls 1392-96,* 36.
(7)   BL, *Calendar of Patent Rolls 1381-85,* 569.
(8)   King's Bench 27/385 Rex m.15; also B.H. Putnam, *The Place in Legal History of Sir William Shareshull, Chief Justice of the King's Bench, 1350-1361*(Cambridge, 1950) 148.
(9)   Inq. post mort, 4 R.II., Rot. 59, No. 7.
(10)   BL: *Chronicon Angliae*, 291.
(11)   Common Pleas – CP 40/490 m.489.
(12)   CP 40/490 m.458.
(13)   HALS, D/EWe 4/16.
(14)   Raphael Hollinshed, *Chronicles of England, Scotland and Ireland*, II, 765.
(15)   Nigel Saul, *Richard II* (New Haven, 1997), 408; *Chronicles of the Revolution, 1397-1400*, ed. C.Given-Wilson (Manchester, 1933), 32.
(16)   Raphael Hollinshed, *op.cit.*, III, 19 – quoting Thomas Walsingham.

Chapter 8 – 1400s: Ware governs itself

(1)   BL, *Calendar of Close Rolls, 6 Henry IV,* 449.
(2)   Susan Reynolds, *An Introduction to the History of English Medieval Towns* (Oxford, 1977) 84.
(3)   J.E. Brown, *Chantry Certificates for Hertfordshire* (Hertford, no date) 49; also Hunt, *op.cit.,* 61.
(4)   HALS, D/EWe 4/26.
(5)   HALS, D/EWe 4/20.
(6)   HALS, D/EWe 4/107.
(7)   Chaucer, *The Canterbury Tales, The Prologue,* lines 382-386.
(8)   HALS, D/EWe4/59.
(9)   Augmentation Off., Misc. Bks, vol.114, fol.130.
(10)   HALS, D/EWe 4/56-4/58 and 4/59-4/61.
(11)   HALS, D/EWe 4/61-4/65.
(12)   BL, Ad.MS 27976, 23b.
(13)   HALS, D/EWe 4/26.
(14)   *The Paston Letters, 1422-1461,* ed. J. Gairdner (London, 1872) Letter no. 243.
(15)   Andrew Little, *The Grey Friars in Oxford,* (Oxford, 1891) 259.
(16)   HALS, 63803.
(17)   HALS, 26823-4.
(18)   BL, Add Ch. 36070.
(19)   I am indebted to Kathy Sanders for information about this banner.
(20)   Wills 1 Dogett.

Chapter 9 – Life under the Early Tudors

(1)   Hunt, *op.cit.,* 6-7.
(2)   Michael K. Jones and Malcolm G. Underwood, *The King's Mother, Lady Margaret Beaufort, Countess of Richmond and Derby* (Cambridge, 1992) 102.
(3)   *Wills 29 Bennett p222ff.*
(4)   BL, Letters Patent 1 Hen.VII, *1. pars. 1, mem 27.*
(5)   Hunt, *op.cit.,* 64-65.
(6)   HALS, D/EWe4/107.
(7)   Wills 4 Holgrave.
(8)   Exch. Inq. (ser.2), file 299, No.9,10; Chan.Inq.p.m. (ser.2) xxviii,71.
(9)   BL, Ad.MS 27976, 46.
(10)   BL, Ad.MS 27976, 4; also Mins. Accts. Hen VIII, 1593 and 6869; G.E.C. *Complete Peerage,* Salisbury; *L and P Hen.VIII, xiv (s),* 1354 (15).
(11)   Michael Dunn, *Churchgate House, Ware, Hertfordshire, The History and Architectural Development of a Late Medieval Timber Framed Building,* (BEAMS, Hertford, 2001).
(12)   BL, *L and P Hen. VIII,* vii, no.665.
(13)   BL, *Mins. Accts. Hen.VIII,* no.1617; *32 & 33 Hen.VIII,* no.71,m.2.
(14)   BL, *L and P Hen.VIII, xix (I), 610 (68).*
(15)   BL, *L.& P. Hen.VIII,* vii,1251 (15).
(16)   RHMC, 24, vol iv, 290.

Chapter 10 – Weathering Two Extremes

(1)   Brown, *op.cit.*, 8-10.
(2)   Brown, *op.cit.*, 35.
(3)   Augmentation Off., Misc. Bks, vol.114, fol.130. For some reason, Edith Hunt missed this contentious document which is two folios after the later hearing, which she did quote at length (Hunt, *op.cit.*, 63).
(4)   Augmentation Off., Misc. Bks, vol.114, fol.128.
(5)   BL, *Acts of the Privy Council, 1550-52*, 228, 467; *1552-54*, 101.
(6)   BL, *Acts of the Privy Council, 1550–52*, 264.
(7)   BL, *Warrants of the Great Seal*, Chancery Series, 2, 16, f.979.
(8)   John Foxe, *Book of Martyrs*, (1563).
(9)   BL, *Letters Patent. I, Mary, pt vii, m.20*.
(10)   J.T. Smith, *Hertfordshire Houses, Selective Inventory* (Royal Commission on the Historical Monuments of England, 1993) 199.
(11)   Trinity College, Cambridge, MSS Box 44, 14.
(12)   Stephen G. Doree (ed.), *The Parish Register and Tithing Book of Thomas Hassall of Amwell*, (Hertfordshire Record Society, 1989) 185.

Chapter 11 – 'The Guested Town of Ware'

(1)   BL, Ad.MS 27976, 109.
(2)   *Memoirs of Ann, Lady Fanshawe, wife of Sir Richard Fanshawe, bart. 1600-1672* (privately printed, 1907), 9.
(3)   Star Chamber Proceedings, Elizabeth, Fanshawe v Harvye, F.16/35, F31/2.
(4)   Proceedings in Chancery, Elizabeth F.f.4.
(5)   BL, Lansdowne MS 38 & 35 (letter from Thomas Hodder); also David Pam, *A Parish near London* (Enfield Preservation Society, 1990) 76.
(6)   BL, Lansdowne MS 32 & 98.
(7)   BL, *Court of Star Chamber, 1594*.
(8)   CLRO, *Calendar Middlesex Session Rolls, 1609*.
(9)   BL, Lansdowne MS 105 & 38, No 32; Pam, *op.cit.*, I, 7; VCH *Hertfordshire iv. 209*.
(10)   BL, Harleian MS 6,768.
(11)   A.G. Davies, *Liberty, Loyalty, Property: the Landed Gentry of Hertfordshire from 1588 to 1688* (Hertford Museum) Appx. A.5.
(12)   BL, *Calendar of Cecil Papers*, vii, 303.
(13)   H.C. Andrews, *The Chronicles of Hertford Castle* (Hertford, 1947) 70-74.
(14)   An earlier version of this plan appeared in *Hertfordshire's Past 31* (Autumn 1991) 27 – 'The Inns of Ware under the Tudors' by the author.
(15   RCHM, W.M. Molyneux Collection, Eliz. 5 Nov. 1593.
(15)   BL, *Acts of Privy Council*, 1565.
(16)   BL, *Calendar of Cecil Papers*, ii, 214.
(17)   P.K. Thornton, *Victoria & Albert Museum Masterpieces, Sheet 8 The Great Bed of Ware*.
(18)   There are no modern editions of Dekker and Webster's play, but it is available online at *www.en.wikipedia.org/wiki/Northward_Ho*. I am indebted to Derek Forbes, the theatre historian, for drawing my attention to this remarkable play.
(19)   Stephen G. Doree, *op.cit.*, 109.

Chapter 12 – James I and VI

(1) Hunt, *op.cit.*, 29.
(2) Alan Thomson, 'Progress, Retreat and Pursuit: James I in Hertfordshire' in *Hertfordshire in History, Papers presented to Lionel Munby* (Hertford, 1991) 93.
(3) Elizabeth McClure Thomson, ed., *The Chamberlain Letters, A Selection of the Letters of John Chamberlain concerning life in England from 1597 to 1626* (London , 1966) Letter 89.
(4) BL, *CSP Domestic 1619-23*, 39.
(5) *Ibid.*, 495.
(6) HALS, D/We5/8.
(7) Hunt, *op.cit.*, 37-38.
(8) HALS, D/EWe/4/93.
(9) HALS, D/EWe/4/94.
(10) Elizabeth McClure Thomson, *op.cit.*, Letter 89.
(11) L.P. Smith, ed., *Henry Wotton: Life and Letters* (1907) 196.
(12) Elizabeth McClure Thomson, *op.cit.*, Letter 124.
(13) L.P. Smith, *op.cit.*, 196.
(14) *Memoirs of Ann Fanshawe*, 9.
(15) BL, *CSP Dom. 1611-1618,* 584.
(16) *Memoirs of Ann Fanshawe*, 9.
(17) *Memoirs of Ann Fanshawe*, Notes, 285.

Chapter 13 – Religious and Political Turmoil

(1) See online: *www.earlystuartlibels.net/htdocs/pdf/esl.pdf.*
(2) BL, *CSP Domestic, 1635-1636*, 123-4.
(3) BL, *CSP Domestic, 1635-1636*, 494.
(4) Hunt, *op.cit.,* 123.
(5) BL, Ad MS 27,977 f.11 – see also Violet Rowe, 'Place House, Ware, in the seventeenth century' (*Hertfordshire's Past 15*, Autumn 1983).
(6) BL, *CSP Domestic, 1638-1639*, 633.
(7) BL, *CSP Domestic, 1639,* 196.
(8) BL, *House of Commons Journal Volume 2*: 1 September 1641.
(9) *Ibid.,* 15 August 1642.
(10) Stephen G. Doree (ed.) *op.cit.,* 109.
(11) BL, *CSP Domestic, 1637,*126.
(12) Quoted in Alfred Kingston, *Hertfordshire during the Great Civil War* (Hertford, 1894) 17.
(13) *Memoirs of Ann Fanshawe*, 474.
(14) *Ibid.*, 295, and *'A perfect Diurnall of the Proceedings in Hertfordshire from the 15th August to the 29th, 1642'* quoted by Hunt, *op.cit.,*11.
(15) BL, *House of Commons Journal Volume 2*: 17 November 1642.
(16) *Ibid.,* 1640-1643, 720-22; and 1660-1667, 36-8.
(17) *Hertford and Ware Local History Society Newsletter* No 18 (Winter 1988).
(18) Alan Thomson, *The Ware Mutiny: Order Restored or Revolution Defeated?* (Ware Museum, 1996) 41.
(19) BL, *House of Lords Journal Volume 9*: 30 June 1647.
(20) BL Thomason Tracts E414 (13).

(21) *Memoirs of Ann Fanshawe*, 474.
(22) *Ibid.*, 80.
(23) *Ibid.*, 87.

Chapter 14 – Ware under the Commonwealth

(1) Stephen G. Doree (ed.) *op.cit.,* xxiii.
(2) BL, *CSP Dom 1655-565*, 305.
(3) *Oxford Dictionary of National Biography (DNB).*
(4) Kingston, *op.cit.*, 185.

Chapter 15 – The Restoration

(1) *The diary of Samuel Pepys. A new and complete transcription*, ed. Robert Latham and William Matthews (London, 1971).
(2) James Smith, 'An English Country Town in 1835' in *A Quaint Old-Fashioned Place*, ed. David Perman (Hertford, 1990) 18.
(3) BL, *Journal of the House of Commons: volume 8: 1660-1667*, 36-8.
(4) BL, Add MS 29586 f.26.
(5) Violet A. Rowe, *The First Hertford Quakers*, (Hertford, 1970), *passim*.
(6) Rowe, *op. cit.*, 14.
(7) Rowe, *op. cit.*, 18.
(8) *Memoirs of Ann Fanshawe*, 11.
(9) *East Herts Archaeological Society (EHAS) Newsletter* No. 18, 1966 – edited by Gordon E. Moodey.
(10) HALS, *Herts. Sessions Rolls, 1, 86 and 128.*
(11) Hunt, *op.cit.,* 32.
(12) *'The Turnpike Act'* – 15 Cha. 2, c.14.
(13) Izaak Walton, *The Compleat Angler*, 57.
(14) *DNB*
(15) BL, *CSP Domestic, 1667*, 268.
(16) BL, *CSP Domestic, 1665-66*, 528.
(17) BL Add MS 27977, f.21.
(18) *Dictionary of National Biography.*
(19) Hunt, *op. cit.*, 125.
(20) BL, *CSP Domestic, 1667*, 494.
(21) BL, *CSP Domestic, 1668-69*, 89.
(22) HALS, D/P116 29/9 – Richard Benyon Croft, *A Short Note on the Fanshawe Vault in Ware Parish Church* (1908)
(23) Violet A. Rowe, 'Place House, Ware, in the seventeenth century', *Hertfordshire Past and Present 15* (1983).
(24) Violet A. Rowe, *The Bluecoat Children in Ware 1564-1761* (Ware Museum, 1983).
(25) CLRO, III WAR/PLA.
(26) HALS, 72206
(27) HALS, *Herts Sessions Books No.1 1581-1698*, 380.
(28) *Travels through England of Dr. Pococke* (Camden Society, 1888).
(29) *A Quaint Old Fashioned Place*, 13.

(30)   HALS, Ware Parish Register (microfilm), 2 June 1690.

(31)   HALS, D/EP F.92.

Chapter 16 – A Century of Commerce

(1)   F.M. Page, *History of Hertford* (1959), 107.

(2)   Peter Mathias, *The Brewing Industry in England 1700-1830*, (Cambridge, 1959) 439.

(3)   Rowe, *The Bluecoat Children in Ware 1564-1761*, 22.

(4)   Mathias, *op.cit.*, 256-7; also F.A. King, *Story of the Cannon Brewery 1751-1951*, 2-3.

(5)   Desmond Chapman-Huston & Ernest C. Cripps, *Through a City Archway, The Story of Allen and Hanburys 1715-1954* (London, 1954) 140.

(6)   *EHAS Newsletter 36*, 1975.

(7)   David Perman 'The Mystery of the French Horn Inn' in *EHAS Newsletter New Series No. 18* (September, 1996), 6-8.

(8)   R.G. Simons, *Cricket in Hertfordshire* (Herts County Cricket Association, 1996) 9.

(9)   12.George II.c.32.

(10)   7.George III.c.51.

(11)   'A report by Mr. Smeaton on the new making and completing of the navigation of the river Lea, from the river Thames through Stanstead and Ware, to the town of Hertford, dated 24 Sept. 1766', Royal Society, Smeaton, 6, ff 84v and 85.

(12)   32.George II and 6.George III.

Chapter 17 – Improving the Roads

(1)   BL, 8245.bb.14 – 'A Letter to the Inhabitants of Hertford'.

(2)   Letter to Joseph Cockfield, dated 2 September 1764, Friends House, London, Dimsdale Coll., Folder 11/11 – quoted in David Perman, *Scott of Amwell: Dr. Johnson's Quaker Critic* (Ware, 2001) 75.

(3)   see *Hertfordshire 1731-1800, as recorded in the Gentleman's Magazine*, edited by Arthur Jones (Hertfordshire Publications, 1993), 46-48.

(4)   BL, *The Review*, 25 June 1709.

(5)   HALS, Acc.3855.137.

(6)   HALS, Acc.3855.81

(7)   *Calendar of the Papers of Benjamin Franklin in the Library of the American Philosophical Society* (Philadelphia, 1908), iii, XXVI, 76.

(8)   *The Monthly Ledger or Literary Deposit*, I (December 1773) 261-262 – the only copy appears to be in Friends House, London.

(9)   Lettsom's letter to Sir Robert Barker FRS and G. Stacpoole, quoted in Charles Creighton, *A History of Epidemics in Britain* (Cambridge, 1894) ii, 511.

(10)   Shirley Lavender, *Churches, Chapels and Faiths of Ware* (Ware Museum, 1989) 39.

(11)   BL, *Monthly Repository*, 1817, 90.

(12)   Thomas Clarkson, *The History of the Rise, Progress and Accomplishment of the Abolition of the African Slave-Trade, by the British Parliament* (1839) cap. 23.

(13)   H.R. Wilton Hall, *Herts Archaeological Notes and Queries*, (1918).

Chapter 18 – Malt and the Malt Tax

(1) Mathias, *op.cit.*, 339.
(2) RCHM, MSS of Earl of Verulam, Gorhambury, 133, 136-9.
(3) Mathias, *op.cit.,* 409-411.
(4) Mathias, *op.cit.,* 461-462.
(5) Mathias, *op.cit.,* 459.
(6) Aline Burgess, *The History of a Ware Family, Part I: Chuck and Collins*, (Ware Museum, 1994) 22.
(7) Jonathan Brown, *Steeped in Tradition: The malting industry in England since the railway age* (University of Reading, 1983) 59-60.
(8) Brown, *op.cit.,* 21-22.
(9) HALS: Russ and Minns pamphlet, *Water Supply & Drainage of Towns and Villages*, (1869).
(10) Family tradition – Henry Page also rode his cob to the Mark Lane cornmarket in London every week: Lord Croft, *My Life of Strife* (1948) 17.
(11) Letter quoted in the *Souvenir Brochure of the Ware Exhibition (Trades and Hobbies)* 1950 – Ware Museum.

Chapter 19 – Before the Railway came

(1) *A Quaint Old-Fashioned Place* – Chapter 2. James Smith first published his reminiscences of Ware in the *Melbourne Argus* on 6 March 1880 and then sent it to the *Hertfordshire Mercury*, which published it on 19 June 1880 under the title 'Ware As It Was Forty-five Years Ago'.
(2) *ibid.*, 17.
(3) *ibid.*, 39.
(4) *ibid.*, 27.
(5) *ibid.*, 19.
(6) Perman, *600 Years of Charity,* 19-29.
(7) *The Reformer*, 6 April 1839.
(8) *The Reformer*, 28 March 1840.
(9) *John Bull*, 16 November 1844, 725.
(10) David Dent, *150 Years of the Hertford and Ware Railway* (Ware, 1993) 14.
(11) *The Reformer*, 21 October 1843.

Chapter 20 – Reform and Renewal

(1) 11 & 12 Vict. c.63 – brought in by the incoming Liberal government, in response to the urging of the social reformer, Edwin Chadwick.
(2) MH 13/195/2092/49 – J. W. Blakesley to General Board of Health, 23 May 1849.
(3) HALS, D/EX716, 3 – *Report to the General Board of Health on a Preliminary Inquiry into the Sewerage, Drainage and Supply of Water, and the Sanitary Condition of the Inhabitants of the Parishes of Ware and Great Amwell*, 1849.
(4) *ibid.*, 6.
(5) *Hertford Mercury,* 1 January 1847; quoted in Hunt, *op.cit.,* 49.
(6) *The Ecclesiologist, LXXIII, August 1849,* 76.

(7)   Nikolaus Pevsner, rev. Bridget Cherry, *The Buildings of England, Hertfordshire,* 377.
(8)   HALS, Acc. 3855.108.
(9)   HALS, D/Ex317 p8-14.
(10)   *The Builder*, vol. VII (21 July 1849), 342. Godwin's drawing of the roof is reproduced in Hunt *op.cit.*
(11)   Pevsner *op.cit.,* 380.
(12)   *A Quaint Old-Fashioned Place,* 15.
(13)   EHAS Newsletter, No.3 1953.
(14)   HALS, D/ELc P3.
(15)   Kain, Chapman and Oliver, *The Enclosure Maps of England & Wales, 1595-1918,* (Cambridge 1995).
(16)   Jack Parker, *Nothing for Nothing for Nobody, A History of Hertfordshire Banks and Banking* (Hertford, 1986) 39.
(17)   HALS, D/EHp T178.
(18)   *Hertfordshire Mercury*, 20 January 1894.
(19)   Perman, *Scott of Amwell*, 300 – information based on a flyer in Hoddesdon Library Local Collection.
(20)   John Smallshaw, *Henry Rydon and the Highbury New Park Estate*, privately printed pamphlet.
(21)   *Hertfordshire Mercury*, 1 July 1865. This story was first brought to light by Dr. Violet Rowe, a keen follower of Victorian politics in Hertford and Ware, in 'The Bells of St. Mary's – an Election with Musical Overtones' (*Hertfordshire's Past, 35,* Autumn 1993).

Chapter 21 – An Explosion of Churches

(1)   Some of the information in this chapter is based on the booklet, *Churches, Chapels and Faiths of Ware* by Shirley Lavender, edited by the present author (Ware Museum, 1989).
(2)   Andrew Wang, *Christ Church, Ware. A History 1858-1958* (Ware, 1958) 8.
(3)   *Christ Church Chronicle*, March 1963, quoted in Wang, *op.cit.,* 17.
(4)   I am indebted to Eileen Lynch, a life member of the Ware Society and former deputy County Archivist, for bringing to my attention the story of Jack Dye and the Papal Effigy. Eileen's mother was Florence Dye, whose parents were lockkeepers and named their daughter after the first boat to go through Ware Lock after the birth.
(4)   From the Salvation Army's newspaper, *The War Cry*, 1888.
(5)   *Reminiscences of Ware's Past No. 1* (Ware Society, 1982) 30.

Chapter 22 – The Schools Revolution

(1)   Trinity College, Cambridge, Box 44, DDE/71.
(2)   HALS, D/P116 25/14.
(3)   *A Quaint Old Fashioned Place,* 33.
(4)   *Ibid.,* 38.
(5)   BL Parliamentary Papers, *Schools Inquiry Commission*, XXVIII, pt.x, 1.
(6)   HALS, Pamphlet collection.
(7)   A full account of the rivalry of the two grammar schools and the fate of the unfortunate Mr. Lilley is given in David Perman *600 Years of Charity – a Brief History of the Ware Charity Trustees* (Ware Museum, 1991).

Chapter 23 – A Sense of Civic Pride

(1)   HALS, Pamphlet collection.
(2)   Aline Burgess, *The History of a Ware Family, Part II: Page, Croft & Collins* (Ware Museum, 1994) 9.
(3)   Lord Croft, *My Life of Strife* (1948) 24.
(4)   A.Charles Sewter, *The Stained Glass of William Morris and his Circle: a Catalogue* (1975) 71.
(5)   Pevsner rev. Cherry, *op.cit.,* 377.
(6)   Geoffrey Tweedale, *At the Sign of the Plough, Allen & Hanburys and the British Pharmaceutical Industry, 1715-1990* (London, 1990) 87-93.
(7)   *EHAS Newsletter New Series,* No.21, 1967.
(8)   Hunt, *op.cit.,* 16.

Chapter 24 – Before 1914

(1)   *Hertfordshire Mercury,* 30 December 1911.

Chapter 25 – A World War and its Aftermath

(1)   *Hertfordshire Mercury,* 7 August 1914.
(2)   I am happy to acknowledge the meticulous research by Mrs. Grace Kay into electricity and other utilities in Ware – now in a series of folders at Ware Museum.
(3)   *Hertfordshire Mercury,* 27 March 1931, 15.

Chapter 26 – The Thirties

(1)   Christine Clark, *The British Malting Industry since 1830* (London, 1998) 150.
(2)   Tweedale, *op.cit.,* 151-159.
(3)   Loxley G. Ford and James Cooper Jr., *Wickham of Ware: a history of D. Wickham & Co. Ltd. Railcar Manufacturers* (Ware, 2003) 38-40.
(4)   HALS, NQ 1A/52 page 91 for the Friends' conditions and HALS, UDC19 3/1 page18 for the council's agreement.
(5)   Owen Hamilton, *The Heart of Hertfordshire* (London, 1938) 23-24.

Chapter 28 – Post-war Progress

(1)   Tweedale, *op.cit.,*170-172, 187-191, 222-234.
(2)   Clark, *op.cit.,* 190.
(3)   *Ibid.,* 194.
(4)   *EHAS Newsletter New Series, No.9,* 1958.
(5)   The Ware Society's archive is stored on the top floor of Ware Library, along with some of the Collection of the Ware Museum.
(6)   This plan appeared in *People and Traffic – a study of conflict and congestion in Ware,* published jointly by Hertfordshire County Council and Ware Urban District Council in May 1970. This study put forward a number of proposals, including complete pedestrianisation of the High Street, but the preferred option was as shown on this plan, Figure D on page 12.

(7)   BL, *New Roads in Towns, Report of the Urban Motorways Committee to the Secretary of State for the Environment*, July 1972.

(8)   I am grateful to Christine Adams for permitting me to use this photograph of May Savidge, which appeared on the cover of *A Lifetime in the Building – the extraordinary story of May Savidge and the house she moved*, by Christine Adams and Michael McMahon (London, 2009).

(9)   In July 2009, the Public Accounts Committee of the House of Commons described the handling of the national college building programme by the Learning and Skills Council as "a catastrophic mismanagement".

Chapter 29 – A Period of Restoration

(1)   Ware Museum, at 89 High Street, Ware, is a registered charity and is run by volunteers. It is open to the public on Tuesdays, Thursdays, Saturdays and Sundays – tel. 01920 487848 and *www.waremuseum.org.uk*.

(2)   For other opening times please email *info@scotts-grotto.org*.

(3)   *Reminiscences of Ware's Past Number 1* (Ware Society, 1983), 10. The eight booklets in the series are no longer in print, but should be obtainable at HALS or Ware Library.

(4)   *Reminiscences of Ware's Past Number 3* (Ware Society, 1983), 23.

(5)   *Reminiscences of Ware's Past Number 4* (Ware Society, 1984), 20.

(6)   *Reminiscences of Ware's Past Number 5* (Ware Society, 1985), 26.

(7)   *Saving Ware's Historic Priory* (Ware, 1992), 21.

Chapter 30 – Epilogue

(1)   The Meads between Ware and Hertford are now a Nature Reserve, in the care of the Hertfordshire and Middlesex Wildlife Trust, and go under the name of King's Meads. But that is not a Ware name. So, it is worth recording here the original names of the Ware Meads. The largest area was Broadmeads, extending from Amwell End to the Chadwell Spring, with one area of about an acre to the south being known as Dewrod Mead. Chadwell Mead incorporated all the land between the New River and the Hertford Road, to the west of Chadwell Spring. To the north of this were Lady's Mead and Widow's Mead, later known collectively as Cowbridge Mead. The island to the east of Ware Lock is still known as Mill Mead and is owned by GlaxoSmithKline.

Index